ßS

OLD TESTAMENT TODAY

OLD TESTAMENT TODAY

A JOURNEY
FROM ORIGINAL
MEANING TO
CONTEMPORARY
SIGNIFICANCE

JOHN H. WALTON · ANDREW E. HILL

GRAND RAPIDS, MICHIGAN 49530 USA

Old Testament Today
Copyright © 2004 by John H. Walton and Andrew E. Hill

Requests for information should be addressed to:
Zondervan, *Grand Rapids, Michigan 49530*

Library of Congress Cataloging-in-Publication Data

Walton, John H., 1952–
    Old Testament today : a journey from original meaning to contemporary significance / John H. Walton and Andrew
E. Hill.
       p. cm.
    Includes bibliographical references and index.
    ISBN 0-310-23826-9
    1. Bible. O.T.—Textbooks.   I. Hill, Andrew E.   II. Title.
BS1194.W33 2004
221.6'1—dc22
                                                                          2003017823

This edition printed on acid-free paper.

Interior design by Tracey Moran

Printed in China

---

04 05 06 07 08 09 10 /❖ CH/ 15 14 13 12 11 10 9 8 7 6 5 4 3 2 1

CONTENTS

List of Maps and Tables   ix

The Design and Use of the Book   xi

Acknowledgments   xix

Abbreviations   xx

1 FUNDAMENTALS

About the Old Testament   2

The Big Story Line/Plotline   3

Reorientation   6

Expectations and Procedures   8

Writing and Books   19

2 PENTATEUCH

Original Meaning

Old Testament Story Line   28

History Story Line   41

Literary Perspective   51

Bridging Contexts

Plotline of the Pentateuch   67

Purpose of Each Book   70

Dealing with Story   83

Theological Perspectives   86

Contrast: Religious Belief
in the Ancient World   102

Contemporary Significance

Scenario: Evolution and the Bible   108

Recapitulation   110

The Fall Today   114

Significance of the Faith of Abraham   115

Old Covenant/New Covenant   117

What Are All of These Laws Doing
in My Bible If the Law Is Obsolete?   117

Scenario: Law   118

Recapitulation   120

What Does Sacred Space
Mean to Me?   121

A Sense of the Holy   124

3 HISTORICAL LITERATURE

Original Meaning

Old Testament Story Line   136

World History Story Line   155

Literary Perspective   173

Bridging Contexts

Plotline of the Historical Literature   180

Purpose of Each Book   189

Understanding Historical Literature   196

Pedestals and Role Models   200

Theological Perspectives   205

Contemporary Significance

History Seems Boring and
Irrelevant to Me—Help!   213

Scenario: Using Historical
Literature Today   216

Recapitulation   217

How Can We View
History Biblically?   220

How Should We View
the Bible Historically?   224

4 PROPHETS

Original Meaning

Story Line of the Prophets
in Their Times   232

Literary Perspective   237

Bridging Contexts

Purpose of Prophetic Books   244

Prediction, Prophets, and God   250

Fulfillment and Revelation   252

Theological Perspectives   254

Contemporary Significance

Scenario: Read Today's
Headlines in the Bible   264

Thinking about Prophecy   265

Indictment Today   267

Judgment Today   274

Instruction Today   275

Aftermath Today   276

Recapitulation   283

5 WISDOM LITERATURE

Original Meaning

What Is Wisdom?   283

Retribution Principle   292

Story Line: Job   293

Literary Perspective   295

Bridging Contexts

Proverbs and Truth   301

Purpose Book by Book   305

Theological Perspectives   316

Contemporary Significance

Scenario: Retribution
Principle Today   321

Recapitulation   322

When Life Goes Wrong   322

Seeking Fulfillment in Life   327

Proverbs and the Family   331

The Power of Sex   335

6 PSALMS

Original Meaning

Summary of Content   343

Literary Perspective   346

Bridging Contexts

Purpose: Kingship in Psalms   355

Psalms as Revelation   361

Theological Perspectives   362

Contemporary Significance

Contemporary Worship
and the Psalms   371

What Do We Expect from God and
What Does He Expect from Us?   372

Scenario: Trusting God When He
Doesn't Seem to Hear   373

Recapitulation   374

Devotional Use of Psalms   377

7 EPILOGUE

Plotline of the Old Testament
Continued to the New Testament   382

How Do the Old and
New Testaments Relate?   384

Were Israelites "Saved"?   388

Interpreting the Old Testament
in Light of the New and the
New in Light of the Old   389

What Have We Learned?   392

Overall Theme   394

What to Do with It   394

You Will Know That I Am Yahweh   396

*Appendix: Reading through
the Old Testament*   398

Glossary   401

Index   405

LIST OF MAPS AND TABLES

Maps

Ancient Near East about 2000 BC 27
Travels of the Patriarchs 34
Trade Routes in Fertile Crescent 43
Akkadian Empire 44
Locating Ebla, Mari, Nuzi, Amarna, Emar, Nineveh,
    Hattusha 48
Route of the Exodus 53
Reed Sea Map 74
Three World Empires 135
Map of Conquest 136
Tribal Territories 139
Two Stages of the United Monarchy 141
Borders of Israel and Judah in the Middle of the
    Eighth Century 150
Jerusalem in Post-Exilic Period 154
Egypt in New Kingdom 156
Ancient Near East Late Bronze 158
Solomon's Trade Districts 161
Neo-Assyrian Empire 164
Neo-Babylonian Empire 167
Medo-Persian Empire 170

Tables

Semitic Languages 12
Contrast in Values and Perspectives 16
Pictograms in Early Civilizations 20
Patriarchal Family Tree 30

(Tables continued)

The Plagues and the Gods of Egypt	38
Ancient Near Eastern Story Line	46–47
Covenant and Treaty Format	64
Flow of the Pentateuch	68–69
Sacrificial System	76
Jewish Calendar	79
Structure of Deuteronomy	82
Key Theological Distinctions Between Israel and Its Neighbors	106
The Ten Commandments for Today	122
The Kings of Israel (Northern Kingdom)	148
The Kings of Judah (Southern Kingdom)	149
The Prophetic Voice in Kings	186
Baal (of the Canaanites) vs. Elijah and Elisha (of Yahweh)	187
Sinai Covenant and Davidic Covenant	191
Kings and Chronicles	194
Major Archaeological Texts	199
Function of the Prophets	233
Categories of Prophetic Oracle	239
Minor Prophets	246
Messianic Prophecy	247
The Nations in Prophecy	258
Retribution Principle	292
Structure of Job	296
Psalm Types	349
A Cantata about the Davidic Covenant	356

PREFACE

THE DESIGN AND USE OF THE BOOK

The NIV Application Commentary Series established an approach to the biblical text that has received wide appreciation and acclaim. The basic idea that it developed was that the Bible would be most accessible to pastors and students if it could be approached from three different perspectives. To represent these perspectives, the headings Original Meaning, Bridging Contexts, and Contemporary Significance were chosen. Using these headings, the text's meaning and significance could be traced from the original author and audience to our contemporary setting. This approach allows us to understand the content of the Bible as well as its message, theology, and relevance for today. We have used these same three headings as our way of telling the story of the entire Old Testament. In so doing, we hope that we will be able to make plain the connectedness of the text.

When we speak of connectedness, we refer to several different levels of connectedness. First, each book is coherent and has an inner connectedness. We want our readers to understand that connectedness. Second, there is a connectedness between the books of the Old Testament that we want to clarify. Third, there is a connectedness between the Old Testament and the New Testament that we must understand in order to appreciate either one. Fourth, there is a connectedness of believers across the millennia for which the Bible, as the common heritage for our faith, provides the foundation. Finally, there is a connectedness to all the levels of significance as the content serves as the basis for the message and theology and as all of them then provide the foundation for our appropriation and application of the text's teaching to our lives.

To convey most effectively all of these levels of connectedness, we have chosen to present the material in units connected to canonical categories rather than book by book. The five units are Pentateuch, Historical Literature, Prophetic Literature, Wisdom Literature, and Psalms.

ORIGINAL MEANING

Under Original Meaning we present the details of content, addressing the question "What's it all about?" This section focuses on the story line, historical background, and literary information. Comments here will address the original setting and the original audience of the biblical material.

BRIDGING CONTEXTS

Under Bridging Contexts we present the details of meaning, addressing the questions "What's it here for?" and "How does this function as God's revelation?" Here the focus extends to the plotline, theological perspectives, and the issues of the author's purpose and the universal message of the text. This section also gives the student some methodological direction, addressing the question "How do I handle it?" This section is called "Bridging Contexts" because it seeks to build a bridge between the original audience and today's audience. This is necessary because of the historical and cultural differences that separate us. Though the books were written in specific contexts and circumstances, their message is important to us today. If we truly believe that the Old Testament is God's revelation of himself, we must acknowledge that it carries a message across time and culture for all of God's people. The timeless nature of Scripture enables it to speak with power in every time and every culture.

CONTEMPORARY SIGNIFICANCE

Under Contemporary Significance we present the details concerning the impact of the Old Testament on the modern reader. Here we try to answer the question "What is it supposed to mean to the church, to my family, to my world, and to me?" This section focuses on developing an awareness of the relevance of this literature for the Christian. In the process we explain how we may gain access to the Old Testament's message so we can have confidence that God's Word is getting through to us loud and clear. So often when Christians read the Old Testament they have questions like "What is this doing in my Bible?" or "What am I supposed to do with that?" or even "What is that supposed to mean to me?" Worst of all, we too often hear "That's not the God I know!" It is precisely these difficulties that inspired the vision for this book.

VISION

The Old Testament has been largely lost to the church. For the most part, this is because people simply don't know what to do with it. Not only do the people in the pew have this struggle; many pastors do as well as they labor to figure out how to make these texts relevant to their congregations. Unfortunately, books and survey courses on the Old Testament sometimes do little to rectify this situation if they present the Old Testament as if it were a haphazard collection of moralistic lessons or endless lists of names and dates. Somehow people have imagined that if students are introduced to the history of the Old Testament and have learned the names of all the patriarchs, judges, kings, and prophets, they have been adequately introduced to the Old Testament! Other courses might focus on the arguments that can be made against the critics or on trying to understand the Bible as a great piece of literature. All of these pursuits have their place, but they often leave us empty and still mystified about the place of the Old Testament in our lives.

For many their experience with the Old Testament is similar to the piñata game. There is a target out there that they are aiming at, but they are blindfolded and turned around so many times that they are entirely disoriented. They flail wildly at the air and become frustrated with an exercise that offers so little return for their effort. In this book we want to remove the blindfold and point the student in the right direction. Perhaps we can even take their hands in ours and give them a bigger stick so that the prize becomes achievable.

Our vision for this book is that we would be able to introduce students to the Old Testament by going beyond basic content to help them know just what they are supposed to do with it and what it is supposed to mean to them. It is hoped that this approach will remedy the all-too-frequent caricature of the Old Testament as little more than endless trivia, irrelevant history, and obscure prophecies only alleviated by some comforting psalms and models for living from the heroes and heroines of the faith. Students will not be overwhelmed by names and dates, but in contrast will be impressed with the way the Old

Testament uniquely reveals the God of the universe. They will gain an appreciation for the central importance of this sacred text and in doing so will come to appreciate the literature, theology, and history for the contribution they make and, most of all, the role they play in the greater story of God's plan for reconciling his creation to himself.

Finally, we hope that students will actually become equipped to handle Old Testament texts with confidence that extends beyond trivia tests. This text will help schools to move beyond the outcome objectives of the past that wanted to ensure that students knew which books were in the Pentateuch, who the left-handed judge was, and when the fall of Samaria took place. Instead, results will include an understanding of God as revealed in the Old Testament, a grasp of methodological approaches to the specialized genres of revelation found in the Old Testament, and a comprehension of the theological, cultural, and historical aspects of the plotline of the Old Testament and how it merges with the plotline of the New Testament. In short, the Old Testament will become central to their theology and their spiritual growth.

THE OBJECTIVES OF THE BOOK

In summary, then, our objectives are to present an orientation to the concepts of the Old Testament through this textbook. First, we will introduce students to the content of the Old Testament, always showing how to move beyond the details of names, places, events, and dates. Second, we will provide an orientation to the world of the Old Testament through pictures, maps, and other visuals. These will often take students beyond the focus of the textbook and into the world behind the Old Testament text. Third, we will provide an orientation to the study of the Old Testament through principles and methods that will help students read the Bible with confidence. Finally, we will offer an orientation to the theology of the Old Testament in its own right but also as a prelude to the New Testament and as a section of the church's canon.

UNIT DESIGN

We have introduced each of the five units with a carefully chosen quote about the literature of the chapter and a summary of the key terms the chapter will include. We then offer some of the important concepts for the unit in an "Orientation" box and include a "Yahweh

Focus" box that highlights some of the key theological teachings of the unit. Ample use is made of time lines, maps, pictures, and charts to aid in the pedagogical process.

A wide array of sidebars and callouts have been used throughout the text. Each section concludes with study questions ("Reflections"). After each Original Meaning section, the study questions focus on review of the facts from that section. After each Bridging Contexts section, the "Reflections" focus on conceptual questions. After each Contemporary Significance section, the "Reflections" focus on challenges for living. In addition, each unit concludes with a very basic list of books that is designed to take students to the next level.

THE USE OF THE BOOK

Sample Aims for a Course Using This Book*

- to acquaint students with the purpose and themes of the books of the Old Testament

- to acquaint students with the major characters of the Old Testament

- to acquaint students with important locations in Israel and the ancient world

- to familiarize students with the chronological framework of the Old Testament

- to nurture in students an understanding of God as revealed in the Old Testament

- to equip students with methodological approaches to the specialized genres of revelation found in the Old Testament

- to acquaint students with some of the important aspects of interpretation of the Old Testament

- to familiarize students with the theological, cultural, and historical aspects of the plotline of the Old Testament

- to familiarize students with how the Old Testament plotline merges with that of the New Testament

* These aims are just samples based on some of what we attempt to achieve through this book and in our courses. Individual institutions and accrediting agencies have varying guidelines for course objectives. For instance, some prefer objectives to be worded in terms of expected student outcomes. To address outcomes, the wording of these aims would have to be adjusted.

The desired outcome is that the Old Testament will become central to students' theology and spiritual growth.

Sample Course Schedules

Semester Class of Forty Class Periods

If *Old Testament Today* is the main textbook, we recommend completing one section per class period. If it is being read in conjunction with a survey text that goes book by book (such as our *Survey of the Old Testament*), or if there is still the desire to proceed book by book through the course, units can be given together as assignments, though the Pentateuch unit, being the longest, may have to be spread out to make it manageable. This approach is represented in the first list on the facing page. In that approach the "Overview" class periods may address the three segments of the textbook.

What should happen in class if students are reading this book in preparation for each class?

1. Much of the information presented in the book will require radical changes in the way the students have previously thought about the Old Testament; therefore the professor will need to summarize, target important points, and probe for areas that need further clarification and explanation.

2. Once it appears that the concepts are understood, class time may be spent on working through specific examples in the Old Testament and trying to pursue the implications for Bible reading, theology, the church, the students' personal lives, and so on.

3. Some class time may be devoted to developing areas that the textbook has only touched on in a sidebar, such as the date of the exodus or the Ten Commandments.

4. Alternatively, discussion might target particularly difficult (though familiar) passages, such as Isaiah 7:14 or Genesis 22 as interpretive case studies.

5. Certain issues are not addressed at all in the book, such as the extent of the flood or the archaeology of Jericho. Such topics offer additional possibilities for discussion.

6. Visuals in the text may be used as prompts for discussion of various issues.

Covering the Old Testament Book by Book

1. Fundamentals
2. Pentateuch Overview
3. Genesis
4. Exodus
5. Leviticus/Numbers
6. Deuteronomy
7. Historical Literature Overview
8. Joshua
9. Judges/Ruth
10. 1 and 2 Samuel
11. 1 and 2 Kings
12. 1 and 2 Chronicles
13. Ezra/Nehemiah
14. Esther
15. Wisdom Literature Overview
16. Job
17. Psalms
18. Proverbs
19. Ecclesiastes
20. Song of Songs
21. Prophetic Literature Overview
22. Isaiah
23. Jeremiah/Lamentations
24. Ezekiel
25. Daniel
26. Hosea/Amos
27. Jonah
28. Micah
29. Nahum/Zephaniah
30. Habakkuk
31. Haggai
32. Zechariah
33. Joel/Obadiah
34. Malachi
35. Epilogue

Covering the Old Testament Section by Section

1. Fundamentals
2. Geographical Overview of Bible Lands

3. Pentateuch: Original Meaning
4. Pentateuch: Bridging Contexts
5. Pentateuch: Contemporary Significance
6. Pentateuch: Sample Book Overview
7. Pentateuch: Sample Passage
8. Discussion of Issues in Critical Scholarship
9. Unit Quiz
10. Historical Literature: Original Meaning
11. Historical Literature: Bridging Contexts
12. Historical Literature: Contemporary Significance
13. Historical Literature: Sample Book Overview
14. Historical Literature: Sample Passage
15. Archaeology and the Bible
16. Unit Quiz
17. Wisdom Literature: Original Meaning
18. Wisdom Literature: Bridging Contexts
19. Wisdom Literature: Contemporary Significance
20. Wisdom Literature: Sample Book Overview
21. Wisdom Literature: Sample Passage
22. The Canon of the Old Testament
23. Unit Quiz
24. Prophetic Literature: Original Meaning
25. Prophetic Literature: Bridging Contexts
26. Prophetic Literature: Contemporary Significance
27. Prophetic Literature: Sample Book Overview
28. Prophetic Literature: Sample Passage
29. Unit Quiz
30. Psalms: Original Meaning
31. Psalms: Bridging Contexts
32. Psalms: Contemporary Significance
33. Psalms: Sample Passage Interpretation
34. Unit Quiz
35. Epilogue

These leave several classes for tests or supplementary topics, such as Geography, Archaeology, Issues of Authorship, Critical Scholarship, Manuscripts and the Development of the Canon, or Old Testament/New Testament Issues, to whatever extent the professor feels they are important or has the expertise to address them.

ACKNOWLEDGMENTS

A book like this does not come together easily—it is a group project that many hands help to shape. The writing is only the beginning. We have both been helped by student assistants, particularly Kyle Keimer, Caryn Reeder, Liz Klassen, and Heiko Wenzel, who each spent countless hours helping track down pictures, collect captions, and organize the work.

Artists have also made a contribution to the beauty of the book. Our special thanks to Alva Steffler, Susanne Vagt, and Hugh Claycombe for lending us their artistic skills and their attention to detail.

The staff at Zondervan has worked tirelessly to bring this book to completion. Layout director Tracey Moran and editorial assistant Katya Covrett deserve special mention. At the top of the list, however, is project manager, Angela Scheff, who guided the production of the book with grace and patience. We are also grateful to others on the staff who have had significant roles, Ron Huizinga, Alicia Mey, and Jack Kragt. Of course, we must thank Stan Gundry and Jack Kuhatschek for allowing us to tackle this project in the first place.

Finally, we are both in debt, as always, to our wives, Kim (Walton) and Teri (Hill) for their support and their help in dozens of ways. From reading the manuscript at various junctures, to giving opinions and suggestions, to helping out with some of the mechanical details, they are ever our strong right hands.

ABBREVIATIONS

AEL	*Ancient Egyptian Literature*, ed. Miriam Lichtheim (Berkeley: Univ. of California Press, 1975–80.)
ANET	*Ancient Near Eastern Texts*, ed. James Pritchard (Princeton: Princeton University Press, 1974).
COS	*The Context of Scripture*, eds. W. W. Hallo and K. Lawson Younger (Leiden, The Netherlands: Brill, 1997–2002).
HUCA	*Hebrew Union College Annual*
JETS	*Journal of the Evangelical Theological Society*
JSOT	*Journal for the Study of the Old Testament*
NICOT	New International Commentary on the Old Testament
NIVAC	NIV Application Commentary
RB	*Revue biblique*
SBL	Society of Biblical Literature
VT Supp	Vetus Testamentum Supplements
ZAW	*Zeitschrif fur die alttestamentliche Wissenchaft*

Caves near the site of Qumran.

1 FUNDAMENTALS

ABOUT THE OLD TESTAMENT

The Old Testament can be considered a *book*, a *part* of a book, and a *collection* of books. It is a *book* to the extent that its parts form a single whole. This book is often referred to today as the Hebrew Bible because it constitutes the Scripture of the Jewish people. As history progressed and Jesus Christ came, taught, died, and rose again, a whole new round of Scripture was formed to document the life of Christ and the rise of the church and to explore the theological and practical implications of what Christ had done. This New Testament was joined with the Old to become the Christian Bible, and so the Old Testament has become *part* of that book.

We also understand that the Old Testament is a *collection* of books—thirty-nine books by various authors written over the span of a millennium. These books share a common religious perspective, but they vary widely in the types of literature they represent and the functions they serve. In the pages of these books the reader will find consideration of origins, tribal and national histories, collections of laws,

collections of poetry, philosophical discussions, and prophetic sermons. But in all of these and through all of these, the reader will find theology—or, more appropriately put, God. Though the genres (types of literature) may vary, each is theological throughout. So, for instance, the discussion of origins is not about science; it is about God. The presentation of history is not concerned with facts or events in themselves; it is concerned with God's role. And perhaps most important, rather than simply being human thoughts and opinions about God, the Old Testament is God's presentation of himself, that is, his self-revelation.

> The Old Testament can be considered a *book*, a *part* of a book, and a *collection* of books.

THE BIG STORY LINE/PLOTLINE

God made the world operational and put people into it. Adam and Eve disobeyed his command, resulting in their being driven from the Garden of Eden. Thus begins the story of dislocation. Over time the "Eden Problem," sin, became so pervasive that God sent a flood to destroy all but Noah and his family. The Tower of Babel represents the next step as people imagined that God had needs and saw themselves as providing the way for God to come down and have his needs met. This misperception of God can be called the "Babel Problem." Consequently, God chose Abraham to be the ancestor of a chosen people through whom he would reveal himself

Sequence

Creation
Fall
Flood
Tower of Babel
Patriarchs
Sojourn
Exodus
Wilderness
Conquest
Judges
United Kingdom
Divided Kingdom
Exile
Return

and correct the distortion represented at Babel. He brought Abraham to the land of Canaan, where his family lived on the brink of extinction for three generations before going down to Egypt. There they lived for more than four hundred years and became a large nation. God brought them out of great oppression in Egypt, and they began their journey back to the land of Canaan, the Promised Land. After stopping at Mount Sinai, where Moses received the law—God's next phase in revealing himself—they were waylaid in the wilderness for a generation because they lacked the faith to let God lead them into the land.

Under the command of Joshua, the Israelites returned to the land and, in a series of battles, God won them control of the land. Joshua divided the land among the tribes, and they began to settle in. Over the next several centuries, known as the period of the judges, there was no king. Each tribe had its own tribal leadership, but they constantly fell prey to the surrounding nations. God allowed this because of the failure of the Israelites to be faithful to God in their beliefs.

Finally, the people initiated a move to a monarchy form of government. The first attempt, in which Saul was crowned king, failed because of unrealistic and theologically misguided expectations of the king and his role. At his death, Israel was just as bad off politically and spiritually as when he came to the throne. The second attempt was more successful. David was chosen by the Lord to be king, his dynasty became established through a covenant with the Lord, and Jerusalem was made the capital city. As the empire of David expanded, Israel finally came into control of the land that had been promised to Abraham nearly a millennium earlier. He successfully passed this empire to his son Solomon, but Solomon's misjudgments and excesses in both political and theological terms eroded the empire as well as the support of the people. After Solomon's death in 931 BC, his son Rehoboam retained control of only a small section of the kingdom from Jerusalem south, while God gave a new dynasty control of the much larger northern kingdom. The southern kingdom was now designated "Judah," and the northern kingdom, under Jeroboam, was designated Israel.

For just over two hundred years, this situation continued. The Davidic dynasty remained in control in Judah, while the northern kingdom, Israel, experienced a series of dynastic lines. When the Assyrians extended their control across the ancient world in the middle of the eighth century, Israel joined a coalition against the Assyrians and eventually lost the war. The capital city, Samaria, was destroyed in 722 BC, and the northern kingdom was assimilated into the Assyrian Empire. Judah remained an independent nation but was for the most part under Assyrian control. During this time there were kings who were faithful to the Lord (such as Hezekiah), but for the middle fifty-five years, Manasseh forged a regime that accepted not only Assyrian rule, but foreign religious practice as well. The Assyrian Empire lasted for another century until it weakened and was taken over by the Medes and the Babylonians.

Already as the Assyrian Empire receded, the prophetic voices in Judah, such as Jeremiah, were calling on the people to return to the Lord and were warning of impending doom at the hands of the Babylonians. The Assyrian Empire breathed its last gasp in the fall of Carchemish in 605 BC, and the Babylonians began to exert their control into Judah. For several years it was uncertain whether Babylon or Egypt would have the greatest influence, and the kings of Judah rocked back and forth. Eventually Babylon prevailed as the army under Nebuchadnezzar moved west to punish the rebellious King Jehoiakim. His son Jehoiachin was taken into exile in Babylon along with many others in the administration, but the kingdom was left intact. In the next decade, however, the lure of rebellion became too strong, and King Zedekiah joined a conspiracy against the Babylonians. This time there was no mercy. The result of the Babylonian invasion in 587 was the destruction of Jerusalem and its temple, the massive deportation of the Israelites, and the incorporation of Judah as a Babylonian province. The prophets' warnings had come to pass, and for the first time in more than four hundred years, there was no king on David's throne.

The seventy years that were spent in exile were given very little treatment in the text. Prophetic voices such as Ezekiel and Daniel continued to speak, but no historical literature discussed the situation in either Israel or Babylon. When the Babylonian Empire fell to the Persian king Cyrus in 539 BC, a new policy of tolerance allowed the exiles to return to Israel and rebuild their temple. In this postexilic period they had no king, but a governor ruled the small state of Yehud on behalf of the Persian king. Under the leadership of individuals such as Ezra and Nehemiah, the city of Jerusalem was rebuilt and the people recommitted themselves to the covenant and the Lord. Yet they remained a state under Persian rule until Alexander the Great overthrew the Persians and they became part of another empire. As Daniel had indicated, empire followed empire as the people waited for their deliverance and the return of a Davidic king, their Messiah.

REORIENTATION

Picture of a typical Hebrew scroll. The Jewish people wrote their script from right to left on individual pieces of parchment, which were then sewn or glued together and rolled up.

Z. Radovan, Jerusalem

It is not enough to know what the Old Testament is; we need it be reoriented to what the Old Testament does.

If it is true that the Bible is God's self-revelation, we must move beyond the superficial levels of description in the previous paragraphs. It is not enough to say, "The Old Testament is a collection of thirty-nine books written in Hebrew (and Aramaic) that became the Scriptures of the Jewish people as well as Christians," although this certainly is true. That is what the Old Testament *is;* we need it be reoriented to what the Old Testament *does.*

Revelation

When we say that the Old Testament is God's revelation of himself, we are affirming that in the Old Testament God is telling us his story. So begins our quest in the Bible. We need to know God, and the Bible is his story. When we first come to know someone, we become acquainted by relating parts of our stories to one another. The first pages we open include our name, our hometown, and other basic information. As acquaintances become friends, they unfold more and more of their stories to one another. They discover likes and dislikes, past history, present struggles and joys, and future hopes and dreams. We gauge how well we know a person by how much we know of his or her story. When people come to love one another, they want to know every story, and they delight in hearing those stories over and over again.[1]

How can we come to know God? By relating stories to one another. God relates his story through his Word, the Bible. We relate our stories through prayer. God's story is intended to help us to know him. When we see his attributes in action, we come to understand the implications of those attributes. If I were to boast of a friend's kindness, my assessment would be most persuasive if I were able to tell of some of the incidents in which that kindness was evident in unique ways. Once in an initial conversation with a real estate agent, we discovered that we had a mutual acquaintance. My statement that this mutual acquaintance was a good friend could have been understood at various levels. But when I elaborated by saying that his family lived at our house for three weeks while their house was being remodeled, the person had a lot better idea of the level of our friendship. So it is with God. It is not enough to say simply that he is sovereign, just, faithful, loving, gracious, compassionate, or anything else. We know God by hearing his story and by others telling us of things that he has done. We know God by seeing his attributes in action and thereby gaining insight into the warp and woof of his character. The Bible accomplishes this for us, and that is why we refer to it as God's revelation of himself.

If we had no revelation, we would only be able to guess what God is like. We would have to infer from the world around us or from philosophical deduction or from the circumstances of human experience. Like ancients who had no revelation, moderns who refuse to acknowledge the Bible as God's revelation are mired in this bog of uncertainty. If they believe there is a God, the world around them may suggest he is arbitrary or distant. Human experience may suggest to them that he is cruel or meddling. Speculation may conclude that he is like a genie in a bottle, a cosmic cop, or a kind grandparent.

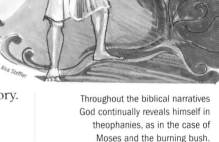

Only revelation can correct these misperceptions. Without the Bible we would know nothing about God with any confidence. Only revelation can offer information outside of ourselves by which we can form a confident and accurate image of God in our minds. As we proceed through our orientation to the Old Testament, one of the most important tasks we will face is to understand how God's story is presented or advanced through each book and how the different genres function to offer us this story.

Throughout the biblical narratives God continually reveals himself in theophanies, as in the case of Moses and the burning bush.

Scripture

In many ways and in various places—from Sinai and the prophets in the Old Testament to the statements of the apostles in 2 Timothy 3:16 and 2 Peter 1:20–21—the Bible presents itself as God's self-disclosure. It is because we accept these claims of the Bible to be God's revelation, God's story, that we label it Scripture. It is not like any other book; it is not just good or classic literature; it is not just a repository of traditions; it is not just entertainment. Once we label it as Scripture, it is no longer *just* anything. Yet even among the books that the major religions of the world label as scripture, the Bible holds a unique position. Even most other scriptures are not revered as the self-revelation of deity—they are simply seen as sacred books. If we were left with a Bible that was just a sacred book, our confidence in our faith would be badly compromised. If the Bible were reduced to

> Without the Bible we would know nothing about God.

being the wise thoughts of spiritual people about God, our hope would be shattered.

But how can we be so confident that the Bible *is* revealed Scripture? Normal responses include reference to fulfilled prophecies and historical accuracy—these have an important role to play, and they help but fall short of offering absolute proof. Skeptics can always find examples of prophecies that don't pair up well with fulfillments, or historical statements that can be undermined. Moreover, even if everyone agreed that every historical statement was above reproach, that would not prove that the book was God's revelation of himself. In the end, the confidence that we have derives from Christ. The Old Testament was the Bible to him—his basis for teaching who God is, what he is like, and what he did. If we believe that Jesus is the Christ, the Son of God, his testimony seals our acceptance of the Old Testament as revealed Scripture.

Authority

The implication of the belief that the Bible is God's revelation of himself is that we must accept it as authoritative. At the center of this authority is not what the Bible tells us to do, though its commands and instructions cannot be ignored. The center of its authority is found in what it tells us to think and believe. It is true that if the Bible says something happened, we believe it happened; if the Bible says someone existed, we believe he or she existed; these are implications of its authority. But the core of its authority is to be found in what it tells us God is like. We are compelled by its authority to accept this picture of God, place it in the center of our worldview, and make it the basis for everything we think and do. Its picture of God is true, and this picture demands our response. In our reorientation to the Old Testament, we need to come to know the Old Testament not as laws and history, psalms and prophecy, but as God's authoritative revelation of himself. If we can do this, the end result will not just be that we will be educated; we will be transformed—godly people living holy lives committed to imitating and serving the God we have come to know through the Bible.

EXPECTATIONS AND PROCEDURES

Most people come to the Old Testament with certain expectations. Some are skeptics and expect myths or legends. Some are believers who have had bad experiences with the Old Testament—frustrated by its laws, bored by its history, or confused by its prophecy. Many have written off the Old Testament as irrelevant to the modern world, and many have concluded that the God of the Old Testament is a tyrant. Some expect moralizing stories of saints and sinners, while others want to find mystical guidance for life. These expectations coupled with our past experiences with the Bible have given us a collection of assumptions about the Old Testament. Whether those presuppositions are insubstantial and blurred or extensive and dogmatic, we must be willing to recognize them and set them aside as we approach the text as if for the first time.

One of the ways we can readjust our expectations is to learn to study the text with an eye toward the big picture. Imagine a large tapestry portraying an expansive view of the countryside with harbor and shore on the one side and steep mountain ranges on the other. In the middle is pictured a castle surrounded by a forest. This landscape is also a snapshot of a momentous historical event, for the castle is under siege. The battlements and towers of the castle are not only festooned with flags and banners; they are swarming with the fully armored defenders who look out on the encampment of the enemy. One can see scattered throughout the forest the tents of the would-be conquerors, including the grand pavilion of their king and the line of tethered horses anticipating the upcoming clash. Over by the sea the harbor is busy as an army disembarks from dozens of ships loaded with supplies and weaponry. And through the mountains on the other side, yet another army wends its way to the aid of one of the combatants. But at the center, the focus of the tapestry is the lowered drawbridge of the castle where the king of the besieged fortress leads a sortie out to engage the enemy, perhaps to catch him unaware and unprepared, turn the tide of the war, and gain a victory for his demoralized people. As his proud white horse gallops across the drawbridge, the banner flaps in the wind and the sun glints off each spear but mostly off the golden crown that indicates the royalty of the one who leads the charge.

This tapestry is not only made up of a combination of smaller pictures rolled into one but is also woven from many different colored threads that make up each smaller picture as well as the whole scene that is frozen in time. Let us imagine that we could go up to this tapestry and work loose the golden thread used to stitch the crown of the king and pull it from its place. I now hold in my hand a golden thread that is about eight inches long. I could conduct numerous tests on this thread. I could discover the material that it was made from, the dye that was used to give it color, and its precise length and thickness. But there is no test that could be performed that could tell me it was a crown, for that was a role it played in the context of the tapestry. Furthermore, if I now turn my attention back to the tapestry, the lead figure on the white horse no longer has a crown on his head, and as a result, something important has been taken away.

Each book of the Old Testament (and in some ways, the Old Testament as a whole) is something like a tapestry. Too often we think we are studying it when we pull out the threads (individual verses or stories) and conduct all of our tests. And in the end, we have a huge pile of threads on the floor at our feet and we know nothing of the tapestry. In fact, we have destroyed it. If we want to understand the tapestry, we need to examine each thread in its place and come to understand the role and function it has in the tapestry. Each thread is important, but its importance derives from its contribution to the tapestry, not from itself. When we apply this concept to the Old Testament, we will become aware that each law, for instance, is most significant with regard to its contribution to the tapestry of law; each narrative is most significant with regard to its contribution to the book in which it is found and the use the author has for it. In the tapestry, whether an individual thread is the crown of the king or the leaf on a tree, it has an important role to play. So it is with the "threads" of the Old Testament, though obviously some have more notable roles to play than others do.

Many have become disillusioned with the Old Testament because they were looking at a pile of threads that had been extracted from the tapestry. In our reorientation, we will try to focus on the tapestry without ignoring the contributions of each picture and thread. Focus is the operative term. When we look at a subject through a camera lens, the focus is important. If we focus on the foreground, the background blurs; if we focus on something at a distance, that which is close to the camera becomes blurred. A good photographer must decide what needs to be clear and what can be blurred. The larger picture of the Old Testament, from a literary standpoint, is seen in the purpose of each author in the book that he is writing. As we keep that in focus, the individual verses and stories must be seen in relation to it. From a theological perspective, the larger picture is God. Individuals fade into the background as we see the Old Testament not as a compilation of stories about Abraham or David or Esther, but a single story about God. If we bring David too much into focus, the picture of God may blur.

It is instructive to think of the Old Testament in terms of a photo-mosaic. The computer has made photo-mosaics common. Whether on jigsaw puzzles, posters, or TV commercials, we have seen the technique in which many small pictures (e.g., from the life of Lincoln) are arranged to make one large picture (e.g., a portrait of Lincoln). Using this technique, we could take thousands of small pictures of various Bible stories and characters and sort and arrange them so that they depict Michelangelo's fresco on the ceiling of the Sistine Chapel showing God reaching out his hand to Adam—a picture not only of creation, but also of revelation and redemption, three ideas that comprise the most important ways God has reached out to us. The study of each picture would prominently include coming to an understanding of the role it played in the larger picture of God reaching out to humankind. This is the plotline of the Old Testament.

What Is a Plotline?

A plotline traces the big picture. It is the tapestry. For the Old Testament, the most important big picture is not a historical one, it is a theological one. The big picture is God, not history. The story line traces the content; the plotline traces the message. In the end, the plotline offers us a worldview—an understanding of God and ourselves. A story line is made up of an array of facts; a plotline is made up of an array of convictions. The objective of the story line is to let the reader know what happened; the objective of the plotline is to persuade the reader what to believe.

Story line: content

Plotline: message

Old Testament Study

What is involved in arriving at an understanding of the story line and plotline of the Old Testament? It is actually a complex and multifaceted field of study. Since the Old Testament was written mostly in Hebrew (small sections in Aramaic), the study of that language is important. Further understanding of Hebrew can come from studying related Semitic languages such as Akkadian (spoken by Babylonians and Assyrians and written in cuneiform) and Ugaritic (a language spoken by some Canaanites). These related languages are referred to as cognate languages. The study of ancient Near Eastern history and

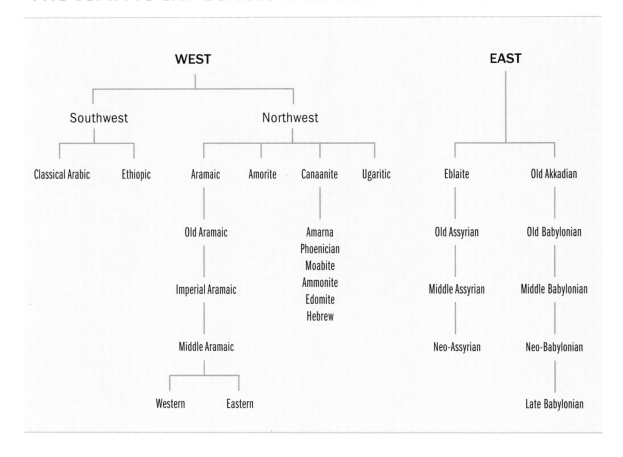

literature is another specialized field (called comparative studies) that can shed light on the cultural background of the Old Testament. These studies use texts as a window to culture and try to fill in the whole area of manners and customs in the ancient world. Historical geography is a type of study that targets the locations that appear in the text and tries to understand the events in relation to the places in which they occurred. These places can be further explored by archaeologists who not only learn about the various sites, but also attempt to reconstruct the history of a site and the lifestyle and culture of the peoples who inhabited that site. Sociological specialists seek to understand the institutions of the ancient world (priesthood, families, sacrifice), while those specializing in the history of religion explore the religious beliefs of the Israelites and their neighbors. All of these fields involve the people, events, and cultures that are portrayed in the texts.

The study of the texts themselves takes us into an entirely different realm. Textual critics seek to compare the modern state of the text as we have received it and the ancient form of the text as it is evidenced in manuscripts. Their task is to study variations between manuscripts to determine what the original or earliest canonical form of the text looked like. Other scholars investigate the sources that may have been used in the compilation of a book or the individual(s) that authored or compiled the book. Almost all of the specialists we have mentioned so far focus on the individual threads of the tapestry of the Old Testament. The study of the tapestry as a whole involves still other specialties. The literary analysis of a book is often essential in order to arrive at the author's purpose. From a study of the literary form of a book will emerge observations about the author's selection and arrangement of his material. Working with these and paying attention to the emphasis the author gives to the material can help the interpreter to deduce the author's purpose. The theologian will combine all of these elements to try to distill the theological message of the text. What is the text teaching? What is it revealing about God? What beliefs are being presented authoritatively to the reader?

All of these methodological approaches are designed to help us to understand the *face value* of the text. They are *exegetical* tasks governed by principles of *hermeneutics* that guide us in the process of interpretation. We need to spend a little time on each of these three terms.

Face Value

Evangelicals are committed to taking the text at face value, that is, we do not try to read anything into the text or squeeze something out of the text. We are not trying to sidestep the text or to avoid what it makes obvious. We are not trying to subordinate the text to our own agenda or purpose, nor are we trying to commandeer it for our theology or make it answer our questions. We are simply trying to understand the text in the way that the author wanted to be understood by his audience. This means that we have to be alert to a wide array of factors that could inadvertently lead us to misconstrue the face value and therefore distort the communication. After we make adjustments for these factors, however, we should have a clear idea of what the text asks of us. Following is a brief discussion of three of the principal factors for determining face value.

> **Face Value:**
>
> Not trying to read anything into the text or trying to squeeze something out of the text.

> **Face Value Issues:**
>
> - genre
> - cultural background
> - focus of revelation

Nature (Genre) of Literature Issues

The first item that must be taken into account when determining the face value is the type of literature represented in the text. Language and literature can be used to represent, express, or persuade, and we must be sensitive to which function is reflected in any particular genre. In our culture, the function of a mystery novel would certainly be different than the function of a biography. As we consider the various genres, we need to become informed about how those genres were used and understood in the ancient world. For example, let us briefly consider one of the Bible's most baffling genres, genealogy. We have certain expectations of a genealogy based on the way our culture uses the genre. A genealogy in our culture represents a line of descent for the purpose of identifying ancestors in their sequential order. Interestingly, anthropologists studying genealogies in primitive cultures found that sequential order was not a major concern of the genealogical representations.[2] The order was more representative of the relative significance of the various ancestors. As a result, liquidity (switching around the order) could be observed. Likewise, the ages attributed to various ancestors did not necessarily represent the years of life. Other considerations were factors in assigning years. Consequently, though it goes against our understanding of the genre of genealogy, we could hardly label a genealogy of these cultures as false or deceptive if it was found to be out of order or to list ages that differed from "reality."

What about narrative? As with genealogy, we need to try our best to understand how narrative works in Israel rather than just to assume it works the same as it does in English. We know that narrative style can be used for mythology, epic, folktale, parable, and fable as well as for history. As a result, identifying something as narrative is not the same as identifying it as history. Within a given genre, language can be used for different purposes. A narrator may be using his language to represent events, to express truths, or to persuade of some point. Sometimes it is difficult to assess what expectations the narrator has of his audience, making literary analysis to no avail. For instance, when we read Judges 9, we easily label Jotham's narrative as fable because the trees talk, and we all know trees don't talk. By the same criterion, some have concluded that Genesis 3 ought also to be considered fable because of the talking serpent. Obviously the issues are complex. If we are going to take the text of Genesis 3 at face value, we must go beyond a

Genre:

Classification identifying what type of literature a work is.

single criterion and ask what the Israelite audience believed about it. In this case, neither literary analysis nor understanding of the culture gives a clear indication of how the Israelites would have heard this narrative. Continuing revelation, however, suggests that they did not understand it as fable, because in the rest of Scripture the surrounding narrative (trees, garden, temptation, sin) is all taken with the seriousness of fact. That leads us to conclude that taking the narrative at face value precludes classifying it as fable despite the presence of literary elements that might otherwise point in that direction.

Cultural Background Issues

The cultural dimension must also be considered when trying to discern the face value of a text. As an example, we may consider the issue of the sons of God in Genesis 6:2. If the face value of the text suggests that angels intermarried with mortals, we must be prepared to accept that and defend it. Some interpreters, however, have concluded that an understanding of the culture and literature of the ancient Near East suggests that the text was making reference to the heroic, but oppressive, kings of old. If the latter were true, then familiarity with the culture would have provided a face value for the text that was not immediately obvious to the modern reader but may have been intuitive to the author and his audience. Consequently, the historical intermarriage of angels with mortals would not have to be defended.

In general we have to be aware that the ancient culture was far different from our own. They had different values and different ways of thinking about themselves in relation to the world and the people around them. The chart on page 14 offers a sampling of some of the differences.

Focus of Revelation Issues

An understanding of the focus of revelation is a third element that is essential for gaining a clear comprehension of face value. For instance, the Bible often speaks of the heart as the center of intelligence and the organ of thought. The function of the brain was unknown

The Sumerian King List records the names and years of rule for the early kings of Mesopotamia. The reigns are exceedingly long, and are often compared to the lengthy life spans mentioned in Genesis.

Courtesy Ashmolean Museum, University of Oxford

The Old Babylonian map of the world is one of the oldest known maps. It portrays Babylon as the center of the world and provides insight into the geographical perspective of the ancients.

Z. Radovan, Jerusalem

in the ancient world, and rather than redress their physiological ignorance, God felt free to speak of the heart as the organ of thought. As modern readers with better knowledge of physiology, we are not obligated to believe that we think with our hearts. Physiology was not the focus of revelation, and therefore the revelation at its face value had no intentions of making physiological statements.

CONTRAST IN VALUES AND PERSPECTIVES*

MODERN WESTERN	NEAR EASTERN
• Egocentric identity	• Group-centric identity
• Promote independence	• Promote interdependence
• See the parts	• See the whole
• Urge uniqueness	• Urge conformity
• Seek autonomy from social solidarity	• Seek integration into social reality
• Primary responsibility to self and individual potential	• Primary obligation to others and development of the group
• Behavior is governed by rights and duties specified by one's goals	• Behavior is dictated by the group or the leader
• Individual worth is based on achievements and possessions	• Individual worth is rooted in family status, social position, class, or caste
• Status is achieved	• Status is ascribed
• Achieving and competing are motivational necessities	• Achieving and competing are disruptive to the group
• Equality is a key value	• Hierarchy is a key value
• A group is viewed as a collection of individuals	• A group is viewed as an organismic unit
• Individual self is a separate entity from physical world and others	• Individual self is organically connected with physical world and others
• Private autonomy	• Corporate solidarity
• Strong personal identity	• Strong familial identity
• Self-reliant achievement	• Interdependent collaboration
• Desire to be personally satisfied	• Desire to be interpersonally satisfying or satisfactory

*From John Pilch, *Introducing the Cultural Context of the Old Testament* (Mahweh, NJ: Paulist, 1991), 97.

Exegesis and Hermeneutics. Exegesis is simply the detailed study of the biblical text. Exegesis proper deals most specifically with the linguistic and literary features of the text, but the general exegetical task includes any study that is necessary for the interpretation of the text. Hermeneutics is the science that governs the exegetical process. Principles of biblical hermeneutics generally promote objectivity such that anyone who applies these principles can arrive at the same conclusion. It operates on the basis of evidence, not on feeling. In this way we treat the text as using conceptual language that expects to be read in a forthright manner. This is in contrast to symbolic language that is coded or mystical—that is not the Bible's way. An acceptable or correct interpretation is arrived at by thorough exegesis (using all the tools available) guided by sound hermeneutics and premised on presuppositions that have been evaluated and judged valid.

Nevertheless, we do not mean to suggest that everyone can always arrive at and agree on *the* true interpretation of a passage. Different interpreters will judge different presuppositions to be valid. One will accept presuppositionally the nature of the text as the Word of God with all the implications that that has; others will not. One will accept the essential unity of the text; others will not. One might feel comfortable imposing a New Testament grid on the interpretation of the Old Testament; others will not. Even if two interpreters agree in the area of presuppositions, there are often times when the evidence is insufficient to arrive at a confident conclusion. In this case, different interpreters might give greater weight to different elements. One might consider a word study that is inconclusive but suggestive as leading in one direction, while the other might consider the weight of archaeological and cultural considerations as overriding the word study and leading elsewhere. Thus, in the study of the Old Testament, we are faced with many texts for which there will be a number of possible alternative interpretations. The challenge to readers of the text is to foster a commitment to keep an open mind where the data fail to establish a firm case.

Confidence in the Results of Old Testament Study. We have seen that studying the Old Testament is a complex task with many potential pitfalls. How can we arrive at any sense of confidence about our reading of God's Word? Amid the prospect of uncertainty in the adequacy of our knowledge, the sufficiency of our methods, and the details of our presuppositions, it is important to bear in mind that the revelation of God stands untainted by ambiguity. Granted there are times when we might have difficulty understanding why God does what he does (e.g., allow for the ruin of Job or order the killing of entire families). But though we occasionally may be uncertain about how his attributes are consistent with his actions, there is no question what his attributes are. The problems usually come not when the text is incomprehensible, but when we are too ready to discount the claims of the text about God—to consider God as having the same weaknesses and the same motivations as we do.

One of the facts that humans have yet to master is that we cannot outperform God. In the movie *Patch Adams*, starring Robin Williams, the main character is an unconventional medical student who believes that humor and compassion are the most significant tools of the doctor's trade. His idealism is shattered when his girlfriend, who has helped him start a free clinic based on these principles, is murdered by one of the psychotic patients. As Patch stands on a high cliff pondering suicide, he has the following monologue with God: "So answer me please—tell me what you're doing. . . . You create man; man suffers enormous amounts of pain; man dies. Maybe you should have had just a few more brainstorming sessions prior to creation. You rested on the seventh day—maybe you should have spent that day on compassion."

As he looks down into the valley far below, again considering the possibility of jumping, he says, tragically, "You know what? You're not worth it."

Whenever we raise questions about God's justice, we tacitly suggest, as Patch did, that, given the chance, we would be more just. When we question the love of God, we imply that we could be more loving. Name whatever attribute you will—his grace, his mercy, his patience. If we think we can do it better than God, we have a defective view of God (not to mention an unrealistic conceit and a superficial and simplistic knowledge of the problem). Talk to any adult on the street and you likely will hear how unfair it is of God to do this or that. In today's climate of tolerance, it is common to be told that only an ogre of a God would so limit the range of salvation that only those who happened to hear of Jesus could benefit. So, for instance, our own sentiments become hopelessly entangled with our theology as we try to address the difficult issue of the plight of the aborted unborn in eternity. One year in a doctrine class for sixth graders at church, one of the students in the heat of the debate about the fate of babies declared forcefully, "If I were God, all babies would go to heaven!"

We all know that revelation only takes us so far and our theology does not provide ironclad answers for every question. But where revelation is silent and the logic of our theology fails, we are not without recourse. Here is where faith begins. Will not the Judge of all the earth do right? Of course he will. We don't have to worry that God is less fair, less just, less merciful, less loving, or less gracious than we would be. The "If I were God . . ." option will always fall far short of the option of letting him be God. This is our faith. We never have all the information, and we are never wise enough to apply what information we have infallibly to whatever issue is at hand. Faith has to step in and cover the ground where exegesis and hermeneutics are insufficient.

WRITING AND BOOKS

Before we conclude this introductory chapter, we need to say a few words about how the Old Testament came together and was recognized as the Word of God. If we go all the way back to the beginning of the process, we must start with the invention of writing toward the end of the fourth millennium BC. The Sumerians in Mesopotamia and the Egyptians both used a pictographic script that represented objects and then syllables as pictures. These syllabic scripts were complex, and consequently, very few could read. The invention of alphabetic script did not come until about 1600 BC—a period roughly between the patriarchs and Moses. It was invented by Semitic peoples for Semitic languages, and the Israelites would therefore have had early access to the advances it offered. Now with only about thirty signs rather than hundreds, more people could learn to read, though literacy may still have been somewhat limited.

Words for "King" in Various Scripts

The word *king* Lugal in Sumerian script.

The word *king* nesu in Egyptian Hieroglyphic script.

The word *king* melek in Iron Age Hebrew script.

The word *king* šarru in Neo-Assyrian Akkadian script.

PICTORIAL SIGNS

Chart of early forms of writing: Sumerian, Egyptian, Hittite, Chinese.

	Sumerian	Egyptian	Hittite	Chinese
MAN				
KING				
DEITY				
OX				
SHEEP				
SKY				
STAR				
SUN				
WATER				
WOOD				
HOUSE				
ROAD				
CITY				
LAND				

From Martha L. Carter and Keith N. Schoville, eds., *Sign, Symbol, Script* (Madison: Office of the Exhibit, Univ. of Wisconsin, 1984), 3. Used by permission.

Many different surfaces were used for writing, including stone, clay, pottery, wood, metal, leather, and papyrus. Only the latter two materials were suitable for scrolls. An average papyrus scroll contained about twenty pages of papyrus sheets glued together. The resulting scroll was about fifteen feet long and one foot tall. Parchment (using animal skins) was much less in use during the Old Testament period but was known.

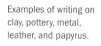

Examples of writing on clay, pottery, metal, leather, and papyrus.

The transition from scrolls to books with pages did not take place until well after the Old Testament period, so Old Testament "books" actually would have been scrolls.

Some of the books of the Old Testament, including many of Moses' words in the Pentateuch as well as the sermons of the prophets, were originally presented orally as the word of God. If a prophet was accepted as a true messenger of the true God, his words immediately would have attained the status of Scripture and been preserved. Other books of the Old Testament have far more obscure origins. For instance, though many psalms are associated with David, others were not written until after the exile. Consequently, the book could not have reached its final form until centuries after the earliest parts were written. Other books were not put together until long after the events recorded in them took place. The books of Kings, for example, trace history from the reign of Solomon until after the fall of Jerusalem. The books could not have achieved their final form until the middle of the sixth century BC, even though the events of Solomon's reign are in the tenth century BC.

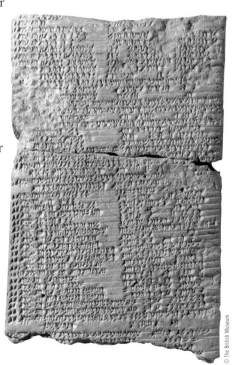

Old Testament manuscripts date back to only the second century BC (among the Dead Sea Scrolls), so we cannot glimpse the development of the Old Testament through that type of evidence. In the end, we must admit that the information at our disposal is extremely limited. We find the confidence to accept the Old Testament as God's Word not because we have full access to the information regarding the writing, editing, and collecting of each book into the canon, but because we consider the Old Testament to have been validated by Jesus. It is this Bible that Jesus read, knew, and used that will now be the subject of our study.

© The British Museum

© The British Museum

Samples of early writings: Egyptian Hieroglyphic (above left) and Sumerian Barley ration tablet (above right).

Erich Lessing, Courtesy of Art Resources

The Dead Sea Scrolls contain the oldest extant copies of the books of the Old Testament (except Esther). Fragments have been found scattered throughout numerous caves near the site of Qumran.

Copyright: ROHR Productions Ltd.

- authority
- comparative studies
- Dead Sea Scrolls
- exegesis
- face value
- genre
- hermeneutics
- inspiration
- revelation
- Scripture

GOING TO THE NEXT LEVEL

Bill Arnold and Bryan Beyer, *Encountering the Old Testament* (Baker).

Albert Baylis, *From Creation to the Cross* (Zondervan).

Daniel Doriani, *Getting the Message* (Presbyterian and Reformed).

Gordon Fee and Douglas Stuart, *How to Read the Bible for All Its Worth* (Zondervan).

Andrew Hill and John Walton, *Survey of the Old Testament* (Zondervan).

Tremper Longman III, *Reading the Bible with Heart and Mind* (Navpress).

Leland Ryken, *How to Read the Bible as Literature* (Zondervan).

Leland Ryken and Tremper Longman III, *A Complete Literary Guide to the Bible* (Zondervan).

Gordon Wenham, *Story as Torah* (Baker).

Notes

1. Tim Stafford, *Knowing the Face of God*, rev. ed. (Grand Rapids: Zondervan, 1989), 122–29.
2. For a full discussion of primitive as well as ancient societies, see Robert R. Wilson, *Genealogy and History in the Biblical World* (New Haven, CT: Yale University Press, 1977).

2 PENTATEUCH

Kadesh Barnea.

The Pentateuch is made up of the first five books of the Bible—Genesis, Exodus, Leviticus, Numbers, and Deuteronomy. The ancient Israelites and the Jewish people of today refer to the Pentateuch as the Torah. *Torah* is a Hebrew word that is often translated "law" and may be more widely understood as "instruction." In the traditions of Israel and of the church, Moses is considered the author of these books. The face value of the texts therefore sees them as addressed to the Israelites on their way from Egypt to the promised land of Canaan. If we were to use a modern metaphor, we might say that in the Pentateuch we have a five-part mini-series (the five books) and one that expects a sequel (for they have yet to enter the land).

"What you think about God—not what you *say* you think about God, but what you really think deep down inside—is the most important determination of your character."

ORIENTATION

- The covenant is God's program of revelation.
- The stories in the Bible are stories about God.
- The law is God's revelation of his character.

YAHWEH FOCUS

- God established and maintains order in the cosmos.
- God overcomes obstacles to carry out his purposes.
- God has determined to reveal himself to his people.
- God's grace exceeds all logic.
- God is holy.

KEY VERSES

- Genesis 12:1–3   Covenant offer
- Exodus 3:16–17   God's intentions to bring Israel out of Egypt
- Leviticus 19:2   Call to holiness
- Numbers 6:24–26   Priestly benediction
- Deuteronomy 6:4–9   Israel's responsibility

OUTLINE

ORIGINAL MEANING

Old Testament Story Line, Adam through Moses

History Story Line, 3000–1400 BC

Literary Perspective

BRIDGING CONTEXTS

Plotline of the Pentateuch

Purpose of Each Book

Dealing with Story

Theological Perspectives

Contrast: Religious Belief in the Ancient World

CONTEMPORARY SIGNIFICANCE

Scenario: Evolution and the Bible

Recapitulation

The Fall Today

Significance of the Faith of Abraham

Old Covenant/New Covenant

What Are All of These Laws Doing in My Bible if the Law is Obsolete?

Scenario: Law

Recapitulation

What Does Sacred Space Mean to Me?

A Sense of the Holy

KEY PLOTLINE TERMS

- cosmology
- fall
- flood
- Tower of Babel
- covenant
- patriarchs
- exodus
- Law/Torah
- holiness
- sacred space
- Yahweh

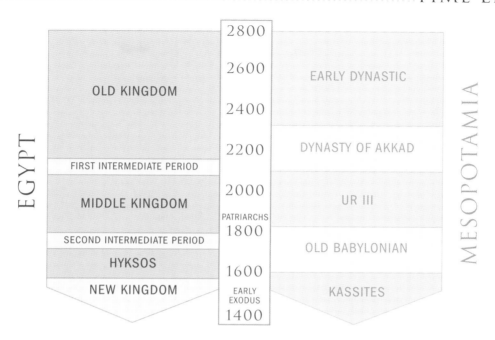

EGYPT

2800	
OLD KINGDOM	2600 · 2400 · EARLY DYNASTIC
	2200 · DYNASTY OF AKKAD
FIRST INTERMEDIATE PERIOD	
MIDDLE KINGDOM	2000 · UR III
	PATRIARCHS
SECOND INTERMEDIATE PERIOD	1800 · OLD BABYLONIAN
HYKSOS	1600
NEW KINGDOM	EARLY EXODUS · KASSITES
	1400

MESOPOTAMIA

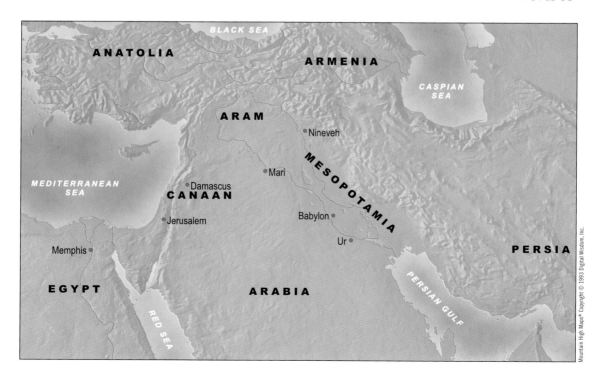

ANATOLIA

BLACK SEA

ARMENIA

CASPIAN SEA

ARAM

Nineveh

MESOPOTAMIA

Mari

MEDITERRANEAN SEA

Damascus

CANAAN

Jerusalem

Babylon

Ur

PERSIA

Memphis

EGYPT

ARABIA

PERSIAN GULF

RED SEA

1 ORIGINAL MEANING

OLD TESTAMENT STORY LINE

Beginnings

The first eleven chapters of Genesis record events that took place before the ancestors of the Israelites were chosen by God. Logically, the story of creation opens the section with the account of God bringing the orderly cosmos out of chaos. Once people had been placed in this well-organized world, God blessed them with the privileges of multiplying and of acquiring food for themselves from that which he had created. Chapter 2 shows how this blessing was made possible as the Garden of Eden was planted for food and the woman was created from the man so that it would be possible to be fruitful and multiply.

The serenity of paradise is broken in chapter 3 as the serpent came on the scene and enticed the woman to eat fruit from the only tree that was forbidden, the tree of the knowledge of good and evil. Man followed her lead, and their disobedience resulted in God's expelling them from the garden and from his presence. They were now cut off from the tree of life and subject to death. Moreover, they would now experience considerable difficulty and anguish in appropriating the blessing, as reproducing and acquiring food would be burdened with obstacles.

Sin escalated in the next generation. As Adam and Eve's sons Cain and Abel offered their gifts to God, Cain became angry that his brother's was deemed acceptable while his was not. The result was premeditated murder, for which Cain was driven away. The next chapters use genealogies of Cain and Seth (a "replacement" son) to bridge the gap to Noah, a descendant of Seth, in whose time the flood came. Chapters 6 through 9 are taken up with the flood account, with Noah, his immediate family, and animals being delivered in the ark. When the waters subsided and order was restored, God once more extended the blessings of reproduction and food acquisition.

Again a genealogical type of record is used to list the descendants of Noah's sons who repopulated the world. The resulting "Table of Nations" in chapter 10 classifies all the known peoples of the ancient world according to which of Noah's sons they descended from. This leads into the last narrative of the section, the story of the Tower of Babel. The people were reluctant to separate from one another and decided that if they built a city more of them could survive in one place. Like the ancient ziggurats of Mesopotamia, the tower they built along with the city was designed as a way to allow their God to come down and bless them. But when God came down, he was displeased and diversified their languages, making their cooperative living plans impossible. They thus scattered abroad. Chapters 1 through 11 come to a conclusion as yet another genealogy bridges the space from Noah to Abram and the beginning of the covenant relationship.

Reconstruction of a ziggurat.

Patriarchs and Matriarchs of Israel

The remainder of the book of Genesis traces the four generations from Abraham (Abram) through the sons of Jacob, who were the patriarchal originators of the twelve tribes of Israel. Called late in life by a God previously unknown to him, Abram left his home in Mesopotamia and traveled with his wife, Sarai, and his nephew Lot to the land God had promised would be given to him. The text

Ivory plaque from Assyria that depicts a deity from whom the four life-giving waters flow, flanked by trees and guardian creatures.

Garden of Eden

In the ancient world, palaces and temples often had adjoining park-like gardens. These were not primarily for growing vegetables. Rather, they were pleasant places to relax and spend time. They featured shady areas, waterways, exotic trees, birds, and wildlife that contributed to a peaceful atmosphere. Fruit trees provided refreshment while paths and pavilions served as places to meet and talk. This is the type of garden

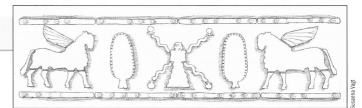

described in Genesis 2. Eden is portrayed as the place of God's presence. As was commonly understood in the ancient world, water flowed out of the presence of God and brought life to everything around.

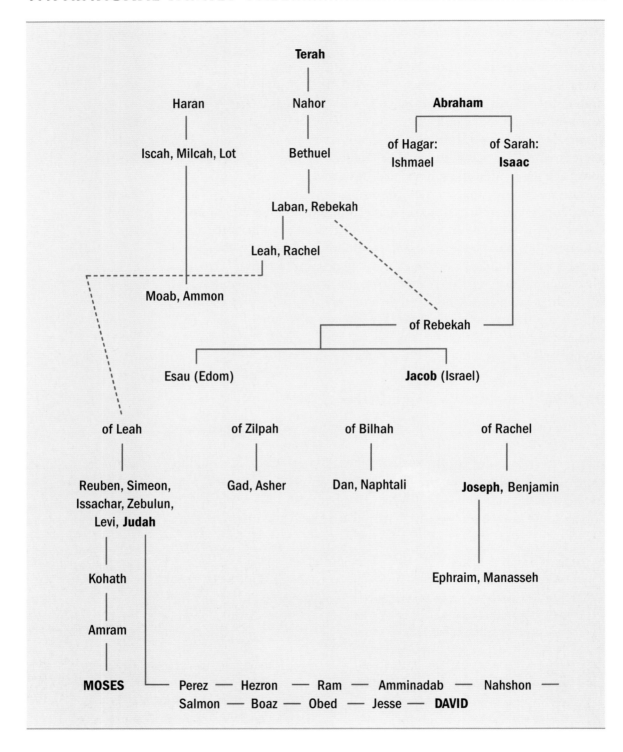

Terah

Haran   Nahor   **Abraham**

Iscah, Milcah, Lot   Bethuel   of Hagar: of Sarah:
Ishmael   **Isaac**

Laban, Rebekah

Leah, Rachel

Moab, Ammon   of Rebekah

Esau (Edom)   **Jacob** (Israel)

of Leah   of Zilpah   of Bilhah   of Rachel

Reuben, Simeon,   Gad, Asher   Dan, Naphtali   **Joseph**, Benjamin
Issachar, Zebulun,
Levi, **Judah**

Kohath   Ephraim, Manasseh

Amram

MOSES   Perez — Hezron — Ram — Amminadab — Nahshon —
Salmon — Boaz — Obed — Jesse — **DAVID**

documents his travels and his adventures as he gained a foothold in the land of Canaan and struggled with Sarai's childlessness. He found it difficult to understand how someone whose wife could bear no children (a repeated motif in these narratives) could become the father of a great nation as God had promised him. Lot eventually left Abram to settle in Sodom and was spared because of Abram when the Lord destroyed Sodom and Gomorrah. In an attempt to produce an heir, Abram had a son by Sarai's servant, Hagar, and named him Ishmael. Though this was a standard solution to a wife's barrenness at that time, God had other plans. When Abraham was one hundred years old and Sarah was ninety, a son, Isaac, was born to them.

Most of Isaac's story is intertwined with either his father's or his sons'. Though his wife, Rebekah, was also unable to have children for a time, eventually the twins, Esau and Jacob, were born. The conflict between Esau and Jacob took center stage as Jacob exploited his older brother and deceived his elderly father to gain the advantages that normally belonged to the firstborn. At last he had so angered his brother that he fled back to Mesopotamia to protect his life.

Abraham in Real Life

Tomb painting from Beni Hassan of Semitic merchants in Egypt.

After Abraham moved to Canaan, he spent most of his life in the desolate southern regions of the country. He was not a farmer; he was a keeper of herds and flocks. Since the land of this region had limited vegetation, he moved the herds and flocks around throughout the year from one area of grazing land and water supply to another. This was an isolated and lonely way of life. Visitors were rare, and news from the outside world was occasional at best. The places where Abraham stayed were not along major trade routes, and therefore he had little opportunity for trade. Abraham's tent was likely made of black goat hides. His meals probably consisted of vegetables, ghee (a refined form of butterfat), and bread from barley grain. Daytime heat required frequent drinks of water. From the size of Abraham's household, we can assume that his tent was one in what was practically a village of tents. Evenings were likely spent gathered around the remains of cooking fires. These were not campfires like we build today, for wood was scarce in the region and shade was too valuable to consider cutting down any trees. In short, the wilderness was a region where survival required a lot of attention and left little time for anything else.

We should not think of Abraham as having daily devotions and regular times of conversation face to face with God. Neither should we think of him worshiping in a temple. He had no Scripture to read (if indeed he could read) and no temple to visit. On special occasions, however, he made sacrifices on altars that he built. His personal conversations with God were extremely rare—often decades apart. We can know little about his religious life but can assume that aside from the probability of daily prayers, it was very limited.

Before Jacob left, God spoke to him in a dream and told him that he would take care of him and bring him back to the land. Jacob spent twenty years in Paddan Aram (northern Mesopotamia) working for his Uncle Laban and marrying Laban's daughters, Leah and Rachel. While he was there, eleven of his twelve sons were born. But conflict followed wherever Jacob went, and over twenty years he and his uncle/father-in-law developed irreconcilable differences. Jacob took his family and goods and stole away while Laban was off shearing his sheep.

Families in the Ancient World

Most families in the ancient world were either farmers or pastoralists. Urban centers were relatively few and were generally very small. Major cities such as Jerusalem were only twelve to fifteen acres. Even the largest cities did not exceed two hundred acres. Nothing was truly metropolitan in modern terms. A large majority of the population lived in either rural or village settings. A typical village might be between one and three acres in size. Population experts estimate that usually villages averaged one hundred people per acre.

While pastoralists lived in tents, farmers and village folk lived in pillared houses. The common designation for the style of house in Israel is the "four-room house."

These pillared houses were small, rectilinear structures. Access was through a door leading into the largest room. On one or sometimes both sides of the entryway was a row of crude pillars (or piers). Sometimes there was a low partition wall connecting the pillars. The central area of the large room usually had a beaten earth floor, with the area between pillars and side walls having a cobbled surface. At the end of the main room, or along one side in some cases, were one or more doorways leading to one of the three smaller rooms, usually with beaten earth floors. Stairways, usually attached

Model of the layout of a four room house.

Reconstruction of typical four-room house.

to exterior walls, indicate upper stories. The central room sometimes had ovens, cooking pits, or hearths. *

Recent study has suggested that most of the ground floor was for storage and supplies while the living quarters were on the second floor. The large central room may have sometimes been at least partially open to the sky, but courtyards were more often outside the structure. Groups of houses often shared common walls and probably shared central courtyard space, allowing extended families including several generations to live together yet not share a single house. A typical small village would contain several housing compounds with most of the members of the village being related to one another (constituting the clan). Each housing compound would be made up of two to three houses with the extended family numbering perhaps fifteen.

Family activity was task oriented, focusing on all of the details necessary for daily subsistence: caring for animals, processing food (from planting to storage to meal preparation), making tools, providing water, manufacturing textiles, and maintaining property.

*Carol Meyers, "The Family in Early Israel," in *Families in Ancient Israel,* ed. L. G. Perdue et al. (Louisville: Westminster John Knox, 1997), 14. Most of the information for this entry was drawn from Meyers's article.

The personal name of the God of Israel was Yahweh. This is not a name that can be applied to any other god. In most English translations it is represented by LORD (in all uppercase letters). *Yahweh* often used to be represented in English as "Jehovah," but now it is recognized that such a rendering is the result of a misinformed reading of the Hebrew. Other countries and peoples had patron gods of nations or cities, cosmic gods (connected to the heavenly bodies), fertility gods (responsible for crops and reproduction), and family or personal gods. In Israel Yahweh served all of these functions, though it often was difficult for the Israelites to retain him in each of these categories. They were especially inclined to adopt Baal as their fertility god even when they recognized that Yahweh was their national god. The meaning of the name *Yahweh* is uncertain, though it is generally accepted that it is a form of the verb "to be," thus Yahweh's statement to Moses, "This is what you are to say to the Israelites: 'I AM has sent me to you'" (Exod. 3:14).

Since Israel's faith was monotheistic, Israel's God was understood to be the ultimate force in the universe. There were no other gods to compete with. In the polytheistic beliefs of Israel's neighbors, none of the individual gods,

Name of YHWH in Ancient Hebrew Script

or even all the gods rolled into one, operated in the unrestricted realm of ultimate power. In Israel this was the realm occupied by Yahweh. He was accountable to no one, dependent on no one, underived, and totally autonomous. In contrast, the realm of ultimate power in the polytheistic pagan mentality was impersonal. Yet this elevated view of the Bible was not all laid out at once. It was not until the Ten Commandments were given at Sinai that the issue of other gods was addressed forthrightly. But even there it is only said that they should worship no other gods along with Yahweh. When he said that they should have no other gods before him, he indicated, perhaps among other things, that there were no other gods in his presence serving as a divine assembly (a view that was common in the ancient Near East). As the role of Yahweh was made clearer and clearer, the Israelites came to understand the central and ultimate position of their God, Yahweh—but it was a long road with many detours along the way.

Jebel Musa. "You saw no form of any kind the day the LORD spoke to you at Horeb out of the fire" (Deut. 4:15).

2 PENTATEUCH

Shechem is the first Canaanite site mentioned in relation to the travels of Abram. It is also where Abram built is first altar to the Lord (Gen. 12:6-7).

Copyright: ROHR Productions Ltd.

Terah, the father of Abram, took his family from Ur of the Chaldeans to Haran. There is scholarly debate over the location of this Ur. Some believe it is to be located in southern Mesopotamia (the traditional location), while others believe Ur was farther north and much nearer Haran. It is from Haran that Abram began his journey to Canaan.

Laban, unwilling to let his daughters and grandchildren escape so easily, pursued Jacob and caught up to him as they approached the northeastern boundary of Canaan. After dredging up each other's list of supposed offenses, they finally came to an uneasy agreement, and Laban went back home while Jacob and his family turned their attention to the next problem: Esau. Jacob's uneasiness about how Esau felt after all of these years led him to make a number of gestures designed to foster reconciliation, but on the eve of their reunion, he remained anxious about his brother's intentions. The tension made him vulnerable to God's influence, and an angel wrestled his self-sufficiency away from him. The reunion with Esau went astonishingly well, and Jacob resettled in the land.

When Jacob's favorite wife, Rachel, died while giving birth to his twelfth son, Benjamin, he transferred his favoritism to Rachel's oldest, Joseph. The special coat Jacob gave to Joseph designated him as having a leadership role over his older brothers. Their resentment grew when he related his dreams to them in which they bowed down to him. Finally, when they found themselves alone with Joseph far from home, their envy asserted itself and they sold him to a caravan going to Egypt. In Egypt Joseph was sold as a slave to an official named Potiphar. Potiphar was impressed by Joseph, who proved to be competent and reliable, and Potiphar quickly promoted him to a place of significant responsibility. When Potiphar's wife attempted to seduce Joseph, he retained his integrity. This humiliated and angered her so that she accused him of mistreating her. The false charge landed Joseph in prison. Again advancing to a position of responsibility, Joseph encountered two of Pharaoh's officials who had had baffling dreams. Joseph found that he could interpret them with God's help. When Pharaoh himself had dreams several years later, Joseph was able to interpret them and was elevated to one of the highest positions in Egypt. The dreams had been a message concerning a coming famine, and Pharaoh commissioned Joseph to prepare for that famine through years of plenty so that Egypt would survive.

The famine struck Canaan as well and drove Joseph's brothers to Egypt to buy food for their families. And so it was that they

Beersheba is where the Lord appeared to Isaac (Gen. 21:23-24).

encountered Joseph again, though they didn't recognize him as they bowed before one they knew only as an important Egyptian officer. Eventually Joseph identified himself to his brothers (once he was persuaded that they had changed for the better), and Jacob's entire family moved to Egypt. There they were given a region in which to live, and for a time they prospered as Joseph and his powerful friends took care of them. So ends the book of Genesis.

Egypt

No Old Testament book details the more than four hundred years Jacob's family spent in Egypt growing into the Israelite nation. When we pick up the narrative in the opening chapters of Exodus, they are near the end of their sojourn there. The situation had changed dramatically in four centuries. No longer enjoying the benefits of a friend in a position of power, the Israelites were enslaved and oppressed; stretched to the limits of human endurance. Infant sons were ordered cast into the river to reduce the male population. But one mother creatively cast her son into the river in a small reed basket as protection. Pharaoh's daughter found him afloat, named him Moses, and raised him as her son.

The Great Pyramids of Giza were already a thousand years old when Abraham visited Egypt (Gen. 12:10–20).

©Copyright 1995-1999 Phoenix Data Systems, portions copyright 1999 Imspace Systems Corporation

The Nile River.

We are not told the extent to which Moses was aware of the plight of his people as he was growing up. He may not even have known they were his people. Whether he intended to make a choice or not, what he saw one day changed his life and the course of history. When he saw an Egyptian beating one of the Israelite slaves, he reacted with force and killed the Egyptian. Before long he fled Egypt for his life and took refuge in the wilderness among the people of Midian, where he met a tribal chieftain (Jethro), met his wife (Jethro's daughter Zipporah), and met Yahweh, his God, the God of Abraham, Isaac, and Jacob. As a bush blazed but was not consumed, Moses received the commission he had been prepared to take up all his life—he was to be the deliverer of Israel.

Moses in Real Life

Perhaps Moses often reflected back on his early life when he was taking care of the people of Israel in the wilderness. Life in Pharaoh's palace had been relatively easy. His days were busy with his education and training in practical skills. Pharaoh's sons were expected to be scholars and warriors. Sometimes his studies were boring, and always they were challenging; they filled his days with activities that would prepare him for future service to the kingdom. But at the same time he had enjoyed all of the comforts life had to offer—luxurious living quarters, the finest food, and clothing of the most expensive materials. How different life was now. Of course, living in a tent was nothing new anymore—his years as a shepherd in Midian had accustomed him to that. But the responsibility of providing leadership for so many people was far more complicated than taking care of sheep. A large part of his days now was taken up with resolving disputes and making decisions. Ever since he had come back down from Sinai, people had been making constant demands on his time. Even though he had appointed judges to help him, many cases called for his personal attention. Some of these required him to go directly to God for an answer. In addition, the tabernacle was being constructed and the builders were always asking about details. Supplies were

Egyptian scribe at work.

Z. Radovan, Jerusalem

a constant concern, and keeping records was time-consuming as well. Perhaps all of this would be more tolerable if the people were content—content with him, content with what they were doing and where they were going, content with God. But no change in their attitude appeared on the horizon. Maybe when they got to Canaan things would get better.

Only screenwriters' speculation has forged a brotherly link between Moses and the pharaoh to whom he declared, "Let my people go!" Ten plagues were needed to soften Pharaoh's resolve sufficiently that he agreed to release the Israelites. It took the death of Egypt's firstborn sons, but God's covenant people were finally on their way back to the land of Abraham,

A tomb painting portraying brick makers. The Israelites were enslaved and forced to make bricks for the Egyptians (Exod. 1:14).

Isaac, and Jacob. When Pharaoh changed his mind and charged after his escaping slaves, the Lord parted the sea for his people and then brought it crashing down in destruction on Pharaoh's army. Then God provided water and manna for the Israelites in the wilderness as they made their way to the holy mountain, Mount Sinai.

THE PLAGUES AND THE GODS OF EGYPT*

PLAGUE	REFERENCE	POSSIBLE EGYPTIAN DEITY DIRECTED AGAINST
NILE TURNED TO BLOOD	Exodus 7:14–25	Khnum: guardian of the Nile; Hapi: spirit of the Nile; Osiris: Nile was bloodstream
FROGS	Exodus 8:1–15	Heqt: form of frog, god of resurrection
GNATS (MOSQUITOES)	Exodus 8:16–19	
FLIES	Exodus 8:20–32	
PLAGUE ON CATTLE	Exodus 9:1–7	Hathor: mother-goddess, form of cow; Apis: bull of god Ptah, symbol of fertility; Mnevis: sacred bull of Heliopolis
BOILS	Exodus 9:8–12	†Imhotep: god of medicine
HAIL	Exodus 9:13–35	Nut: sky goddess; Isis: goddess of life; Seth: protector of crops
LOCUSTS	Exodus 10:1–20	Isis: goddess of life; Seth: protector of crops
DARKNESS	Exodus 10:21–29	Re, Aten, Atum, Horus: all sun gods of sorts
DEATH OF FIRSTBORN	Exodus 11:1–12:36	The deity of Pharaoh: Osiris, the giver of life

*These are only some of the gods whom the plagues may have been directed against. The list is not necessarily conclusive.
†Perhaps too early for this deity to have been involved.

Sinai and the Wilderness

The remainder of the books of Exodus and Leviticus occur during the year that Israel was camped at the base of Mount Sinai. There they received not only the Ten Commandments, but many other laws as well. In addition, instructions were given for construction of the tabernacle (their portable sanctuary), the priesthood, and the rituals of their religious practice. It was also, of course, at Mount Sinai that the golden calf was constructed by Moses' brother, Aaron (at the insistence of the people). When the Israelites broke camp (recorded in the book of Numbers), they continued their journey to the land promised to their ancestors.

As the Israelites came near to their destination, they sent a representative of each tribe to scout out the land. The scouts' report indicated that the produce of the land was bountiful but that the inhabitants were intimidating. The faithless reluctance of the people to trust God to overcome their obstacles resulted in God dooming the unbelieving generation to die in the wilderness. For nearly forty years they inhabited the wilderness in the vicinity of Kadesh Barnea as all who were adults when they came out of Egypt gradually died. Aaron, Moses, and their sister, Miriam, were among the last to die. During those wandering years, the Israelites often complained, rebelled, and failed to trust the Lord. They were characterized by a spirit of quarrelsome grumbling.

The plain by Jebel Musa. If Jebel Musa is Mt. Sinai, this would have been where the Israelites camped for the year that they stayed.

Jebel Serbal is one of the possible identifications of Mt. Sinai.

As the time of wandering came to a close, the group made its way around the southern end of the Dead Sea and camped on the east side of the Jordan River. There on the plains of Moab they received the final words from their aged leader Moses before he went up into Mount Nebo to view the land and there died. His last words make up the book of Deuteronomy.

Mount Nebo.

Kadesh Barnea.

HISTORY STORY LINE

Mesopotamia: Sumer through Old Babylonia

Sumerians. It is not possible at this time to put the first eleven chapters of Genesis into a specific place in the historical record. Our history of the ancient Near East begins in earnest after writing had been invented, and the earliest civilization that is known to us in the historical record is that of the Sumerians. This culture dominated southern Mesopotamia for more than five hundred years during the first half of the third millennium BC (2900–2350), known as the Early Dynastic Period. The Sumerians have become known through the excavation of several of their principal cities, which include Eridu, Uruk, and Ur. They are credited with many of the important developments in civilization, including the foundations of mathematics, astronomy, law, and medicine. Urbanization was also first witnessed among the Sumerians. By the time of Abraham, the Sumerians no longer dominated the ancient Near East politically, but their culture continued to influence the region. Other cultures replaced them in the political arena, benefiting from the advances they made.

Sumerian statuettes from Tell Asmar were used as votive offerings.

It was not uncommon in the ancient world for people to spend whole days walking. That was how they got from place to place. When Abraham or Jacob left Haran to go to Canaan, he would have had to travel more than five hundred miles. With a family and flocks and herds, he could probably cover only six to eight miles per day, stopping for food and water. Walking most of the day every day, this would mean about eight weeks on the road. Even once they settled in Canaan they had much walking to do. When Joseph went looking for his brothers, he had to travel from their home base at Bethel to Shechem, more than twenty miles. Then when he didn't find them, he was directed to Dothan, another fifteen miles. By the time he was done, he would have spent several days on the road.

The terrain and climate added to the difficulty of getting around. Much of Israel is mountainous. This means that travelers either have to wind through valleys or climb over mountains. Most of the roads involve some combination of the two. This makes paths longer and more strenuous than the actual mileage suggests. In addition, during the summer months, temperatures in the nineties and one hundreds Fahrenheit are common. Heat exhaustion, sun-stroke, and dehydration are real dangers, and precautions are essential.

Typically using major trade routes, merchants and armies could travel twenty to twenty-three miles per day. The merchant routes taken were dictated by the topography of the various regions (avoiding disease-infected swamps and uneven and deeply cut hill country) as well as political situations and potential markets. From Egypt the major trade route, known as the Great Trunk Road or the Coastal Road, started in Memphis on the Nile, crossed the northern Sinai Peninsula, turned north up the coastal plain of Canaan, then jogged east through the Valley of Jezreel at Megiddo and then north to Hazor. From there the route went northeast to Damascus, passed Ebla and Aleppo in Syria, and then came to the northwestern spur of the Euphrates River, which then served as a guide southward into the major cities of Mesopotamia. The other major route, known as the King's Highway, was picked up by caravans coming north through Arabia, as it traversed the Transjordanian region from the Red Sea port of Ezion Geber north through Edom, Moab, and Ammon to join the Trunk Road at Damascus.

Valley of Jezreel with Mt. Tabor in center.

Since the northern and central deserts of Arabia were so inhospitable, trade routes skirted them to the north, traveling up the Tigris and Euphrates river valleys, west to Palmyra and Damascus, and then south along either the coastal highway through Palestine (the Great Trunk Road) or down the King's Highway in Transjordan. Caravans transporting spices (myrrh, frankincense) and indigo traced the western coast of Arabia, transshipped to Ethiopia and further north to Egypt, and traveled up the Nile. Eventually these merchants reached deep-water seaports (various ports used between 2500 and 100 BC: Byblos, Tyre, Sidon, Acco, Ugarit, Aqaba, and Alexandria), which gave them access to markets in the Mediterranean (Crete, Cyprus, the Aegean and Ionian islands, the coasts of Turkey and North Africa) as well as along the Arabian Peninsula and East Africa and to sources of natural resources (such as the copper mines of Cyprus).

Familiarity with the climate, terrain, and conditions in Israel easily prompt the question "Why should there be so much interest in this land?" It is not known for its natural resources, its fertile soil, or its aesthetic beauty (though it is not totally devoid of any of these). Rather, the wide interest in the land needs to be understood with regard to its strategic location. It is the crossroads of the continents, sometimes referred to as the "Land Between." All travelers (military or merchant) from Africa (especially Egypt) to Asia (especially Anatolia and Mesopotamia) and back had to use this land bridge. This meant that armies would want garrisons along this route to provide a supply line. Merchants would pass through selling and buying their wares. Control of this region meant control of the trade routes and the economic advantages such control provided.

With the entire ancient world constantly passing through this region, it was also a strategic location in terms of communication. God had chosen Abraham and his family as a means by which he would reach the world with his revelation of himself. But he didn't have to send the Israelites throughout the world. Instead, he gave them a land to which the world would come. In this way, because the land was politically and economically strategic, it became theologically strategic as well.

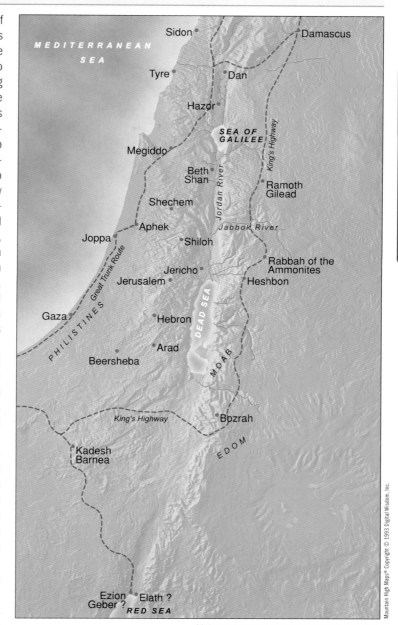

Major trade routes through the Fertile Crescent.

Stele of
Naram-Sin,
King of Akkad.

Shaded area shows the extent
of the empire of Sargon, King
of Akkad, about 2300 BC.

Dynasty of Akkad. In the middle of the twenty-fourth century,[1] the Sumerian culture was overrun by the formation of an empire under the kingship of Sargon I, who established his capital at Akkad. He ruled all of southern Mesopotamia and ranged eastward into Elam and northwest to the Mediterranean on campaigns of a military and economic nature. The empire lasted for almost 150 years before being apparently overthrown by the Gutians (a barbaric people from the Zagros Mountains east of the Tigris), though other factors, including internal dissent, may have contributed to the downfall.

Naram-Sin.

Ur III. Little is known of the next century when more than twenty Gutian kings succeeded one another. Just before 2100 BC, the city of Ur took control of southern Mesopotamia under the kingship of Ur-Nammu, and for the next century there was a Sumerian renaissance in what has been called the Ur III period. It is difficult to ascertain the limits of territorial control of the Ur III kings,

BLACK SEA

Hattusa

Kanish
Puruskhanda

CASPIAN
SEA

Carchemish

Ebla

Nineveh

Asshur

ASSYRIA

MEDITERRANEAN
SEA

Sidon   Yarmuti
Tyre

Mari

S U M E R   E L A M

CANAAN

Kish
Babylon
Nippur
Umma
Uruk

Lagash

Ur

Marhasi

On
Memphis

EGYPT

PERSIAN GULF

Thebes

RED SEA

though the territory does not seem to have been as extensive as that of the dynasty of Akkad. Under Ur-Nammu's son, Shulgi, the region enjoyed almost a half-century of peace. Shulgi exercised absolute rule through provincial governors and distinguished himself in sportsmanship, music, and literature. He himself was reputed to have composed a hymn and was trained in scribal arts. Decline and fall came late in the twenty-first century through the infiltration of the Amorites and the increased aggression of the Elamites to the east, who finally overthrew the city.

It is against this backdrop of history that the Old Testament patriarchs emerge. Some have pictured Abraham as leaving the sophisticated Ur, the center of the powerful Ur III period, to settle in the unknown wilderness of Canaan, but that involves both chronological and geographical speculation. By the highest chronology (that is, the earliest dates attributed to him), Abraham probably would have traveled from Ur to Haran during the reign of Ur-Nammu, but many scholars are inclined to place Abraham in the later Isin-Larsa period or even the Old Babylonian period. From a geographical standpoint, it is difficult to be sure that the Ur mentioned in the Bible is the famous city in southern Mesopotamia. Reference to it as Ur of the Chaldeans has led some to identify it with a northern city referred to as Ur mentioned in contemporary sources. All this makes it impossible to give a precise background of Abraham.

The Ur III period came to a close in southern Mesopotamia as the last king of Ur, Ibbi-Sin, lost the support of one city after another and was finally overthrown by the Elamites, who lived just east of the Tigris. In the ensuing two centuries (roughly 2000–1800 BC), power was again returned to city-states that controlled more local areas. Isin, Larsa, Eshnunna, Lagash, Mari, Assur, and Babylon all served as major political centers.

Old Babylonian Period. Thanks substantially to the royal archives from the town of Mari, the eighteenth century BC has become thoroughly documented. As the century opened, there was an

This bull-headed harp is one example of the exquisite wealth and artwork coming from the Ur III period.

Sumerian collection of laws from the Ur III period—probably the time of Shulgi.

The Standard of Ur. This box, overlaid with gold and other precious metals and stones, depicts battle sequences on one side and banquet sequences on the other.

1550–1069	New Kingdom Egypt
1479–1445	Thutmose III (Egypt)
1375–1350	Amarna
1352–1336	Akhenaten (Egypt)
1279–1213	Rameses II (Egypt)
1550–1200	Late Bronze Age
1500–1350	Mitanni
1370–1330	Shuppiluliuma I (Hittite)
1350–1200	Ugarit
1200–539	Iron Age
1200	Sea Peoples Incursion
858–824	Shalmaneser III (Assyria)
853	Battle of Qarqar
841–806	Hazael (Syria)
745–727	Tiglath-Pileser III (Assyria)
727–722	Shalmaneser V (Assyria)
722	Fall of Samaria
721–705	Sargon II (Assyria)
704–681	Sennacherib (Assyria)

Hammurabi acting as judge.

National Geographic

uneasy balance of power among four cities: Larsa ruled by Rim-Sin, Mari ruled by Yahdun-Lim (and later, Zimri-Lim), Assur ruled by Shamshi-Adad I, and Babylon ruled by Hammurabi. Through a generation of political intrigue and diplomatic strategy, Hammurabi eventually emerged to establish the prominence of the first dynasty of Babylon.

The Old Babylonian period covered the time from the fall of the Ur III dynasty about 2000 BC to the fall of the first dynasty of Babylon just after 1600 BC. The rulers of the first dynasty of Babylon were Amorites. The Amorites had been coming into Mesopotamia as early as the Ur III period, at first being fought as enemies, then gradually taking their place within the society of the Near East. With the accession of Hammurabi to the throne, they reached the height of success. Despite his impressive military accomplishments, Hammurabi is most widely known today for his collection of laws. His was the first major collection uncovered from the ancient Near East and is still the most extensive, with about 450 laws preserved. They predate Moses by at least three hundred years. The first dynasty of Babylon extends for more than a century beyond the time of Hammurabi, though decline began soon after his death and continued unabated, culminating in the Hittite sack of Babylon in 1595. This was nothing more than an incursion on the part of the Hittites, but it dealt the final blow to the Amorite dynasty, opening the doors of power for another group, the Kassites.

Canaan: Middle Bronze Age

Abraham entered Canaan during the Middle Bronze Age (2200–1550 BC), when it was dominated by scattered city-states much as Mesopotamia had been, though it was not as densely populated or as extensively urbanized. The period began about the time of the fall of the dynasty of Akkad in Mesopotamia (ca. 2200) and extended until about 1500 (plus or minus fifty years, depending on the theories followed). In Syria there were power centers at Yamhad, Qatna, Alalakh, and Mari; and the coastal centers of Ugarit and Byblos seemed to be already thriving. In Palestine only Hazor is mentioned in prominence. Contemporary records from Palestine are scarce, though the Egyptian story of Sinuhe has Middle Bronze Age Palestine as a backdrop and therefore offers general information. Lists of cities in Palestine are also given in the Egyptian texts. Most are otherwise unknown, though Jerusalem and Shechem are mentioned. As the period progresses there is more and more contact with Egypt and extensive caravan travel between Egypt and Palestine.

701	Assyrian Siege of Jerusalem
710–703	Merodach-baladan (Babylon)
681–669	Esarhaddon (Assyria)
669–630	Ashurbanipal (Assyria)
626–605	Nabopolassar (Babylon)
612	Fall of Nineveh
610–595	Necho (Egypt)
605	Battle of Carchemish
605–562	Nebuchadnezzar (Babylon)
597	First Babylonian Siege of Jerusalem
587	Fall of Jerusalem
556–539	Nabonidus (Babylon)
539	Fall of Babylon
539–530	Cyrus (Persia)
522–486	Darius II (Persia)
490	Battle of Marathon
486–464	Xerxes (Persia)
464–423	Artaxerxes (Persia)

Hazor was strategically located on the plain of Huleh, and it controlled the trade route connecting Egypt and Syria.

Ebla, Mari, Emar, and Nuzi are ancient cities in whose ruins archaeologists have discovered major archives of texts that shed light on the world associated with the Pentateuch. The texts are generally written in the cuneiform script and inscribed on small clay tablets. Additional important archives were found in Ugarit, Amarna, Hattusha, and Nineveh. What sort of information do they offer?

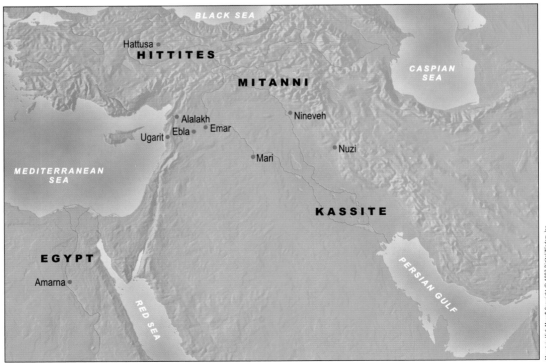

Ebla Tablet.

Erich Lessing, Courtesy of Art Resources

- The *Ebla* archive is the oldest, dating to the middle of the third millennium, somewhere between the Tower of Babel and Abraham. Located in modern Syria, Ebla was a city of economic and political importance. The seventeen thousand texts do not have any direct connection to the Bible, but they give a good idea of the historical and cultural background of the period.

- The twenty thousand texts from *Mari* date to what is called the Old Babylonian period (1800–1600 BC). Mari was one of the major cities along the Euphrates River. The archives provided extensive historical information for the period of Hammurabi and also contain the largest collection of prophetic texts outside the Bible.

- The *Hittite* texts from the ancient capital of Hattusha revealed the history and culture of the Hittite Empire that was one of the dominant political forces of the Late Bronze Age (1500–1200 BC). The international treaties found there showed the same format as used in biblical covenant documents.

- The *Nuzi* tablets provided family records in contrast to the national and royal archives of most of the other cities. Some four thousand tablets dating to the fifteenth century BC offer details of many personal legal matters, such as marriage, adoption, and inheritance.

BLACK SEA

Hattusa •

HITTITES

CASPIAN SEA

MITANNI

• Nineveh

• Alalakh
Ebla • Emar

Ugarit •

• Nuzi

MEDITERRANEAN SEA

• Mari

KASSITE

EGYPT

Amarna •

RED SEA

PERSIAN GULF

Mountain High Maps® Copyright © 1993 Digital Wisdom, Inc.

They serve as a good source for some of the customs that were practiced in the ancient world.

- The Late Bronze Age town of *Emar* was located at the bend on the Upper Euphrates. Among the most important texts found there were ritual texts from the temple library that help us to understand worship at Emar and the festivals and rituals the residents observed. Many legal texts found there continue to shed light on daily life.

- The texts from the coastal town of *Ugarit* also date to the Late Bronze Age (1550–1200 BC). The population of Ugarit was probably what the Bible would refer to as Canaanite. These texts therefore give us our best picture of Canaanite culture. Most significant among the fourteen hundred tablets are the literary texts: *The Tale of Keret, The Tale of Aqhat,* and the mythological *Baal Cycle.*

- The *Amarna* texts were found in the ruins of the short-lived capital city of Egypt's Pharaoh Akhenaten. Nearly four hundred texts make up this collection of letters, many of them from the kings of Canaanite city-states to the pharaohs of the fourteenth century. This international correspondence details the political situation in Canaan during a critical period sometime around the Israelite conquest of the land. Depending on how one dates the exodus, they could offer some snapshots of the kind of situation Israel's spies would have observed or that the tribes would have encountered.

- The texts from Assyrian king Ashurbanipal's library at *Nineveh* also provide much important information for the Pentateuch even though he reigned in the seventh century BC. His library attempted to collect all the great literary works of history, so it provided copies of pieces like the Gilgamesh Epic and the Babylonian Creation Epic, which are two of the most important literary works that shed light on Genesis.

Nuzi Tablets.

Egypt: Old and Middle Kingdoms

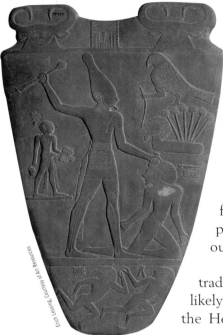

The Narmer palette gives early evidence of the uniting of upper and lower Egypt.

Roughly concurrent to the Early Dynastic Period in Mesopotamia was the formative Old Kingdom in Egypt that permanently shaped Egypt both politically and culturally. This was the age of the great pyramids. During Egypt's Sixth Dynasty, contemporary with the dynasty of Akkad in Mesopotamia, disintegration of central government became evident. From the mid twenty-second century until about 2000 BC, Egypt was plunged into a dark period known as the First Intermediate Period, which was characterized by disunity and at times anarchy. Order was finally restored when Mentuhotep reunited Egypt and Amenemhet I founded the Twelfth Dynasty, beginning a period of more than two centuries of prosperous growth and development.

The Twelfth Dynasty developed extensive trade relations with Syro-Palestine and is the most likely period for initial contacts between Egypt and the Hebrew patriarchs. By the most conservative

Egyptian Tale of Sinuhe*

I was an attendant who attended his lord, a servant of the royal harem. . . .

Year 30 . . . day 7 . . . The King of Upper and Lower Egypt flew to heaven. . . .

My heart fluttered. . . . I removed myself in leaps, to seek a hiding place. . . .

I set out at night. . . . Land gave me to land. I traveled to Byblos; I returned to Qedem. I spent a year and a half there. Then Ammunenshi, the ruler of Upper Retenu, took me to him. . . .

He set me at the head of his children. He married me to his eldest daughter. He let me choose for myself of his land, of the best that was his. . . .

I passed many years, my children becoming strong men. . . .

I gave water to the thirsty; I showed the way to him who had strayed; I rescued him who had been robbed. . . .

This ruler of Retenu made me carry out numerous missions as commander of his troops. . . .

Now when the majesty of King Kheperkare was told of the condition in which I was, his majesty sent word to me with royal gifts. . . . Come back to Egypt! See the residence in which you lived! . . . I found his majesty on the great throne in a kiosk of gold. . . . His majesty said, "He shall be a companion among the nobles." . . . I was given a house that had belonged to a courtier. . . . A stone pyramid was built for me in the midst of the pyramids. . . . I was in the favor of the king until the day of landing came.

*From Miriam Lichtheim, *Ancient Egyptian Literature*, vol. 1 (Berkeley: University of California Press, 1974), 222–33.

estimates, Sesostris III would have been the pharaoh who elevated Joseph to his high administrative post. Others would be more inclined to place the emigration of the Israelites to Egypt during the time of the Hyksos. The Hyksos were Semitic peoples who had begun moving into Egypt (particularly the delta region) as early as the First Intermediate Period. As the Thirteenth Dynasty ushered in a gradual decline, the reins of power eventually fell to the Hyksos (whether by conquest, coup, or consent is still indeterminable), who then controlled Egypt from about the middle of the eighteenth century to the middle of the sixteenth century. It was during this time that the Israelites began to prosper and multiply in the delta region, waiting for the covenant promises to be fulfilled.

Syrian tribute bearers
Thebes, Tuthmosis IV.

After nearly two centuries of foreign domination at the hands of the Hyksos, the Egyptians finally set about recovering control of their nation. In an explosion of nationalistic fervor, the Hyksos were driven from the land around 1550 BC and the Eighteenth Dynasty was established under the Egyptian pharaoh Ahmose. It was perhaps in a reaction against foreigners that the Israelites were reduced to slavery by the newly established regime. The Egyptians did not fear the military might of the Israelites, but rather were afraid that the Israelites would join forces with the enemy and be driven out (Exod. 1:10). The Egyptians did not want the Israelites to leave, perhaps having become economically dependent on them in some way (see Gen. 47:6). Nevertheless, God was insistent, and the Israelites began their move back to the land that had been promised to them.

LITERARY PERSPECTIVE

Literary perspectives can be found both from an investigation of the internal characteristics of a book and from an investigation of similar pieces of literature. The former offers an appreciation of the literary art of the author (and/or editor). The latter provides a spectrum of comparable works from which the student can come to recognize the patterns and features inherent in the particular type of literature as well as gain an appreciation for the unique contributions of the literature of the Old Testament.

The exodus is one of the pivotal events in the history of Israel. Unfortunately, the text of Exodus never names any of the pharaohs involved. Moreover, historical records from Egypt, not surprisingly, mention nothing of what only could have been viewed by them as a national embarrassment. Consequently, assigning a date to the exodus has long stood as a bone of contention in biblical studies. The information given in the Bible would most logically favor a date in the middle of the fifteenth century. This would be calculated from 1 Kings 6:1, which locates the exodus 480 years before the dedication of Solomon's temple in 966 BC. Simple arithmetic would then arrive at a date of 1446 BC. Some consider this too simple, because 480 has the appearance of being a schematic number (twelve generations of forty years each) that may not have been intended to be used in a precise equation.

When we turn to the information that can be gleaned outside the Bible, many interpreters find the thirteenth century a more attractive option based on archaeological excavations and texts from fourteenth-century Canaan. The texts, the Amarna Tablets, give no clear indication of an Israelite presence in the land, and archaeology finds no fortified cities in the fifteenth century for the Israelites to conquer. On balance, however, it must be noted that the thirteenth century does not offer any greater number of fortified cities. Rameses II in the thirteenth century offers a convincing portrait of the kind of pharaoh presented in the Exodus narrative, but his chronology is difficult to mesh with the details given in the text. The Merneptah Stele, reflecting the accomplishments of Rameses' successor, shows that Israel was in the land by the end of the thirteenth century at the latest. If the excavations at Jericho are considered seriously, the only city walls attested there in the middle of the second millennium are currently dated to the second half of the sixteenth century. Unless one considers the biblical account greatly exaggerated, or the walls that fell are entirely eroded away, these walls must somehow be related to the conquest of Joshua. Until more definitive information becomes available, the controversy will undoubtedly remain.*

---

*For a more detailed treatment, see "Exodus, Date of," in *Dictionary of the Pentateuch* (Downers Grove: InterVarsity Press, 2002).

National Geographic

Scholars adhering to an early date for the Hebrew exodus from Egypt identify Thutmose III (depicted in painting) as the Pharaoh of the oppression. Those who adhere to a late date identify Ramesses II (statue) as this pharaoh.

Z. Radovan, Jerusalem

©Copyright 1995-1999 Phoenix Data Systems, portions copyright 1999 Imspace Systems Corporation

The large granite stele discovered at the temple tomb of Pharaoh Merneptah in Egypt, significant because it contains one of the rare references to Israel in ancient nonbiblical documents and complements the history of the days of the judges. *(Encyclopaedia Judaica)*

Alternatives for the route of the Exodus and for the location of Mt. Sinai.

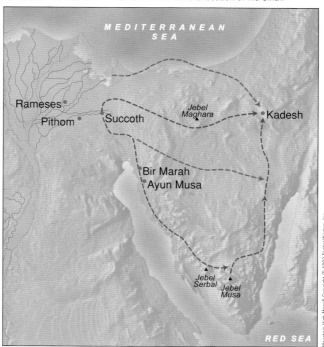

Mountain High Maps® Copyright © 1993 Digital Wisdom, Inc.

Internal Characteristics

Even though the Pentateuch is made up of five books, there is a sense in which it is a single book (earlier we spoke of it as a five-part mini-series). Each book has an independent structure and can function as an autonomous piece of literature even though there is an obvious continuity in the story line. On the other hand, especially the three middle books (Exodus, Leviticus, Numbers) can be seen as bound closely together in style, subject, and perspective. Moreover, just as Deuteronomy is a fitting conclusion (the final message of Moses), the book of Genesis serves as a fitting introduction that is closely connected to the other books. When literary and thematic motifs are considered, building blocks such as promise, election, deliverance, covenant, law, and land can be seen as central to the Pentateuch as a whole. The case for the original autonomy of each book currently is stronger than the suggestion that the entire Pentateuch was written to be a single book. Nevertheless, it is clear that after all five books were completed, they were soon merged into a single entity that came to be known as the "Book of the Law" (Josh. 1:8).

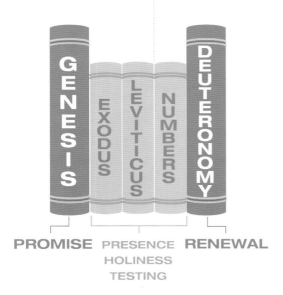

PROMISE PRESENCE RENEWAL
HOLINESS
TESTING

By means of analogy, we can look at another well-known composite piece of ancient literature. The *1001 Arabian Nights* represents many traditional tales unified editorially by the scenario (a frame narrative) involving the king Shahbriar and his clever story-telling princess, Sheherezade. This frame narrative is a secondary scheme used only as an anthologizing technique. It offers an artificial occasion for the preservation of the desired traditions. We do not consider the frame of the Pentateuch to be artificial. But while there are some indications of editorial activity, there is no discernible purpose of the whole other than to bring together the material from this stage of God's program of revelation.

Comparative Literature

Cosmologies. A number of pieces of literature from Egypt and Mesopotamia talk about the origins of the cosmos. The first impression we gain from reading these is how different their view of God is from what we find in the Old Testament. A second observation would notice how different their ideas about the cosmos are from those that make up our worldview today. If we are to understand the original meaning of the text, we must sort out the similarities and differences between the modern worldview, the ancient worldview, and the biblical worldview. It would be a mistake to think that the Israelites and the biblical writers thought about the world the same way we do. Such a misperception would inevitably lead to distorted interpretation.

Egyptian representation of the cosmos. The goddess Nut symbolizes the sky, which is held up by the god Shu. The sun god Re rides his royal bark over the back of Nut, symbolizing the rising and setting of the sun.

The Bible's revelation of God clearly presents a different picture of deity from that which was current in the creation accounts of the ancient Near East. For instance, in the ancient accounts, creation of the major parts of the cosmos occurs when the gods of that sphere are born. In sharp contrast, Genesis has only one God who has no beginning and who brings the cosmos into existence with no gods associated with the various spheres. Another example where a clear difference exists is that, in Mesopotamia especially, creation occurs within the context of conflict. Chaos among the gods is reflected in rebellion. When the rebellion is subdued and the chaos is controlled, the creator deity reestablishes order in the cosmos. In these and other important ways, the role and character of the God of the Bible is shown to be unique in the ancient world. Since the role and character of God as shown in the Bible are the foundation for our own modern beliefs, we should expect for the biblical perspective in this case to be more similar to our modern perspective and in contrast to the general ancient perspective.

A tablet containing the *Enuma Elish*, the Mesopotamian creation story.

As might be expected, however, when the view of God was not involved, it was not unusual for the Israelites to share the worldview of their neighbors. Often this worldview was very different from our own. For instance, the Israelites were more inclined to think of creation as an ongoing action of God establishing and preserving order in the cosmos rather than as a one-time act of making something. With the rest of the ancient world, they would have considered an act of creation to involve the assignment of a role and function to something rather than seeing it as the manufacture of a piece of matter, as our scientifically oriented culture is more inclined. They would have thought of God's creation of the cosmos as his making a temple for himself and his Sabbath rest as his taking up residence in this temple from which control and order would be maintained. The emphasis of creation in the ancient world—and the Bible—was bringing order out of chaos rather than bringing something out of nothing or something out of something else. That is why Genesis 1:2 starts with "formless and void" (= "chaos") rather than with nothing.

Ancient View of the Cosmos

In the ancient Near East, people believed that there was a single disk-shaped continent. This continent had high mountains at the edges that both kept out the waters of the cosmic ocean and held up the sky. The heavens were understood to be made up of three superimposed disks with pavements of various materials. The sun moved through the sky during the day and then moved into the netherworld during the night, where it traversed under the earth to its place of rising for the next day. Flowing all around this cosmos were the cosmic waters that were held out by the mountains, held back by the sky, and on which the earth floated. Similar views of the structure of the cosmos were common throughout the ancient world and persisted in popular perception until the Copernican revolution and the Enlightenment. The language of the Old Testament text reflects this view, and there is no revelation in the Bible that seeks to correct this view. Without revelation to the contrary, we must consider it likely that this is the view of the cosmos that Israelites would have held in common with their neighbors.

Artistic rendering of how the Israelites envisioned their world.

© John H. Walton,
drawing by Alva Steffler

ALVA W. STEFFLER

We find our own perspectives to be in contrast to the Bible's because, along with the rest of the ancient world, the Bible's focus in creation was on the purpose of the Creator. In our world, we are more inclined to make the focus of creation the physical makeup, structure, and laws of the creation. This is because the scientific community that sets the standards for culture often rejects the idea of a creator and therefore cannot accept the concept of a purpose for the cosmos. Since the Bible insists on the involvement of a creator, it is then, by definition, in opposition to the naturalistic worldview of today that insists on seeing the cosmos only in "natural" terms (that is, nothing supernatural).

God's revelation of himself in the Bible did not seek to change the Israelites' worldview by offering new scientific perspectives or by raising them above their "primitive" understanding of the cosmos. No verse in the Bible reveals or assumes a level of scientific knowledge that supersedes what was known in the ancient world. Rather than correcting or enhancing their scientific understanding, God used what they understood to clarify his role and character. They did not need to know the fundamentals of physics, chemistry, or biology to believe that God set everything up to function the way that it does and that he presides over the moment-by-moment operation of the cosmos. In fact, our scientific understanding often hinders our belief of this important truth.

In summary then, the original meaning of the cosmology of the early chapters of Genesis can be identified only as we combine an understanding of the unique presentation of the role and character of God in creation with an understanding of the ancient worldview that served as the context for the Bible's teaching.

Genealogies. Genealogies are not primarily a way of record-keeping in the Pentateuch or in the ancient world. In Genesis particularly, they not only establish continuity from one era to another, but they show the continuation of God's blessing in allowing the human race to be fruitful and multiply. They therefore serve a theological role. In the ancient world, genealogies most frequently had a political role. They were used to establish the legitimacy of a king and his dynastic line. Research has shown that genealogical lists in the ancient world could at times be liquid—that is, that there could be rearrangement of the order of the names, telescoping (leaving names out), or even changes in the ages or lengths of reign assigned to the individuals in the list. While, aside from telescoping, such variations are difficult to substantiate in biblical genealogies, knowledge of the ancient Near East leaves open

Genesis and Mythology

Mythology in the ancient world served the same function as science in our modern world—it offered an explanation of how the world came into being and how it worked. In the mythological approach, the functions of natural phenomena were interrelated to the purposes of the gods and inseparable from them. Our modern scientific approach attempts to understand cause and effect entirely based on natural laws and human nature. In contrast, when ancient people thought about cause and effect, the purposes and activities of the gods were considered the most important causes. Ancient Israelites thought in this same way, except that they believed in just one God who was at the foundation of cause and effect. Mythology is a window to culture because it reflects the worldview and values of the culture that forged it. Many of the writings we find in the Old Testament performed the same function as mythology did in other cultures in the sense that they gave Israelites a literary mechanism for preserving and transmitting their worldview and values. Israel was part of a larger cultural complex that existed across the ancient Near East. Israelites shared many aspects of that cultural complex with their neighbors, though each individual culture had its distinguishing features.

When we seek to understand the culture and literature of Israel, we rightly expect to find help in the larger cultural arena, whether from the mythology, wisdom writings, legal documents, or royal inscriptions. The community of faith need not fear the use of such methods to inform us of the common cultural heritage of the Near East. Neither the theological message of the text nor its status as God's Word is jeopardized by these comparative studies. In fact, since revelation involves effective communication, we would expect that God would use known and familiar elements when possible to communicate with his people. Identification of similarities as well as differences can provide important background for a proper understanding of the text.

Cylinder seals portraying Gilgamesh.

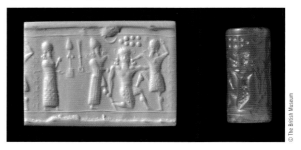

Hero fighting a seven-headed dragon.

Shamash, the sun god, on his throne.

the possibility that order and precise numbers were not as significant to their sense of a genealogy's function as those aspects are to ours.

However much Israel may have shared the general ancient perspective on genealogies, that which Genesis conveys through the genealogies is in stark contrast to what we find in Mesopotamian literature. In the Mesopotamian Atrahasis Epic, for example, the creation account leads into a problem with overpopulation. The gods become distressed at how their quality of life is diminished because there are so many people. Several different strategies are used to try to reduce the size of the human population. This is the complete opposite of the biblical idea that it was through God's blessing that the population increased.

The Atrahasis Epic.

© The British Museum

In summary, by examining ancient genealogies, we have discovered ways in which the genealogies of the Bible may be different than our initial inclinations would have led us to believe. By examining the ancient literature, we have discovered a theological contrast that the genealogies provided for the Israelites that we could not have otherwise appreciated.

Flood Stories. We have already referred to the Atrahasis Epic. This Babylonian work contains an account of creation and presents the problem of human overpopulation and how the gods tried to deal with it. The final tactic used by the gods was to send a flood. They had intended that all people would be destroyed, but through a ruse by one of the gods, Atrahasis and a few others saved their lives by building a large boat. This story is used as a source for the later variant of the flood story that plays a minor role in the wide-ranging and popular Gilgamesh Epic. These Babylonian flood traditions show the most similarities to the biblical account. There is a destructive flood, from which a small number, warned by deity, are spared in a boat. When the flood ends, birds are sent out and a sacrifice is offered. In the end, deity makes promises. In these superficial details of story line, the traditions have much in common.

Yet, as we might expect, there are still significant differences. The gods of the Mesopotamian accounts appear as caricatures with their petty and quirky behavior. Their shortsightedness and self-absorption leads them to the decision to entirely wipe out the human race—forgetting that they have become dependent on humans to supply their needs. In contrast, the Bible offers an elevated portrait of a deity

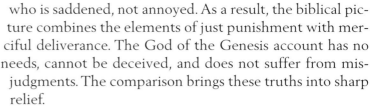

The tablet that contains the flood account from the Gilgamesh Epic.

The stele bearing the Code of Hammurabi.

who is saddened, not annoyed. As a result, the biblical picture combines the elements of just punishment with merciful deliverance. The God of the Genesis account has no needs, cannot be deceived, and does not suffer from misjudgments. The comparison brings these truths into sharp relief.

Law Collections. When the stele engraved with the laws of the Babylonian king Hammurabi was found around AD 1900, scholars noticed how similar the laws were in many ways to those found in the Pentateuch. This opened up a whole new level of discussion regarding the law God delivered to Moses at Mount Sinai. Since Hammurabi lived several centuries before Moses, people began to wonder whether there was any uniqueness left to the law in the Bible. It appeared to some that Moses had been preempted. Subsequent discoveries produced law collections that came centuries before Hammurabi. So what light have these discoveries shed on the Bible? What makes the laws of the Pentateuch different from the standard law collections of the ancient Near East?

When God said to the Israelites at Mount Sinai, "You shall not murder" (Exod. 20:13), were they startled at the innovation and stunned by how that would change their way of life? When God gave them regulations for sacrifice, was he initiating a whole new institution? No. Sacrifice was regularly practiced throughout the ancient world and by Israel itself long before the exodus. Murder was prohibited in all societies and would have been contrary to law among the Israelite tribes during their centuries of life in Egypt. Israel must have had legislation by which society was governed and guidelines that regulated worship from the beginning. We would assume that that legislation, developed in the context of ancient Near Eastern thinking and culture, would have looked very much like the legislation that has survived from the ancient world, preserved in the laws of Hammurabi, Eshnunna, and the like. And indeed, as already mentioned, many of the laws preserved in the Pentateuch show a striking resemblance to laws that are preserved in other ancient Near Eastern sources.

What, then, is God doing at Sinai? Is he giving Israel legislation? If it is very similar to the legislation under which they already were operating and to the common legislation of other contemporary societies, what is the point? To answer this we must explore the respective functions of the legal sections of the Pentateuch and the law collections of the ancient Near East.

In the ancient Near East, law was seen as a way to create harmony between people and the cosmos. People believed that law and order had been built into the cosmos and that the laws that were set forth described how harmony could be achieved. Strictly speaking, the law collections of the ancient Near East were not instruments of legislation, but of instruction.[2] The major goal of the collections was for the king to present evidence that he was a good and just king, discharging his duty to the gods to maintain order in society and to do justice. The basis of the relationship between the king and the gods was that the king would be granted the authority to rule and that he, in return, would rule justly. The gods were the guardians of the cosmic law, which was built into the fabric of the natural world. As guardians they granted authority to human kings to make laws that would reflect the cosmic order of things. The law collections served as the king's defense that he was doing just that. They included illustrations of the kind of laws that were enacted and/or enforced under the king's administration. By collecting such exemplary laws, the king intended to reveal something about himself as the promulgator of those laws. He was under obligation to promulgate and enforce such laws so as to retain his official relationship with the gods under whose auspices he ruled.

The law collection of Lipi-Ishtar.

Erich Lessing, Courtesy of Art Resources

Comparison of Sample Laws from Various Cultures*

Lipit-Ishtar 17: "If a man, without grounds, accuses another man of a matter of which he has no knowledge, and that man does not prove it, he shall bear the penalty of the matter for which he made the accusation." (Compare Exod. 21:12–14.)

Ur-Namma 1: "If a man commits a homicide, they shall kill that man." (Compare Exod. 21:16.)

Hammurabi 14: "If a man should kidnap the young child of another man, he shall be killed." (Compare Deut. 24:7.)

Hammurabi 117: "If an obligation is outstanding against a man and he sells or gives into debt service his wife, his son, or his daughter, they shall perform service in the house of their buyer or of the one who holds them in debt service for three years; their release shall be secured in the fourth year." (Compare Exod. 21:2–11; Deut. 15:12–18.)

Hammurabi 132: "If a man's wife should have a finger pointed against her in accusation involving another male, although she has not been seized lying with another male, she shall submit to the divine River Ordeal for her husband." (Compare Num. 5:11–31.)

Eshnunna 54: "If an ox is a gorer and the ward authorities so notify its owner, but he fails to keep his ox in check and it gores a man and causes his death, the owner of the ox shall weigh and deliver 40 shekels of silver." (Compare Exod. 21:28–29, 35–36.)

Middle Assyrian A21: "If a man strikes a woman of the *a'ilu* class, thereby causing her to abort her fetus, and they prove the charges against him and find him guilty—he shall pay 9,000 shekels of lead; they shall strike him 50 blows with rods; he shall perform the king's service for one full month." (Compare Exod. 21:22–25.)

Hittite XXXV (late version): "If anyone finds implements or an ox, a sheep, a horse, or an ass, he shall drive it back to its owner, and the owner will lead it away. But if he cannot find its owner, he shall secure witnesses." (Compare Deut. 22:1–3.)

*From Martha Roth, *Law Collections from Mesopotamia and Asia Minor* (Atlanta: SBL, 1995).

In a similar manner, the biblical law collections present illustrations of legislation that are intended to reveal something about the promulgator of the laws. A key difference here, however, is that God is the promulgator of law in Israel. Hammurabi set his laws before Shamash, the god of justice, to illustrate what a just king he was. The Lord set his laws before Moses to illustrate what a holy God he was. Therefore, rather than revealing the justice of the king, the law in Israel reveals the holiness of God. Beyond mandating justice for society, Yahweh mandates holiness for his people. Just as the king's enforcement of his legislation maintained his elect relationship with the gods, so Israel's enforcement of God's law as it had been promulgated would maintain their elect relationship with God.

Most important, God's law reveals what God is like and is given in the context of a covenant relationship that asks people to reflect and imitate God's holiness. The covenant established the relationship and the law regulated the relationship. The collections of laws in the Pentateuch are not there to serve as actual legislation for any and all readers but represent the foundation for the ever-changing legislation required for a society to operate. In that sense, it is like our constitution, which is not legislation, but the foundation for legislation.

> Most important, God's law reveals what God is like and asks people to reflect and imitate God's holiness.

Law in Israel has a divine authorship; it is not a "humanly authored safeguard of cosmic truth." . . . God alone is the ultimate source and sanction of law. The entire law is ascribed directly to him. "Here God is not merely the custodian of justice or the dispenser of truths to man, he is the fountainhead of the law; the law is a statement of his will. . . . The only legislator the Bible knows of is God." God, furthermore, is not merely the guarantor of the covenant, as the deities are in the epilogues to Mesopotamian legal collections and treaties; he is the author of the covenant who directly addresses his people.[3]

Hammurabi Prologue*

The gods Anu and Enlil, for the enhancement of the well-being of the people, named me by my name: Hammurabi, the pious prince, who venerates the gods, to make justice prevail in the land, to abolish the wicked and the evil, to prevent the strong from oppressing the weak. . . . When the god Marduk commanded me to provide just ways for the people of the land (in order to attain) appropriate behavior, I established truth and justice as the declaration of the land, I enhanced the well-being of the people.

*From the Prologue to Hammurabi's law collection, found in Martha Roth, *Law Collections from Mesopotamia and Asia Minor* (Atlanta: SBL, 1997), 77, 81.

Erich Lessing, Courtesy of Art Resources

The different approaches to law can be understood in terms of three baseball umpires describing how they call balls and strikes. The first claims, "I call 'em how I see 'em." This represents a subjective perspective like that found in the ancient Near Eastern law collections. They tried to perceive what were good laws as well as they could. The second umpire insists, "I call 'em how they are." This is more like the Israelite view that saw law objectively. Their law was based on an absolute standard that must be adhered to. The third umpire declares stubbornly, "They ain't neither balls nor strikes till I call 'em." This is closest to how law is viewed in American culture where there is no such thing as law until Congress declares it to be a law. Whatever Congress says is law, is law.

In summary, the uniqueness of Israelite law is not to be found in the laws themselves, but in what the laws represent. They are God's revelation of the nature of his holiness.

Priestly Regulations. Just as Leviticus contains many regulations, procedures, and instructions for priests and rituals, there are documents from the ancient Near East that serve the same function. These offer information about sacrifices and rituals, provide instructions for priests, and address the issue of impurity. This information usually must be gleaned in bits and pieces from many different sources. There are, however, a few major ritual texts available that serve as significant sources of information. Among the most helpful is the Hittite Instructions for the Temple Officials from the mid second millennium. This text details the means that should be used to protect the sanctuary from sacrilege and trespass. From Mesopotamia we have incantations as well as one tablet of rituals connected to the incantations. Other texts concerned purification, royal ablutions, and rituals of undoing. Most of these texts assume a background of magic and divination where witchcraft, demonic forces, and incantations represented powerful threats in society. Israelites ideally did not accept this worldview, and their concepts

Ancient Near East	Israel
• *Law:* Amoral and meant to insure the smooth running of society; offenses of the law were considered as offenses against civilization. • *Law Collections:* Propagandistic report to deity; a theoretical development of some of the forms justice might take.	• *Law:* Meant to be a guide to godlikeness; offenses of the law were considered offenses against God. • *Law Collections:* Development of the forms morality or holiness would take; civil law tied to moral absolutes.

of purity and impurity can be seen as distinct from those evident in the rest of the ancient world. Even though the biblical literature purged the rituals of the magical element, the religious practices of the people and the words used to describe them often still echoed the larger cultural context.

Covenant/Treaty Format. Over fifty treaties between nations and their vassals have been recovered by archaeologists. These date to the second and first millennia BC. The treaties from the second millennium are largely from Hittite archives, while the first millennium examples come during the time of Assyrian kings Esarhaddon and Ashurbanipal (seventh century BC). These are important for Bible study in that the format used in these treaties shows striking similarity to the format of the covenant documents in the Bible, most notably, to the book of Deuteronomy.

COVENANT AND TREATY FORMAT*

Order of Sections	Description	Exodus-Leviticus	Deuteronomy	Joshua 24
Introduction of Speaker	Identifying author and his right to proclaim treaty	Exodus 20:1	1:1–5	24:1–2
Historical Prologue	Survey of past relationship between parties	Exodus 20:2	1:6–3:29	24:2–13
Stipulations	Listing of obligations	(Decalogue) Exodus 20:1–17 Covenant Code, Exodus 20:22–23:19 Ritual, Exodus 34:10–26; Leviticus 1–25	4–26	24:14–25
Statement Concerning Document	Storage and public reading instructions	Exodus 25:16?	27:2–3	24:26
Witnesses	Usually identifying the gods who are called to witness the oath	None	31–32	24:22, 27
Curses and Blessings	How deity will respond to adherence to or violation of treaty	Leviticus 26:1–33	28	24:20

*Taken from John H. Walton, *Chronological and Background Charts of the Old Testament* (Grand Rapids: Zondervan, 1994), 86.

These treaties begin with a preamble that identifies the suzerain who is making the treaty. Besides giving his titles and attributes, it emphasizes his greatness and his right to proclaim the treaty. Next the treaties offer a historical prologue in which the relationship between the parties is reviewed. It explores what has brought them to the point of this agreement. The kindness and power of the suzerain is generally emphasized. The main section of the treaty, the stipulations, details the obligations that each party will have to the other as a result of the treaty. The last three sections contain legal material including instructions concerning the document, witnesses to the agreement, and blessings and curses that will result from either honoring or violating the treaty. As we become aware of this format, we can see that the Lord used a very familiar literary form to communicate his covenant to Israel. Israelites would have recognized that the Lord was putting himself in the place of the suzerain and that they should respond as faithful vassals would. The covenant-treaty relationship provides support and protection to the vassal in return for his loyalty to the suzerain.

Summary and Conclusions. The comparative literature affords us an opportunity to read various parts of the Pentateuch a little more like the Israelites would have read them. It helps us to gain entry into their worldview and to begin to understand the culture that formed the backdrop to the Bible. As we become acquainted

2 PENTATEUCH

Hittite Instructions*

"The first fruits of animals which you, the farmers, present for the pleasure of the gods, present them promptly at the right time." (Compare Exod. 88:19–20; Deut 18:19.)

---

*COS, 1.88 #18.

Hittite Treaties*

Shuppululiuma, King of Hatti, Hero, Beloved of the Storm-god, . . . I spoke thus: . . . I have taken up Shattiwaza, son of King Tushratta, in my hand, I will seat him upon the throne of his father, so that the land of Mittanni, the great land, does not go to ruin. . . .

As someone is the enemy of the land of Mittanni, he shall be the enemy of Hatti. The friend of the King of Hatti shall be the friend of the king of the land of Mittanni. . . .

And I, the Great King, King of Hatti, will revive the dead land of Mittanni, and I will restore it to its place. You shall not act again independently, nor transgress your treaty. . . .

A duplicate of this tablet is deposited before the Sun-goddess of Arinna. . . . And in the land of Mittanni a duplicate is deposited before the Storm-god. . . . It shall be read repeatedly, for ever and ever, before the king of the land of Mittanni and before the Hurrians. Whoever, before the Storm-god . . . alters this tablet, or sets it in a secret location—if he breaks it, if he changes the words of the text of the tablet—in regard to this treaty we have summoned the gods of the secrets and the gods who are guarantors of the oath. . . .

If you, Prince Shattiwaza, and you Hurrians do not observe the words of this treaty, the gods, lords of the oath, shall destroy you and you Hurrians, together with your land, your wives and your possessions. . . .

If you, Prince Shattiwaza, and you Hurrians observe this treaty and oath, these gods shall protect you. . . . And the land of Mittanni shall return to its former state. It shall prosper and expand. And you, Shattiwaza, your sons and your grandsons . . . the Hurrians shall accept you for kingship for eternity.

---

*From Gary Beckman, *Hittite Diplomatic Texts* (Atlanta: SBL, 1996), 38–44.

with how the ancient world thought about creation and the cosmos or about law, we become informed about how issues would most naturally be addressed as the biblical writers communicated with their audience.

1. Who are the patriarchs and matriarchs of Israel, and what is their significance?

2. What general sequence of events bridges the time period from the promise of the land to Abraham in Mesopotamia to the preparation to enter the land after Moses?

3. What important periods of ancient Egyptian and Mesopotamian history overlap the patriarchs?

4. How would you describe the relationship of the five books of the Pentateuch?

5. What is the significance of comparative studies for interpreting the Bible?

6. How can cuneiform archives help us understand the Old Testament better?

7. How is law in the Old Testament different from law in the ancient Near East?

8. Is there any legitimate definition of "mythology" that would allow Genesis to be so categorized? If so, explain.

9. What is the significance of geography in understanding the Old Testament?

10. Discuss what might be considered the central theme or themes of the Pentateuch.

Notes

1. Students should note that labeling of centuries in BC works the same as in AD, so the twenty-fourth century is 2399–2300. Additionally, since the numbers are going backwards, "late" in the century refers to the lower 2300 numbers (e.g., 2315).
2. D. Patrick, *Old Testament Law* (Atlanta: John Knox, 1985), 198.
3. Shalom Paul, *Studies in the Book of the Covenant in the Light of Cuneiform and Biblical Law*, VT Supp 18 (Leiden, The Netherlands: Brill, 1970), 36–37.

BRIDGING CONTEXTS

PLOTLINE OF THE PENTATEUCH

The plotline of the Pentateuch is firmly grounded in the covenant. The early chapters of Genesis lay the foundation for understanding the covenant. God brought an orderly cosmos out of chaos and took his place at the helm. He created people in relationship with him. He blessed them and set them up as his representatives. It is therefore logical to infer that God desired people to be in relationship with him. When sin entered through disobedience, relationship was lost. Rather than scrapping the whole operation, God began weaving a plan for reconciliation. Instead of human disobedience being a glitch, it became a habit and a debilitating condition. The orderliness of the cosmos remained, but chaos reigned in the human context. In time the human chaos of sin and violence became overwhelming, and God responded to that chaos by flooding the world and returning it to its pre-Creation watery state of chaos. But he saved a few in the ark. After the flood, order was restored to the cosmos, but the disorder of sin remained. It resulted not only in continued rebellion against God, but in the corruption of the perception of God and therefore in loss of the knowledge of God. Consequently, as a prelude to his program of reconciliation, God found it necessary to initiate a plan of revelation in the covenant. God chose Abraham and established the covenant with him, promising that the blessing of revelation would come to the world through Abraham and his family. They, in turn, as they were faithful to God, would enjoy the benefits of the covenant: God's blessings in a land that he would give to their growing family.

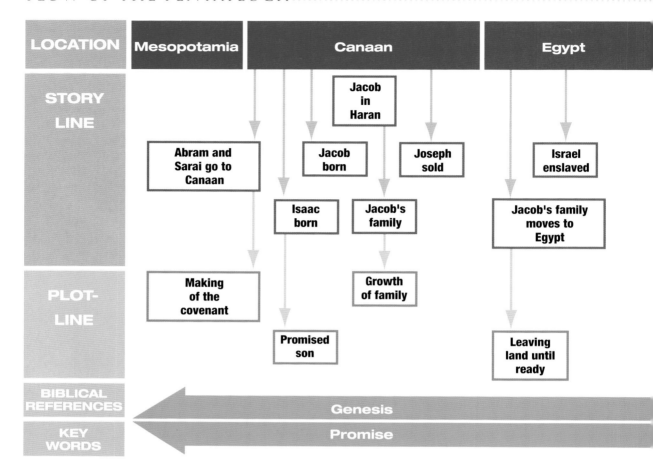

Through many obstacles, God brought Abraham's family to the land and began to establish them as his people. But the land was not yet ready for them, so he brought them down to Egypt at the time of Joseph, where they could grow into the large family the Lord had promised they would be, and where they could wait for the proper time to enter the land the Lord had promised to give them.

After Abraham's descendants had spent more than four centuries in Egypt, however, the covenant appeared to be in disarray. They were in slavery, and God was nowhere in evidence. If God was with them, they certainly did not recognize him. As he had previously overcome the obstacles to establishing Abraham's family as his chosen people, the Lord now began working on overcoming obstacles that would prevent him from dwelling in the midst of his people. He showed that

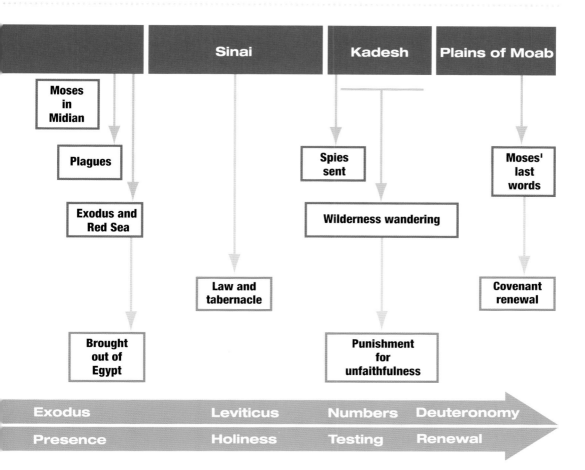

	Sinai	Kadesh	Plains of Moab
Moses in Midian			
Plagues		Spies sent	Moses' last words
Exodus and Red Sea		Wilderness wandering	
	Law and tabernacle		Covenant renewal
Brought out of Egypt		Punishment for unfaithfulness	

Exodus	Leviticus	Numbers	Deuteronomy
Presence	Holiness	Testing	Renewal

he was with them as he delivered them from the grip of Egyptian slavery. Then he revealed himself to them through the law so they would know how to honor and imitate his holiness. Finally, he was able to come and dwell in their midst in an appropriate dwelling place, the tabernacle, which had been built to specifications that would elevate and preserve his holiness. The people were instructed in how purity was to be maintained so that God's presence could remain in their midst.

There was a one-generation detour in the wilderness as a result of the Israelites' disbelief, but at the close of the Pentateuch, they were poised on the border of the Promised Land as they received Moses' farewell instructions and final admonitions. In all of this, God was continually revealing himself to and through Israel. It is only as God

View from Mount Nebo (in modern-day Jordan). This view is similar to the one Moses would have seen, as mentioned in Deuteronomy 34:1–4. The Israelites crossed over the Jordan River near Mount Nebo as they began their conquest of the Promised Land.

becomes known that people will come to desire a relationship with him. God showed Israel his justice (both in theory and in practice), holiness, faithfulness, power to deliver, anger against sin, and love for them in mercy and grace.

PURPOSE OF EACH BOOK

As we present the purpose of each book, we will attempt to provide in a little more detail its role and unique contribution to the plotline of the segment of the canon it is in.

Authors and Books

Authorship in the ancient world is not as straightforward an issue as it is in today's society. Authorship had no entitlements such as copyright or royalties attached to it. In addition, many of the literary pieces in the ancient world were commissioned by the palace or the temple, and a scribe was employed to do the writing. In such cases, the responsibility for authorship was not easy to establish. Finally, many of the literary pieces that have come down to us are composite. That is, they were compiled from a number of different traditions or sources over time by many different hands. As a result, many books in the ancient world, and in the Bible for that matter, must be considered anonymous.

In light of this, we must often expand our ideas about what is meant by authorship with regard to a biblical book. In many parts of the Pentateuch, for instance, the material is clearly presented as having derived from Moses. On the other hand, Moses is generally referred to in the third person. The exceptions are in embedded speeches. For instance, the book of Deuteronomy might say something like, "So Moses began to expound this law, saying: 'The LORD our God said to us at Horeb.'" In this construction the one writing the book has referred to Moses in the third person ("Moses began"), but then has Moses speak in the first person ("God said to us"). In this way, it could be understood that the material in the book derives from Moses, but it would be reasonable to see the one recording Moses' words as someone other than Moses. These issues make the determination of authorship a very complex matter; yet on the basis of the statements of the text, we would defend an essential Mosaic authorship of the Pentateuch.

Genesis

The purpose of Genesis is to begin the story of the covenant. Though God created everything just right, sin drew people away from God—so much that they no longer had an accurate idea of what God was like. This was why God decided to make a covenant. The covenant would be with a chosen people, Abraham and his descendants. God would use them to give the world an accurate picture of what he was like. Genesis tells how the covenant was established despite many obstacles.

Genesis 1 through 11 traces the blessing from Genesis 1:28–30 as the genealogies show people being fruitful and multiplying. At the same time, these chapters trace the advance of sin as they recount the disobedience of Adam and Eve, Cain's murder of his brother Abel, and the escalation of violence that finally eventuates in the flood. After the flood, the people not only continue their movement away from God, but they corrupt and distort their picture of God, resulting in a god they expect to come down and be worshiped by having his needs met (the function of the Tower of Babel). Now, in addition to the problem of bringing people back to God (the Eden Problem), there is the problem that they have lost the accurate knowledge of what God is like (the Babel Problem). Human initiative, first by Adam and Eve, then by the builders of Babel, has had devastating results.

The covenant represents God's initiative and intends to correct the Babel Problem by providing a means by which God can reveal himself to the world through Abraham and his family—in this way all the world would be blessed through them. The covenant in the Old Testament addresses the Babel Problem, while the covenant in the New Testament addresses the Eden Problem. The covenant blessings that serve as benefits to Abraham and his family are extensions of the original blessing in Genesis 1. The patriarchal narratives in Genesis 12 through 50 trace the advance of the covenant and its blessings and at the same time show the many obstacles to the covenant and its blessings. Obstacles interfere with Abraham getting a footing in the land and with having a family. Many times the whole covenant appears to dangle from a fragile thread. Conflict and character flaws within the family also present obstacles that must be overcome. As these obstacles are overcome one by one, God demonstrates his mastery.

Genesis begins by showing God's mastery in bringing order out of chaos. It continues with the development of the covenant that brought order to his relationship with the world through revelation and the overcoming of obstacles. The book concludes by showing God as the one who brought order to the world through his chosen people (battling the chaos of famine and providing food). God has thus shown his mastery in creation, covenant, and history. Genesis can therefore be seen to begin to provide answers to the question of what must be subdued for God's mastery of his kingdom to be secured. And, of course, all of this is just the beginning. The biblical narratives continue to pursue this quest through the history of Israel as well as theologically through the redemptive history that culminates in the work of Christ. Salvation shows God's mastery over the chaos that came about because of sin. Eventually all chaos will be subdued as God establishes his kingdom forever and the forces of chaos are finally destroyed, not just balanced, limited, or contained. This is the story of biblical eschatology—the story begun in Genesis.

Tower of Babel

Most interpreters agree that the Tower of Babel was a ziggurat. Ziggurats characterized many of the early cities in Mesopotamia and, as in Genesis 11, were the main feature of the city. Ziggurats were solid—brick frames filled in with rubble. They did not have passages and chambers the way the pyramids did. Ziggurats usually were built alongside a temple. They served as an architectural representation of the stairways that are found in the mythology of Mesopotamia. These stairways were used for the gods and their messengers to pass from one realm to another. This function is indicated in the names given to some of the ziggurats: "Sacred place of the foundation of heaven and earth" (Babylon), "Sacred place that links heaven and earth" (Larsa), "Sacred place of the stairway to pure heaven" (Sippar).

The shrine at the top was not a place of worship. It housed a bed and a table stocked with food for the deity to refresh himself as he came down from the heavens to be worshiped in his temple. It is this same sort of stairway that Jacob saw in his dream in Genesis 28. People did not use the ziggurat for any purpose—it was holy ground meant only for use by the gods. It is important in this connection that Genesis 11:5 indicates that God "came

The Epic of Enmerkar and the Lord of Aratta, which contains a Sumerian account of languages being confused.

University of Pennsylvania Museum (neg. #82150)

down" to see what the people were doing. That is precisely what the tower was designed for. But instead of bringing blessing on the people for providing this passageway for him, God was displeased. It is easy to understand why he was displeased when we consider that the ziggurat represented a system of belief in which the gods have needs. The people would meet the needs of the gods and expect that they had earned blessing in return. In this way it can be seen that the Tower of Babel account represents distortion of the nature of God. They had corrupted the image of God by reshaping him as having needs and flaws like people have needs and flaws. This is why it was necessary for God to implement a program of revelation like that represented by the covenant.

Exodus

The purpose of Exodus is to explain how God's presence came to dwell among his chosen people, Israel. In Egypt they were enslaved and felt abandoned by God. God made his presence known through the plagues and the deliverance from Egypt. The intended result was that both Egypt and Israel would know and acknowledge that Yahweh was God. God's presence guided and protected the Israelites through the wilderness. God led them from place to place by a pillar of cloud during the day and a pillar of fire by night, and he saved them from the Egyptians at the Red Sea. He also gave them food (manna) and water in the wilderness. At Sinai he told them how they needed

The Names of God

During Old Testament times, names described the being, existence, character, personality, reputation, and authority of individuals. This meant that the name of a thing or a person embodied the reality of that entity in one sense. The process of naming a child was connected with religious ritual in most ancient societies, because the ascribing of a name was important to one's identity, existence, and destiny (e.g., God changed Abram's name to Abraham, Gen. 17:5).

Likewise, the changing of a name usually signified a corresponding change of fortune, character, or circumstance in that individual's life (e.g., Jacob's name was changed to Israel after his encounter with God, Gen. 32:28). More drastic was the "forgetting" of a name or "erasing" of a name—since such an act denied existence and blotted out the memory of one cursed in this fasion (e.g., Pss. 9:5; 109:13).

Given this context, it is only natural that God would choose to reveal himself to the Hebrews using a variety of divine names and titles. So when people encounter God in Old Testament narratives, we should not be surprised to find that aspects of his nature, character, personality, and work are disclosed through names and titles specific to the historical circumstance of his people (see, e.g., Exod. 3:14-15; 6:3; 15:3; 20:7). To know God more fully, it becomes important to understand the names he used to communicate himself and his purposes to humanity. A list of the more prominent Old Testament divine names and titles is included below:

1. God (Heb. *Elohim*): names the transcendent creator of all that exists (Gen. 1:2).
2. God Most High (Heb. *El-Elyon*): indicates God's superior position above all the other gods of the nations (Gen. 14:18-20).
3. Lord (Heb. *YHWH* or *Yahweh*): names the "I AM" God of the burning bush episode (Exod. 3:14-15). The name is associated with God's covenant with Israel and speaks to the personal and relational nature of his character.
4. Lord (Heb. *Adonai*): reveals God as owner and master of all his creation (Josh. 3:11).
5. God Almighty (Heb. *El-Shaddai*): recalls God's power in creating and sustaining all life (Gen. 17:1).
6. God Everlasting (Heb. *El-Olam*): emphasizes God's immensity and eternality (Gen. 21:33).
7. God, the One Who Sees (Heb. *El-Roeh*): reveals God's beneficent omniscience, a God who sees the needs of his people and cares enough to respond with help and deliverance (Gen. 16:13).
8. God, the God of Israel (Heb. *El Elohe Israel*): attests God's sovereignty and providential watch and care over Israel as his elect people (Gen. 33:19-20).
9. The Lord Our Provision (Heb. *YHWH/Yahweh-Yireh* or *Jehovah Jireh*): witnesses to God's ability to sustain the faithful in trial and testing (Gen. 22:13-14).
10. The Lord of Hosts (Heb. *YHWH/Yahweh-Sabaoth*): designates God as the creator and leader of the angel armies of heaven (1 Sam. 17:45).

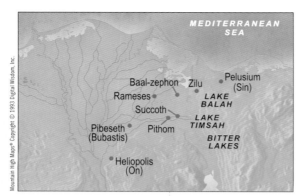

Mountain High Maps® Copyright © 1993 Digital Wisdom, Inc.

MEDITERRANEAN SEA

Baal-zephon • Zilu • Pelusium (Sin)
Rameses •
Succoth • • LAKE BALAH
LAKE TIMSAH
Pibeseth (Bubastis) • • Pithom
BITTER LAKES
• Heliopolis (On)

There are varying opinions about the body of water that the Israelites crossed (referred to in Hebrew as the Reed Sea). Many favor Balah or Timsah, given the description of their travel route.

to live so that his presence could dwell among them. The tabernacle was built and the priesthood prepared so that God could come and take up residence. God had chosen them to be his people (Exod. 6:7), and he intended to reveal himself to them and to the world by living in their midst.

Leviticus

The purpose of Leviticus is to detail the management of sacred space, sacred status, and sacred time. Frank Gorman has indicated that ritual, by its nature, seeks to uphold creation by maintaining equilibrium, referring to harmony and balance in the cosmos.[1] In this regard, the three most important

Calf/Bull Icons*

When the Israelites built a golden calf at the foot of Mount Sinai after they concluded that Moses was not going to return, they were following a practice well known in the ancient world. Bronze or composite bull or calf figurines have been found in several archaeological excavations (Mount Gilboa, Hazor, and Ashkelon) but only three to seven inches long. The calf symbol was well known in the Canaanite context of the second millennium and represented fertility and strength. The gods typically were not depicted in the form of bulls or calves but were portrayed standing on the back of the animal. Nevertheless, worship of the animal image was not unknown, and there is little in the biblical text to suggest they understood the figure merely as a pedestal (as the ark was a footstool for the throne of Yahweh).

Moses had been their sole contact with Yahweh and the mediator of Yahweh's power and guidance, and for all the people knew, Moses might be dead. With him gone, they feared that contact with Yahweh might be lost and that they therefore needed a replacement mediator to serve the role of "going before them." The fact that the calf is worshiped in the context of a feast to Yahweh suggests that this may be a violation of the second commandment rather than the first. The proclamation "These are your gods" implies that the calf is in some way representative of Yahweh—history is not being rewritten by suggesting a

different deity was responsible for the deliverance. But just as the worship of Yahweh had been corrupted by introducing an image as the means of representation, so it was also corrupted in their conduct in worship, tainted with coarse and excessive carousing, a typical feature of pagan fertility festivals.

This bronze and silver bull was discovered at the site of Ashkelon.

Z. Radovan, Jerusalem

*Adapted from J. Walton, V. Matthews, and M. Chavalas, *The IVP Bible Background Commentary: Old Testament* (Downers Grove, InterVarsity Press, 2000), 115.

aspects of rituals are time, space, and status.[2] These categories can also be used in reference to the larger issue of how God desires equilibrium to be maintained in his sanctuary through ritual. Sacred times must be identified, maintained by the priests, and observed by the people. Sacred space must be delineated and its sanctity preserved. Status of priests and people must be regulated by specific guidelines. These guidelines enable the priests to determine who has access to sacred time and sacred space and how particular levels of status can be achieved or maintained. Leviticus deals with these issues of equilibrium zone by zone as it speaks of space, status, and time, and the qualifications and procedures associated with each. The overall criteria define and relate to "holiness"—God is holy, and Israel is expected to be holy. Chapters 1 through 23 concern equilibrium relative to deity, and chapters 24 through 27 concern equilibrium relative to Israel.

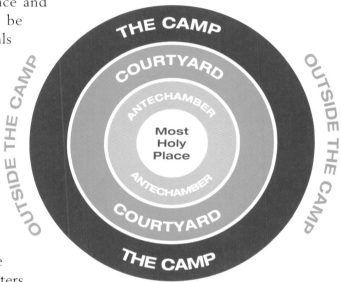

The first sequence in the divine equilibrium section is covered in chapters 1 through 17, where qualifications and procedures pertinent to maintaining equilibrium in sacred space are established. Within this sequence, the first section is, of course, the discussion of sacrifices in chapters 1 through 7. Each sacrifice is treated in terms of the materials and procedures that will render it acceptable. These sacrifices either constitute gifts to God (e.g., the fellowship offering) or serve to purify the sancta (sacred things). As such the sacrifices pertain to the holiest central zone (from ark to altar), which they maintain.

With chapters 8 through 10, the installation of the priests provides for the maintenance of the second zone, the enclosure area (courtyard). These chapters talk about the qualifications and procedures for the priests. Chapters 11 through 15 concern purity in the camp, the third zone. These chapters talk about the various ways that Israelites can become unclean and what procedures are necessary to resolve their uncleanness.

Once each of the concentric zones of the sacred compass (see diagram on p. 75) has been addressed, chapter 16 offers a description of the annual ritual that was designed to reset the equilibrium of the entire sacred compass. The rituals of the day were intended to disinfect sacred space from whatever desecration had occurred that had not been cared for by specific rituals throughout the year. The ritual prescribed for Yom Kippur features the high priest moving into the center of the sacred zone, bringing the accumulated impurities out, and finally sending them outside the camp.

Last, chapter 17 deals with behavior outside the camp. As chapter 16 moved from the center zone to outside the camp, chapter 17

SACRIFICIAL SYSTEM

NAME	PORTION BURNT	OTHER PORTIONS	ANIMALS	OCCASION OR REASON	REFERENCE
Burnt Offering	All	None	Male without blemish; animal according to wealth	Propitiation for general sin; demonstrates dedication	Leviticus 1
Meal Offering or Tribute Offering	Token portion	Eaten by priest	Unleavened cakes or grains, must be salted	General thankfulness for firstfruits	Leviticus 2
Peace Offering **a. Thank Offering** **b. Vow Offering** **c. Freewill Offering**	Fat portions	Shared in fellowship meal by priest and offerer	Male or femal without blemish according to wealth; freewill: slight blemish allowed	Fellowship a. For an unexpected blessing b. For deliverance when a vow was made on that condition c. For general thankfulness	Leviticus 3 Leviticus 22:18–30
Sin Offering	Fat portions	Eaten by priest	Priest or congregation: bull king: he-goat individual: she-goat	Applies basically to situation where purification is needed	Leviticus 4
Guilt Offering	Fat portions	Eaten by priest	Ram without blemish	Applies to situation where there has been desecration or desacralization of something holy or where there is objective guilt	Leviticus 5–6:7

moves from outside the camp to the center zone. The first sequence, chapters 1 through 17, then can be seen to move through the sacred compass zone by zone, addressing required procedures and guidelines for maintenance of sanctity for each zone. In this way equilibrium can be preserved. The emphasis is more on sacred space than on personal relationship with God.

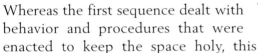

Chapters 18 through 22 cover the second sequence of the divine equilibrium section of the book. This sequence discusses the issues of disqualification, and it moves from the outer zone (the camp) to the center. This section is concerned with status. Whereas the first sequence dealt with behavior and procedures that were enacted to keep the space holy, this sequence deals with behavior that would render a person's status unacceptable for the respective zones of the compass and thereby jeopardize the desired equilibrium.

Priests in Israel

Though it is true that priests were responsible for teaching the people and making decisions as leaders of the people, their primary role concerned the performance of duties in the sanctuary. Instead of thinking of them as clergy, similar to today's pastors or priests, we should consider them to be the ritual experts of Israel. Their job was to do whatever was necessary to preserve the sanctity of God's temple. This meant guarding the access to sacred space, maintaining the pure status of the people, and overseeing the observances connected to sacred times, the festivals of Israel.

Perhaps we can understand their role better if we compare them to the Secret Service agents who protect the White House and the president of the United States. The Secret Service is responsible for the security of the president and his residence. They limit access to the president and protect him with their lives. Only certain people with specific business are allowed access to the president. Specific guidelines dictate how people act in the presence of the president. All of these elements also describe how the priests served the presence of God.

High Priest laying hands on the scapegoat.

LEVITICUS 11-15

LEVITICUS 8-10

LEVITICUS 1-7

LEVITICUS 17

LEVITICUS 16

Most Holy Zone

Courtyard   Camp

Enclosure

LEVITICUS 22:17-31

LEVITICUS 21-22:16

LEVITICUS 18-20

Sacred Status
Disqualifications
Leviticus 18-22

Chapter 23 addresses the third category of equilibrium, that concerned with time. Maintaining the sacred times of the calendar contributed just as much to order and equilibrium as maintaining sacred space. This chapter brings a conclusion to the three elements connected with equilibrium relative to deity (sacred space, sacred status, and sacred time).

In chapters 24 through 27 the book's attention turns to equilibrium in Israelite society. Leviticus 24:1–9 speaks of Israel's duties in the central zone. Equilibrium is maintained by performing their sacred duties in sacred space. In 24:10–22 the text moves to the camp zone (v. 10) and moves from the issue of space to the issue of status. Chapter 25 deals with the issue of time by delineating the sabbatical year law and the Year of Jubilee. Both of these are premised on preserving equilibrium by being cognizant of the passage of time and managing activities related to it.

The blessings and curses of chapter 26 delineate God's ability and willingness to either establish equilibrium for Israel or disrupt its equilibrium. This chapter serves a purpose similar to that of chapter 16—

Kosher Diet: Clean and Unclean Animals*

The main criteria used to distinguish between clean and unclean animals were (1) means of locomotion and (2) physical characteristics. Nothing is mentioned of the eating habits of the animals (e.g., whether they ate carrion, meat, or plants) or the conditions of their habitat. Anthropologists have suggested that animals were considered clean or unclean depending on whether they possessed all the features that made them "normal" in their category. Other suggestions have concerned health and hygiene. The weakness of each of these is that there are too many examples that don't fit the explanation. A popular traditional explanation suggested that the animals prohibited had some connection to pagan rituals. While this may explain a few of the examples, the sacrificial practices of Israel's neighbors appear strikingly similar to

Israel's. A recent promising suggestion is that the Israelite diet is modeled after God's "diet"—that is, if they could not offer it in sacrifice to God, then it was not suitable for human consumption either. This would understand the dietary laws as a further attempt by the Israelites to be holy as God is holy. This view is likewise not without problems, since some of the permitted animals are not the sort typically found in sacrifices.

Hugh Claycombe

*Adapted from J. Walton, V. Matthews, and M. Chavalas, *The IVP Bible Background Commentary: Old Testament* (Downers Grove: InterVarsity Press, 2000), 128.

that is, it encompasses all of the zones and issues (cf. vv. 1–2) and in so doing addresses the total equilibrium picture.

Finally, chapter 27 can be understood as parallel to chapter 17. In chapter 27 the topic is vows. As in chapter 17, the situation concerns movement of objects through the zones. When something is dedicated to the Lord, its location shifts from the camp zone, for instance, to the enclosure zone. Just as the handling of the blood was the significant issue for maintaining the equilibrium in chapter 17, the setting of valuations (or substitutions of other sorts) is the significant issue in chapter 27. In both the question is, What belongs to the Lord? Equilibrium in the sacred compass is maintained when everything is in the zone where it belongs.

The Gezer Calendar is one of the earliest examples of Hebrew writing (written ca. 925 BC). It lists the twelve months and the agricultural chores associated with each month.

JEWISH CALENDAR

RELIGIOUS YEAR	CIVIL YEAR	HEBREW MONTH	WESTERN CORRELATION	FARM SEASONS	CLIMATE	SPECIAL DAYS
1	7	**Nisan**	March-April	Barley harvest	Latter Rains (Malqosh)	14–Passover 21–Firstfruits
2	8	**Iyyar**	April-May	General harvest		
3	9	**Sivan**	May-June	Wheat harvest Vine tending	D R Y S E A S O N	6–Pentecost
4	10	**Tammuz**	June-July	First grapes		
5	11	**Ab**	July-August	Grapes, figs, olives		9–Destruction of Temple
6	12	**Elul**	August-September	Vintage		
7	1	**Tishri**	September-October	Ploughing		1–New Year 10–Day of Atonement 15-21–Feast of Tabernacles
8	2	**Marchesvan**	October-November	Grain planting	Early Rains (Yoreh)	
9	3	**Kislev**	November-December			25–Dedication
10	4	**Tebet**	December-January	Spring growth		
11	5	**Shebat**	January-February	Winter figs	Rain Season	
12	6	**Adar**	February-March	Pulling flax Almonds bloom		13-14–Purim
		Adar Sheni	Intercalary Month			

Numbers

The purpose of Numbers is to contrast the faithfulness of God with the faithlessness and rebellion of the Israelites. God kept his covenant promises to make them a numerous people (shown by the census) and to bring them to the land. But the people grumbled from the very beginning, rebelled against God's leadership, and refused to enter the land. They not only ended up wandering in the wilderness, but they wandered into false worship as well. Thus the people tested God at every level even while God was providing their needs.

There are two major transitions in the book:

1. From traveling with God's presence in their midst to preparing to settle in the land with God's presence in their midst.

2. From God's provision for the old generation and their resultant failures (Aaron, Miriam, spies, Korah, Moses) and dying in the

---

Sacred Times and Seasons

The Hebrew religious calendar established distinct rhythms of time for worship as part of God's larger plan of redemption that would eventually restore all of creation to its prefall "goodness." The fixed patterns of time designated for worship included daily, weekly, monthly, seasonal, or annual cycles. Many of these Old Testament rhythms were adopted by the Christian church in the development of the church year, a Christian rhythm of worship designed to "sanctify" or set apart time as God's domain. These biblical rhythms may be outlined as follows:

Daily Cycle

Old Testament sacrifice, morning and evening (Exod. 29:39)
Old Testament prayer, morning, noon, and evening (Ps. 55:17)
New Testament sacrifice and prayer seem to adopt the theological idea of Psalm 119:164, prayer seven times a day or continually (i.e., the Christian offers his or her life as a living sacrifice and prays always; Rom. 12:1-2; 1 Thess. 5:17)

Weekly Cycle

Old Testament Sabbath (creation/rest) (Gen. 2:2-3; Exod. 20:8-11)

New Testament Sunday (Christ's resurrection) (John 20:1; Acts 20:7)

Monthly Cycle

New Moon Festival (Num. 10:10)
Seasonal festivals/annual cycle
Old Testament: Passover, Pentecost, Tabernacles (Exod. 23:14-17)
New Testament: Advent, Easter, Pentecost

Multiyear Cycle

Sabbath year (every seventh year) (Lev. 25:1-7)
Jubilee year (every fiftieth year) (Lev. 25:8-13)

The rhythms of time for worship, especially festival time, are a rejection of death and the impact of the fall. The rejoicing and sharing associated with the feasts asserted the quality of life and value of community and affirmed the goodness of God's original creation. The rhythms of time for worship are a return to creation principles, in that "redeeming" the time in this way conquers "chaos" and recovers "cosmos" or order in the fallen world.

wilderness to God's provision for the new generation and their preparation for entrance into the land.

Leadership was provided for both generations (old: Aaron's family; new: Joshua), and genealogies are presented for both, yet an extended contrast can be seen between the two. The Balaam section signals the transition, giving blessing instead of the deserved cursing and showing the zeal of the new generation (Phinehas, chap. 25). The first generation was provided with God's presence. The second generation is introduced with God's blessing (through Balaam).

Chapters 1 through 10 concern the presence of the Lord in relation to the traveling arrangements as the people leave Sinai (now with the law and with their new portable sanctuary). Chapters 11 through 21 report constant complaints from all sectors—from the common folks to the top leadership—and detail God's provision for their needs. The failure of the people reaches a climax when they refuse to trust God to bring them into the land.

The blessing of Balaam in chapters 22 through 24 serves as the transition to the second generation and introduces the blessing of God that will establish Israel in the land as his covenant people. The new census prepares the way for inheritance and is followed by inheritance law. The text then proceeds to detail some of the calendrical ritual obligations for living in the land (daily, weekly, monthly, and yearly) in chapters 28 and 29. The book draws to a conclusion with information concerning boundaries and claims in the land (chaps. 32–36).

©Copyright 1995, 1999 Phoenix Data Systems, portions copyright 1999 Imspace Systems Corporation

A model of the tabernacle set up in the Negev.

Deuteronomy

The purpose of Deuteronomy is to summarize and renew the covenant in preparation for entering into the land. In the process, the book organizes laws in such a way that the spirit behind the Ten Commandments will be understood. It emphasizes the issues of one God, one people, one sanctuary, and one law.

Deuteronomy can be viewed in a number of different ways:

- As a vassal treaty that delineates the vassal relationship between Israel and the Lord. This can be observed in that it follows a common format of treaties between nations.

- As a constitution type of document that provides the foundation of Israel as a nation. In this sense, it is a charter document giving Israel its mission statement, values, and by-laws.

- As a speech of exhortation by Moses to the generation that is ready to enter the land. As such it reminds them of God's faithfulness and of their obligation to love God and obey his law.

- As an exposition of the Ten Commandments (Decalogue) showing how all of the various laws offer explanatory detail of the

STRUCTURE OF DEUTERONOMY

Speech Segment	Treaty Components	Decalogue	Miscellaneous Elements
First Speech (1:1–4:43)	Preamble (1:1–5)		
	Historical Prologue (1:6–3:29)		
			Exhortation to obey (4:1–43)
Second Speech (4:44–28:68)			Introduction (4:44–5:5)
	Stipulations (5:6–26:19)		
		Decalogue (5:6–33)	
		#1 (6–11)	
		#2 (12)	
		#3 (13:1–14:21)	
		#4 (14:22–16:17)	
		#5 (16:18–18:22)	
		#6 (19–21)	
		#7 (22:1–23:14)	
		#8 (23:15–24:7)	
		#9 (24:8–16)	
		#10 (24:17–26:15)	
			Concluding exhortation (26:16–19)
	Document Clause (27:1–10)		
	Curses & Blessings (27:11–28:68)		
Third Speech (29–30)			Last words of Moses (31–33)
			Death of Moses (34)

implications of the Ten Commandments. Particularly chapters 6 through 26 constitute a legislative portfolio for each of the Ten Commandments in order to discuss their implications, nuances, and broader ramifications.

DEALING WITH STORY

Large sections of the Pentateuch are in narrative form and therefore constitute "story." As interpreters it is important that we become aware of literary elements that play a significant role in any genre. We can begin by identifying four important elements of story and four important guides to the author's intentions in the presentation of story.

Elements

Every story must have certain ingredients. First, it must have a *plot*—the flow of action or events that provide a framework for the story. The plot describes what happens in the story. Any plot must have at least one setting, but most plots have many different settings. The *setting* is defined by the geographical places of the plot, by the time period in which the plot is set, and by the types of places that are featured (e.g., the living room of the neighbor's house). The third ingredient is comprised of the *characters* in the story. They are the ones involved in the plot, and through the story we come to know them to various degrees. Finally, any story must be told from a *point of view*. If the point of view is from one of the characters, we might learn what that character is thinking, but we will know only what he or she knows. Some stories adopt varying points of view at different places in the narrative so that the reader gets the perspective of several different characters. Alternatively, the story may be told from the perspective of the narrator, who is capable of revealing any of the characters' thoughts and motives.

In the world of literature, some authors emphasize plot. A good action novel will keep the reader in suspense and create a sense of the dramatic. This can be seen in modern novelists such as Michael Crichton or John Grisham. Other authors are more interested in developing characters. They want readers to feel like they know the people in the story and will profit from the insights into human nature that are thereby provided. Classic novelists such as Charles Dickens or John Steinbeck are known for their skill in this area. A novelist such as

> **Story Ingredients**
> - plot
> - setting
> - characters
> - point of view

James Michener seeks to use plot and character development to explore interesting settings.

When we move from the world of the novelist to the realm of historical writing, all three elements are combined (the events of the period = plot; the place of the events = setting; the historical figures = characters), but still the writer may emphasize one over the others. One writer may be more concerned that readers understand the course of events (plot emphasis), while another writer may be more concerned that the people of this period of history become better known to readers as real people with feelings and choices—people who make mistakes but achieve certain things (character emphasis; historical *fiction* puts imaginary people in real historical settings or creatively develops the real people). Whichever emphasis the author chooses, in nonfictional historical writing, he expects readers to believe that what is written actually happened in real time and real space—that people who were there would have seen such things and known such people.

In that sense, biblical stories are more like nonfictional historical writing than they are like a novel. The biblical authors relate real events that happened in the lives of real people in real space and time. They are not inventing characters, nor are they attributing to them artificial actions or thoughts. Biblical stories are almost always told from the narrator's point of view, but would we say that the biblical authors have a plot emphasis or a character emphasis?

On the human level, we would have to say that the biblical stories offer more plot emphasis than character development. Biblical stories infrequently explore the motives and attitudes of characters. But the belief that the Bible is God's revelation of himself places

ANE Stories: Birth of Sargon*

Sargon, the mighty king, king of Akkade, am I.

My mother was an en-priestess, my father I never knew....

She conceived me, my en-priestess mother, in concealment she gave me birth.

She set me in a wicker basket, with bitumen she made my opening watertight.

She cast me down into the river from which I could not ascend.

The river bore me, to Aqqi, the water-drawer, it brought me.

Aqqi, the water-drawer, when lowering his bucket did lift me up,

Aqqi, the water-drawer, did raise me as his adopted son,

Aqqi, the water-drawer, did set me to his gardening.

While I was still a gardener, Ishtar did grow fond of me;

And so for [56] years I did reign as king.

---

*From Joan Goodnick Westenholz, *Legends of the Kings of Akkade* (Winona Lake, IN: Eisenbrauns, 1997), 39–41.

the biblical story in a different category than either novel or historical writing. In the category of plot, the author is not just interested that his readers understand what happened in a sequence of events; he is interested in familiarizing readers with what God was doing. In the category of character, the author's main concern is not that his readers get to know Abraham or David, Rachel or Ruth—he wants us to get to know God. In that sense, both plot and character should be seen as oriented toward God. If we are content with the development of plot in human terms or the character development of mortal men and women, we are missing the point of the biblical literature.

Guides

Any story has a number of different guides that help reveal the author's main concerns to the reader. The first is *selection*. An author must choose what to include and what not to include in his story. This choice cannot help but reveal what issues are important to him. Once the story and the material for the story have been selected, the author must choose the *arrangement* of the material into the story. In a straightforward telling, a reader would expect the events to be in sequence, that is, in chronological order. But in complex stories, such an arrangement may not always be possible or desirable. At times, the author may choose to hold back some events for dramatic effect. At other times, he may tell different parts of the story together, not because they happened sequentially, but because there is an important correlation between them that the author wants to develop.

In seeking to understand the motives for the author's selection and arrangement, we are trying to discern his or her emphasis. The *emphasis* can be found not only in the selection of what to tell and the arrangement of what is being told, but simply in the aspects of the story that the author highlights. If there is no development of the motives and attitudes of the characters in general, but then the story suddenly slows down and explores in detail the characters' thoughts in one particular place, the author's interests become transparent. If the plot covers several years in a very short space, then is developed minute by minute on one particular day, it is evident that the author is drawing our attention to the events of that day. The author's emphasis can be identified by what he commits more time to developing.

Guides

- selection
- arrangement
- emphasis

In biblical storytelling, one of the more frequently observed emphases of the authors is dialogue. Consider, for example, the story of David and Abigail in 1 Samuel 25. A quick tally of the verses shows that four verses track the setting (vv. 1, 4–5, 20); five verses deal specifically with character, mostly the character of Abigail's no-good husband, Nabal (vv. 2–3, 17, 21, 25); and about twenty-seven verses trace the plot of the story (vv. 4–23, 36–42). The remaining twelve verses contain the dialogue between David and Abigail and serve as the heart of the story. It should be further observed, however, that more than half of the plot verses (twelve) are speeches by the characters. Here we can see that speech or dialogue is the means the storyteller uses to do most of his plot and character development. In addition, the dialogue complements the placement of this story between the two accounts of David having a chance to kill Saul, because it indicates how God takes care of punishing David's enemies. In the Pentateuch, more extensive examples can be found in the Joseph story (Gen. 37:1–46:7) and in the story of Moses before Pharaoh (Ex. 5–12).

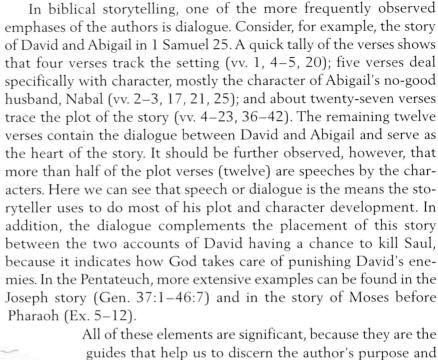

Artist's representation of the way Israel viewed the cosmos.

All of these elements are significant, because they are the guides that help us to discern the author's purpose and intentions. This is especially important in biblical narrative, because we believe that the author's intentions are inspired by God and that his purposes represent the authoritative teaching of the text.

THEOLOGICAL PERSPECTIVES

Creator

In the biblical world, the most important aspect of creation was that God brought order from disorder. He gave everything a function and a role as he imposed his will and purpose on the world. In our worldview, we most often emphasize the aspect of making something. The problem with this is that once a thing is made, the job of creation is done. In the biblical view, the order that was brought from chaos has to be maintained day by day, moment by moment. God does not disengage after creation. He takes his

Alva Steffler

place at the helm of the cosmos and maintains the equilibrium that he has established.

In one sense, God made the world for us, but in another, he made the world for himself. The cosmos was created to be his temple, and people were placed in the garden to serve, but not as slaves. Since the garden was sacred space, serving in the garden was similar to serving

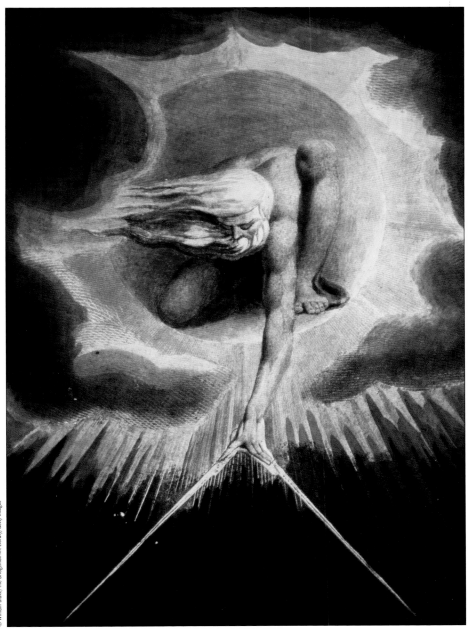

Ancient of Days
by William Blake.

© William Blake/The Bridgeman Art Library/Getty Images

in the temple—it involved caring for sacred space. In fact, the Hebrew terms used in Genesis 2:15 are often connected with priestly service.

If the world is God's temple where he has established and continually maintains equilibrium as his ongoing creative activity, we can understand that the biblical view of God is that he is intensely engaged in every aspect of the universe. To illustrate the implications of this, consider the question "What would happen to us and the world if God 'turned himself off'?" Some might think that goodness would dwindle away or that nature would begin to malfunction. But if we follow the biblical way of thinking, we would have to answer that we and everything in the world would immediately cease to exist (see, e.g., Col. 1:16–17). It would be like pulling the plug on the TV—the people on the screen would not just move more slowly, the screen would go blank and cold.[3]

The Fall

The fall was caused by disobedience. In popular Christian thought, we tend to consider the fall in terms of what it did to us: forfeited paradise, made us vulnerable to death, and established our sinful nature. These are all true, but there are other aspects that Israelites would have considered just as significant. First of all, the greatest loss was not paradise, it was access to God's presence. It was God's presence that made Eden so desirable. When a family goes through a divorce and mom and the kids have to move from their luxurious home to a two-bedroom apartment, whatever sense of longing they have for their prior *house* is insignificant compared to the loss of their *home*—the family relationship that has been shattered. We get closer to this in Christian theology when we speak of sin causing separation from God, but even then we often think in legal terms rather than sensing that ache deep inside and the feeling that life will never be good again. For readers who have lived through such circumstances, this illustration is hard to read without experiencing emotion. In the same way, we should experience a sense of loss, regret, and emptiness—the sense that nothing will be right again—when we think of the fall.

Second, what sin did to us is not as important as what sin did to God. The fall desecrated God's presence. In the Israelite worldview, the sanctity of God's presence was much more of a reality than it is to us. Their concern about the purity and holiness required in sacred space is only matched today by the concerns we find in laboratory

There is perhaps no book in the Bible (dare we say in the world?) for which the issue of historical authenticity is more crucial than Genesis. For centuries it framed the beliefs of Western culture concerning the natural world and the history of civilization. Only in the aftermath of the Enlightenment did its tenets begin to be subjected to inquiry under the onslaught of rationalism and empiricism. Over the last few centuries, then, Christians have been challenged with regard to the correlation between the Bible and history. Were the patriarchs real flesh-and-blood people or were they literary-cultural constructs whose legends grew up to embody the cultural heritage of a small but influential ethnic group? Did God really have conversations with these people? Did Adam and Eve actually exist, and did all people come from them? Was there really a garden with such marvelous trees? Did the serpent really talk? Are the many diverse languages of the earth the result of God's judgment? Was there a worldwide flood? It is testimony to the powerful impact of the Bible on Western civilization that we continue to address these questions.

The only way to get to the specific questions is through the big issues. As we discussed in the opening chapter, our commitment is to take the text at *face value.* We approach this face value from a *worldview of faith.* It is important to establish the first before applying the second. We must determine what the text asks us to believe in order to make an informed commitment. To do this, it is essential to understand that discerning the face value of a text is dependent on the reader's awareness of the vehicles that are used in delivering the message of the text. As mentioned in the chapter on fundamentals, when we say we take the text at face value, it means that we are not trying to read anything into the text, nor are we trying to squeeze something out of the text. We are not trying to sidestep the text or to avoid what it makes obvious. We are not trying to subordinate the text to our own agenda or purpose, nor are we trying to co-opt it for our theology or make it answer our questions. We are simply trying to understand the text in the way the author wanted it to be understood by his audience.

Here the three main vehicles that provide the face value that we discussed in the first chapter come into play. A brief review is in order. The first is the *genre* of the literature. If the author intended something to be a parable, we want to read it as parable. If the text was intended to be poetically figurative, that is how we want to read it. Second is the issue of *cultural perspective.* Cultures have ways to communicate that might differentiate them from other cultures. There may be features in the text that are part of the communication framework without representing the message, and those need to be identified in the search for face value. For instance, the Bible can talk about the heart as what one thinks with (communication framework) without teaching that the heart actually does the work of the brain. Third, we must try to assess the *focus of the revelation.* There may be a difference between what Israelites believed and what the text is communicating. Though we can at times discern the former, it may not impact the latter. So when the text speaks of the windows of heaven, we may conclude that the Israelites believed there were windows of heaven, but we need not conclude that the Bible is teaching that there are such windows. That is not the focus of revelation. When we understand the face value, we have arrived at an informed understanding of literature, culture, and the intent of the revelation. Then we can identify what mandates of belief the text is placing on us based on our worldview of faith.

How does this worldview of faith work? With no apologies or embarrassment, we accept the Bible as God's revelation of himself. It is a supernatural book, and its affirmations of God's involvement in the world are unassailable. He is the source from which Scripture flows, enabling it to emerge as true and authoritative. As a result, we are committed to accepting without question whatever God has revealed. If we should be convinced, for instance, that the Bible teaches a global flood, the worldview of faith dictates that whatever scientific or logical problems may exist must be set aside in deference to the text. While this firm commitment is not subject to compromise or equivocation, it cannot afford to be naïve. The last thing we want to do is to bring the text to disrepute and subject it and ourselves to ridicule by making claims for the Bible that it never made for itself. Examples of such misplaced faith litter the landscape of history. Perhaps the best known is the case of Galileo, who suffered persecution at the hands of the church because of its conviction that his heliocentric theories contradicted the teachings of Scripture. We must bring an informed discernment to the table when we address such issues. Without being simple, we must remain without guile.

work where scientists are dealing with hazardous materials. Sin was not just a momentary problem that a swipe of antiseptic could remove. It was more like a Chernobyl nuclear accident that caused radiation damage that had lasting effects. While there was certainly human tragedy at Chernobyl in the people who were irradiated and driven from their homes, there was also the tragedy of the ruined land. This is similar to the desecration that sin brought to God's temple-cosmos. In the ancient world, when a conquering army destroyed a temple, it often took steps to contaminate the site so that it could never be used as a temple again (see, e.g., 2 Kings 10:26–27). Similarly, God's temple-cosmos had been desecrated in apparently irreparable ways.

Covenant

We have already introduced the idea of the covenant as God's program of revelation. In Genesis 12 the promises offered to Abram have an obvious association with the original blessing to all people. They differ, however, in the way they indicate the ability to appropriate the blessing successfully. God did not just offer the blessing to be fruitful and multiply; he said that Abram would indeed be fruitful and multiply, with the result that he would become a great nation. God did not just give permission to eat food; he promised a land that would provide bountifully for his people. God intended to be more than one who granted privileges; he assured success and personally imparted the benefits to Abram and his family.

The Covenant and Abram. God did not ask Abram to give up anything that he was not going to replace. God asked Abram to leave his land, and God promised to take Abram to a new land. After Abram arrived there, God said he would give him that land. God also asked Abram to leave his kinship group. This meant giving up the protection and security that a kinship group provided. He was leaving his roots and putting aside all that was familiar to him. In return, God offered Abram a family that would become a great nation. Eventually God told him that his descendants would be as numerous as the stars. The third thing God asked Abram to leave behind was the "house of his father." This could be identified as his inheritance. In the ancient Near East, household gods were passed down generation to generation. There were ancestors to make offerings to and to care for. Most important was the care of elderly parents and eventually their burial. The inheritance one received included not only material possessions and ownership of land. It involved taking one's place in the family line and appropriating the blessings that had been passed down through the family line. As Abram put all of this behind him, God offered a threefold blessing for him. God would bless Abram, he would be a blessing, and he would be a channel of blessing. The first meant that Abram would come under God's care, protection, and favor, which would bring him safety and prosperity. The second meant that Abram would provide care and protection to those in favor with him. And the third meant that God would bring blessing to other people through Abram and his family.

The Covenant and God. Why did God make a covenant with Abram and his family? How would God bring blessing to other people through Abram and his family? When God created people, he created them in relationship to him. When sin disrupted that relationship, God determined to restore it and embarked on a course of action that would eventually accomplish reclamation, redemption, and reconciliation. While God's ultimate goal is relationship through redemption, there may be many objectives that work toward that goal, and not all of them are directly involved with restoring relationship. The covenant may be viewed not as directly tied to the redemption/relationship goal, but as addressing one of the secondary objectives. That is, the covenant does not announce salvation or provide salvation. It is not a mechanism for any part of the redemption program. It establishes a relationship with Israel, but only a relationship in the human realm; it does not solve the sin problem and restore the relationship broken by sin.

Before God resolved the Eden Problem (sin), he determined to resolve the Babel Problem (deity falsely construed). Calvary resolves

Leaves
country
people
father's house

Receives
land
family
blessing

Household gods were small statuettes that represented the patron deity.

Z. Radovan, Jerusalem

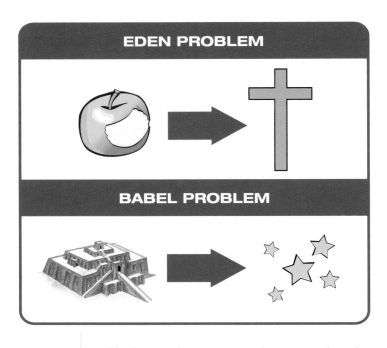

EDEN PROBLEM

BABEL PROBLEM

the Eden Problem, while the covenant resolves the Babel Problem by revealing what God is truly like. In this way, the covenant fills the gap that stretches between Babel and Calvary. On the Babel side, the problem is that people have corrupted the concept of God. On the Calvary side, God has provided a way to redeem humans and bring them back into relationship with himself. This is what we mean by saying that the covenant is God's revelatory program. People cannot enter into a relationship with a God they do not know. Revelation is a necessary step to reaching the goal of relationship.

Since the beginning of the church, the answer to the second question, identifying the blessing that comes through Abraham, has seemed obvious. God brought blessing to the world through Abraham and his family by means of the child born in the Bethlehem manger, the God-man who hung on a cross and died and then left a tomb empty on the third day (Gal. 3:8–9). Everything else pales before this blessing above all blessings. But though this is surely the climax of all of God's blessings, we must doggedly investigate whether the life and work of Christ is the sum total of the blessing that was to come through Abraham's family. We can start this investigation by inquiring about the range of blessings brought through Christ. Was salvation the only blessing he brought? (Certainly it would be enough if it were the only one, but we don't want to neglect other important aspects.) Our next thought might be of the blessing he provided to individuals as he healed them. But as we think about his ministry, we must expand his blessing to the way he taught about God and his kingdom. Indeed, there is no place to stop, and we begin to realize what a blessing it was for him to come and live. As important as Christ's death was, his life was also a blessing.

**Covenant/
Revelation
Blessings**

• law
• Israelite history
• Bible
• Jesus
• salvation

When we pause to think about it, we discover that all nations of the earth were blessed in Christ, not just by the salvation he brought, but by the revelation he brought. Through him we know the Father and we have a model for living. Through him we become aware of what God's kingdom is like and how its citizens ought to conduct themselves.

Was Christ the beginning of that revelation? Not at all; he was the culmination of it. As we consider the law and the prophets, the long process of revelation, we realize that every aspect of God's blessing of special revelation came through Abraham and his family. We find passages such as Joshua 4:21–24, where the Israelites are told that the partings of the Jordan and the Red Sea were done "so that all the peoples of the earth might know that the hand of the Lord is powerful." Again in Isaiah 49:26 the Lord speaks of the victory over enemies that he will bring so that "all mankind will know that I, the Lord, am your Savior, your Redeemer, the Mighty One of Jacob." In Ezekiel 36:23 the nations receive revelation through the punishment that comes on Israel: "Then the nations will know that I am the Lord . . . when I show myself holy through you before their eyes." And in Ezekiel 37:28, "Then the nations will know that I the Lord make Israel holy, when my sanctuary is among them forever."

In this way we can understand that the nature of the blessing on the nations is that, through Abraham's family, God revealed himself to the world. The law was given through them, the prophets were from among their number, the Scripture was written by them, and their history became a public record of God's attributes in action. Then to climax it all, his own Son came through them and revealed the Father and the kingdom through his life and a plan of salvation for the world through his death. God chose one nation to bless many nations. In Abraham all the nations of the earth were blessed as they were shown what God was like and as the means were provided for them to become justified, reconciled to God, and forgiven of their sins.

The answers to both questions then converge into one. God's purpose in making the covenant was to use the covenant as a mechanism of revelation. Through the instrument of elect Israel, he would reveal himself to the world.[4] The blessing that comes through Abraham and his family is that "through you, they will know that I am Yahweh." Israel would be a light to the nations (Isa. 60:1–3), and through them would come the oracles of God (Rom. 3:1–2).

Abraham: His Heritage and His Legacy

The biblical text is clear on the point that Abraham came from a family that was not monotheistic (see Josh. 24:2, 14). We must assume that he was brought up sharing the polytheistic beliefs of the ancient world. In this type of system the gods were connected to the forces of nature and showed themselves through natural phenomena. These gods did not reveal their natures or give any idea of what would bring their favor or wrath. They were worshiped by being flattered, cajoled, humored, and appeased. *Manipulation* was the operative term. They were gods with needs made in the image of man. As we have suggested, one of the main reasons God made a covenant with Abraham was to reveal what he was really like—to correct the false view of deity that people had developed. But this was projected to take place in stages, not all at once.

A standing stone, or *mazzebah* in Hebrew. Jacob erected a *mazzebah* at Bethel after a dream from the Lord (Gen. 28:18).

In the article "Yahweh, the God of Israel" (p. 33), we introduced the idea of "personal god" that was current in the ancient Near East at the time of Abram. It is possible that Abram's first responses to Yahweh may have been along these lines—that Abram may have viewed Yahweh as a personal god who was willing to become his "divine sponsor." The Lord would provide for Abram and protect him, and Abram would give his obedience and loyalty in return. One major difference, however, is that our clearest picture of the personal god in Mesopotamia comes from the many laments that were offered as individuals sought favors from deity or complained about his neglect of them. There was no hint of this in Abram's approach to Yahweh. Abram maintained an elevated view of deity that was much more characteristic of the overall biblical view of deity than it was of the Mesopotamian perspective. Though we are given no indication that Yahweh explained or demanded a monotheistic belief, or that Abram responded with one, it is clear that the worship of Yahweh dominated Abram's religious experience. By making a break with his land, his family, and his inheritance, Abram was also breaking all of his religious ties, because deities were associated with geographical, political, and ethnic divisions. In his new land, Abraham would have no territorial gods; as a new people, he would have brought no family gods;[5] having left his country, he would have no national or city gods; and it was Yahweh who filled this void, becoming the "God of Abraham, Isaac and Jacob."[6]

Offering scene from Ur.

Election: A Chosen People

The Israelites' most enduring understanding of themselves is found in their belief that they are God's chosen people. What did they understand themselves as chosen for? Christians today understand themselves as the elect of God in that they are chosen for salvation (Eph. 1:4–5). But this was not the Israelite understanding of their election. Their sense of election was connected to the covenant. God chose Abram and made a covenant with him (Gen. 12, 15). Subsequently, God chose Israel as his people through the covenant with Abraham (Ex. 6:3–8). To them this meant that he would deliver them, provide for them, and protect them. That is, they were chosen to be favored by God. In addition, it was communicated to them that God planned for them to be a "kingdom of priests and a holy nation" (Ex. 19:6). Finally, they were chosen to be a channel of blessing: through them all the world would be blessed (Gen. 12:3). In summary they were chosen to receive blessing and favor if they were faithful to God. They were not chosen to receive eternal salvation,[7] but to be God's instrument of revelation through the covenant, his revelatory program as God's blessing of revelation came through them.

Mesopotamian Land Grant

Alalakh Royal Land Grant*

From the present day on, Niqmaddu . . . King of Ugarit has taken the house of Yatarmu, son of Sharupshu, and the fields of Sariru with all that they have, and has given them to Bin-ilu, Yasiru, and Abi-irshi, and their sons forever. In the future nobody shall take it from their hands. It is a grant forever.

*COS, 3.108.

Law as Grace

Some readers of the New Testament have adopted a low opinion of the Old Testament law. But if we read the Psalms, we cannot help but be impressed with the fact that the psalmist cherishes the law (see Ps. 119:16, 20, 24, 40, 47, 48, 97, 127, 143, 159, 167). Why the difference? A careful reading shows that the New Testament writers did not condemn or reject the law itself. The difference is to be found in what role the law is serving. In the New Testament the law is seen to be defective if it is thought to provide the way to achieve and/or maintain lasting favor with God. In this view it can become an impossible burden, and the New Testament writers instead commend the idea of salvation through grace by faith. In contrast, while the psalmists understood the need to obey the law and its importance for pleasing God, the reason they cherished the law was that it represented God's revelation of himself. As such, the giving of the law is an act of grace.

In Christian thinking, law and grace are often seen on opposite sides of the spectrum. We are not saved by law but by grace. We do

---

I have hidden your word in my heart
that I might not sin against you.
Praise be to you, O LORD;
teach me your decrees.
With my lips I recount
all the laws that come from your mouth.
I rejoice in following your statutes
as one rejoices in great riches.
I meditate on your precepts
and consider your ways.
I delight in your decrees;
I will not neglect your word. . . .
Oh, how I love your law!
I meditate on it all day long. . . .

Your statutes are my heritage forever;
they are the joy of my heart.
My heart is set on keeping your decrees
to the very end.

Ps. 119:11–16, 97, 111–112

---

not live under the law but under grace. This dichotomy is based on the understanding of law as a guide to salvation. In the Old Testament, the law is best understood as a guide to knowing God. In his grace, God gave the law so that his people might know what he is like; he is holy and expects his people to be like him. Without the law and the rest of God's revelation of himself, we would have no idea of what God is like.

Sanctuary and the Presence of God

The presence of God is an important theological theme throughout the Bible. From the Garden of Eden through the various sanctuaries and temples and into the New Testament, the concept of God dwelling in the midst of his people was one of the most cherished. For the Israelites, God's presence came with the covenant and was represented in the tabernacle. The role of the tabernacle in Israel was far different from the role of church for the Christian. The tabernacle was the place of God's presence. As such it was the place where the Israelites came to bring their gifts to God. Individual worship took place there when people brought their sacrificial gifts to be offered.

Corporate worship took place three ways. First, the priests offered daily sacrifices on behalf of the people. This worship was corporate in focus, but the people did not gather for it. Second, the king was

Living the Law by the Categories

Even as early as the New Testament church, there were controversies about how much of the law was to be kept by Christians (especially gentile Christians; Acts 15). One of the early strategies, popularized by Thomas Aquinas, was to distinguish laws into three categories: ritual law, civil law, and moral law. After such a division was made, decisions could be made about which part of the law needed to be kept. It was commonly claimed that the ritual law became invalid with the sacrifice of Christ, and the civil law was applicable only to Israel as a state, leaving the moral law as that which had to be obeyed by all of God's people. As convenient as this approach seems, there are a number of problems with it. First, even the New Testament appears to make no such distinction. When Christ speaks of fulfilling the law (Matt. 5:17-18), he indicates that not a single part of it will pass away until all is fulfilled. Paul likewise makes no categories. Second, it is not easy to assign laws to single categories in consistent ways. How can laws be civil without being moral? Wasn't the ritual law a moral issue to the Israelites? In light of these difficulties, it is preferable to see the whole law as applicable today but applicable as a guide to understanding the holiness of God (for further discussion, see the Contemporary Significance chapter, pp. 108-31). This does not, however, turn the Ten Commandments into the Ten Suggestions. Laws like the Ten Commandments that we would have been most inclined to consider moral laws carry the same obligation for us today because the law told us that God disapproved of murder. God has not changed, and therefore murder is still something we would not do if we were seeking to please God.

involved in rites that corporately involved the nation, but again, the performance of these was public yet not an occasion for gathering. Third, the large pilgrimage festivals often brought people into the vicinity of the sanctuary for celebration of the festival. It is only in this last situation that large corporate groups gathered at the tabernacle. Neither the tabernacle nor the temple was constructed with the idea of accommodating large groups of worshipers. The inside was off-limits for all but priests fulfilling particular tasks. The outer court was for the sacrificial procedures and the purification necessary to perform sacrifices. These were not places where the common worshiper came to participate in services as we do at church. Since communal meals were often associated with sacrifices, there must have been places to accommodate them. But there was nothing to compare to the modern church auditorium or even to the New Testament synagogue that provided enough seating for people to gather for singing praise, offering corporate prayer, and hearing exhortation and instruction from God's Word.

Biblical Theology of the Divine Presence

Garden of Eden (Gen. 3:8)
Build me a tent (Exod. 25:8)
The glory of the Lord filled the temple (1 Kings 8)
You will call him Immanuel, God with us (Isa. 7:14)
The glory of the Lord departed from the temple (Ezek. 10:18)

The Word became flesh (John 1:14)
He will give you another Helper to be with you forever (John 14:15)
You are the temple of the Holy Spirit (1 Cor. 3:16)
God himself will be with his people (Rev. 21:3)

National Geographic

Reconstruction of the White Temple at Uruk dedicated to the god An. Various activities were associated with the sanctuaries in Mesopotamia.

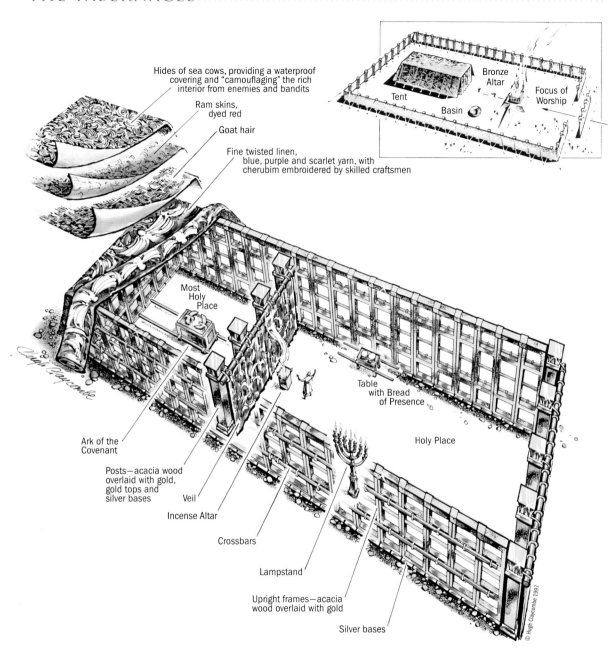

Hides of sea cows, providing a waterproof covering and "camouflaging" the rich interior from enemies and bandits

Ram skins, dyed red

Goat hair

Fine twisted linen, blue, purple and scarlet yarn, with cherubim embroidered by skilled craftsmen

Bronze Altar

Tent

Basin

Focus of Worship

Most Holy Place

Ark of the Covenant

Posts—acacia wood overlaid with gold, gold tops and silver bases

Veil

Incense Altar

Crossbars

Lampstand

Upright frames—acacia wood overlaid with gold

Silver bases

Table with Bread of Presence

Holy Place

© Hugh Claycombe 1997

We might compare the tabernacle to a bank. The bank is where the money is kept in the central vault. No one—not even most of the employees—can go into the vault anytime he or she wants. The bank building serves the banking public, housing the money and providing what is necessary for tellers and bank officials to conduct bank business, that is, managing the money appropriately and effectively. A person comes to a bank primarily to make deposits or withdrawals, not to learn about personal finance. In the same way, the tabernacle was built primarily to house God. Few people had direct access. It was designed to provide what was necessary for the priests to conduct the business of managing God's presence appropriately and effectively.

Holy Land and Sacred Space

Since the sanctuary was built to house the presence of God, it was a holy place where certain standards of purity had to be maintained. Therefore an area around it was in effect cordoned off. Access was restricted, and the closer one came to the Holy Place, the greater the demands of purity were. This resulted in a concept of sacred space. Sacred space can be understood by using a model of concentric circles. In the center circle is the most holy area, the Holy of Holies, the place of God's presence. The next concentric circle defines the area that is limited to priestly access. In Israelite sanctuaries this area was the antechamber and, at least eventually, the area between the altar and the portico. Leviticus treats these two areas as one in light of the fact that they are limited to priestly access. The third circle was the courtyard where people of determined status (i.e., a particular level of purity) were allowed access for particular purposes (sacrifices at the altar). The fourth circle is represented in the Pentateuch as the "camp of Israel," which is clearly distinguished from the area "outside the camp." Those who had contracted impurity were driven out of the camp until their impurity could be resolved.

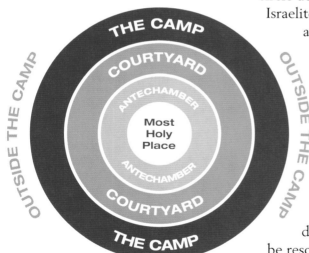

Sacred Compass

THE CAMP

COURTYARD

ANTECHAMBER

Most Holy Place

ANTECHAMBER

COURTYARD

THE CAMP

OUTSIDE THE CAMP

OUTSIDE THE CAMP

Each section of sacred space had its own standards of purity that had to be maintained. Many of the regulations in Leviticus are designed to indicate what those standards are and what procedures should be used to preserve them. The purpose of all of the rules of sacred space was to preserve the level of sanctity that was necessary for God's presence to remain in their midst. They were to be holy as God is holy.

We can best identify with Israel's concerns with the need for purity in sacred space when we think of our modern-day view of contagious bacteria. When a surgeon scrubs down for surgery, it is routine (could we say ritual?), but we would be horrified if he did not do so, and we would recognize how dangerous such an oversight would be. Surgery requires an absolutely germ-free environment, and all sorts of precautions are taken to assure that condition. That is how the Israelites thought about sin, purity, and God's presence. Eventually the concept of sacred space extended to the settled areas of the land of Israel. The settled areas became identified as "the camp," and to be driven out of the camp was accomplished by being driven into the wilderness or driven out of the land.

Yom Kippur—the Day of Atonement.

Hugh Claycombe

Priests and Sacrifice

The principal job of the priests was to preserve the sanctity of sacred space and thereby ensure the continued presence of God. They were the specialists on standards of purity and procedures for the maintenance of purity. As such, they supervised the sacrificial system. What is difficult for modern Christians to understand is that the sacrificial system only secondarily focused on the individual who had sin or impurity to deal with. The blood of sacrifices was dabbed or wiped or poured on the sacred things that had been desecrated or compromised by the sin or impurity. The primary goal of the sacrificial system was to restore the purity of the sacred space or object. The objective went beyond removing a person's sin to reversing the impact of the sin on the presence of God. Other sacrifices were offered more directly as gifts in an act of worship. These resulted in sacred meals with the officiating priest. The main sacrifices, the burnt offerings, usually accompanied petitions, either general or specific. Even the sacrifices intended for gifts or accompanying petitions had regulations that had to be followed so that God's holiness would not be compromised in the process. In summary, sacrifices were intended as a means to praise God, make requests of God, and maintain the holiness of God's presence.

CONTRAST: RELIGIOUS BELIEF IN THE ANCIENT WORLD

There is no doubt that in many areas Israelites thought like the peoples around them. Their views of the cosmos as a temple of God, of God bringing order out of chaos, of the temple as sacred space, and of the need for purity to preserve sacred space are all concepts that show significant similarities. The vast difference that made Israel stand out in the ancient world was the view of God that had been offered in their sacred texts. This concept of God that was urged upon them, when adopted, had ripple effects through every aspect of their worldview. In this section we will look at six areas and contrast the general ancient Near Eastern view to the ideal view that the Scriptures proposed to the ancient Israelites.

Ultimate Power

In the religious understanding of the ancient world, no entity possessed ultimate power in the cosmos. Polytheism by its very nature withheld ultimate power from any being since power, authority, and jurisdiction had to be shared among the gods. Each god was accountable to the decisions and decrees of the assembly of the gods. Beyond that, however, if we were able to lump all the gods together into one entity labeled "Deity,"

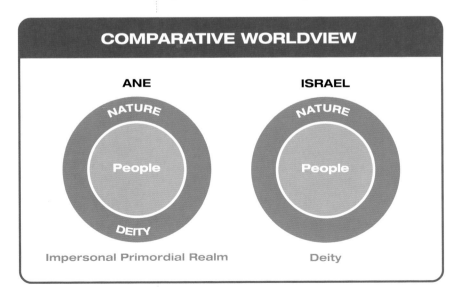

COMPARATIVE WORLDVIEW

ANE

NATURE

People

DEITY

Impersonal Primordial Realm

ISRAEL

NATURE

People

Deity

even then Mesopotamian belief would not have attributed ultimate power in the cosmos to deity. They believed in a realm that was outside of the gods and independent of them that the gods had not created and could not alter. This was an impersonal realm that gave structure to the cosmos. Law was built into the fabric of this realm, and it was a source of power and knowledge that could be tapped if one knew how.

Relief from Malataya that shows a procession of gods perched on the backs of animals.

In contrast, Yahweh, the God of Israel, was presented as the ultimate power and authority in the cosmos. When the first commandment says, "You shall have no other gods before me" (Exod. 20:3), it means that there are no other gods in God's presence. There is no pantheon, no assembly of gods, no sharing of power. He is accountable to no one, and there is nothing over which he does not have jurisdiction. Law comes from him, and there is no knowledge or power outside of him.

Manifestation of Deity

The gods of the ancient Near East were manifested in the heavenly bodies, the powers of nature, and the images that had been made to house their essence. In Israel, Yahweh is not associated with any image, and he controls the powers of nature but is not manifest in them. The second commandment forbids that Yahweh be associated in this way with any created thing.

Disposition of Deity

We have mentioned several times that the people of the ancient Near East believed their gods had needs. In this way, the gods were more like humans. In a similar manner, the gods often were viewed as conducting themselves in much the same way as humans do—with the same shortcomings, weaknesses, desires, and frustrations. This made them inconsistent and unpredictable. They were not

Prayer to Inanna

To pester, insult, deride, desecrate—and to venerate—is your domain, Inanna.

Downheartedness, calamity, heartache—and joy and good cheer—is your domain, Inanna.

Trembling, affright, terror—dazzling and glory—is your domain, Inanna.*

---

*From T. Jacobsen, *The Treasures of Darkness* (New Haven, CT: Yale University Press, 1976), 141.

The man who
sacrifices to his
god is satisfied
with the
bargain—he is
making loan
upon loan.

The man who
does not
sacrifice to his
god can teach
the god to run
after him like
a dog.*

*From W. G. Lambert,
*Babylonian Wisdom
Literature* (Oxford:
Clarendon, 1960),
147, 149.

understood to be moral, ethical, or fair, and integrity was not the norm. In contrast, Yahweh is seen as holy in all his ways. All ethics and morality are embodied in him. He is not like a man, does not change, and is consistent in all his ways. That does not mean that people can always comprehend his ways. His ways may be unfathomable, but they cannot be written off as simply arbitrary or motivated by needs or moods.

Autonomy of Deity

Once it was imagined that the gods had needs, it was not far to the concept that people could meet the needs of the gods. As people were seen to meet those needs, the gods were seen as becoming dependent on people. This gave people a certain amount of bargaining power when dealing with the gods. The gods needed food, housing, and clothing, and the people provided those things in their sacrifices and temples and in their clothing of the images. In contrast, the prophets had to remind Israel continually that Yahweh did not depend on them for anything. Yahweh indicates this clearly in Psalm 50:7–15, where he retorts that if he were hungry, he wouldn't tell them—he owns the cattle on a thousand hills.

Requirements of Deity

Though the gods were perceived as willing to answer inquiries about situations at hand through oracular questioning, they offered no permanent revelation of their character. Humans therefore had little guidance regarding what the gods expected of them. The gods had ordained justice, and people tried to live within the status quo of society. But the gods could become angry very suddenly, and the causes for divine anger were impossible to discern. All the people knew for

Prayer to Every God*

The transgression I have committed I do not know;
The sin I have done I do not know;
The forbidden thing I have eaten I do not know;
The prohibited place on which I have set foot I do not know;
The god whom I know or do not know has oppressed me;

Man is dumb; he knows nothing;
Mankind, everyone that exists—what does he know?
Whether he is committing sin or doing good, he does not even know.

*ANET 391–92

sure was that the gods wanted their needs met. As a result, when things were going badly, they assumed some deity was angry, and they attempted to appease the angry deity by trying to meet more of his or her needs. An additional problem, however, was that in pleasing one god, the worshiper risked making another god jealous and thereby multiplying offenses. A person would not hesitate to admit any sort of offense if he thought that by doing so he might be able to get back in the god's good graces. People usually thought in terms of ritual offenses, but ethical or social offenses were not ruled out. The contrast here is obvious, for in giving Israel the law, Yahweh revealed what his expectations were. The Israelites always knew what was required of them (see Deut. 10:12–14; Mic. 6:8).

Response to Deity

What sort of conduct did the gods expect from their worshipers? Alternatives ranged from a schedule of carefully choreographed rituals or planned periods of mystical meditation to generally ethical behavior or adherence to a wide range of rules. Still today some religions require pilgrimages or acts of piety, while others emphasize the need for good deeds and charitable works. A religion will be characterized by the features that have priority and make the greatest claims on the worshiper.

In the ancient Near East, the texts that are currently available to researchers testify most strongly to the ritual aspects of their religious practice. There is little to suggest that the rituals were expected to be accompanied by a sense of personal piety. There is even less to indicate that they believed that their religious beliefs made demands on their personal morality. Certainly the gods appreciated ethical behavior since justice and the preservation of a civilized society were important values. But ritual is seen to be sufficient and efficacious as

Babylonian Counsels of Wisdom*

Every day worship your god.
Sacrifice and benediction are the proper accompaniment of incense.
Present your free-will offering to your god,
For this is proper toward the gods.
Prayer, supplication, and prostration offer him daily, and you will get your reward.

Then you will have full communion with your god.
In your wisdom study the tablet.
Reverence begets favor,
Sacrifice prolongs life,
Prayer atones for guilt.

*Lambert, *BWL* 105.

a religious response. The Mesopotamian worshiper was expected to play whatever role was open to him in the performance of cultic ritual. That is the way he shared the responsibility for the care and feeding of the gods. This required no particular lifestyle or faith. He was, however, also expected to play his part in maintaining a well-ordered society by conforming to social expectations.

In contrast, the Israelite was expected to observe the covenant by abiding by the stipulations of the law. This involved the performance of rituals but also gave detailed guidelines for ethical behavior and community life. In addition, it was expected that the Israelites would love the Lord their God and live a life of faith in him. Many texts make it clear that ritual may be efficacious, but it is not sufficient. Any attempt to approach God with ritual alone was thoroughly condemned.

KEY THEOLOGICAL DISTINCTIONS BETWEEN ISRAEL AND ITS NEIGHBORS

ISSUE	ISRAEL IDEAL	POLYTHEISM
Ultimate of deity	Yahweh is the ultimate power in the universe. He answers to no one, and his jurisdiction has no limitations.	The gods have competing agendas and limited jurisdiction. Even as a corporate body they do not exercise ultimate sovereignty.
Manifestation of deity	Yahweh cannot be represented in material form or in the form of any natural phenomena.	Deities are represented iconically, anthropomorphically, or in natural phenomena.
Disposition of deity	Yahweh is consistent in character and has bound himself by his attributes.	Deities are not bound by any code of conduct. They are inconsistent, unpredictable, and accountable only marginally to the divine assembly.
Autonomy of Deity	Yahweh is not dependent on people for the provision of any needs.	People provide food and housing for deities (sacrifices and temples).
Requirements of Deity	Yahweh makes his requirements known in detail through the giving of the law.	Deities do not reveal any requirements; they can be inferred from one's fortune.
Response to Deity	Yahweh expects conformity to the law and to his holiness and justice.	Response to the gods is ritualistic, though maintaining an ordered society is important.

*From J. Walton, *Chronological and Background Charts of the Old Testament*, rev. ed. (Grand Rapids: Zondervan, 1994).

1. What are the major elements and guides to story?

2. State briefly the main purpose of each of the books of the Pentateuch.

3. What is the function of Genesis 1 through 11?

4. What are the three main vehicles that communicate the face value of the text?

5. What is the purpose of the covenant?

6. Describe some of the differences between the beliefs of Israel and its neighbors.

Notes

1. Frank Gorman, *The Ideology of Ritual* (Sheffield: *JSOT*, 1990), 28–29.
2. Ibid., 32–37, 55–59.
3. Richard H. Bube, *The Human Quest* (Waco: Word, 1971), 27–28.
4. I have developed this idea in depth in John H. Walton, *Covenant: God's Purpose, God's Plan* (Grand Rapids: Zondervan, 1994).
5. Though notice that Rachel attempted to bring hers (Gen. 31:19).
6. These paragraphs are adapted from J. Walton, V. Matthews, and M. Chavalas, *The IVP Bible Background Commentary: Old Testament* (Downers Grove: Inter-Varsity Press, 2000), 46–47.
7. Though certainly we are right to expect to see the Old Testament saints in heaven. See discussion in the epilogue, p. 388.

CHAPTER

CONTEMPORARY SIGNIFICANCE

Scenario: Evolution and the Bible

The scene is a biology classroom. The teacher has been busy explaining how natural selection and random mutations were responsible for gradual changes that over millions of years brought about the development of the first truly human species. He has traced the molecular evolution of the species from the emergence of single-celled organisms through the lower phyla to the emergence onto dry land and has been very explicit about the nature of our human ancestors.

Beth, a Christian sitting in the back of the room, has grown increasingly troubled. She recognizes that this challenges the fundamentals

Genesis and Science

Science has taken upon itself the task of accounting for everything in the universe by using only what is known about natural cause-and-effect processes. There is no place in which, as a discipline, it is content to say, "And this part was done by God." If something cannot be explained by natural laws and natural cause-and-effect principles, science can only admit its limitations.

In contrast the Bible has the function of revealing the role of God. There is no place in which the text is content to say, "And this part, God had nothing to do with." If something has no information to offer about God, it ceases to be a matter for textual discussion.

Given these definitions, it is easy to see why it is difficult, if not impossible, to get the Bible to take account of science or to get science to take account of God. To require that from either would drive them out of their domain.

The result of this is that phrases such as "theistic evolution" or "scientific creationism" as commonly used can be oxymorons. Both try to involve God in scientific description when scientific description, by its nature, cannot address the role of God.

The Bible does not offer any new revelation to the Israelites about science, nor does it ever assume a more sophisticated scientific outlook than the Israelites possessed. Instead, God was always content to communicate on the basis of how they understood the world to work.

of the faith that she has been taught her whole life. She agonizes over whether she should speak up and what she should say. Finally, despite the objections of her self-consciousness, she tentatively raises her hand, hoping deep down inside that perhaps the teacher won't call on her and she can walk away feeling as if she at least tried. No such luck. He pauses and calls her name. The whole class pivots heads to look at her—she has never spoken up in class before.

"Mr. Compton," she hears her voice say as she quickly tries to remember the arguments that her youth pastor taught last month, "all that you have just told us seems to go to a lot of trouble to edge God out of the picture. There are a lot of flaws in the science behind evolution that are often overlooked. For instance, doesn't the second law of thermodynamics contradict the evolutionary scenario of going from the simple to the complex? If the system is moving from order to disorder, we wouldn't expect an evolutionary spiral moving upward . . . would we?" As she finished talking, she smiled tentatively—that hadn't come out sounding too bad.

Mr. Compton paused before answering, and a grim look passed over his face as he heaved a sigh. He hated this kind of situation. Beth was nice enough, and a decent student, but she was obviously misled and her comment had been naïve. He hated to be the one to burst the bubbles, but too often it came to this.

"Beth, and the rest of you too, listen carefully. First of all, it is a gross oversimplification to represent the second law of thermodynamics by describing it as the movement from order to disorder. The second law of thermodynamics refers to energy, not matter. Whatever the complexity of the organism, it operates by taking in energy and using that energy up through its life processes. As the energy is used up, it dissipates in the form of heat. That is the second law in action. Nothing in this law concerns the process of evolution. Evolution is a fact of science, and you may as well get used to it. Science has no room for God and no need for God. What you believe in is your own business, but don't try to bring your Bible into my classroom."

© Comstock Images

As many of her classmates turned back to face the front, snickering and sneering, Beth sank lower in her seat in deep humiliation. Her confidence was shaken, her resolve weakened, her emotions raw. Her faith was teetering on the edge.

RECAPITULATION

What should Beth have said? What would have been appropriate for her to say? How can she stand up for her beliefs when she feels they are being threatened?

The essence of apologetics is defense, not attack. What is it that we defend? Mr. Compton has not suggested that God does not exist—he would not legally be able to do that. Instead, he has set forth a view that leaves God out of the picture. When we think about it, however, every meteorologist leaves God out of the picture when he or she gives the evening weather report, and we don't take that as an attack on God, even though we believe that God controls the weather, good and bad. There are no court cases trying to force the evening news to offer the alternative of God-controlled weather patterns alongside the meteorologist's godless speculations about pressure systems.

We believe that God is active even when natural processes are capable of offering an explanation for what we see. We do not have to choose between a natural explanation and a supernatural explanation. The two are not mutually exclusive in a view that sees God at work in every process whether it has a natural explanation or not. This does not suggest, however, that we simply accept an evolutionary model alongside our beliefs. The biggest difference between the biblical view and the secular naturalism of the world around us is the belief in purpose. Science is only equipped to identify cause, not purpose. In contrast, when considering the normal operation of the world, the Bible is most interested in purpose without regard to cause.

Instead of viewing the origins issue as a pie that has to be cut up and divided between that which is supernatural and that which is scientifically explained by means of natural cause and effect, it is more helpful to view it as a layer cake. The bottom layer would represent the cause-and-effect process as scientists could observe it. Their discipline can only explore that bottom layer. Everything in that bottom layer is matched by the top layer—representing God's activity. God's involvement does

not require that no scientific explanation be possible. When the psalmist says that God "knit me together in my mother's womb" (Ps. 139:13), he is not negating the normal developments recognized by embryologists. God's activity is represented by these "natural" occurrences. But none of these natural occurrences can be considered to take place independently of God and his purposes.

In many ways, then, it is fruitless for Beth to try to argue with Mr. Compton about the scientific deficiencies of the theory of evolution. Whatever scientific deficiencies it may have, it still represents the best that naturalistic science has, and nothing can be said in a science classroom to dismantle the theory and "save the faith." If evolution were proven defective, something just as neglectful of the role of God would be put in its place, because science operates totally within the realm of the natural. Likewise, it is pointless to try to get a science teacher to put God in the picture somewhere or allow for God. Since modern science is committed to describing things without God (the bottom layer of the cake), putting in God immediately moves one into a different sphere of thought.

What Beth can do is ask questions that will help define the scientific fundamentals more carefully. First, all science is open to development and change. Mr. Compton would do well to speak of consensus or generally recognized principles rather than call any scientific proposal or reconstruction a fact. On this any careful scientist would agree. Moreover, without the ability to repeat something, science can only suggest what might have happened. Second, science does not prove there is no God, and in fairness to the Mr. Comptons of the world, he has not suggested that it has proved any such thing. Science only tries to describe the operations of a closed cause-and-effect system that does not allow itself the luxury of resorting to the "God factor" to explain how things worked or

Models of Relating Science to Theology and the Bible

Conflict: Science and theology say the same kinds of things about the same things (dividing a single pie) but offer competing views.

Compartmentalization: Science and theology say different kinds of things about different things—people must decide which is which (two pies).

Complementarity: Science and theology say different kinds of things about the same things (layer cake).

Concordist: Science and theology are both really saying the same thing. People who adhere to this concept try to see scientific statements behind the biblical verses and then construct scientific theories that will confirm those readings (the Bible is the crust of the pie containing science as the fruit).

happened. Mr. Compton is only half right though—it is true that science as it is typically defined today has no room for God. But many scientists would admit that there are places where God could nicely fill a gap that present knowledge leaves gaping. It is these gaps that are often targeted by the scientists arguing the case for intelligent design. But simply targeting gaps does not help a theistic point of view. Our theology is not helped by a God who just fills in the gaps when science fails to offer an explanation. Returning to the layer cake analogy, there may be places where there is no bottom layer (i.e., no scientifically determined explanation), such as in the incarnation or the resurrection.

Other issues that perplex scientists (such as the stimulation of the Big Bang or the jump from nonlife to life) can also be included in this list. It is in this latter category that the intelligent design movement has been most helpful. Although there are places where either science or theology tells us there is no bottom layer, there are no places where there is only a bottom layer—we believe that God is involved at all levels at all times. Finally, science cannot prove there is no purpose to the created world; scientists can only confess that their discipline is not suited to identify a purpose. This is the key to the impasse between the Bible and science, for the Bible is most interested in and insistent upon the issue of purpose.

When we express our biblical conviction that God created with a purpose, and that he is involved in maintaining order in the cosmos moment by moment, we have not made a statement that science can either confirm or falsify. If we are to defend the faith, it is these concepts that are the core biblical values that we ought to be prepared to defend, and we need to realize that science per se is not attacking them. The greatest disagreement the Bible has with evolution is found in the difference between changes brought about by random chance (which evolution has no choice but to accept) and purposeful intentionality and thoroughgoing providence (which are foundational to a biblical faith). Perhaps it is less important for us to argue against evolution and more

Intelligent Design

Intelligent design is a theory that suggests that the universe as a whole as well as many mechanisms within the universe shows evidence of design. Many of these can be recognized by their irreducible complexity. It is difficult to imagine how something irreducibly complex could have evolved piece by piece or stage by stage since its function can only be accomplished as all the complex parts work together.

important for us to promote the picture of a God who is actively engaged in carrying out his purposes. But the science classroom is not the most appropriate context for those discussions.

As Beth listens to Mr. Compton present the evolutionary model, she ought to be reminding herself that he is presenting the sort of sequence that would have to take place if God were not involved and natural cause and effect were all that could be considered (investigation of the bottom layer). She can mentally confirm her belief that God was involved and still is involved in every step (existence of a top layer), and that science will never be able to detect every aspect of his role. Once there is an option to put God in the picture, the shape of any model seeking to explain the world we live in is characterized by radically different parameters.

Finally, teachers in public schools can be challenged if they are promoting a belief that there is no God or that there is no purpose. They need to be held accountable to sticking with science rather than encroaching on metaphysics. Beth could ask questions such as:

- Has science proved or is it even capable of proving that there is no purposeful direction driving the natural processes that scientists observe?

- Have scientists observed anything that rules out the existence of a higher being or that being's involvement in the origins and operation of the universe?

- What are the implications of the fact that such a large number of scientists (40 percent by some recent surveys) believe in a personal God who acts in miraculous ways?

In effect, these questions ask only that the teachers and school systems present the existence of the metaphysical debate fairly without taking sides—that there be an acknowledgment of a variety of worldviews. The indoctrination with "secular religion" is just

Questions to Clarify That Science Is Always "in Process" and Represents a Combination of Scientists' Best Explanations

- The evolutionary models of today look significantly different from Darwin's model. What changes might we anticipate in the coming decades?
- How are scientists integrating the observations of irreducible complexity at the cellular level into evolutionary theory?

- The proposal of punctuated equilibrium to account for the Cambrian explosion has offered alternatives and modifications to the shape of evolutionary theory. Given these variations, what do you mean when you call evolution a "fact of science"?

as unacceptable in the public arena as indoctrination with Christianity, Judaism, Islam, or Hinduism.

THE FALL TODAY

Without the Fall

We're madmen
all.

We watch the
stars

That creep and
crawl

Like dying flies

Across the wall

Of night and
shriek

And that is all.

Without the
Fall . . .*

---

*A. MacLeish, *J. B.*
(Boston: Houghton-Mifflin,
1958), scene 9, 127.

In the politically correct climate of the day, the word *sin* has dropped out of our vocabulary. We can speak of crime or corruption, but even in those cases, it would be considered unacceptably judgmental in our society to label people involved in those activities as sinners. As has been observed in Cornelius Plantinga's masterful book on sin, "The word *sin* now finds its home mostly on dessert menus. 'Peanut Butter Binge' and 'Chocolate Challenge' are sinful; lying is not."[1] In this sense, we could describe ourselves as living in the days of sin's decline, unfortunately referring to the word, not the behavior.

In contrast, the behavior now is sometimes seen as something to be encouraged. A recent newspaper advertisement for Las Vegas boasted: "Seven Deadly Sins. One Convenient Location." Where sin used to be taken seriously by society, it is fast becoming something to snicker at and to indulge in. Self-indulgence has established itself as a societal value.

One sign of the erosion has been evident for decades in advertising. Some product, activity, or fashion is accepted as attractive if it can produce envy or lust in someone else. In effect, this suggests that the capability of making someone else sin is a worthwhile pursuit. Another sign is the official promotion of greed by the state lotteries. What about the other four of the seven deadly sins—can most of us even name them? Pride, gluttony, anger, and sloth are all promoted in various ways in our society. We used to regret that we live in a fallen world—more recently we have come to revel in it. Both Old and New Testaments recognize the essential sinfulness of the human race. Paul's lengthy discussions in Romans 1 through 6 return often to the Old Testament to make his points (Ps. 14:1–3; Rom. 3:11–12).

It is important to continually remind ourselves that we live in a fallen world. This recognition gives us hope that there is something else. If we have no belief in a fall, we can only despair over the meaninglessness of life and resort to wallowing in the self-indulgence and self-absorption that have come to characterize our society.

SIGNIFICANCE OF THE FAITH OF ABRAHAM

Abraham's faith does not simply provide an example of what faith looks like; it gives an idea of the kind of faith God expects from us. If a student preparing for a final exam were permitted to look at a student's exam paper from the previous year, how would he best use that opportunity? On the one hand, he could try hard to memorize the answers his friend had given just in case the professor asked the same or similar questions. On the other hand, he could look a little deeper and try to discern the kind of understanding the professor expected and the kinds of answers that pleased her. In this second way, the student could prepare for whatever questions were asked. Likewise, as we look at Abraham's faith, we should not be as interested in imitating Abraham as we are in understanding the nature of God. We hasten to say that there would be much benefit in learning faith from Abraham (cf. Rom. 4; Gal. 3:6–18; Heb. 11:8–19), but the most important objective of the text is that we understand the nature of God.

Abraham's faith was demonstrated by his response to a test. If we wanted to devise a test that would be comparable to Abraham's, we would not ask, "Would you be willing to give up your child?" That falls far short of this test (remember that Abraham had already given up a dear son when he sent Ishmael away). Instead, we would have to ask, "Would you give up eternity in heaven for God?" In the 1970s a popular spiritual by Andrae Crouch explored this question:

Why Doesn't God Talk to Me Like He Did to Abraham?

Eight conversations are recorded between God and Abraham from God's first conversation with Abraham when Abraham was 75 until his death at the age of 175 (Gen. 12:1-3; 12:7; 13:14-17; 15:1-21; 17:1-22; 18:1-33; 21:12-13; 22:1-18)—several conversations in one hundred years, and sometimes with decades of silence in between! We cannot say conclusively that there were not other occasions, but God speaking is a significant enough event that we would think that it would be noted. And rarely were the conversations about those things that we long to hear from God about. Abraham did not control those meetings or have open Q & A times.

What if you were to make an offer to Abraham: "Which would you prefer, Abraham—a very brief conversation directly with God eight times in your life during which he spoke whatever was on his mind or a book that programmatically showed you what God was like and explained his plans and expectations?" God has given us far more revelation and guidance than Abraham ever dreamed was possible. Though God can still speak in theophanies, we should easily see the advantage of the Bible over random theophanies, and I expect Abraham would too.

You may ask me, why do I serve the Lord.
Is it just for heaven's gain?
Or to walk those mighty streets of gold,
And to hear the angels sing?
Is it just to drink from that fountain
That never shall run dry?
Or just to live forever, ever and ever
In that sweet old by and by?
But if heaven never were promised to me;
Neither God's promise to live eternally;
It's been worth just having the Lord in my life—
Living in a world of darkness he came and brought me
    the light.[2]

What a challenging lyric that is! We could just as easily sit with John Lennon for a moment and imagine. Though Lennon would have seen heaven and hell as fantasies that prevented people from living in the real world, his words can function differently to help us think of what our faith might be like without the hope or threat of eternity factored in.

Imagine there's no heaven,
It's easy if you try,
No hell below us,
Above us only sky,
Imagine all the people
living for today . . .[3]

Would we give God a chance if there were nothing in it for us? Would we give God our lives if he gave nothing back but himself? Would our lives have a place for God if we were "living for today"? It should be our aspiration to respond to those questions with a resounding "yes!" That is what Abraham did when he built his altar on Mount Moriah and bound his son. God asks no less of us than that he be our all in all. Job also was called upon to demonstrate that there was such a thing as faith that was not motivated by personal gain. When all is stripped away and no hope remains; in the dark, in the loneliness, in the emptiness, there is God. That is when faith stands up and is counted. Many times I have heard those whom I consider spiritual to express a longing to hear the coveted accolade, "Well done, good and faithful servant." Is our faith impetuous enough that we could long to hear the words God said to Abraham, "Now I know that you fear God"?[4]

OLD COVENANT/NEW COVENANT

The law was part of the old covenant, the covenant of God with Israel. We are under the new covenant of Christ's blood. In this new covenant, Christ is the new law who perfectly fulfills the Old Testament law. In this way, when Christ indwells us as believers, we have the law in our hearts (Jer. 31:33). In Christ the covenant relationship is redefined, but the basic thrust of the covenant is not changed. The character of God that was previously revealed through the law is now revealed more effectively by Christ, God's Son, who came and lived among us (Gal. 3:24). The old covenant with its law was like a map leading God's people to know how to be like him. In the new covenant and the law of Christ, the map has been replaced by a guide. That does not make the map wrong; it just makes it easier to get to the destination. Christ fulfills the law by serving as the climax of God's revelation of his character. This is what the author of Hebrews means when he says that "by calling this covenant 'new,' he has made the first one obsolete" (Heb. 8:13).

WHAT ARE ALL OF THESE LAWS DOING IN MY BIBLE IF THE LAW IS OBSOLETE?

What is the significance of Christ's fulfilling of the law for our understanding of those parts of the Pentateuch that represent the old

What Sort of Government Does the Bible Endorse?

In America we like to think that democracy is God's way. But it doesn't take much reading in the Bible to recognize that there is not much that is democratic about how Israel or the church operated. Leadership in Israel took many forms, from prophetic leadership to tribal leadership through elder members of the tribe, to priestly rule, to kingship through a divinely sanctioned dynasty. Does biblical law endorse a particular type of government as the norm to be followed? The short answer is no, but that does not mean that the Pentateuch has nothing to say about government. It is clear from Deuteronomy 16 through 18 that leadership institutions have an inclination to get in the way of God's rule and to usurp his authority. The more power that is attached to an office, the more likely it is that that power will be abused. Common folk are no less inclined to abuse power than important officials,

but as power is more broadly distributed, it becomes more difficult to abuse. The advantage of democracy is that it puts in more checks and balances and distributes power most broadly, thereby offering the greatest number of safeguards against abuse of power. As it becomes less possible to provide godly leadership, it becomes desirable to limit corruption by whatever means possible.

God is neither a Republican nor a Democrat, and neither party ranks godliness high on its platform. Parties are not godly; people are. Christians need to recognize that neither party offers to establish America as a godly nation, though in the platforms of both parties worthy causes can be found for Christians to stand behind. Our responsibility is to participate in holding our leaders accountable to justice and trying to make an impact on society for godliness.

covenant? When Hebrews 8 presents Christ as a mediator of a "better" covenant, it does not imply that the "first" (old) covenant was defective. The new covenant was better because it offered additional benefits: the law in the heart and the taking away of sins. That the old covenant did not offer salvation does not make it defective, for it was not designed to offer salvation. As we have already discussed, the purpose of the covenant was to offer revelation. The old covenant has been superseded in that it no longer provides the framework for relating to God. It is still capable of providing revelation about the character of God. In fact, Christ made it clear that he came to fulfill the law, not do away with it (Matt. 5:17–18). In addition, Paul affirms that "the law is holy, and the commandment is holy, righteous and good" (Rom. 7:12).

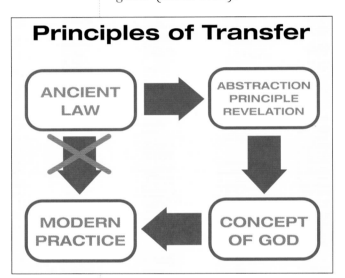

So what are we to do with all of these laws? We have to approach them as revelation of God (which they still are), not as rules for society (which they once were) or means of salvation (which they never were). That means that as we look at each law, whether it is one of the Ten Commandments or a law about mildew on the wall of a house, our first step is to try to understand what that law revealed about God to the Israelites. Once we understand that, we must make a cultural transfer to formulate a general principle about what that law reveals about God to us. Then we can use that principle to try to apply the revelation to our world in specific ways of acting or thinking. It is not the ancient law itself that carries the authority of the text. Authority is found in the revelation of God that is offered through the principle behind the law.

Scenario: Law

The church was in an uproar and so was the youth group. An abortion clinic had just opened up for business in their town—and just a block from the church! Bob went to Al, the youth pastor, to begin discussing what they could do as a youth group to take a stand. Should they picket the site? What about writing editorials and sending them to the local newspaper? Maybe a prayer vigil in front of the building would work. Al listened carefully and then suggested that maybe they should brainstorm some strategies as a youth group: "In preparation for that, Bob, why don't you do a little biblical research so you can present the Bible's case to the group as they begin to think of possible responses?" That sounded like a good idea, so Bob went home that night and began digging around in his Bible.

Sunday night came all too quickly, but Bob gathered up his notes and went to youth group to offer his findings. After some preliminary comments about the situation by Al, Bob was introduced and began his presentation. "First of all," he said, "we have to begin with the Ten Commandments. Number six is very clear—'You shall not murder.' According to Genesis 9:6, people are made in God's image, and taking a human life is punishable by death." He was feeling strong, so now he was ready to pull out the stops on his specific example from the Bible. "If you turn to Exodus 21:22–25, you will see an important case. Let me read it to you: 'If men who are fighting hit a pregnant woman and she gives birth prematurely but there is no serious injury, the offender must be fined whatever the woman's husband demands and the court allows. But if there is serious injury, you are to take life for life, eye for eye, tooth for tooth, hand for hand, foot for foot, burn for burn, wound for wound, bruise for bruise.' In this case," he concluded, "the death of the baby results in the death of those who hit the woman. Here there was only carelessness; how much more then does the Bible require serious action against those who purposely take the life of an unborn child? It is clear that the Bible forbids abortion and that we should do whatever we can to shut down this clinic."

As Bob took his seat, Al asked if there were any questions or if anyone else had anything to add. Elise raised her hand. "I am really upset about what is going on in that abortion clinic and truly believe that God is against abortion, so I would love to be able to open up my Bible and show them all how they are disobeying God's law. But something wasn't making sense as you pointed us to these passages. The case in Exodus wasn't really about abortion, even in your translation. And my translation says she had a miscarriage. Also, that law talks about specific punishments. If you are saying that this law tells us how God demands that we act, are you saying that we need to do this 'burn for burn and bruise for bruise' thing? And even in the Ten Commandments, where it says that we shouldn't murder—wouldn't those who are doing abortions say that the fetus is still part of the woman's body, so it is not murder? I guess I'm just confused, that's all."

RECAPITULATION

What can Bob say? How can Elise's questions be resolved? How can Al give clear direction to his youth group? Can the Bible help?

If we apply the principles we have learned in this chapter, we will have to agree with Elise on some of the weaknesses of Bob's presentation, though she was not able to articulate the issues clearly. Citing biblical laws against one action or another is not going to resolve an issue outright. Israel's laws are not our laws, and the Bible does not intend them to be. We cannot confidently use Israelite law as prece-

---

Clauses for Causes: Biblical Law and Contemporary Social Issues

Many controversial discussions are taking place in society today. Topics include abortion, homosexuality, and divorce and remarriage, just to name a few. If biblical law is understood as offering revelation rather than legislation, can we still use its verses to formulate "the biblical position" on these contemporary social issues? If Israelite law considered the unborn to enjoy the protection of the law, does that mean that the Bible is pro-life? If homosexuality is considered an abomination in Leviticus, do we adopt that as the biblical view? How do we determine that these statements constitute biblical teachings when we easily dismiss the regulations forbidding the eating of pork or requiring houses with mildew to be torn down? The answers are not easy or straightforward, but a couple of guidelines will help.

1. There is a difference between how we handle laws that focus on management of sacred space and how we handle those that govern society. The mildew and pork laws are both part of the guidelines for managing sacred space. Since there is no geographical sacred space, and since the guidelines for sacred space were to some extent governed by cultural norms, these laws can be handled in different ways.

2. We must be cautious to differentiate between statements of the law and inferences that we draw from the law. So, for instance, the identification of homosexuality as an abomination (Lev. 18:22; 20:13) is a statement; the personhood of the unborn (from Ex. 21:22–23) is an inference. Inferences are not binding statements of the text.

3. We must be careful to treat the text and context with integrity instead of seeking to use it to further our own agendas, however noble they may be. The text cannot be commandeered and forced to speak to issues it has chosen not to address clearly. If we violate the text to make it fit the case we want to make, we have paid too high a price. We may have gained a point, but we have lost the ability to identify the text as God's Word, because we have turned it into our own word.

4. We must conscientiously persist in the process of transfer as traced in the Principles of Transfer figure on page 118 so that we can confidently identify what cultural adjustments need to be made, what principles underlie the law, and what is revealed about God in the law.

In summary, yes, the laws can be used to address the issues, but not glibly or naïvely. We must be careful in our methods, consistent in our decisions, and respectful of the text's purposes.

dent law in our system to dictate how a case should be judged. Israel's laws help us to see the heart of God and begin to point the way toward faithfulness, holiness, and justice by showing us God's sense of those virtues.

What else can Bob do to build a biblical case against abortion? He should look to how God reveals himself rather than to a specific case law or commandment. For example, God reveals himself as one who defends the defenseless (Deut. 24:6–22). And no justification can be found in the Bible for the attitude that this is my body and I can do whatever I want with it. God's justice is represented in the insistence that people are punished for their own sins, not for the sins of others (Deut. 24:16; Ezek.18). These are aspects of the character of God that constitute God's revelation of himself. In this way, the law is used not for legal proof texts, but as an indicator of what God is like. Al, Bob, Elise, and the rest of the youth group will have to make their case against abortion using the Old Testament law to portray the heart of God, not as defining what our laws should be.

What Does Sacred Space Mean to Me?

God's presence does not dwell in a sanctuary today—there is no building that is sacred space. The temple is no more, and church buildings do not represent sacred space. It is fair to say that sacred

---

Sample Analysis: Deuteronomy 23:24–25

Law: "If you enter your neighbor's vineyard, you may eat all the grapes you want, but do not put any in your basket. If you enter your neighbor's grainfield, you may pick kernels with your hands, but you must not put a sickle to his standing grain."

Abstraction, principle, revelation: The idea here is clearly to make provision for the poor or the wayfarer. The law distinguishes between receiving hospitality and taking advantage. The obligation is placed both on the landowner who is instructed to consider this a form of hospitality and care and on the recipient who is instructed to show gratitude through restraint rather than imposing on his benefactor's generosity.

Concept of God: On the basis of this law, God could be seen as one who cares about generous hospitality and at the same time cares about the recipient not being lazy or greedy. These passages reveal values that God is seeking to reinforce.

Practical Application: In one specific context, very much like the biblical scenario, the school cafeteria may have a policy of allowing students to eat as much as they would like on the premises but will not allow students to head back to the dorm with three cakes for a floor party they are holding later that evening.

In an extended context we could say that the law would provide guidance in a situation in which a man's lawnmower broke down and he went next door to borrow his neighbor's. The spirit of this law would be violated if the man never bothered getting a new lawnmower but just assumed he could use his neighbor's each time.

Consider other passages connected to this law: Ruth 2; Luke 6:1-5.

To understand the impact the commandments should have on us today, many of them have to be put through the process of cultural transfer. With that process in mind, this is how the commandments might look today:

	THEN	NOW	CONCEPT
1	You shall have no other gods before me.	You shall not dilute my power by distributing it to other beings, forces, or principles.	God's being in the presence of another god indicates a pantheon working in a divine council with power distributed among the members. There was no pantheon with Yahweh.
2	You shall not make for yourself an idol of anything in heaven, on earth, or in the waters.	You shall not think of me as having needs that I am dependent on you to supply.	Idols were viewed as mediating the presence of the deity to the people and mediating the worship of the people to the deity as they tried to meet the needs of the gods, thus representing the limitations of the deity.
3	You shall not misuse the name of the Lord your God.	You shall not use the power of my name to accomplish your own plans.	The name of a god had efficacious power just as modern day credit card numbers—it could be used properly or illicitly.
4	Remember the Sabbath day by keeping it holy.	Set aside time regularly and often to turn your attention away from your own needs and take stock of God's role in the big picture of your life and world.	The Sabbath was a means of recognizing God's place in the cosmos and giving honor to him.
5	Honor your father and mother.	Honor those who are responsible for transmitting your spiritual heritage to you and be receptive to their guidance.	Parents were responsible for the transmission of the covenant from one generation to the next.
6	You shall not murder.	Respect others' right to life.	Dignity of life must be respected.
7	You shall not commit adultery.	Preserve and respect the integrity of family identity.	Dignity of the family must be respected.
8	You shall not steal.	You must not take what belongs to someone else.	Personal dignity must be respected, including a person's freedom, and self-respect.
9	You shall not give false testimony.	You must not slander others or defame them to others.	A person's name and reputation must be respected.
10	You shall not covet.	You must not infringe on the rights of others.	Rights must be respected.

space has not been a central plank in the theological platform of Protestant Christianity. There is, of course, good reason for that. A generation before the temple was destroyed by the Romans in AD 70, a remarkable event took place. The Gospels report that at the moment Jesus died, the curtain of the temple was torn in two (Matt. 27:51; Mark 15:38; Luke 23:45). Often Christians do not recognize the significance of this event because we have so little understanding of sacred space. The tearing of the veil indicated the end of restricted access to God. Hebrews 10:20 clarifies the new situation further as it uses the imagery of Christ's flesh as the veil that gives us access. Through the blood of Christ we are able to enter the holy place of God's presence. Paul works out some of the ramifications of this in Ephesians 2:11–22 as he explains that the Gentiles had been excluded from God's presence (i.e., outside the camp), but now were brought near. Access that had been denied was now available as the barrier or wall was broken down (v. 14). He goes even further to make it clear that there is still sacred space on earth. Continuing in Ephesians 2, Paul says that through him we all have access (v. 18), and built together *we* become a "holy temple" (v. 21) and a "dwelling in which God lives by his Spirit" (v. 22). Paul further develops this issue in 1 Corinthians, where he identifies the corporate church as God's temple (3:16–17) and each individual Christian as a temple of the Holy Spirit (6:19). Just as God's presence in the temple had the role of maintaining equilibrium and order in the cosmos, Christ came as our peace (Eph. 2:14–16; similar to equilibrium).

Peter proclaims that we are a royal priesthood (1 Peter 2:9). Since this is true, the church has taken its place in the long tradition of the priests as ones who uphold creation through their acts of worship and preservation of purity. Eden, the original sacred space, is restored in us as God's presence has taken up his dwelling in his people. We have

Temple and Church

The temple was sacred space because God's presence was there in a unique way. In contrast, God is not in the church building in a unique way. Instead, he indwells his people. When we sing about "God being in this place" or refer to church as God's house, it is important to understand the distinction. The temple was always the place of God's presence whether people were there or not. The church building is the place of God's presence only when his people are gathered there. The temple was holy because of God's presence. The church building has no holiness attached to it. The function of the temple was to provide a place of residence for God among his people; very little corporate worship took place there. The function of the church is to provide a place for God's people to gather in corporate worship. Priests performed the rituals necessary to maintain the holiness required for God's presence. Pastors instruct and care for God's people.

been given access to the fruit of the tree of life and thereby have been granted eternal life; the function of the fruit of the tree of the knowledge of good and evil takes root in us as the indwelling Spirit leads us to make godly choices. We are the heirs to the Garden of Eden. Our sacred status has been permanently set as we are in Christ and Christ is in us. The unfortunate dimension of this significant change in status is that we no longer understand the dynamics of the Israelite theology concerning sacred space. The status issue, our status in Christ, has become, in one sense, the only issue, and it absorbs most of our theological attention.

A SENSE OF THE HOLY

Since we, the church, are God's sacred space (both individually and corporately), we must renew our attention to holiness.[5] In an earlier section, we compared the importance of purity in sacred space to the importance of a germ-free environment in a hospital operating room. What does this ask of us? Where do we have to improve?

In Old Testament ritual laws the presence of God in a physical sanctuary required steps to maintain physical purity. Everyday issues such as the location of the latrine, mildew on the walls of houses, skin conditions, or bodily emissions could result in physical impurity. While the law was concerned with internal matters as well, much of Leviticus deals with external matters.

Whenever I Try to Read through the Bible in a Year, I Always Get Stuck in Leviticus

If we were to read the state regulations that have been imposed on the food handlers in restaurant kitchens, we would be very impressed with the thorough detail we found there. Those people have thought of everything, because they understand what is at risk if food is not handled properly. We would not read those regulations so that we could follow them in our home kitchens (though some of them might be relevant). Instead, we might read them to gain an appreciation of the nature of food preservation and to feel confidence that when we eat in a restaurant the food has not spoiled or been contaminated. We would not want food to become a threat to our health rather than nourishment for our bodies.

This might help us when we try to read through Leviticus. We need to keep in mind that we are not reading it to find out what we should do. As food could become spoiled or contaminated, God's presence could become spoiled (by sin) or contaminated (by impurity). In a spoiled or contaminated state, there was danger, not benefit. By familiarizing ourselves with the regulations, we should be impressed with the thorough detail that we find and through them seek to gain a greater appreciation of the nature of God's holiness.

Reading food-handling regulations helps us to understand how sensitive food is to contamination and will make us more careful with our own food handling. Reading "holiness handling" regulations can help us to understand how very holy God is and will make us more sensitive to ways that we can honor God's holiness in our own lives.

Now, with God's presence within, holiness has become almost entirely an internal matter. Personal holiness concerns not only what we do, but how we think and what motivates us. Passages such as Philippians 4:8 point us in the right direction: "Whatever is true, whatever is noble, whatever is right, whatever is pure, whatever is lovely, whatever is admirable—if anything is excellent or praiseworthy—think about such things." As Peter urges us to holiness, he talks about issues such as self-control, turning away from evil desires, obeying the truth, and loving one another. In addition, he encourages us to rid ourselves of malice, deceit, hypocrisy, envy, and slander (1 Pet. 1:13–2:1).

We can discipline ourselves to practice the presence of God by attending to the following three tasks:

1. Keep the space pure.

2. Maintain an environment and routine of worship.

3. Monitor the status of the inhabitants of sacred space.

Keep the Space Pure

The priests kept sacred space pure by carrying out rites of cleansing and purification. In following the mandate of holiness, we must keep careful accounts and be sure to deal with sin or impurity in our lives. Even though the defilement of sin or impurity has been taken care of through Christ's blood, our sin can still draw us away from God. That is why we must continue to seek his forgiveness (which is guaranteed for the asking) and the restoring of our fellowship with him.

What Is Holiness?

Holiness is not a separate individual attribute of God but is the result of the sum total of God's attributes. That is, all of God's attributes are what make him holy. Holiness is a term that implies comparison. God is holy in relation to the people he created. His holiness is defined as the distance between him and his creatures. That distance is defined by his attributes. His sovereignty, omniscience, love, righteousness, and the like are the things that distinguish him from people and give specificity to his holiness.

God asks his people to be holy as he is holy—that means we are to maintain distinctions between ourselves and the world around us. The distance between ourselves and the world is defined by the attributes of God that we are able to imitate (i.e., fruit of the Spirit). As we become more godlike in love, grace, faithfulness, mercy, and so on, we are becoming holy by distinguishing ourselves from the fallen world. As we are able to accomplish this, however, we do not close the distance between God and ourselves. His holiness is not reduced as we become holier.

We must also preserve the purity of the church. This means that we cannot allow sin to take root and fester (compare the letters to the churches in Revelation 2 and 3). In the permissive and litigious society in which we live, it has become more and more difficult to carry out church discipline. As a result, accountability is at an all-time low. Just as the priests sought to restore wholeness to those who had contracted impurity, so the church must seek to maintain its purity not just by driving some "outside the camp" but by engaging in procedures that will bring the disenfranchised back into the camp.

Maintain an Environment and Routine of Worship

Priests ministered daily in God's presence as they offered the sacrifices (morning and evening) for the nation and assisted the people who brought their sacrifices day by day. But they also maintained the details of the worship calendar from Sabbath to New Moon to the great annual pilgrimage festivals. The worship environment of our personal sacred space needs also to be maintained through the "times" of our schedules and calendars. The routine of worship should proceed day to day. This may take the form of "devotions," but our routine devotions, whatever they are comprised of, should not be isolated from the rest of the day. The routine of worship should engage us in some sense throughout the day.

Beyond our daily routine of worship, however, is our involvement in special opportunities for renewing our commitment, and expressing our adoration in our regular participation in weekly worship and the events of the liturgical calendar. In all of this, we cannot afford to become mechanical. The routine of worship only carries out the mandate as we maintain the environment of worship. If our thoughts are

Reading the Law

When a Christian reads the law, it is again like a student looking at previous tests that a professor has given in a course to get an idea of what she is to expect in the upcoming exam. The student does not actually have to take that past test—she is only using it to learn what is important to the professor. In the same way, we read the law not to find out what our law should be, but to understand the issues that are important to God. Just as an earlier test question may show up again in future tests

and others may be slightly revised, some laws carry the same importance for us, while others may be revised and still others may not carry over at all. For example, laws in Leviticus that had to do with the preservation of geographical sacred space will not be directly applicable to us because we have no geographical sacred space to maintain. Yet the principles will be important as we think about what it means to maintain our lives as sacred space.

full of ourselves and our plans, the environment of our minds has no room for another to be adored. In the temple complex of Israel, this focus was represented in centrality. The temple complex could be divided into two squares. At the center of one sat the ark; at the center of the other was the altar. This was believed to create the proper environment for worship. In the sacred space of our lives, an environment for worship is also created by making God central in our worldview. Everything in our lives should revolve around God and be under the influence of his gravity. It is too easy to allow God to drift to the outer edges of our personal world and make something else our center of gravity.

In the church, it is also true that God must be firmly in the center of who we are and what we do. Many causes are worthy of the church's attention, and we should not just huddle in our pews singing hymns. But we cannot allow any distraction, as noble or worthy or necessary as it may be, to usurp the central role from Christ. Nevertheless, we go out into the world to extend and expand sacred space. This is the missionary mandate that will involve us not only in evangelism, but in addressing the needs and wounds of our fallen world.

Monitor the Status of the Inhabitants of Sacred Space

In our personal lives we must take very seriously the priestly role of gatekeeper, preventing that which is impure from taking up

---

The Liturgical Year

For the Israelites, maintaining the calendar of sacred times was as important as maintaining sacred space. We are probably inclined to see Sundays and religious holidays more as traditions than as sacred duties. After all, there are no commandments to observe even holidays commemorating the birth of Christ or his resurrection, let alone some of the "lesser" holidays such as Pentecost Sunday or All Saints' Day.

Nevertheless, observance of sacred times is not without significance. For Israel, the festivals commemorated certain seasons as well as important events. When commands were given for the observance of the festivals, the emphasis was on remembering what God had done for them. Our culture is becoming increasingly a culture of the present. Each passing generation seems to be less concerned with history than the one before it. The speed of travel has brought the world to our doorstep, while the computer and the Internet have brought us to focus on smaller and smaller increments of time. It is easy to become lost in the present and disconnected from the past. This is all the more reason to be concerned about remembering—not just remembering the traditions of our past, but remembering the mighty acts of God. The church is not just made up of the generations of believers alive today. It is made up of all of the followers of Christ from centuries past as well. Liturgies, traditions, and festivals help us to establish continuity with the church of the ages and help us to look beyond ourselves and the issues of our time to the plan of God and the work of his people across the millennia.

residence in, or even gaining entry to, God's sacred space, our lives. On the individual level, this means self-examination. There was nobody to regulate the status of the priesthood but the priests. This extends beyond our behavior (Paul's subject in 1 Corinthians 6) to our thoughts. This is very difficult to accomplish because of the great amount of impurity that is all around us. Sometimes a very entertaining movie or a well-written novel may be tainted with less than desirable elements. How many movies or TV shows would we watch if we engaged in the discipline of imagining ourselves in God's presence—the Eternal One sitting on the couch in the den? How many inappropriate pictures do we allow to take their place in the photo albums of our minds? The biblical mandate is still in force: We are to be holy as God is holy (Lev. 19:2).

We must also keep the corporate sacred space pure. How is the church (the corporate body of Christ) in danger of allowing defiling influences in its midst? When the church allows qualities to become characteristic of it that are an offense to God's presence, we risk defilement. In ages past, we could point to abhorrent behavior reflected in endeavors undertaken in the name of the church such as the Crusades, the Inquisition and, in more recent times, the Holocaust. But we need to look closer to home. Can political alliances defile the church? Can social apathy? Can worldliness or materialism or secularism? Of course, they all can. In *The Subversion of Christianity*, Jacques Ellul decries the many ways in which the familiar Christianity of our age has become too comfortable with culture and spends far too much energy trying to make itself acceptable to and in society, rather than taking the radical narrow path enjoined by Christ on his disciples. "Jesus tells us plainly that if we simply do as the world does, we can expect no thanks, for we are doing nothing out of the ordinary. What we are summoned to do is something out of the ordinary.

Sacred Time and Redeeming the Time

Time
- created by God (Gen. 1:1–5)
- regulators established by God (Gen. 1:14–16)
- sanctified in religious festival calendar (Exod. 20:8–11; 23:14–17; Lev. 25)
- is God's time (Job 12:10; 33:4)
- is a divine gift, an act of grace (Ps. 139)
- has purpose and meaning
- is both cyclical (Eccl. 3) and linear (e.g., "the day of the Lord")
- is short (Ps. 90)
- is for rejoicing (Ps. 118:24)
- is for praising God (Ps. 119:175)
- God stands outside of time (Ps. 90:4; 2 Pet. 3:8) and Christ entered time (John 1)

We are to be perfect as our Father in heaven is perfect. No less. All else is perversion."[6]

The holiness mandate calls us to the narrow way of self-sacrificing service, of purity, of practicing God's presence minute by minute, of worship and adoration. It does not call for a method; it calls for a lifestyle. It does not call for establishing a devotional time to touch

Sabbath and Sunday

Christians commonly ask, "Is the Sabbath a law that we Christians have to keep?" The answer is, if we have to be reminded, commanded, or coerced to observe it, it ceases to serve its function. Sabbath isn't the sort of thing that should have to be regulated by rules. It is the way that we acknowledge that God is on the throne, that this world is his world, that our time is his gift to us. It is "big picture time." And the big picture is not me, my family, my country, my world, or even the history of my world. The big picture is God. We need to stop looking at Christianity as being defined as a set of rules we have to keep. Christian freedom doesn't say there are no rules, but that we shouldn't need rules. The Bible is not a book of rules; it reveals the God that we serve, and we serve him gladly.

Scripture tells us very little about what we are to do on the Sabbath. It gives us a clue by indicating what we are not to do, but if the Sabbath has its total focus in recognition of God, it would detract considerably if he had to tell us what to do. Be creative! Do whatever will reflect your love, appreciation, respect, and awe of the God of all the cosmos (this is the thrust of Isa. 58:13–14). Worship is a great idea, but it can't be mechanical, and it may only be the beginning.

Think for a moment about the cultural phenomenon of holidays. Let's take Memorial Day as an example. This is a day that has been set aside to honor Americans who have died in wars, who have given their lives to preserve the ideals and the freedom we enjoy. A significant aspect of the honor accorded is the fact that the day is designated as a federal holiday when, as a rule, people don't go to work. But, as with the Sabbath, that defines what we don't do rather than what we do. So what do we do on Memorial Day to give honor? For the most part it depends on whether one has loved ones who gave their lives. The more gratitude one feels toward the sacrifice of those who died,

the more effort will go into planning ways to give honor. Some have parades; some have graveside services; some buy flowers to plant by tombstones. Taking a day off from work is just the beginning—a societal response. What should be the personal response? The more the day means to a person, the more deliberate he or she will be about scheduling appropriate activities.

This is very similar to how the Sabbath works. A society-wide response designates it as a holiday and dictates that it be work-free. But it is up to the individual to determine what his or her personal response will be in order to give the honor that is due. The parades and ceremonies of a holiday are matched by the worship services of the Sabbath. The more gratitude we feel toward God and the more we desire to honor him, the more the ceremonies will mean and the more we will seek out ways to observe the Sabbath. The main difference between a holiday like Memorial Day and the Sabbath is that Memorial Day is important enough to have an official day set aside once a year; the Sabbath is important enough to have an official day set aside once a week. Additionally, holy days, unlike holidays, celebrate past events in worship and adopt a spiritual posture toward time and history.

Gathering together to worship on our Sabbath, Sunday, however, should be something we do for God, not for ourselves. C. S. Lewis suggests that "the perfect church service would be one that we were almost unaware of; our attention would have been on God."* Worship is about giving, not getting. When we choose a gift for someone, are we only to think about how good we will feel giving it?

---

*C. S. Lewis, *Letters to Malcolm, Chiefly on Prayer* (New York: Harcourt, 1964), 4.

base with God before we go on with our day; it calls for an attitude that fills our day with God. Too often our "devotional" time with God serves as an excuse to neglect him the rest of the day. Instead, it should help us set the course for being continually mindful of him. Brother Lawrence was a seventeenth-century Carmelite monk whose writings and life challenged us to practice the presence of God. He offered the advice that we focus totally on God.

> I have read many books on how to go to God and how to practice the spiritual life. It seems these methods serve more to puzzle me than to help, for what I sought after was simply how to become wholly God's. So I resolved to give all for ALL. Then I gave myself wholly to God; I renounced everything that was not His. I did this to deal with my sins, and because of my love for Him. *I began to live as if there were nothing, absolutely nothing but Him.* So upon this earth I began to seek to live as though there were only the Lord and me in the whole world.[7]

We are not only the priests of this sacred space, but we also are, in some sense, the sacrifices. Christ is the sacrifice that provided justification, atonement, and forgiveness, but we learn that we are to make our lives sacrifices of thanksgiving and that we are to do this by being transformed (Rom. 12:1–2). In addition, we offer our sacrifices of praise and of doing good (Heb. 13:15–16) as we carry out our functions as priests upholding sacred space.

REFLECTIONS

1. What steps can a person take to start moving from a me-centered faith to a God-centered faith?

2. Discuss homosexuality using the biblical law appropriately.

3. Discuss the importance of the law for a Christian today and develop the principles you set forth using a specific example.

4. Discuss how principles of holiness from Leviticus can offer guidance for Christians trying to live a holy life today.

5. What are some specific strategies that represent a legitimate observance of the Sabbath (Sunday) in today's world?

6. Discuss some of the ways Jesus can be considered the fulfillment of the law.

Biblical Characters: Aaron, Abraham and Sarah, Adam and Eve, Isaac and Rebekah, Jacob, Joseph, Moses, Noah

Extrabiblical Characters: Hammurabi, Rameses II, Sargon, Thutmose III

Peoples: Hyksos, Sumerians

Biblical Places: Beersheba, Bethel, Hebron, Kadesh Barnea, Paddan Aram, Sinai

Extrabiblical Texts: *Atrahasis Epic, Enuma Elish,* Gilgamesh Epic

Concepts: covenant-treaty format, mythology, three-tiered cosmos

GOING TO THE NEXT LEVEL

T. Desmond Alexander, *From Paradise to the Promised Land* (Baker).

T. Desmond Alexander and David Baker, *Dictionary of the Pentateuch* (InterVarsity Press).

Bill T. Arnold, *Encountering the Book of Genesis* (Baker).

David J. A. Clines, *The Theme of the Pentateuch* (Sheffield Academic Press).

Henri Frankfort et al. eds., *The Intellectual Adventure of Ancient Man* (University of Chicago Press).

Victor Hamilton, *Handbook on the Pentateuch* (Baker).

Alan Millard and D. J. Wiseman, eds., *Essays on the Patriarchal Narratives* (Eisenbrauns).

Karen Rhea Nemet-Nejat, *Daily Life in Ancient Mesopotamia* (Greenwood).

Carl Rasmussen, *NIV Atlas of the Bible* (Zondervan).

John H. Walton, *Ancient Israelite Literature in Its Cultural Context* (Zondervan).

John H. Walton, *Covenant: God's Purpose, God's Plan* (Zondervan).

Gordon Wenham, *Exploring the Old Testament: A Guide to the Pentateuch* (InterVarsity Press).

Herbert Wolf, *Introduction to the Old Testament Pentateuch* (Moody Press).

Notes

1. Cornelius Plantinga Jr., *Not the Way It's Supposed to Be* (Grand Rapids: Eerdmans, 1995), x, quoting sociologist James Dawson Hunter.
2. Andrae Crouch, "If Heaven Never Was Promised to Me," *Best of Andrae Crouch* (Lexicon Music, 1975).
3. John Lennon, "Imagine," *Imagine* (Apple Records, 1971).
4. Elements of this section were adapted from John Walton, *Genesis,* NIVAC (Grand Rapids: Zondervan, 2001).
5. This section uses material adapted from Walton, *Genesis.*
6. Jacques Ellul, *The Subversion of Christianity* (Grand Rapids: Eerdmans, 1986), 173.
7. Brother Lawrence, *The Practice of the Presence of God,* letter 1.

2 PENTATEUCH

2

3 HISTORICAL LITERATURE

Mounts Ebal and Gerizim near Shechem.

Twelve books of the Old Testament are classified as historical literature: Joshua, Judges, Ruth, 1 and 2 Samuel, 1 and 2 Kings, 1 and 2 Chronicles, Ezra, Nehemiah, and Esther. None of these books indicates who its author was. Joshua, Judges, Samuel, and Kings are often grouped together and referred to as the Deuteronomistic History because of their obvious reflection of the theological concerns and literary style of Deuteronomy. They function as a history from the conquest of the land to the exile from the land. Chronicles, Ezra, and Nehemiah are also often grouped together and assigned a single author. They represent a view of history from the period after the return from exile and relate some of the history of the period. Ruth and Esther are narratives about what God accomplished in two particular crisis situations in Israel's history. Ruth is set in the period of the judges, and Esther is set in Persia in the postexilic period.

"If we didn't have the Bible, we would know nothing about God but what we could infer from the world around us."

ORIENTATION

- Historical literature focuses on God, not people or events.
- Davidic covenant reveals God's kingship as kings serve as his vice-regents.
- Historical literature reflects a long-range plan of God.

YAHWEH FOCUS

- God is the active force behind history.
- God is patient but will not tolerate unfaithfulness.
- God is faithful to his covenant promises.
- God's kingship is supreme, and the nations are under his command.
- God can weave evil actions of people into his good plan.

KEY VERSES

- Joshua 24:14–15   Covenant renewal and commitment
- Judges 21:25   Lack of leadership
- Ruth 1:16–17   Affirmation of faithfulness
- 1 Samuel 16:7   God's criteria
- 2 Samuel 7:8–16   Davidic covenant
- 1 Kings 18:36–37   Yahweh's supremacy over Baal

- 2 Kings 17:7-15   Offenses of Israel
- 1 Chronicles 28:9-10   God searches the heart
- 2 Chronicles 7:14   God's willingness to forgive and heal
- Ezra 1:2-3   Decree to return
- Nehemiah 6:15-16   God aids completion of wall
- Esther 4:14   God will find a way to deliver

OUTLINE

ORIGINAL MEANING

Old Testament Story Line, Joshua-Nehemiah

World History Story Line, 1400-330

Literary Perspective: Historiography

BRIDGING CONTEXTS

Plotline of the Historical Literature

Purpose of Each Book

Understanding Historical Literature

Pedestals and Role Models

Theological Perspectives

CONTEMPORARY SIGNIFICANCE

History Seems Boring and Irrelevant to Me—Help!

Scenario: Using Historical Literature Today

Recapitulation

How Can We View History Biblically?

How Should We View the Bible Historically?

KEY PLOTLINE TERMS

- historiography
- conquest
- ban
- judges cycle

- polytheism
- syncretism
- kingship
- theocracy

- Davidic covenant
- ark
- temple
- exile

TIME LINE

EGYPT	LEVANT		ISRAEL	MESOPOTAMIA
NEW KINGDOM	HITTITES	**1400**	CONQUEST AND JUDGES	KASSITES
		LATE EXODUS		
	SEA PEOPLES	**1200**		MIDDLE ASSYRIAN
THIRD INTERMEDIATE PERIOD	ARAMAEANS	**1000**	UNITED MONARCHY	
			DIVIDED MONARCHY	RISE OF ASSYRIA
		800		NEO-ASSYRIAN
LATE KINGDOM		JERUSALEM FALLS	EXILE	NEO-BABYLONIAN
		600		
			POSTEXILIC	PERSIAN
		400		

MAP

Three world empires.

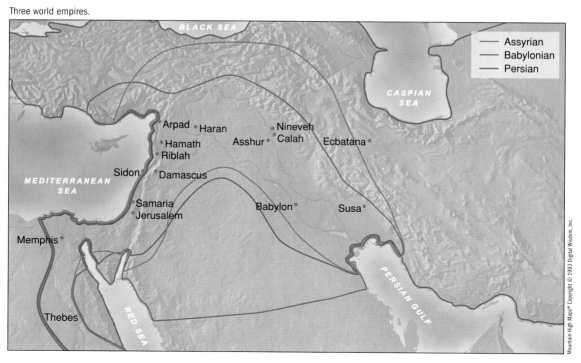

Assyrian
Babylonian
Persian

BLACK SEA · CASPIAN SEA · MEDITERRANEAN SEA · PERSIAN GULF · RED SEA

Arpad · Haran · Nineveh · Calah · Asshur · Ecbatana · Hamath · Riblah · Sidon · Damascus · Samaria · Jerusalem · Babylon · Susa · Memphis · Thebes

CHAPTER

1 ORIGINAL MEANING

OLD TESTAMENT STORY LINE

The largest segment of the Old Testament's story line (retelling of events) is found in the historical literature. In the next several pages, we will cover about a millennium's worth of story (mid second millennium to the mid first millennium). Consequently, this section will be a little longer. Though every book of the Old Testament contributes to the plotline of the Bible (the theological message that we cover under Bridging Contexts), not every book contributes to the story line. The story line in this chapter will take us to the end of the Old Testament period.

Conquest

After the Israelites had been brought out of Egypt, they came to the border of the Promised Land but were intimidated by the report the scouts brought back. Their lack of faith led to a period in which they remained in the wilderness. A generation later, after Moses had died and now under the leadership of Joshua, they were ready for the Lord to bring them into the land he had promised. After crossing the Jordan River (which parted for them as the Red Sea had a generation earlier), they entered the land now inhabited by a number of people groups, most notably Canaanites and Amorites. The land was not organized into a single nation but consisted of

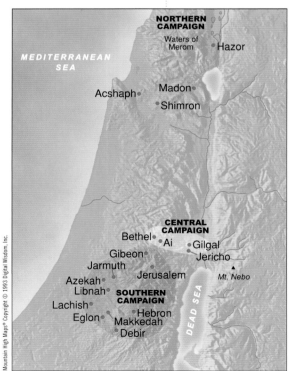

Campaigns of the conquest.

numerous city-states, each with its own territory, government, and army. The term *conquest* refers to the series of wars fought by the Israelites to secure control over the land that had been inhabited by their ancestors, the patriarchs.

The conquest is divided into three major campaigns: central, southern, and northern. The central campaign included conquering the cities of Jericho, Ai, and Bethel from the Israelite base at Gilgal. Jericho was not overcome by siege or breach of defenses through military strategies. God brought the walls down.

Jericho.

The initial battle at Ai was lost because one of the Israelites, Achan, had violated the strict prohibition against taking plunder from Jericho. The second attack was successful, and Ai and Bethel both fell, giving Joshua's army control of a swath of land across the midsection of the country. When a neighboring city in the central region, Gibeon, submitted to Joshua and signed a treaty with Israel, a coalition was

Remains of the Jebusite wall in Jerusalem.

formed by several southern city-states to put a stop to the growing threat represented by the Israelites.

Jerusalem, inhabited by the Jebusites, took the lead in this coalition. Their strategy was to take the offense by initiating a joint attack on the turncoat city of Gibeon. Because of the treaty between them, Joshua came to Gibeon's aid. A forced night march brought the Israelites down on the coalition unexpectedly soon, but it was again God's involvement that brought victory. This campaign and its aftermath brought the southern hill country under Israelite control. The third campaign was against another coalition, this time in the north under the leadership of the city of Hazor.

With the completion of these three campaigns, the entire land nominally came under Israelite control, though there was much work still to be done. The next stage of the conquest would be carried out by the individual tribes of Israel in their respective territories. Consequently, the land was divided among the tribes. They committed themselves to faithfulness to Yahweh and the covenant and went to settle into their new land.

Artist's sketch of Jericho.

Susanna Vagt and Alva Steffler adapted from a sketch by Gene Fackler

Hazor standing stone.

Z. Radovan, Jerusalem

Gezer standing stones.

Z. Radovan, Jerusalem

Judges Period

The judges period occupies the centuries from the division of the land to the initiation of kingship. If the early date of the exodus is correct (see the time line on p. 27), this period is over four hundred years long. In our own American history, this would be like looking back from the present time to before the Pilgrims landed at Plymouth Rock. During this time period, there was no central government for the Israelites. Some of the Canaanite city-states were still in existence, but the Israelites were under the rule of tribal leaders. Since the Israelites failed to drive out the Canaanites and other peoples of the land, this period was characterized by a tendency to combine worship of Yahweh with worship of other gods. Yahweh repeatedly responded to this by allowing Israel to be overrun by its enemies. As often as the Israelites fell prey, they cried to Yahweh for deliverance. The deliverers whom God raised up have been referred to as the Judges because their acts of deliverance established justice for Israel. The period is dominated by this cycle of subservience brought on by apostasy and the subsequent deliverance through the sovereign grace of God (for more information, see Bridging Contexts). Judges who are included in these cycles are called the major judges. Interspersed among them are a number of judges who are not connected to a cycle. The book provides much less information about these minor judges. Enemies included displaced peoples who had come to settle in the area, neighboring nations, and people from the cities of Canaan who had not been driven out.

Division of the land among the tribes.

Mountain High Maps® Copyright © 1993 Digital Wisdom, Inc.

Judges

Major
- Othniel
- Ehud
- Deborah
- Gideon
- Jephthah
- Samson

Minor
- Shamgar
- Tola
- Jair
- Ibzan
- Elon
- Abdon

Judges' Functions

Primary
1. Military leadership

Occasional
2. Judicial decisions
3. Prophetic proclamations
4. Diplomatic negotiations

Transition from this tribal period with intermittent deliverers took place under the leadership of Samuel. The unusual circumstances of Samuel's birth led to his being raised by the priest Eli. He established a prophetic reputation at an early age and functioned as a judge in his adult years as Israel lived under the growing threat of the Philistines. He is the man who became Israel's king-maker.

United Monarchy

When the people requested a king from Samuel, it was a reflection of their frustration. The absence of central authority made them disorganized, and competing interests made it difficult to work for the common good. They too easily became prey for stronger nations. Their political weakness and military needs motivated them to seek a solution in the centralized authority of kingship.

Saul was the first king chosen by God and anointed by Samuel. Though he had many of the qualities and characteristics that the tribal leaders considered important, his lack of spiritual insight and theological sophistication led to some critical errors in judgment. An early victory against the Ammonites was offset by inconsistent results against the Philistines. He defeated the Amalekites but in the process failed to carry out God's instructions. Disappointed with Saul, God directed Samuel to anoint David as the next king. The latter years of Saul's reign deteriorated badly as Saul became paranoid at the prospect that there would be no dynastic succession. He grew obsessed with hunting down the acclaimed heir to the throne, whom he deduced to be David. When Saul was finally killed in battle against the Philistines, the Philistines' control of the land was just as extensive as when he had taken the throne.

David came into Saul's administration at a relatively young age and distinguished himself in a variety of positions. His success led to a close

Philistines among the Sea Peoples in the twelfth century.

Z. Radvan, Jerusalem

friendship with Jonathan, the crown prince, and to a marriage alliance with Saul's daughter. Saul's suspicions that this popular young man would succeed to the throne of Israel turned David into a fugitive.

There followed perhaps a decade of exile for David as he hid out in the wilderness and eventually even served as a mercenary for the Philistines. Nevertheless, he conscientiously refused to take action against Saul, and when the king was killed in battle, David, having been anointed for the task by Samuel many years earlier, began to consolidate a kingdom. He did not immediately become king of all of Israel, because the northern tribes remained loyal to Ishbosheth, a surviving son of Saul. But after the death of Ishbosheth, David was acclaimed king by all the tribes.

United monarchy.

David's reign initiated what was to be considered the golden age of Israel. Taking advantage of the fact that there were no international powers in the ancient Near East, he extended the boundaries of his empire. From the borders of Egypt in the southwest to the bend of the Euphrates in the northeast, David forged his empire of allies, vassals, and conquests; and the economic gains from his imperialistic activities (tribute and trade) resulted in prosperity and peace for Israel. Most notable was his conquest of Jerusalem, which he established as his new capital city.

Unfortunately, David's international success was not matched by domestic stability. Impulsive abuse of his power was evidenced when he took the wife of one of his long-standing military officers and arranged for the officer's death in battle. His sons showed themselves to be headstrong, ambitious, and deficient in character and integrity. Between external conflict initiated by Saul's kin and supporters and internal conflict generated by ambitions to the throne, the latter years of David's reign had their share of instability. Nevertheless, the throne was passed successfully to his son Solomon with the empire intact.

The Judean Wilderness where David fled from Saul.

Having inherited an expansive empire, Solomon turned his attention to domestic building projects. These included improved fortifications at key garrison cities but mostly centered on the public buildings in the capital city of Jerusalem. Most significant were the spectacular temple constructed on the recently purchased acropolis and Solomon's palace on the adjoining plot of land. Solomon's network of political alliances was evidenced by his extensive harem. In the ancient world, the king's harem was built largely through marriages to solidify treaty agreements. He additionally built a reputation for extensive wealth and impressive wisdom.

As time progressed, however, Solomon's hold on outside territories weakened as one country after another broke free from Israelite control. As these satellite states stopped paying tribute, revenues declined and the need for forced labor among the Israelite population increased. This led in turn to increasing unrest among the population, who chafed under the forced labor demands that were necessary to sustain the building efforts. From a political standpoint, it was this latter issue that most directly led to the dismantling of the kingdom. When negotiations with Solomon's son Rehoboam broke down, the northern tribes abandoned the Davidic dynasty and formed their own independent kingdom under the rule of Jeroboam, who had been a member of Solomon's administration. In this new political arrangement, initiated in 931 BC, there were two kingdoms. The northern kingdom continued to carry the name Israel, while the southern kingdom, still under the rule of David's line, was referred to as Judah (after the tribal name of David's line).

Numerous pillared buildings have also been excavated at Solomon's "store cities and towns for his chariots and for his horses" (1 Kings 9:17–19). These pillared buildings were used either as stables or storehouses.

Model of Canaanite Merchant ship, fourteenth century; prototype of the ships of Solomon's fleet.

Massive fortifications have been excavated at Megiddo, Hazor, and Gezer, which date to the tenth century BC, and which are attributed to Solomon in 1 Kings 9:15. Solomon also utilized Phoenician ships and sailors (1 Kings 9:26–28)—both the best in the ancient world.

Solomon's fortifications at Megiddo.

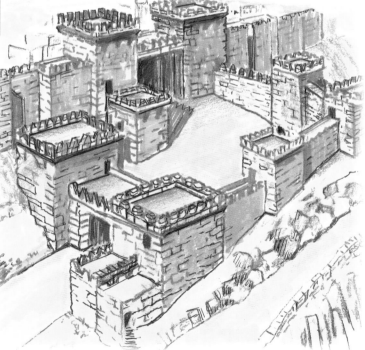

Division—Jehu

In order for the northern kingdom to make a complete break, they had to create an alternative sanctuary to the one in Jerusalem that was so closely associated with the Davidic dynasty. Consequently, two shrines were established, one in the north at Dan, and one in the southern part of this new country at Bethel. The shrine at Bethel was only about twelve miles north of Jerusalem. These shrines featured golden calf images, probably intended to represent a pedestal for the invisible God, Yahweh.[1] Jeroboam also had to create a new priesthood, since most of the Levites (the priestly tribe) had remained loyal to Rehoboam. These and other changes established, in effect, a variant religion for the northern kingdom that was consistently condemned by the prophets.

The split of the kingdom brought an end to the Israelite empire as treaties dissolved and vassals proclaimed their independence. Additionally, it was not long before Israel and Judah became the targets of the imperialism of other would-be powers in the region. The first evidence of this was the invasion of the kingdoms by the Egyptian pharaoh, Shishak, only six years after the division. The most frequent antagonist was the kingdom of the Aramaeans that had now unified and had its capital city in Damascus, just thirty miles northeast of Dan. The southern kingdom had wars with neighbors Philistia to the west and Moab to the east. Mostly, however, they fought with one another.

The southern kingdom continued to be ruled by kings of the Davidic line, with Asa and his son Jehoshaphat among the more prominent ones. In the northern kingdom, dynasties changed rapidly—over the first fifty years, no line lasted into the third generation. Stability was finally achieved with the accession of Omri, whose line was represented by four kings for over forty-five years.

Typical Pattern for the Presentation of Each King

- synchronization with other kingdom
- age at accession
- capital city
- mother's name
- assessment

Archaeology has provided us with numerous calf figurines that were used for worship in the home.

Z. Radovan, Jerusalem

Omri's son Ahab is the best known of these. During this period, peace was finally achieved between Israel and Judah, and a marriage alliance brought a daughter of Ahab (Athaliah) to Judah as wife for Jehoshaphat's son, Jehoram.

Toward the end of Ahab's reign, a new military specter appeared on the eastern horizon: the Assyrians. The seriousness of this threat caused the nations of Syro-Palestine to set aside their petty squabbles and unite against the common enemy. The story line of the Old Testament gives little space to the Assyrian conflict of this period, so it will be discussed in more detail under the history story line (see pp. 155–72). The Bible instead shifts its story to focus on Elijah and Elisha. These two great prophets opposed Ahab and his successors in the north who implemented radical changes in Israel's religious orientation. Omri had begun to reestablish political ties with the nations around Israel. This was politically and economically successful but included a marriage alliance with the Phoenicians that brought the Sidonian princess Jezebel to Israel as wife for Ahab. She persuaded her husband to pursue policies and programs intended to depose Yahweh and enthrone Baal as Israel's national God. It was this movement that Elijah and Elisha opposed as they took the role of defenders and champions of Yahweh.

The line of Omri and Ahab was finally overthrown in a coup engineered by Jehu, one of the generals in the army. Jehu represented the traditional and conservative element in Israel. On the religious front, this led him to dismantle the changes implemented by Ahab and

The high place at Dan was one of the two cultic shrines in the northern kingdom.

Relief depicting Aramaeans.

Jezebel by slaughtering the followers of Baal and destroying his temple in the capital city of Samaria. On the political side of the ledger, he immediately accepted vassal status to the still threatening Assyrians, signaling his submission by paying tribute to Shalmaneser III. When Jehu assassinated the king of Israel (Ahab's son, Jehoram),[2] he also assassinated Judah's king (Ahaziah), who, because of the intermarriage a generation earlier, was a grandson of Ahab. At this point, Athaliah (Ahab's daughter who had married into Judah's royal house) decided that she wanted the throne of Judah that had been vacated by her assassinated son, so she seized it by killing all of her offspring who might lay claim to it.

Seal of Jezebel written in the paleo-Hebrew script.

Jehu — Fall of Samaria

In the northern kingdom, Israel, Jehu's dynasty extended for five generations, lasting nearly a century and eventually leading to the most stable period of Israel's history. At first Israel was frequently at war with its Aramaean neighbors to the north. Initially this led to a significant level of Aramaean domination (by 800 BC), but by the time of Jeroboam II, Aram had become a vassal state of Israel. The

The region of Samaria, which was founded by Omri and served as the capital of the northern kingdom until the Assyrians conquered it in 722 BC.

text of 2 Kings indicates that Jeroboam II was able to reestablish control all the way north to the Euphrates as it had been in the days of David and Solomon. This renewed prosperity brought with it two notable problems. The first was a cosmopolitan interest that imported many of the ways and ideas as well as the products of the world and incorporated them into society. The second was the development of a more noticeable structure of classes within society. This period more than any other saw the decline of the agrarian population in favor of a burgeoning upper middle class comprised of merchants and craftsmen. This in turn created economic inequities and hardship for the poorer class as it was increasingly victimized. These two developments were targeted in part by the prophets Hosea and Amos in the middle of the eighth century.

Z. Radovan, Jerusalem

Stele of Shalmaneser III showing the Israelite king Jehu bowing before the Assyrian conqueror.

Chronological Systems

Even with the benefit of some fixed dates and a complex web of synchronisms, establishing a precise chronology for the kings of Israel and Judah is not easy. There are three complicating factors.

1. Coregencies are not always indicated in the historical sources but are assumed in the years granted to each king. If coregencies are not recognized, some years will be counted twice.
2. There are two systems for designating years to kings in the ancient world. The *accession years system* counts the year in which a king dies as a year of his reign. The remainder of the year in which he died is considered the accession year of his successor until New Year's Day officially begins the first year of his

reign. In the *nonaccession year system,* the year in which the transition takes place is counted for both kings. In this system, every transitionary year is counted twice.

3. There were two possibilities for New Year's Day, six months apart. One was near the spring equinox, the other near the fall equinox. Which New Year's Day one used for reckoning could easily make a difference in what year of the king's reign it was.

As a result of these complications and of some of the difficulties reconciling the synchronisms that exist in the historical sources, students will find that textbooks sometimes have different dates for the kings of Israel and Judah.

> She has not acknowledged that I was the one
>   who gave her the grain, the new wine and oil,
> who lavished on her the silver and gold—
>   which they used for Baal.
>
> Hosea 2:8
>
> You hate the one who reproves in court
>   and despise him who tells the truth.
> You trample on the poor
>   and force him to give you grain.
> Therefore, though you have built stone mansions,
>   you will not live in them;
> though you have planted lush vineyards,
>   you will not drink their wine.
>
> Amos 5:10–11

THE KINGS OF ISRAEL (NORTHERN KINGDOM)

	Hayes and Hooker	Thiele	Bright	Cogan and Tadmor
Jeroboam	927–906	931–910	922–901	928–907
Nadab	905–904	910–909	901–900	907–906
Baasha	903–882 (880)	909–886	900–877	906–883
Elah	881–880	886–885	877–876	883–882
Zimri	7 days	885	876	882
Omri	879–869	885–874	876–869	882–871
Ahab	868–854	874–853	869–850	873–852
Ahaziah	853–852	853–852	850–849	852–851
Jehoram (Joram)	851–840	852–841	849–843/2	851–842
Jehu	839–822	841–814	843/2–815	842–814
Jehoahaz	821–805	814–798	815–802	817–800
Jehoash (Joash)	804–789	798–782	802–786	800–784
Jeroboam II	788–748	793–753	786–746	789–748
Zechariah	6 months	753–752	746–745	748–747
Shallum	1 month	752	745	747
Menahem	746–737	752–742	745–737	747–737
Pekahiah	736–735	742–740	737–736	737–735
Pekah	734–731	752–732	736–732	735–732
Hoshea	730–722	732–722	732–724	732–724

During the century of Jehu's dynasty in the north, Judah in the south was also in the process of moving from instability to stability. Athaliah's massacre missed one of the infant heirs to the throne. For six years while she ruled, the young heir, Joash, was raised secretly in the temple. When he reached the age of seven, the priests staged a coup and Athaliah was deposed and executed. Now with a Davidic heir again on the throne, the temple in Jerusalem was repaired and restored. Occasional conflicts arose with Aram and Edom and even with the northern kingdom of Israel. About the time that Jeroboam II was coming to the throne of Israel, Uzziah (also called Azariah) came to the throne of Judah. He reigned for more than fifty years, the first half of the eighth century BC; and like Jeroboam II in the north, he extended the borders to Davidic proportions and brought stability and prosperity to Judah.

THE KINGS OF JUDAH (SOUTHERN KINGDOM)

	Hayes and Hooker	Thiele	Bright	Cogan and Tadmor
Rehoboam	926–910	931–913	922–915	928–911
Abijah	909–907	913–911	915–913	911–908
Asa	906–878 (866)	911–870	913–873	908–867
Jehoshaphat	877–853	872–848	873–849	870–846
Jehoram	852–841	853–841	849–843	851–843
Ahaziah	840	841	843/2	843–842
Athaliah	839–833	841–835	842–837	842–836
Joash (Jehoash)	832–803 (793)	835–796	837–800	836–798
Amaziah	802–786 (774)	796–767	800–783	798–769
Azariah (Uzziah)	785–760 (734)	792–740	783–742	785–733
Jotham	759–744	750–732	750–735	758–743
Ahaz	743–728	735–716	735–715	743–727
Hezekiah	727–699	716–687	715–687/6	727–698
Manasseh	698–644	697–643	687/6–642	698–642
Amon	643–642	643–641	642–640	641–640
Josiah	641–610	641–609	640–609	639–609
Jehoahaz	3 months	609	609	609
Jehoiakim	608–598	609–598	609–598	608–598
Jehoiachin	3 months	598–597	598/7	597
Zedekiah	596–586	597–586	597–587	596–586

Judah and Israel in the mid-eighth century.

The middle of the eighth century brought decline and a destabilized political climate to both Judah and Israel. As we will see in detail in the history story line, Assyria leaped onto the stage of international politics and in a relatively short period became the first of a series of empires that dominated the ancient world. Israel's kings responded to Assyria's western campaigns by paying tribute and accepting vassal status. Judah at first remained anti-Assyrian. Being further removed and economically less attractive, the Davidic kings did not as much pressure or urgency to submit. But when Ahaz came to the throne, a posture was adopted in which they were open to submission if that was needed to achieve peace and security. As Aram and Israel came under increasing pressure from Assyria, however, they banded together in a coalition against Assyria and prepared to lay siege to Jerusalem, perhaps to force Judah to join them. Whatever the reasons, Ahaz resisted and informed Assyria of their actions, inviting Tiglath-Pileser, its king, to come police the region. The result in 734–732 BC was:

1. Aram was invaded, suffered widespread destruction of cities, including its capital, Damascus, and deportation of the population as the country was annexed into the Assyrian Empire.

2. Israel was invaded and all of its territories annexed into the Assyrian Empire with the exception of the capital city, Samaria, and its immediate environs. A new king (Israel's last king), Hoshea, was put on the throne of what was now little more than a small city-state.

3. Judah was also invaded and was forced to submit to vassal status and to pay tribute.

Within a decade, Hoshea, Israel's last king, became embroiled in another anti-Assyrian coalition that resulted in the Assyrians, now

Assyrian Treaty Text*

This treaty which Esarhaddon, king of Assyria, has established with you in a binding fashion, under oath, on behalf of the crown prince designate Ashurbanipal . . . if you do not say and do not give orders to your sons, grandsons, to your offspring, to your descendants, who will live in the future after this treaty, saying: "Keep this treaty, do not sin against this treaty with you, lest you lose your lives, deliver your land to destruction, and your people to be deported."

*From James Pritchard, ed., *Ancient Near Eastern Texts* (Princeton: Princeton University Press, 1969), 537.

under the rule of Shalmaneser V, coming west in 721 BC and destroying Samaria. The northern kingdom was totally annexed and much of the population deported. In their place, peoples from other conquered territories were brought in and forcibly settled in the region. By this time Ahaz's son Hezekiah was on the throne of Judah. Though he represented an anti-Assyrian faction, he had not yet decided to take a public stand against the empire.

Judah—Fall of Jerusalem

Hezekiah was one of the great reformers among the kings of David's line. His faithfulness to the Lord, sponsorship of the temple, and observance of the traditional festival, Passover, are all commented on in the text. Through the long reign of the Assyrian king Sargon, Hezekiah was lured into a couple of anti-Assyrian coalitions but generally kept a low profile. But when Sargon's son Sennacherib succeeded him on the throne, Hezekiah took a leading role among those who tried to break free of the empire's control. This resulted in the pivotal confrontation reported at length in three places in the Old Testament (2 Kings 18–19; 2 Chron. 32; Isa. 37): Sennacherib's siege of Jerusalem. After eliminating (either by force or by agreement) all the other members of the coalition, and after destroying most of the fortified cities of Judah, the massive Assyrian armies made their way to Jerusalem, which was now crammed with refugees. Despite the intimidating rhetoric of Sennacherib and his generals, Hezekiah believed the prophet Isaiah's assurance that Yahweh would bring deliverance if they would only trust him. The tense situation reached its climax when the angel of the Lord went forth and slaughtered the Assyrian army in the night (2 Kings 19:35).

Relief of the siege of Lachish. Numerous panels recording this event were found in the palace of Sennacherib at Nineveh.

Hezekiah's son Manasseh was the longest reigning and the worst of Judah's kings by the criteria of the book of Kings. Despite his theological apostasy, however, his reign was relatively stable, since he adopted the posture of a loyal, tribute-paying Assyrian vassal for most of his fifty-five years. As his reign expired, the Assyrian Empire was also beginning to wear down. By the time Manasseh's grandson Josiah ascended to the throne, the empire was in its death throes.

Josiah, the second of the great reformers, busied himself undoing all the damage from his grandfather's syncretistic religious policies.[3]

The Siloam Inscription (above) relates the building of the Siloam Tunnel (also called Hezekiah's Tunnel, right), which was used to divert water from the Siloam Spring near Jerusalem inside the city's walls.

The Valley of Jezreel has been a battlefield of nations throughout history, especially during the period of the Israelite kingdom(s).

He restored the temple to the pure worship of Yahweh and reinstalled the covenant as the basis for the Israelite worldview. At the same time, he was able to exercise more and more freedom from the Assyrians, who were gradually but noticeably losing their grip on the empire.

When Josiah was killed in battle with the Egyptians in 609 BC (see more detail in history story line on pp. 168–69), he was succeeded by a series of his sons and grandsons over the next two decades. During that time, the world was transformed as the reins of international power shifted from the Assyrians to the Medes and Babylonians, with the latter coming into control of Judah (though there were several years when Egypt was temporarily successful in extending its control over the region). Though Judah submitted to vassal status under the Babylonians, she was not a content vassal. On two occasions, 597 and 588, the

Babylonians had to come west to deal with their rebellions. The second led to a lengthy siege of Jerusalem. In 587 the walls were breached, the city and temple[4] were destroyed, and many of the people were carried off to exile in Babylon, as the prophets had proclaimed.

This Babylonian tablet records the campaign of Nebuchadnezzar to Jerusalem in 597.

© The British Museum

The Babylonian siege of Jerusalem.

Alva Steffler

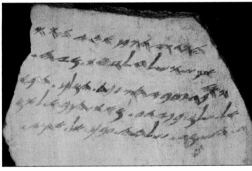

A Lachish Letter. Archaeologists uncovered twenty-two such letters, which all appear to be correspondences between Lachish and Jerusalem around the time of Nebuchadnezzar's campaign in 586 BC.

Z. Radovan, Jerusalem

Lachish.

Copyright: ROHR Productions Ltd.

Exile

The exiled population was resettled in the outskirts of Babylon, but there is little in the biblical story line that represents the events of this half-century. Ezekiel was a member of this community and ministered in his prophetic role in its midst. Daniel also served during this time in the court of the kings of Babylon and Persia. Soon after the Babylonian Empire fell to the Persians, Cyrus decreed that the resettled populations could return to their homeland, and the story picks up again in the newly constituted Persian province of Yehud.

The Cyrus Cylinder.

Postexilic Period

The first group to return numbered nearly fifty thousand. It was led by Zerubbabel, the heir to the Davidic throne who was to be their governor, and Joshua, the high priest. They had not only been granted permission to return, but had been provided with funding to rebuild the temple. Work began at once but then stalled as the community encountered various internal obstacles as well as resistance from some of the local leaders of neighboring territories. Under the encouragement of prophets Haggai and Zechariah, the

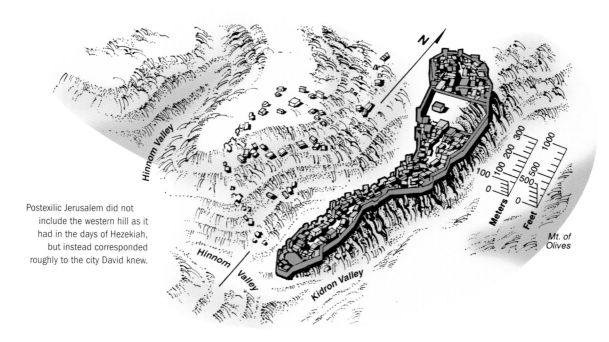

Postexilic Jerusalem did not include the western hill as it had in the days of Hezekiah, but instead corresponded roughly to the city David knew.

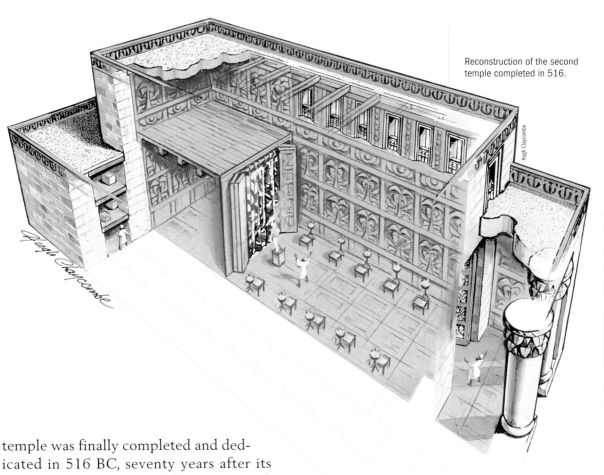

Hugh Claycombe

Reconstruction of the second temple completed in 516.

temple was finally completed and dedicated in 516 BC, seventy years after its destruction. In the mid fifth century, others returned under the leadership of Ezra (458) and Nehemiah (445). During this period, the community renewed its commitment to the law and rebuilt the walls of Jerusalem.

WORLD HISTORY STORY LINE

New Kingdom Egypt

By the close of the fifteenth century, Egypt had reached the limits of its expansion and had begun a decline fostered by military stagnation and an increased standard of living that reduced concern for maintaining foreign interests. The results of this decline are amply documented in the Amarna archives from the fourteenth century BC. The central figure of this period and the one blamed for many of Egypt's

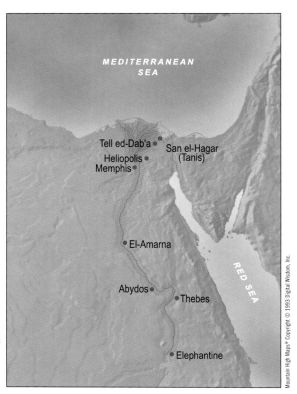
Map of Egypt in the period of the New Kingdom.

troubles was the controversial pharaoh Akhenaten. In an attempt to break the power of the priesthood of Amon-Re, Akhenaten deserted the capital at Thebes, where the cult of Amon-Re was centered, and constructed a new capital city about two hundred miles north at modern el-Amarna (Akhetaten), dedicated to the god Aten (the god of the sun disk). This political strategy was only part of a much larger attempt to establish an almost monotheistic worship of Aten that engulfed art, literature, and nearly every other aspect of Egyptian culture for almost half a century.

The correspondence from the Amarna archives portrays an Egypt that has lost its international respect and is no longer capable of maintaining order among the petty city-states of Palestine, let alone defending its interests against the Hittites in Syria or honoring its treaty with the Mitannian Empire in its death throes in western Mesopotamia. Some holding

Amarna

In the middle of the fourteenth century BC, the Egyptian pharaoh Akhenaten decided to build a new capital city on virgin soil. He named his city Akhetaten and undertook extensive building projects over a period of a dozen years. Three years after his death, his successor, Tutankhamen, abandoned the site, and it fell into ruins. The site today is called Tel el-Amarna, from which almost four hundred letters of international correspondence have been recovered (beginning with an accidental find followed by illegal excavation and eventually supplemented by official excavations). Most of these (over three hundred) are letters written from the kings of the city-states of Canaan who were vassals to Egypt. There are also forty-four letters recording correspondence with the other major powers of the time as well as a number of literary texts. The letters are on clay tablets and are written in Akkadian, though the letters from the Canaanite vassals show dialectal influence from West Semitic.

The Amarna letters provide the most important information available for understanding the stalemate in the international political situation in the latter part of the Late Bronze Age. In addition, they offer a glimpse of the situation in Canaan in the mid fourteenth century—a period either just before or just after the Israelites came into the land (depending on the chronological system one adopts). During this period, Canaanite city-states were controlled by Egyptian garrison cities. While some of the letters concern the relationships between the city-states themselves, others concern the threat to the city-states that is posed by outside groups such as the Hapiru, bands of disenfranchised tribes that were infringing on the territory of the city-states. These groups were generally considered outlaws or brigands. Even though the Hapiru included groups that could not possibly be connected with the Israelites, it is likely that the Israelites would have been classified with the Hapiru by the Canaanites.

Relief of the "heretic" pharaoh Akhenaten, who attempted to install Aten as the major god.

Erich Lessing, Courtesy of Art Resources

to a fifteenth-century date for the exodus contend that the Israelites were making a successful incursion into Canaan at this time, taking advantage of Egyptian neglect of the area. But it is unlikely that the "Habiru" people mentioned as troubling the kings of Palestine should be equated with the "Hebrews." This does not rule out the possibility that the Israelites were among those peoples designated as Habiru who motivated the kings of Canaan to plead with the pharaoh to send auxiliary troops, but usage of the term *Habiru* (or *Hapiru*) shows it cannot be restricted to an identification of the Israelites.

As the thirteenth century began, Egyptian reputation was restored by the Nineteenth Dynasty, primarily by Rameses II (the Great). Most who maintain that the exodus occurred in the thirteenth century would view this pharaoh as the one who witnessed the mighty hand of God in delivering the Israelites from Egypt.

Late Bronze Period Transition to Iron Age: The Sea Peoples

While Egypt was experiencing the decline of the Eighteenth Dynasty and the Amarna age, the Late Bronze Age began in Syro-Palestine. During this period, the Syro-Palestine corridor had a significant role to play. Because this was an age of international trade, control of the trade routes became a great economic advantage. The overland trade routes from Egypt to Anatolia (Asia Minor or modern Turkey) and Mesopotamia all passed through Syro-Palestine, and the growing sea trade on the Mediterranean was dependent on the hospitable ports of the Syrian coast (Byblos, Tyre, Sidon, and Ugarit in

Late Bronze Age (1550-1200 BC)

Stalemate of major international powers

Egypt, Hittites, Mitanni hold power

Syro-Palestine is a buffer they all seek to control

Amarna texts reflect the times

Iron Age I (1200-1000 BC)

Vacuum of major international powers

Sea Peoples incursion

Judges period transitions into monarchy

David's empire fills vacuum

3 HISTORICAL LITERATURE

particular). As a result, each of the military powers desired to expand their control into Syro-Palestine, and many of the great battles of this era took place in Syro-Palestine. According to the earlier chronology, this was the period of the judges of Israel, and the constant burden of foreign oppression described in the book of Judges would fit the profile of this period, though the great political powers are not listed among the oppressors of Israel.

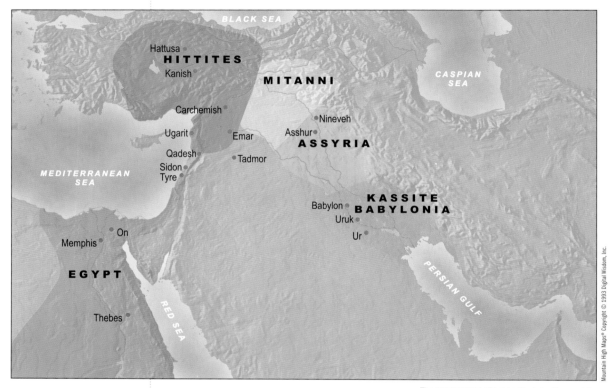

The ancient Near East in the Late Bronze Age.

Vying with Egypt for control of Syria at the beginning of this period was the Hurrian kingdom of Mitanni, located along the upper Tigris and Euphrates in northern Mesopotamia, the area the Bible refers to as Aram-Naharaim (Judg. 3:8–10). Mitanni was soon overshadowed, however, by the emergence of the Hittites in Anatolia, who were to become the dominant political force in the Near East for the next two and a half centuries. As both Egypt and Mitanni reached periods of decline in the latter part of the fifteenth century, they set aside their differences and made an alliance to protect their mutual interests in Syria from the upstart Hittites but to no avail.

The fourteenth century brought expansion of Hittite influence into Syria under the guidance of Shuppiluliuma I, at the expense of the dormant Egyptians and the floundering Hurrians. With the reestablishment of a strong Assyrian state in 1362, Mitanni came under pressure from both east and west, finally breaking apart about 1350. The Assyrians did not, however, attempt to expand to the west, preferring to exert their influence on Urartu to the north and Babylon to the south. Meanwhile, the cities of Syria had gradually come under the control of the Hittites.

The thirteenth century brought the resurgence of Egypt as the Nineteenth Dynasty began to reverse the devastating policies that had characterized the Amarna period. The capital was moved to the delta region in the north, and control over Palestine was exerted more forcefully. In the mid thirteenth century, Rameses the Great began to challenge the Hittite control of Syria. Eventually a treaty was made between Hattushili III (Hittites) and Rameses II, probably motivated by renewed interest in Syria on the part of the Assyrian king Shalmaneser I.

The resulting picture of the Late Bronze Age is an ever-shifting stalemate between major political powers, with Syria and, to a lesser extent, Canaan caught in the middle. If the Israelites were in Canaan during this time, they would have been largely unaffected by the international events. Canaan was too far south and too insignificant (compared with Syria) for the northern powers to be interested. The troop movements of the Egyptians during the thirteenth century would have had little effect, for the Israelites were largely settled in the hill country away from the major travel routes. But the balance of power was about to undergo a dramatic change.

Iron Age I (1200–1000 BC)

The beginning of the Iron Age brought a substantial change to the face of the ancient Near East. The Hittite Empire fell after a century and a half of power. Many of the coveted port cities of Syria were destroyed, including Ugarit, Tyre, and Sidon as well as fortified cities on the southern part of the trade route such as Megiddo and Ashkelon. This period also saw a lull in Assyrian power and a substantial decline in Egyptian influence. Much of this political upheaval has traditionally been blamed on the invasion by a coalition of tribes called the Sea Peoples, who appear to have come from the Aegean region by ship as part of a massive population

A statue of Baal, the Canaanite storm god, found at Ugarit (Ras Shamra) on the Syrian coast.

movement. Conventional historical theory credits them with overthrowing the fortified cities, demolishing the Hittite Empire, and being repelled by the Egyptians only after massive sea battles exacted heavy casualties. More recently, some have expressed some reservations that all of these accomplishments should be attributed to the Sea Peoples, but such disputes remain unsettled. One of the Sea People tribes, the Philistines, occupied the southwest coast of Canaan. It is from them that the name *Palestine* is derived. This is the backdrop for the Israelite period of the judges.

The resulting situation in the Near East was the neutralization of international powers. With no major powers left to exert control, relatively minor skirmishes in localized areas replaced the massive military campaigns of empires. The resulting power vacuum allowed for the development of empire building on a smaller scale such as that most evident in tenth-century Israel.

The Empire of David and Solomon (1000–900 BC)

When David came to the throne, one of his first tasks was to regain control of Israelite territory. This was accomplished from his newly conquered, fortified base in Jerusalem. After the Philistines were subdued, David's military success continued with the eventual subjugation of most of Syro-Palestine. Some countries were annexed, with military governors ruling in place of native kings (e.g., Ammon); others were conquered but became vassal states (e.g., Moab); some paid tribute and became the site for Israelite garrisons

Ugarit

Ugarit is a city located on the coast of the Mediterranean in northern Syria. First excavated in the 1930s, the most significant occupation level of the site (presumably by a Canaanite population) is dated from 1350 to 1200 BC, the period of the biblical judges. The texts found at the site are in a language that has been designated "Ugaritic" and written in an alphabetic cuneiform script (in contrast to Akkadian, which is written in a syllabic cuneiform script). Ugaritic is considered the closest representation we have to the Canaanite language. The literature recovered in these archives has provided researchers with a number of Canaanite epics and myths. The most significant pieces are the Tale of Aqhat, the Tale of Kirta, and the mythological Baal-Anat Cycle. The archives also produced ritual texts, letters, administrative texts, and palace documents. The latter offer insight into the diplomatic and political issues of the day.

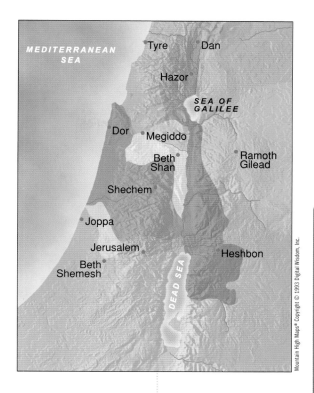

Solomon established trade with Phoenicia and Arabia, and divided his kingdom into twelve administrative districts (1 Kings 4:7–28), which were each required to send rations to the king one month out of the year.

(e.g., Aram-Damascus, Edom); and still others became willing vassals (e.g., Hamath). These events are not yet attested outside of the biblical text from this period of history that is only weakly documented.

As a result of David's successes, Solomon inherited an empire that stretched from the Euphrates in the north to Egypt in the south. Even Egypt entered into a marriage alliance with him (the pharaoh's daughter joined Solomon's harem) as he built a navy and extended his trade to the far reaches of the Mediterranean and south along the full length of the Red Sea. Despite his economic success, Solomon's military capability did not match his father's. Though he fortified strategic cities such as Megiddo, Hazor, and Gezer and built up his cavalry and chariotry, very little military success is recorded for Solomon in the Old Testament (2 Chron. 8:3–6).

Internal unrest and unquenched rebellion among the vassals left Solomon's son Rehoboam little more than the capital city and the wilderness that lay to the south. His kingdom deteriorated even more a few years later when Shishak (known as Sheshonq I in Egyptian records), the pharaoh of Egypt, raided Judah, sacking many of the fortified cities and receiving heavy tribute in return for bypassing Jerusalem.

The inscription from Tel Dan is the first reference outside of the Bible that mentions the "house of David."

House of David.

The Rise of the Aramaeans (950–800 BC)

Hazael, king of Aram.

Even as one of Solomon's officials, Jeroboam, gained control over the northern kingdom of Israel, the reins of political power in the region fell into the hands of the Aramaean states of Syria. The Aramaeans as a people are first mentioned as living along the upper Euphrates toward the end of the Late Bronze Age. In the wake of the incursion of the Sea Peoples, they began to move into Syria. After gaining independence from Israel in the later years of Solomon, Damascus became the center of a new Aramaean state that had achieved unification by the mid ninth century. For much of the ninth century, Aram was the major political power in the west. It led the western states in coalitions against the developing Assyrian threat and served as a buffer between the Assyrians and Israel for much of the time. There were also numerous battles between the Aramaeans and the northern kingdom of Israel, with Aram maintaining a decisive edge. As the century drew to a close, Hazael, the king of Aram, had successfully overrun and occupied most of Israel.

The First Assyrian Threat and the Resurgence of Israel (850–750 BC)

Nearly concurrent with the rise of the Aramaeans came the resurgence of Assyrian imperialism. This began in the reign of Ashurnasirpal

Battle of Qarqar

Though the battle of Qarqar stands as one of the most significant battles in ancient Near Eastern history, it is not mentioned in the Bible. In the sixth year of his reign, 853 BC, Shalmaneser III moved westward with his army, where he was met at Qarqar by an unlikely coalition of twelve kings of western nations who were more used to skirmishing with each other than to fighting side by side. This represents the first successful attempt of the Assyrian Empire to expand its borders beyond the Euphrates, though Shalmaneser's father had engaged in tribute-collecting campaigns. Qarqar on the Orontes was a royal city of Hamath, whose king, Irkhuleni, was one of the members of the coalition. The coalition was led by Hadadezer (= Ben-Hadad II), king of Aram, and joined by Ahab of Israel, who contributed the largest contingent of chariotry (two thousand). Though the Assyrians claim victory in a relief recorded on a six-foot-tall inscription known as

Stele of Shalmaneser III showing the Israelite king Jehu bowing before the Assyrian conqueror.

the Black Obelisk, it was not until the coalition collapsed in the late 840s that Shalmaneser succeeded in establishing his control of the region. By that time, Jehu had overthrown the house of Ahab and paid tribute to accept the role of Assyrian vassal. In the latter part of the century, the Assyrians experienced a series of weak kings until the rise of Tiglath-Pileser III and the Neo-Assyrian Empire in the middle of the eighth century.

II, who undertook a number of annual campaigns along the upper Euphrates, terrorizing the inhabitants through a policy of ruthless intimidation. This was expanded into a more intentional military strategy by his successor, Shalmaneser III, who concentrated on gaining control of the upper Euphrates. Then in 853 Shalmaneser turned his attention to western expansion and launched a campaign into Aram. He was met at Qarqar on the Orontes by a coalition of western states joined by Ben-Hadad of Aram and Ahab, king of Israel. Though Shalmaneser claimed victory, evidence suggests that the coalition had successfully blocked his entry into the west. In 841 the house of Jehu undertook a bloody purge in Israel and also reversed foreign policy. Jehu paid tribute to Shalmaneser III and became a cooperative Assyrian vassal. As Assyrian influence in the west declined toward the end of the century, Jehu's dynasty again became embroiled in skirmishes with the Aramaeans, becoming an occupied Aramaean state by the end of the century. Judah was largely unaffected by the conflicts with either the Aramaeans or the Assyrians. The trade routes skirted their country, which was therefore of little value to foreign powers.

Z. Radovan, Jerusalem

Shalmaneser III depicted in Bronze on the gates of Balawat.

3 HISTORICAL LITERATURE

Chronological Reckoning

Modern chronology designates year names relative to the year of Christ's birth with the system spanning all of history. In the ancient world, chronological designations were almost always made relative to the regnal years of the king ("In the third year of Nebuchadnezzar"). There was no larger scheme by which years were named. A relative chronological system can be pieced together to the extent that events or people from two or more countries can be synchronized (for instance, when a battle is fought and the years of the kings of both countries are stated). Synchronizations can also occur when events affect several countries, such as an earthquake, eclipse, or the execution of two kings on the same day. Even given a fairly complete relative chronology, however, it would be difficult to assign a date to an event using our chronological system. How would we know that Babylon fell in 539 BC?

A series of Assyrian tablets known as the *limmu* lists or the eponym lists gave us the information necessary for moving the chronological web of data from the ancient world into our own chronological system. Throughout the middle of the first millennium, Assyrians would identify one significant individual (the limmu) for whom the year would be named. Predictably, the king was the one who was so designated in the first year of his reign. The importance of this list is that one line indicates that a solar eclipse occurred in that year. This allowed researchers to calculate back and determine that that year was 763 BC, which became a fixed date to provide an anchor for the chronological system. Once the limmu list is aligned with our dates, all the Assyrian kings can be assigned dates in our system. Since the Assyrians interacted with many of the peoples of the ancient world, including the Israelites, synchronisms allowed the establishment of a fairly extensive chronological system for the first millennium BC and selectively back into the second millennium BC.

The early eighth century witnessed the decline of both Assyria and Aram. Assyria was occupied with internal difficulties and pressure from its northern neighbor, Urartu. Jeroboam II, the most successful king of Jehu's dynasty, recovered Israelite territory from the Aramaeans and made vassals of Hamath and Damascus. Meanwhile in the south, Azariah (Uzziah) collected tribute from the Ammonites and was successful against the Philistines and Arabians. Between Jeroboam II and Azariah, the territorial control nearly equaled that of David.

The Neo-Assyrian Empire (750–650)

After a lapse of a half century, the Assyrian Empire returned much stronger under the capable leadership of Tiglath-Pileser III in 745 BC. This was to become the first "world class" empire known to history

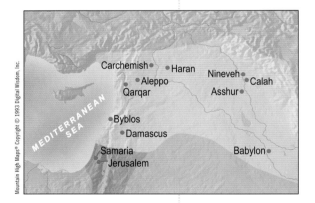

Neo-Assyrian Empire.

and the first of a line of empires that culminated in the Roman Empire. First on the Assyrian king's agenda was to consolidate control of Syria, which had come under the control of Urartu, and thus to regain control of the trade routes. Over his first eight to ten years, the king accomplished this goal and established a strong military presence in Syria. As part of this process, he collected tribute from Menahem, the king of Israel.

While Tiglath-Pileser was pursuing this agenda, however, Rezin, king in Damascus, had his own plan. He had sponsored an upstart, Pekah, from Israel and helped him secure the throne, and together they planned to do the same sort of thing in Judah. Ahaz, the Judean king, though encouraged by the prophet Isaiah to trust the Lord for

Biblical Quotes Concerning Four Assyrian Monarchs

2 Kings 18:9: "In Hezekiah's fourth year, which was the seventh year of Hoshea son of Elah king of Israel, Shalmaneser king of Assyria marched against Samaria and laid siege to it."

2 Kings 18:13: "In the fourteenth year of King Hezekiah's reign, Sennacherib king of Assyria attacked all the fortified cities of Judah and captured them."

2 Chronicles 28:20: "Tiglath-Pileser king of Assyria came to him [Ahaz, king of Judah], but he gave him trou-

ble instead of help. Ahaz took some of the things from the temple of the LORD and from the royal palace and from the princes and presented them to the king of Assyria, but that did not help him."

Isaiah 20:1: "In the year that the supreme commander, sent by Sargon king of Assyria, came to Ashdod and attacked it..."

deliverance from this threat (known as the Syro-Ephraimite War), chose to summon Tiglath-Pileser to deal with the coconspirators. The result was Assyria's second western campaign in the years 734 to 732 BC. Pekah was replaced on the throne of Israel by Hoshea, and all but the environs of Samaria were annexed as part of the Assyrian state. Rezin was killed and Damascus destroyed. In the process, Judah became an Assyrian vassal.

Tiglath-pileser III.

Tiglath-Pileser was succeeded to the throne by Shalmaneser V, who reigned for only about five years. Very little is known of him, but most significantly, it was during his reign that Hoshea of Israel rebelled against Assyria. Shalmaneser's campaign to the west began a three-year siege of Samaria. Upon its fall, the survivors were deported, the city destroyed, and the northern kingdom of Israel annexed entirely to the Assyrian Empire in 722 BC.

When Sargon II came to the throne, the Assyrian Empire was well established. Most of Sargon's attention was focused on Urartu (to the north) and Elam (to the southeast), although there were three major western campaigns. Hezekiah of Judah was anti-Assyrian, but there was little direct action against Judah in these campaigns. That was to change, however, when Sargon's son Sennacherib came to the throne in 704 BC.

During the reign of Sargon, Babylon had declared its independence under the leadership of Merodach-baladan. For twelve years Sargon had been unable to deal with this rebel. Merodach-baladan was finally driven from the throne but escaped. The wily Babylonian had

Sennacherib's Siege of Jerusalem

During much of his reign, Hezekiah was a reluctant but reasonably loyal vassal of Assyrian kings Shalmaneser V and Sargon II. Upon the accession of Sargon's son Sennacherib, however, Hezekiah was persuaded to join a revolt that stretched across the Assyrian Empire. Only when most of the rest of the rebellion was crushed did Sennacherib arrive at Jerusalem. By his account, Sennacherib had by that time taken forty-six of the fortified cities of Judah and deported over two hundred thousand captives, leaving Jerusalem crowded with refugees, exposed, and without ally or possible reinforcements. This made Hezekiah's prospects dismal at best. Sennacherib offers a detailed account of the tribute eventually paid by Hezekiah but makes no claims about the military outcome of the siege. The biblical text, in contrast, headlines this confrontation as an example of Yahweh's ability to deliver against all odds when offended by enemies and trusted by the faithful. Relief came outside the walls of Jerusalem as the angel of the Lord decimated the Assyrian armies during the night.

The Sennacherib Prism recounts the Assyrian monarch's campaign against the kingdom of Judah in 701 BC.

not been idle in the meantime, and when Sennacherib came to power, Merodach-baladan again ascended the throne in Babylon and enjoyed the support of concurrent rebellions against Assyria throughout the empire, including one by Hezekiah of Judah. Sennacherib, however, had learned a lesson from his father's struggles and went immediately to the source of the trouble. Merodach-baladan became the target of a strategic campaign that quickly subdued Babylon.

Having quenched the uprising in the south, Sennacherib undertook a campaign against the western coalition in 701 BC. He came south along the Phoenician coast and collected tribute from Sidon to Acco. After seizing some cities on the coastal plain, he proceeded down into Philistine territory to Ekron. Having cut off the other allies, he was then ready to move against Judah, which was cut off from any potential help. Hezekiah paid tribute at this point but to no avail. Then, when all seemed lost, Hezekiah trusted the Lord for deliverance and the Assyrian army was mysteriously slaughtered during the night. Sennacherib's account does not report the outcome of the siege.

Hezekiah was succeeded by his son Manasseh, who adopted a pro-Assyrian position. His long reign spanning the first half of the seventh century came at the height of Assyrian strength and territorial control. Sennacherib's son Esarhaddon extended the empire to Egypt and successfully subjugated the north, but it was left to Esarhaddon's son Ashurbanipal to capture Thebes in 663 BC. This was the pinnacle of the Assyrian Empire's power, but the cracks of deterioration were already becoming evident.

Empires in Transition (650–600)

Ashurbanipal had inherited an empire at its peak, but decline began in the 650s BC as Pharaoh Psammetichus gradually cleared the Assyrians out of Egypt. About this time also, there was civil war in Babylon, led by Ashurbanipal's brother with the support of the Elamites and the Chaldeans. Though this attempt was unsuccessful, the Assyrian king continued to be worn down by revolts. The last several years of his reign are very confused, and it appears that his son assumed kingship before Ashurbanipal died. Shortly after the death of Ashurbanipal in 627, the Babylonians successfully achieved their independence, and the days of Assyrian strength were gone.

In Judah the decline of Assyria was good news to Josiah, who had ascended the throne at the age of eight, just two years after the death of his grandfather, Manasseh. The reform that Josiah undertook in 628 BC and furthered in 622 took full advantage of the lack of Assyrian presence. At the same time, however, Egypt was strengthening its position in Palestine. Egypt attempted simultaneously to maintain friendly relations with Assyria and to benefit from Assyria's inability to maintain control of the west. As a result, by the 630s the major trade route was controlled by Egypt, and Egypt had a greater presence in Palestine than did Assyria.

Relief of king Ashurbanipal feasting with his queen.

The Neo-Babylonian Empire (600–550 BC)

When the Babylonians declared independence from the Assyrians in 626 BC, it was the Chaldean Nabopolassar who claimed the throne. For the next decade he successfully maintained control of Babylon but was unable to extend his rule any farther into Assyrian territory. It was clear that Assyria was losing its grasp on the empire, however, and Nabopolassar was not the only one scrambling to take over Assyrian interests. To the east, Cyaxares the Mede was also moving against major Assyrian strongholds. In 614 one of those, the city of Assur, fell to the Medes, and outside the ruins of the city, the late-arriving Nabopolassar and the victorious Cyaxares made a pact to join their forces against the floundering Assyrians. Their

Neo-Babylonian Empire.

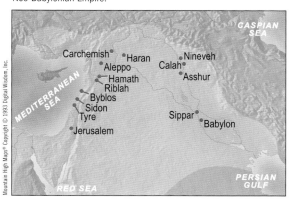

joint armies were able to bring down the mighty capital of Nineveh just two years later, in 612. The beleaguered Assyrian government retreated west and regrouped with its headquarters in Haran.

In 610 BC Haran capitulated, and the Assyrians were forced to retreat another fifty miles west to Carchemish on the west bank of the upper reaches of the Euphrates, just inside modern-day Turkey. Here, though reinforced by the Egyptians under Pharaoh Necho, the Assyrian Empire ended when Nebuchadnezzar, crown prince of Babylon and commander-in-chief of the armies, stormed Carchemish and scattered what was left of the Assyrians, pursuing them as far south as Hamath and claiming Syria for the Babylonian realm. That very year Nabopolassar died, and Nebuchadnezzar rushed back to Babylon, where he assumed the throne of what had now become the Neo-Babylonian Empire.

Nebuchadnezzar was one of the most successful kings known to history. He ruled the Babylonian Empire from 605 to 562 BC and distinguished himself in both military matters and domestic undertakings, foremost of which was the beautification of the city of Babylon. The Assyrian Empire had been divided between the Babylonians and their allies, the Medes. The Babylonians received the Tigris-Euphrates basin from a line just east of the Tigris (approximating the boundary between the modern states of Iraq and Iran) and all of the western states extending as far north as the southeast section of modern Turkey. The Medes ruled the eastern regions (modern-day Iran), Urartu (between the Black and Caspian Seas), and the eastern section of Anatolia (modern Turkey). Eventually Nebuchadnezzar was able to extend his domain to include Egypt (568).

The establishment of the Neo-Babylonian Empire had far-reaching effects on Judah. Apparently hoping to contribute to the downfall of Assyria, Josiah attempted to stop the advance of the Egyptian armies hurrying to provide assistance to Ashuruballit at Carchemish. This proved to be a fatal decision because Josiah, who had accomplished more reform than any of his Davidic predecessors, was killed in the losing effort. He was succeeded to the throne in turn by three sons and a grandson. Jehoahaz, the first son, was taken into exile in Egypt after serving only three months; this occurred upon Necho's return from Syria in 609 BC. Jehoiakim, a second son, was placed on the throne instead. Once Nebuchadnezzar had defeated the Assyrian-Egyptian coalition and claimed control of Syro-Palestine, Jehoiakim became a Babylonian vassal; this lasted until he rebelled in 598. By the time Nebuchadnezzar came west, Jehoiakim had died and his son

Jehoiachin was on the throne. The city of Jerusalem was set under siege and surrendered on March 16, 597. Jehoiachin was taken to exile in Babylon along with many of the people. Nebuchadnezzar set Zedekiah, Josiah's third son, on the throne.

Almost from the start, Zedekiah became involved in seditious schemes against the Babylonians, and finally, with the promise of Egyptian support, he rebelled in 589 BC. The Babylonian army arrived in 588 and blockaded Jerusalem to prevent its stockpiling supplies while other fortified cities were defeated. That summer the siege was lifted briefly, as the Babylonians were diverted to meet an Egyptian force, and then was reinstated. By the following summer, July 587, the walls were breached and Jerusalem was sacked, the temple burned, and the people deported to Babylon.

Cylinder mentioning Belshazzar as coregent with his father Nabonidus.

© The British Museum

The Neo-Babylonian Empire did not long survive the death of Nebuchadnezzar. He was succeeded by four relatively obscure and apparently incompetent kings, and one could say the handwriting was on the wall long before that fateful feast of Belshazzar on the eve of the fall of Babylon the Great. In fact, Cyrus had begun moving to consolidate his power within five years of the death of Nebuchadnezzar.

Battle of Carchemish

Assyria had ruled in the ancient Near East for more than a century before the empire began to unravel. Though it could be said that the empire had officially come to an end with the fall of the capital city of Nineveh in 612 BC, a provisional government had survived and set up base to the west in Haran. Just two years later, though reinforced by Egyptian troops under the command of their new pharaoh Necho (who hoped to gain control of Syro-Palestine by helping the Assyrians survive), Haran also fell. The defeated armies fled for what was to become a final stand at Carchemish, three hundred miles to the west of Nineveh. By this stage, Egypt was the primary opponent

with no Assyrians mentioned. The Babylonian general, the crown prince Nebuchadnezzar, led the surprise attack in 605 on the Egyptian-controlled fortress. The combat took place outside the walls as Necho sent his armies out into the field to engage the Babylonians and avoid a siege. After a heated battle, the Egyptians were forced to flee in retreat, and the Assyrian Empire therefore fell into the control of the Babylonians and Medes. The Babylonians received control of the Tigris-Euphrates basin and the Syro-Palestine corridor. The Medes took the areas east of the Tigris and across the north into Anatolia.

The Medo-Persian Empire (550–450 BC)

Map of the Medo-Persian Empire.

When the Babylonian king Nabonidus negated his treaty with the Medes and realigned himself with Cyrus and the Persians in 556 BC, it gave Cyrus the opportunity he had been waiting for to move against the Medes. He defeated them in 550 and became the ruler of the new Medo-Persian Empire. Over the next decade, he was able

Inscriptions and Prophecies

Jeremiah 24:9: "I will summon all of the peoples of the north, and my servant, Nebuchadnezzar king of Babylon," declares the LORD, "and I will bring them against this land and its inhabitants and against all the surrounding nations. I will completely destroy them."

Jeremiah 29:10: "This is what the LORD says: 'When seventy years are completed for Babylon, I will come to you and fulfill my gracious promise to bring you back to this place.'"

Isaiah 44:24, 28: "This is what the LORD says . . . I am the LORD, . . . who says of Cyrus, 'He is my shepherd and will accomplish all that I please; he will say of Jerusalem, "Let it be rebuilt" and of the temple, "Let its foundations be laid."'"

Babylonian Chronicle: [Nebuchadnezzar] mustered his troops, marched to the Hatti-land, and encamped against (i.e. besieged) the city of Judah and on the second day of the month of Adar he seized the city and captured the king. He appointed there a king of his own choice (i.e., heart), received its heavy tribute and sent (them) to Babylon."*

Cyrus Cylinder: "As to the region from . . . as far as Ashur and Susa, Agade, Eshnunna, the towns Zamban, Me-Turnu, Der as well as the region of the Gutians, I returned to these sacred cities on the other side of the Tigris, the sanctuaries of which have been in ruins for a long time, the images which used to live therein and established for them permanent sanctuaries. I also gathered all their former inhabitants and returned to them their habitations."†

*From D. J. Wiseman, *Chronicles of the Chaldean Kings* (London: British Museum, 1956), 73.

†From ANET, 316.

Praise be to the name of God for ever and ever;
    wisdom and power are his.
He changes times and seasons;
    he sets up kings and deposes them.
He gives wisdom to the wise and knowledge to the discerning.

Daniel 2:20–21

His dominion is an eternal dominion;
    his kingdom endures from generation to generation.
All the peoples of the earth are regarded as nothing.
He does as he pleases with the powers of heaven and the peoples of the earth.

Daniel 4:34–35

The tomb of Cyrus, located near the ruler's capital city of Pasargadae.

Z. Radovan, Jerusalem

to defeat the Lydians, a major political force in western Anatolia, and extend his control in the east as far as the Indus valley. He was now poised to move against Babylon. Since numerous segments of the population had good reason to be disgruntled with the policies and prospects of Nabonidus, Cyrus was welcomed into Babylon (October 16, 539 BC) as deliverer rather than having to resort to a long siege.

Cyrus was anxious to be recognized as a benevolent liberator rather than as a conquering tyrant, and he set policies toward that end. These policies included granting permits for many of the peoples deported by the Babylonians to return to their homelands and rebuild their temples. The Israelites were among them. Nevertheless, such permission assumed loyalty to the Medo-Persian crown and acceptance of its sovereignty; so although Israel was restored to the land, it was still without a king.

Cambyses, the son of Cyrus, was able to add Egypt to the empire in 526 BC, but he died in an unfortunate accident on the return journey. After some struggle, the throne was secured by Darius the Great, who, because of the difficulties surrounding the succession, was now faced with revolts in every quarter of the empire. By 519, however, he was able to put down the revolts and secure his rule.

By the beginning of the fifth century, the Persians were coming into contact with the Athenians because of some rebellions against

Darius seated on throne with crown prince Xerxes behind him.

Darius in the western cities of Anatolia. This led Darius eventually to attempt an invasion of Greece, which failed miserably when his army was driven into the sea at the Battle of Marathon (490 BC). When Darius died in 486, it was left to his son, Xerxes, to renew the attempt. Disaster followed disaster, however, as the Persians were defeated at Thermopylae and Salamis in Greece and continued to suffer losses as they retreated through Anatolia.

Xerxes was assassinated, and he was succeeded by his son, Artaxerxes I, who officially sponsored the rebuilding of the walls of Jerusalem at the request of his Jewish cupbearer, Nehemiah. War with the Greeks dragged on, yet the Persian Empire remained in power for another century until the lightning conquest by the young warrior Alexander the Great in 331 BC.

Fall of Babylon

Fearing the approach of the Persians, Nabonidus had returned to Babylon from his Arabian capital at Tema in 543 BC, where he had spent more than a decade. He gathered the images of the gods from his empire (a defensive act reported on the Cyrus Cylinder) and for the first time in ten years conducted the New Year's festival honoring the god Marduk. But none of his strategies could prevent the fall of the city of Babylon. Cyrus advanced toward Babylon in 539 BC fighting a victorious battle at Opis, about fifty miles north-northeast of Babylon on the Tigris in early October. Nabonidus had been with the army at Opis and fled when the city fell. When Nabonidus was captured, it was in Babylon, but the texts are unclear about when he arrived. Berossus (third century BC Chaldean historian, quoted by Josephus) claims that Nabonidus was trapped in the city of Borsippa (about seventeen miles south of Babylon). On October 11, Sippar (thirty-five miles north of Babylon and one of the last garrisons defending Babylon to the north) surrendered, apparently without a battle. On October 13 the city submitted and the Persian army marched into Babylon peacefully. Persian reports claim they were welcomed by the local populace and that when Cyrus himself entered the city on October 30, he was proclaimed its liberator. But this is standard conqueror's rhetoric and may obscure other facts.

LITERARY PERSPECTIVE

Historiography in the Ancient World

At some point, if a record of events is to be preserved, it must be incorporated into text. Such an undertaking requires the compiler to work under a set of guiding principles, conscious and subconscious. It is this set of guiding principles that constitutes one's historiography. "Historiography" refers to the writing of history and all of the assumptions that such writing entails. Opinions about the appropriate form, content, and structure of a preserved record of events constitute part of this historiography, but they are only the surface issues. What is important about the events of the past? Why is the account being compiled? How do events come to pass? What causes or forces drive history? Are there patterns in history? Is there design in history? The answers to these questions will play a significant role in determining how history will be written. It goes without saying that different individuals and different cultures will answer the questions in different ways. Thus any given historical record will represent a particular perspective about the events of the past. The shape of one's historiography will be determined by the questions the compiler is seeking to answer.

As a result, historiographical analysis includes not only the study of the documents that record history, but also an attempt to understand the philosophy and concepts about history that can be inferred from those documents. We should not be so naïve as to suppose that historiographical documents always have the intention of simply reporting what actually happened. First, there are often significant disagreements about what "actually happened" depending on one's perspective. Second, almost all historical writing is driven by agendas that go beyond simple reporting of the facts.

Relief of Sennacherib seated on throne.

© The British Museum

Tiglath-pileser III.

In the ancient world, historiographical documents were typically produced under the sponsorship of the king. These documents included royal inscriptions (see "Royal Inscriptions," below), chronographic texts (such as chronicles or king lists), and historical literary texts (poetic narratives about a king's accomplishments). They were generally composed to make the king look good. The king's reputation was considered of higher value than the preservation of an objective historical record. Therefore, the historiographical sources of the ancient world need to be treated in large measure as propaganda. The selection of what to report and the perspective and emphasis in the reports all favored the king.

The worldview of the historian will have far-reaching effects on his or her view of history and writing of history. Until the Enlightenment, it was common for a person's worldview to be thoroughly supernaturalistic. People believed that all history was the outcome of the activities of the gods. One could not really speak of the gods intervening in history because there was no neutral, independent cause-and-effect process that the gods were not controlling. In other words, there was no such thing as secular history in the ancient worldview. The role of deity was admitted, and the belief in occurrences that defied natural explanation was commonplace. Therefore, the most important way to ensure that the king's

Royal Inscriptions

Royal inscriptions constitute one of the major sources for historiographical information in the ancient Near East. Documents designated "royal inscriptions" include foundation inscriptions (in temple foundations), annals, chronicles, display monuments, and proclamations. They were produced by scribes for the palace with ideological intentions. Since most of the population was illiterate, and since many of the inscriptions were positioned in inaccessible places, it is generally assumed that they were written to enhance the king's reputation in the eyes of future kings who would encounter the inscriptions. In addition, and

more important, these inscriptions were written for the gods. To the gods, the inscriptions were to give evidence of how the king had enhanced their reputation through his achievements. To the human audience present or future, the inscriptions were to demonstrate how the gods had prospered the king and shown their support for him. As ideological documents, they are not intrinsically trustworthy. The king had much to gain by suppressing some details and embellishing others.

Ashurbanipal carrying ceremonial first brick in basket on head.

reputation was promoted was by demonstrating the ways in which he had been favored by the gods. With the Enlightenment and the philosophies of Machiavelli, Descartes, Spinoza, Hume, Voltaire, and Hegel, a significant shift occurred. The resulting historical-critical method "presupposes that all historical phenomena are subject to analogous experience, in terms of other similar phenomena."[5] It suggests that one can only accept as true that which can be empirically proven. It is concerned only with natural cause and effect in history. So the claims of Spinoza:

> We may be absolutely certain that every event which is truly described in Scripture necessarily happened—like everything else—according to natural law; and if anything is there set down which can be proved in set terms to contravene the order of nature, or not to be deducible therefrom, we must believe it to have been foisted into the sacred writings by irreligious hands, for whatsoever is contrary to nature is contrary to reason, and whatsoever is contrary to reason is absurd.[6]

This is largely the view adopted by our contemporary Western culture. The result of this is that the worldview of society around us differs dramatically from the worldview of the ancient historians. While the ancients would not deny the existence of natural cause and effect in history, they were much more interested in the divine role in history. In his or her skepticism about the role of deity, the modern historian's assessment of Israelite historiography might be "It has

> People believed that all history was the outcome of the activities of the gods.

> The worldview represented in Israel's historiography is one in which the directive activity of God is of primary importance.

Ideas about History

Common ground between the Bible and the ancient Near East:

- The authors did not intend to offer simply an objective report of what happened.
- The role of deity in history was central and assumed.

Contrast between the Bible and the ancient Near East:

- The historical literature of the Old Testament is not produced under the sponsorship of the king and therefore does not have the defense of the king's reputation as a high value. This is obvious from the negative assessment a large majority of kings are given in the text. Religious personnel fare no better, and corporate Israel comes under constant rebuke. The point is that there is no sponsoring individual, group, or institution whose reputation the text seeks to preserve. Nevertheless, the text has a very clear agenda. At every point of historical narrative the authors seek to demonstrate the extent to which God was being honored or dishonored and how God was working through the events and circumstances of history.
- History reflects a long-range plan of Yahweh, not simply the issuing of ad hoc decrees that direct history. The covenant drives history whereas in the Mesopotamian worldview the assembly of the gods decreed destinies year by year.
- Even though the Israelites considered Yahweh to be in total control of both nature and history, they did not see the two as intertwined in the same way as their neighbors did. As a result, omens were not a viable option for Israel.
- Yahweh was involved not only in the events of history, but also in the recording of historiography.

The lines of battle were drawn up, combat was joined on the battlefield.

There was a great commotion, the troops were quivering among them.

Assur went first, the conflagration of defeat burst out upon the enemy,

Enlil was whirling in the midst of the foe, fanning the blaze,

Anu set a pitiless mace to the opponent,

Sin, the luminary, laid upon them the tension of battle.

Adad, the hero, made wind and flood pour down over their fighting,

Shamash, lord of judgment, blinded the eyesight of the army of Sumer and Akkad,

Valiant Ninurta, vanguard of the gods, smashed their weapons,

Ishtar flailed her jump rope, driving the warriors berserk!

Behind the gods, his allies, the king at the head of the army sets to battle.*

---

*From Benjamin Foster, *From Distant Days* (Bethesda, MD: CDL, 1995), 192–93.

not provided information that is reliable." In his ultimate interest in divine activity, the Israelite historian's response to modern historiography might be, "It has not provided information that is worthwhile."

When we study the historiography of a pre-Enlightenment culture, it is important to recognize the worldview that drives that historiography and to respect the integrity of it. The worldview represented in Israel's historiography is one in which the directive activity of God is of primary importance. This view extends far beyond the recognition of occasional supernatural interventions. It sees God's activity in the natural occurrences as well. In fact, it insists that all events are woven into God's plan, which is the driving force of history. This worldview holds much in common with the rest of the ancient world, but some important distinctions exist that must be recognized.

Historical records in Mesopotamia do not claim to be revelation from deity. Nonetheless, they show great interest in discerning the activities of the gods. The polytheistic nature of Mesopotamian religion impedes the development of any concept of a singular divine plan encompassing all of history. At best the reigning dynasty may identify a divine plan in establishing and sustaining that dynasty. Some documents look back into the distant past to see a pattern that led to the

The events of history were intertwined with the events of nature.

present (e.g., the Weidner Chronicle; Akitu Chronicle). These typically concern not what the deity has done, but what has been done to the deity. In Mesopotamia it is assumed that deity plays an active part in the cause-and-effect process that comprises history. The gods are capable of intervention and are expected to intervene. The causation of the gods and the intervention of the gods are understood to be ad hoc rather than in accordance with any overarching plan or grand design. As P. D. Hanson observes:

> An historical sequence spanning centuries in an unbroken development could not be recognized, for in reflecting cosmic events, history was reflecting timeless episodes. The rise and fall of empires reflected decisions in a divine assembly which was not bound by any historical sequence. One decision leads to the rise of Akkad to hegemony over the city states, another to its fall; again to the rise of Babylon, and its fall. No common line connects these separate phases in an unbroken development. They are but separate episodes reflecting isolated decisions in the divine assembly.[7]

An additional element to the worldview of Mesopotamia is the omen mentality. In this way of thinking, the events of history were intertwined with the events of nature. When the gods acted, the effects rippled across both in consistent patterns. Consequently, patterns of occurrences in the natural world could be utilized to predict accompanying occurrences in history. It is interesting to see how this combines empirical methods with supernaturalistic presuppositions. Observations in the world of nature would be meticulously recorded alongside a chronicle of historical events. This served as their database. When the recorded natural occurrences were observed in the future, they would serve as an early warning system to the related historical events. If the anticipated events were negative, attempts would be made to thwart them by means of incantations. In this view of history, the gods were not revealing what they were about, but the omen indicators were used to deduce their activities and intentions. The underlying assumption was that the gods were the causative agents in history.

As in the Mesopotamian view, Israel considered God the cause of every effect and as actively intervening to shape events. Their record of history was not intended to be a record of events but a record of the ways in which God had acted in history. No Israelite historiography is secular. Yahweh is the driving force of history and the raison d'être of historiography.

3 HISTORICAL LITERATURE

A liver omen—so named because it is shaped like an animal's liver. Priests would analyze a real liver and, noting blemishes or other marks, would mark the corresponding region on the clay model. The priests would then read the text boxes that were marked in order to make their predictions.

Susanna Vagt and Alva Steffler

He is not only the primary subject of the historiographical material; he is also understood to be the source of it. In the supernaturalistic view of the ancient world, events were revelation. They were the result of divine activity. Unfortunately, those events required interpretation to discern why the gods were doing what they did. Such interpretation was not provided in the polytheistic cultures surrounding Israel. Mesopotamians were left to their own devices to discern what the gods were up to. In Israel's view, not only were events revelation, but historiography was also revelation. That is, God took it upon himself not only to act, but also to provide an interpretation of his acts, communicating why they were done and what purposes they served. In this way, Yahweh was both the cause of the events and the source of the interpretation of the events. In theological terms, we would say that the general revelation of history was supplemented by the special revelation of historiography. In summary then, Israel shared with the ancient world the idea that events are

Omen Samples

Celestial
- If the moon is red at its appearance and its left horn is blunt, its right horn pointed: you will drive back the enemy land; Adad will devastate
- If on the 15th day the moon and sun are seen together: a strong enemy will raise his weapons; the enemy will tear down my city gate
- When the moon does not wait for the sun and disappears, there will be raging of lions and wolves
- If the moon is eclipsed in Adar, the king of Elam will die
- If a planet becomes visible in Kislev, there will be robbers in the land

Extispicy
- If its "finger" (part of the liver) encloses the tip of the gall bladder, a fire will trap the man in his house

Birth abnormalities
- If a woman gives birth to a male dwarf—troubles; the house of the man will be scattered
- If a woman gives birth to a deaf child—that house will prosper outside its city
- If an anomaly's right shoulder is raised—your enemy will carry off the power of your country; a palace official will die; birth of a moron in your land

Human experiences
- If water is poured out at the door of a man's house, and it looks like a snake, he will experience evil
- If a man is covered with warts, he will have food to eat even in a famine

Behavior of creatures
- If a scorpion kills a snake in a man's house, that man's sons will kill him; he will die
- If pigs gnash their teeth, that town will be scattered
- If a snake crosses from the left of a man to the right, he will have a bad name

City conditions
- If a city's dump makes pigeons murmur, that city's gods will leave it—uprising of an enemy
- If a city's garbage pit is green, that city will go to ruin
- If there is a black fungus in a man's house, the man's house will be rich

Dream contents
- If in a dream the man does the work of a sailor, the god Enlil has a claim against him for a neglected vow
- If a man laughs in his sleep he will become very sick
- If a man repeatedly flies, whatever he owns will be lost
- If someone gives him an empty cup, the poor man will become poorer
- If he dreams a dog rips his garment, he will experience losses

revelation—this in contrast to our modern historiography. The Israelites distinctively believed that their historiography was also revelation—this in contrast to both modern and other ancient historiography.

1. Who were the six major judges, and why were they considered major?

2. What was the significance of the Sea Peoples?

3. Who were the three kings of the united monarchy, and what could be considered the major contributions of each?

4. Identify the major campaigns of the conquest.

5. What were the three major empires of the ancient Near East between the eighth and fifth centuries?

6. What is the Deuteronomistic History?

7. What were the major accomplishments of David?

8. What were the major qualities and accomplishments of Solomon?

9. What were the major religious and political centers of the northern and southern kingdoms?

10. Who were the two most successful reforming kings of Judah, and what did they accomplish?

11. Compare the significance of Sennacherib, Nebuchadnezzar, and Cyrus for history and theology.

12. What is *historiography*, and how does it affect our reading of the Old Testament?

Notes

1. The gods of Canaan were often portrayed standing on the backs of bulls.
2. The history can get pretty confusing here, because through most of the 840s the kings on the thrones of both Israel and Judah are named Jehoram, and they are brothers-in-law.
3. Syncretism is the practice of blending beliefs and practices from different religions.
4. This was the same temple that had been built four centuries earlier by Solomon.
5. Mark Chavalas, "The Historian, the Believer, and the Old Testament: A Study in the Supposed Conflict of Faith and Reason," *JETS* 36 (1993): 145–62.
6. B. Spinoza, *Treatise on Theology and Politics*, Tractatus VI.
7. Paul Hanson, "Jewish Apocalyptic against Its Near Eastern Environment," *RB* 78 (1971): 38–39.

CHAPTER

BRIDGING
CONTEXTS

Hittite god.

© The British Museum

PLOTLINE OF THE HISTORICAL LITERATURE

As the historical literature picks up the plotline from the Pentateuch, the people of Israel are poised on the border of the Promised Land. The text takes every opportunity to detail the theology that God brought victory and gave Israel the land promised to Abraham. The early narratives show little interest in political, military, or personal issues. They focus instead on God's role in overthrowing the cities of Canaan. Furthermore, it is made clear that the destruction of the peoples of the land was not just an arbitrary act to make room for

The Ban: Devoted to Destruction—Kill Them All?

"When the LORD your God has delivered [the nations of the land] over to you and you have defeated them, then you must destroy them totally. Make no treaty with them, and show them no mercy" (Deut. 7:2).

"The city and all that is in it are to be devoted to the LORD. Only Rahab the prostitute and all who are with her in her house shall be spared. . . .' They devoted the city to the LORD and destroyed with the sword every living thing in it— men and women, young and old, cattle, sheep and donkeys" (Josh. 6:17, 21).

How can this be right? It doesn't sound like the God who tells us to love our enemies to command the massacre of innocent women and children. How are we to understand such difficult orders?

First, the text makes it clear that the people of the land have incurred the wrath of God. They have defiled the land (Lev. 18:24–30). Just as the people of Sodom and Gomor-

rah—men, women, and children—were destroyed, such is the decreed fate of these people because of their crimes (Gen. 15:16). God extended to them four hundred years of patience. It makes little difference whether the punishment comes in the form of fire from heaven or armies of God. Second, total destruction cannot be accomplished simply by defeating the army. The influence that is being avoided is transmitted by a culture, and therefore, for the preventive measures to be effective, the culture must be destroyed. Third, we must realize that there was much fuller understanding of corporate identity in the ancient world. The guilt belonged to the corporate group and extended to every member of the group.

Above all, we can rest assured that God acted in justice. As Abraham exclaimed during his discussion with God over the fate of Sodom, "Far be it from you! Will not the Judge of all the earth do right?" (Gen. 18:25).

Gold leaf images of Canaanite deities.

the Israelites. The Canaanites and the others are instead portrayed as having brought upon themselves the judgment of God. The eradication of the peoples of the land was to be seen not as genocidal massacre, but as the judgment of God. God's judgment could take the form of fire from heaven as with Sodom and Gomorrah or the form of invading armies as portrayed here. The text distinguishes the Israelite conquest from typical military action by indicating that God imposed *herem* law on them. This law required that Israel not profit from any of the spoils of the cities. In this way, it was clarified that Israel was not just a pillaging mob ruthlessly driving families from their homes and seeking the spoils of war. The conquest then continued the revelation of God as sovereign in the arena of world events, active on behalf of his people Israel, and faithful to the promises of the covenant.

Once the land had been delivered over to Israel, it was distributed among the clans. The land now assumed its role as each clan and family's private slice of the covenant. Numerous laws and regulations were set up to ensure that land stayed within the family to whom it was granted. This is how land takes on a sacred identity—its possession is seen as the covenant gift of God. Since this land given to Israel by God was connected to a covenant agreement, there were strings attached—stipulations of

Syrian god.

Canaanite god, perhaps El.

Asherah was a Canaanite fertility goddess.

3 HISTORICAL LITERATURE

The Israelites renewed their covenant with God at the base of Mounts Ebal and Gerizim near Shechem (Deut. 27; Josh. 8:30–35).

the covenant that the Israelites were expected to honor. They were to give Yahweh his proper place and live in accordance with his law.

Even as the land is being delivered over to Israel, signs of unfaithfulness begin to become observable. The conquest had delivered control of the land to Israel but had left much work to be done in the tribal territories to secure that control and totally drive out the former inhabitants. Instead of persisting in this task, the Israelites were content to settle alongside of these peoples. This failure not only short-circuited God's judgment program, but it also created a situation in which Israel was continually under the influence of the unacceptable religious practices of the Canaanites. As a result, Baal and other gods were adopted into Israelite worship along with Yahweh, thus corrupting the high view of deity that had been reflected in the ideals of Sinai.

As this problem persisted over several centuries, God continued his program of revelation by showing that he was as faithful to his promises of cursing as he was to his promises of blessing. His grace did not negate his justice. The Israelites found themselves repeatedly troubled by the nations surrounding the land as God judged their

Canaanite Religion

Like most of the religions in the ancient world, Canaanite religion featured a pantheon of male and female deities. Seventy major deities maintained the cosmos through a divine assembly led by the god El (father of them all), where major decisions were made and decrees were pronounced. El is known as a wise judge and as the creator, father, and king. He is a kind and compassionate elder statesman of the gods. Baal is the most familiar of the Canaanite gods in the Bible. Baal is known as the storm god and is portrayed as a divine warrior. Actually, "baal" is a title roughly equivalent to "lord" and could be used in reference to any number of gods. The actual name of the Canaanite storm god was Hadad. Other prominent male deities were Yamm, the god of the sea associated with chaos, and Mot, the lord of the netherworld. These two were sometimes seen as adversaries competing with Baal for power. Female deities included Athirat (Asherah), the consort of El; Anat, the sister of Baal; and Astarte. Canaanite religion, not unexpectedly, was dominated by concerns about fertility in the agricultural cycle. Since this geographical region was so dependent on rainfall for its food supply, Baal naturally emerged as most significant. The sacrificial system shows some similarity to that used by the Israelites but emphasized providing food for the gods. Along with the other polytheistic religions of the ancient world, the Canaanites viewed their gods as having limitations and needs.

Deity (Consort)	Jurisdiction or Attribute
El (Athirat)	father, creator, judge
Baal (Anat)	storm god, divine warrior
Astarte	fertility
Dagon	corn god
Mot	death and netherworld
Yamm	sea and chaos
Kothar-and-Hasis	craftsman
Shapash	sun
Yarikh (Nikkal)	moon
Shahar	dawn
Shalem	dusk
Resheph	plague and disease

Azekah and the Valley of Elah where David fought Goliath.

faithlessness. Yet God periodically raised up deliverers for Israel to show his control and his grace. Even the deliverers became progressively less representative of God's ideals for leadership.[1] In addition, tribal leadership failed to maintain or preserve covenant faithfulness.

The patterns that developed during this period had two significant results. First, God finally became sufficiently outraged that he abandoned Israel. This abandonment took the form of the ark leaving the land. When war erupted with the Philistines, Eli's wicked sons took the ark into battle as a talisman for guaranteeing God's aid, but they lost the battle nonetheless. Furthermore, Eli's sons were killed and the ark was taken captive. Victory in battle usually indicated that the victor's gods were superior to the gods of the defeated. It was conventional for the idol of the defeated army to be taken and placed "in captivity" in the temple of the victorious god. Since Israel had no idol of Yahweh, the ark was taken and placed in the temple of the Philistine god Dagon. Over subsequent days, the idol of Dagon was repeatedly found on its face before the ark and eventually with its head and hands cut off (as would typically be done to defeated kings). The text here and in other places (see Ps. 78:60–61) thereby clarifies that Yahweh had not been defeated by Dagon but had gone into captivity willingly as an act of leaving the land.

Two Results of the Judges Period

1. God abandons the land.
2. Israel becomes frustrated with lack of central leadership.

Ark of the Covenant

The ark of the covenant was the most sacred relic the Israelites possessed. It served as a chest containing the Ten Commandments but also as a footstool for the throne of the Lord. A golden cover, decorated with two winged cherubim, sealed the ark, securing the tablets of the law within it. In Egypt it was common for important documents that were confirmed by oath (e.g., international treaties) to be deposited beneath the feet of the deity. The Book of the Dead even speaks of a formula, written on a metal brick by the hand of the god, being deposited beneath the feet of the god. Therefore the footstool/receptacle combination follows known Egyptian practice. In Egyptian festivals the images of the gods were often carried in procession on portable barques. Paintings portray these as boxes about the size of the ark carried on poles and decorated with or flanked by guardian creatures. A similar sized chest with rings (for carrying with poles) was found in Tutankhamen's tomb.

The ark represented the presence of God in the Most Holy Place in the temple. As such it played a role very similar to that played by the image of the deity in the other cultures around Israel. Consequently, when the Israelites were inclined to compromise on an elevated concept of God, it was easy for them to exploit the ark to manipulate God as their neighbors did with their idols (1 Sam. 4).

After the Israelite conquest in Joshua, the ark figures little in the narrative until the end of the judges period when Eli's sons take it into battle and it is captured by the Philistines. It is shortly brought back to the land but remains in obscure isolation until David returns it to its rightful place (2 Sam. 6). The ark was placed in the temple by Solomon (1 Kings 8:6) but is not referred to in subsequent historical literature. Some believe that it was part of the tribute given to Shishak by Solomon's son Rehoboam, while others believe it sat in the temple until the time of the Babylonian invasion. Second Maccabees 2:4–8 preserves a legend that Jeremiah hid the ark in a cave on Mount Nebo before the Babylonians destroyed Jerusalem. When the second temple was built after the exile, the ark was not replaced.

Battle standards often display the name and/or symbol of the deity leading a people into battle. Israelites occasionally used the ark in the same way.

Susanna Vagt

The Ark of the Covenant.

Hugh Claycombe

The second result was that the people became frustrated with the lack of central leadership. They concluded that their troubles were political and therefore required a political solution. They were discontent with the results of God's leading their armies into battle (it seemed that they always lost), and so they requested a king to lead them. As God indicated to Samuel (who received the request of the people), this was not a rejection of Samuel in his role, but a rejection of God in his role. In other words, they were not replacing Samuel, but God. Unfortunately, the people were blind to the fact that their political problems had a spiritual cause, not a political one, and they therefore should have proceeded with a spiritual solution: renewed faithfulness to Yahweh and the covenant. Yahweh had no objection to the institution of kingship. Kings had been anticipated in the covenant relationship since the beginning (e.g., Gen. 17:6). The problem was in the job description and role that the people chose for the king in their request.

While Saul had been chosen by God, he was chosen with the people's criteria in mind. He was God's choice, but God chose him with reference to the kind of king the people had asked for. In contrast, David was chosen according to God's criteria. The ideal kingship in biblical theology is one in which the king serves as vice-regent to Yahweh, the divine king. David's suitability by this criterion is evidenced in the battle with Goliath, in which he relied on God to bring victory against tremendous odds. He saw clearly that Yahweh was the one who fought the battles. With these ideals in mind, God established

Did God Want Israel to Have a King?

Reading the early narratives of 1 Samuel, one could easily conclude that kingship was bad. When the people requested a king, they were told that in doing so they were rejecting God (1 Sam. 8:7). In the following verses (8:11–18), Samuel warns the people of all of the negative consequences of having a king. When Saul was actually anointed as king, Samuel rebuked the people for their unfaithfulness, and they confessed that asking for a king was an evil thing (12:19).

In contrast to all of these negative indications, the earliest stages of the covenant included the blessing that kings would come from Abraham (Gen. 17:6). Moses' words likewise anticipated kingship and offered guidelines (Deut. 17:14–20). God chose a king for himself in David, and a major covenant resulted, confirming the importance of kingship. As messianic theology developed and unfolded, it became clear that kingship was central to God's eternal plan.

So did God want Israel to have a king? Careful nuanced reading shows that the problem, as is often the case, is not with the issue (kingship) itself, but with the timing and the motivation. Granted that kingship was in the grand scheme, that did not mean that now was the time for its implementation. Furthermore, the request of the people was motivated by discontent with God—they did not trust him to lead their armies successfully in battle. A king who was expected to play the role of God could not help but fail. God did eventually want Israel to have a king—in his time and playing a role that elevated God's kingship rather than undermining it.

a covenant with David that extended a permanent place on the throne to him and his descendants. In David's later career, he came under condemnation when he failed to uphold the ideals of kingship. His adultery with Bathsheba and arrangement for the death of her husband Uriah in battle showed an abuse of power that was the polar opposite of God's kingship rather than an accurate reflection of it.

David was not permitted to build the temple, but he acquired the property just north of the city and gathered materials. The responsibility for building the magnificent structure was left to his son Solomon. With the transition from tabernacle to temple, Yahweh was seen as taking up permanent residence in Jerusalem. In theological terms, this city then became the center of the world from which God maintained order in the cosmos and exercised his rule over all nations. This continues the theme of the presence of God that was begun in Eden and reestablished in the tabernacle at Sinai.

Just as the judges period illustrates the failure of the people to live up to God's ideals as expressed in the law and covenant from Sinai, so the monarchy period illustrates the failure of the kings to live up to God's ideals of kingship expressed in the covenant made with David. As in the judges period, however, God's program of revelation moved forward whether Israel was cooperating or not. As God retracted a large

THE PROPHETIC VOICE IN KINGS

Prophets	Kings	Reference
Nathan	David, Solomon	1 Kings 1
Ahijah	Solomon, Jeroboam, Abijah	1 Kings 11:26–40; 14:1–16
"Man of God"	Jeroboam	1 Kings 13:1–10, 20–32
"Lying Prophet"	Jeroboam	1 Kings 13:11–19
Jehu	Baasha, Elah	1 Kings 16:1–4, 12–13
Elijah	Ahab, Ahaziah, Jehoram	1 Kings 16:29–19:21;
		2 Kings 1:1–2:12
Elisha	Ahaziah, Jehoram, Jehu,	2 Kings 2:13–8:15; 13:14–21
	Jehoahaz, Jehoash	
Zedekiah and other	Jehoshaphat, Ahab	1 Kings 22:5–12
"lying prophets"		
Micaiah	Jehoshaphat, Ahab	1 Kings 22:13–28
Jonah	Jeroboam II	2 Kings 14:25
Isaiah	Hezekiah	2 Kings 19–20
Huldah	Josiah	2 Kings 22:14–20

portion of Israel from Solomon's son, he also graciously preserved the Davidic line. God demonstrated his kingship through his sovereign control of the nations. When Israel was faithful, its people were victorious and prosperous. More often they found themselves struggling to survive as neighbors great and small sought to dominate or obliterate them. In addition, occasional civil wars testified to their continuing inability to unite in faithfulness to Yahweh.

God's role in advising and influencing the kings is represented in the prophets. The continuing revelation of his will took place through these men (and occasionally women) who

Elijah challenged the prophets of Baal at Mt. Carmel (1 Kings 18:16–46).

served as his spokesmen. Prior to the eighth century BC, the prophets interacted mostly with the king. Kings were anointed through the prophets and condemned by the prophets. Prophets advised kings concerning what course of action to take in battle and informed them of what God's plans were for the king and his kingdom. When Ahab and Jezebel attempted to dethrone Yahweh as Israel's national God in favor of Baal, it was the prophet Elijah who became the champion of

BAAL (OF THE CANAANITES) VS. ELIJAH AND ELISHA (OF YAHWEH)

Baal, as storm god, controls the rains.	Elijah commands drought (1 Kings 17:1).
Baal ensures agricultural fertility and bountiful harvests.	Israel experiences famine and drought, yet Elijah and Elisha provide grain and oil miraculously (2 Kings 4:1–7, 42–44).
Baal controls lightning and fire.	Elijah commands fire from heaven in the name of Yahweh (1 Kings 18:38; 2 Kings 1:10–12; 2:11).
Baal controls life and death.	Elijah and Elisha heal and raise the dead in the name of Yahweh (1 Kings 17:7–24; 2 Kings 4:8–37; 5:1–20).

From L. Bronner, *The Stories of Elijah and Elisha* (Leiden, The Netherlands: Brill, 1968).

Yahweh's kingship. Elijah's successor, Elisha, is seen as a surrogate king in many of the biblical accounts. He brought justice for the people and he brought victory over the armies of the enemy. In such cases, God continued to reveal his kingship through the prophets since the kings had proven spiritually derelict.

Once into the eighth century, the prophets turned much of their attention to the people as they began to call them to a renewed faithfulness to the covenant. As the monarchy period progressed, the covenant benefits became increasingly jeopardized. The prophets, as defenders of the covenant, announced the covenant violations of the people and king and gave warning that the covenant curses were about to be enacted. Their messages therefore gradually began to include indications that Samaria or Jerusalem would be destroyed and the people would be taken captive as enemies conquered and overran the land.

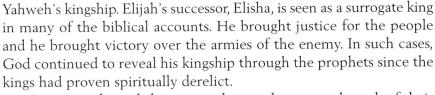

The Assyrians instituted a program of deportation among the peoples they conquered in order to break nationalistic tendencies.

Z. Radovan, Jerusalem

Z. Radovan, Jerusalem

In this way, the Assyrian and Babylonian empires were seen as instruments under the control of Yahweh. If the Israelites would trust their God, relying on him and being faithful to the covenant, they would see that he was able to deliver from the fiercest and largest of enemies. This was demonstrated in the Assyrian siege of Jerusalem under Sennacherib when Hezekiah, advised by the prophet Isaiah, trusted Yahweh in the face of overwhelming disaster and saw his mighty deliverance. On the other hand, if they relied on their own strength and political alliances, or if they sought to achieve peace by compromising their faithfulness to Yahweh, they would be swept away.

After the long and disastrous reign of Manasseh, Judah hovered on the brink of destruction. Their doom was momentarily postponed by the reforming king Josiah. When the Book of the Law was found in the temple restoration, he turned wholeheartedly to the Lord and began to try to undo the web of syncretism that had been woven by his predecessors. His premature death left the job unfinished, and the reform collapsed as Josiah's sons resumed the pattern of unfaithfulness.

Yahweh's kingship is supreme, and the empires are under his command. When Israel fell to the Assyrians, and Judah to the Babylonians nearly a century and a half later, the prophets and the text affirm that this did not happen because Yahweh was inattentive to his people, fickle in his loyalty, or outmatched by stronger gods. Instead, it was testimony to his justice as centuries of repeated faithlessness finally reaped the harvest of God's judgment. When God's presence left the temple and abandoned his people, the nation fell and went into exile.

The exile serves theologically as God's punishment of Israel but also as his purging and purification of Israel. Some may well have decided that the fall of Jerusalem and the temple showed that Yahweh was weak, but the remnant who survived and owned up to their disobedience and unfaithfulness emerged a spiritually refined group. They learned reliance on God, and they finally resolved once and for all the inclination to turn to other gods. In the absence of kings, they learned to focus on God's kingdom.

The group that returned was ready to put the law in its proper place. Though they continued to yearn for a full restoration that included their own Davidic king, they were able to turn attention to important spiritual issues. Worship became more focused, and the spiritual aspects of God's kingdom became more emphasized even as their hopes for the future began to take shape. They came to a clearer sense of their identity as God's people and to a greater appreciation of the significance of the covenant.

Z. Radovan, Jerusalem

By the rivers of Babylon we sat and wept
    when we remembered Zion.
There on the poplars
    we hung our harps,
for there our captors asked us for songs,
    our tormentors demanded songs of joy;
    they said, "Sing us one of the songs of Zion!"

How can we sing the songs of the LORD
    while in a foreign land?
If I forget you, O Jerusalem,
    may my right hand forget its skill.
May my tongue cling to the roof of my mouth
    if I do not remember you,
if I do not consider Jerusalem
    my highest joy.

Psalm 137:1–6

PURPOSE OF EACH BOOK

Joshua

The purpose of Joshua is summarized nicely in Joshua 21:43–45: "So the LORD gave Israel all the land . . . , and they took possession of it and settled there. The LORD gave them rest on every side . . . ; the LORD handed all their enemies over to them. Not one of all the LORD's good promises to the house of Israel failed; every one was fulfilled." The book shows how God kept his covenant promise to give the land to Israel. Consequently, it discusses God's bringing them into

List of cities conquered by Thutmose III.

the land (chaps. 1–5), God's giving them victory over the inhabitants of the land (chaps. 6–12), and God's distributing the land to them for settlement (chaps. 13–22). It concludes with a renewal of the covenant (chaps. 23–24), whereby the people publicly and formally acknowledged that God had fulfilled his promises and that they were indebted to him, obliged by covenant to be faithful. In this way, the book focuses on God's side of the covenant. In the process it shows that God is serious about punishing those who are deserving of judgment. This is true whether it applies to the Canaanite inhabitants of the land or to Israelites who violate God's commands (Josh. 7). The response of Rahab is important in Joshua 2 in that it shows that even one under the judgment of God who responds in faith will be spared.

Judges

The purpose of Judges is to show the failure of the Israelites to keep their part of the covenant. The cycles show how God demonstrated his power and mercy by delivering them time after time after

The high place at Megiddo. This altar dates to the Canaanite occupation of Megiddo.

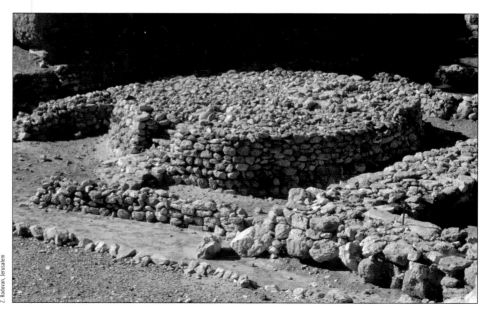

his justice had demanded that he bring punishment. The book shows that neither the leadership of the Judges (chaps. 3–16), nor the tribal leadership (chaps. 17–21) succeeded in helping the people remain faithful. Instead, the leaders were as bad as the people. Both judges and tribes were hampered by the absence of centralized authority. Furthermore, as the cycle of the judges plays out through the book, we see that it was also a downward spiral as each judge was worse than the one before. The theme of turning to idols show the people more and more under the spiritual influence of the native population that they had failed to drive out. As a result, they also were more and more under the political influence of the peoples around them. In every way this shows a pattern that is contrary to the hopes that were associated with the covenant.

Apostasy → Oppression

Deliverance ← Prayer

OTHNIEL

EHUD

DEBORAH

GIDEON

JEPHTHAH

SAMSON

Ruth

The purpose of Ruth is to show that when people are faithful, God is faithful. It provides a poignant contrast to the book of Judges as it shows that faithfulness survived in Israel among some of the common folk. It is interesting that even as Israel suffered under the negative spiritual and political influence of the nations during this period, Ruth was a positive influence from the gentile nations. Her faithfulness stimulated Israelite faithfulness. God responded favorably to her faithfulness, which is even more remarkable since she was an outsider who had no covenant and no law on which to base that faithfulness. God preserved such families of faithfulness, and that is the very background from which David came.

1 and 2 Samuel

The purpose of the books of Samuel is to tell the story of the establishment of the kingship covenant with David. God's plan for kingship was to have a king who would give a good example of what God's kingship was like. It begins by establishing the credentials of Samuel,

Sinai Covenant	Davidic Covenant
Joshua: God **fulfills** his covenant promises	**Samuel:** God establishes covenant with David and **fulfills** covenant promises
Judges: Israel **fails** in its covenant obligations	**Kings:** Kings **fail** in covenant obligations

- Unusual birth showing God's hand
- Raised at the sanctuary in God's presence
- Trained as a priest
- Called as a prophet
- Provided military leadership
- Designated to anoint both Saul and David as kings

who was to become the king-maker (1 Sam. 1–7). The next sequence shows how it came about that Saul became king—how could a king so directly chosen by God be such a failure? The answer is found in the fact that the people were seeking the wrong sort of king and God gave them the kind of king they asked for. After the text addresses the choice of Saul (chaps. 8–12) and the initial successes and eventual failure of Israel's first king (chaps. 13–15), David is introduced. The last half of 1 Samuel demonstrates that David did not usurp the throne of Saul. The author offers numerous evidences showing that David was

Jerusalem from the south. The City of David is the entire spur in the foreground up to the Temple Mount.

Artist's reconstruction of Jerusalem at the time of Solomon (viewed from the southeast). The supporting structure for the palace in the middle can be seen in its modern condition on p. 139. Solomon's palace and the temple are in the top right hand corner.

not antagonistic toward Saul, but that Saul was the one who consistently initiated the conflict. Even the one who stood to lose the most, the crown prince Jonathan, favored David. The text illustrates that everyone acknowledged that David would be king (Samuel [both alive, 1 Sam. 16:12–13, and dead, 1 Sam. 28:17], Jonathan, the people, and even Saul himself). Yet the text shows that David took no action against Saul or his house to make himself king.

Solomon's Temple

Discussion of the sanctuary as sacred space was offered in the chapter on the Pentateuch (see p. 97). The temple serves as the center of God's power on earth. As indicated in Solomon's dedicatory prayer (1 Kings 8; 2 Chron. 6), it is from there that God will see what is happening and will act. In the ancient Near East, the temple was considered to be a microcosm of the land. It represented either the cosmic mountain (Mesopotamia) or the primeval hillock (Egypt) out of which all else emerged. It served as a palace that was the counterpart to the heavenly palace of the deity. Architecturally, Solomon's temple featured an antechamber between the altar and the cella (Most Holy Place) as well as a portico, courtyard, and many side rooms. These were also common features of ancient Near Eastern temple architecture. A temple at Tell Tayanat in Syria from about the

The Temple Mount today.

time of Solomon features the exact structure of a portico with two free-standing pillars, a long antechamber, and a small cella all on a direct axis, 38 feet by 83 feet (Solomon's was 30 feet by 90 feet).

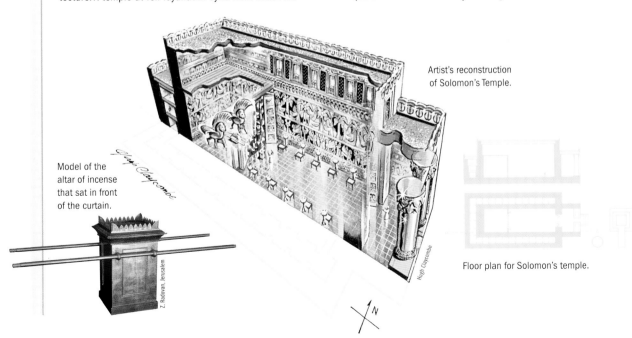

Artist's reconstruction of Solomon's Temple.

Model of the altar of incense that sat in front of the curtain.

Floor plan for Solomon's temple.

1 and 2 Kings

The purpose of the books of Kings is to demonstrate that the kings of Israel and Judah failed to live up to the ideals of the kingship covenant and that God was therefore justified in exiling his people. Just as in the book of Judges, however, God continues to reveal what he is like even through the failures of the kings. Sometimes he does this through punishment or judgment; other times by raising up better representatives of his kingship (like Elisha). The book is written from the exile and seeks to offer an understanding of how Israel and Judah had ended up so far off course with regard to the covenant.

The book can seem a blur of king following king, but it could be argued that that is exactly the effect the author desired to create. One king blends into another as the pattern of failure falls into place. It is evident that the author was more interested in spiritual issues and the kings' relationship to God than in political events. The latter are reported only when they communicate something that God was doing. This demonstrates that the history is only secondary to the theological purpose of tracking covenant failures. In the process, the book shows how God tried to warn and guide them through the prophets, and how Judah prospered under the occasional good king (e.g., Hezekiah and Josiah).

God's presence is more important than a king's presence, and serving God is more important than political and national status.

1 and 2 Chronicles

In contrast to the books of Kings, the books of Chronicles were written after the people returned from the exile. As a result, though it covers almost the same period of history, it does so from an entirely different perspective.[2] The purpose of the books of Chronicles is to

KINGS Overall Theme: Covenant Failure	CHRONICLES Overall Theme: Continuity, Transformation, Theological Stability
· Proclamation of doom	· Proclamation of hope
· Highlights apostasy and idolatry and the role of the kings and prophets	· Highlights retribution theology and role of the priests and Levites
· Ends in judgment and captivity	· Refocuses from monarchy to theocracy
· Addressed to the exiles	· Addressed to postexilic community
· Recurrent themes: sins of Jeroboam, promises to David	· Recurrent themes: reform and repentance as means to God's favor

show that throughout Israel's history, obedience led to blessing and disobedience led to trouble. The chronicler demonstrates that the kingdom is not dependent on a king, but is spiritual. The priests and the temple are therefore of most importance. God's presence is more important than a king's presence, and serving God is more important than political and national status. Rather than focusing on failure the way that Kings did, Chronicles focuses on hope in God's plan.

The lengthy genealogies at the beginning of the book trace the caretakers of the kingdom of God. Beginning with Adam and his descendants, the torch passes to the Israelites, then to the Davidic kings and Levites, and finally to the current community, the remnant of Israel. In this way the community sees itself in the long line of tradition that has stood for the kingdom of God. As they understand their heritage, they can begin to shape their legacy: kingship is not as important as the kingdom of God.

Ezra and Nehemiah

The purpose of the books of Ezra and Nehemiah is to show the many ways that God was at work to restore the people of Israel to their land. God brought favor with the Persian rulers and helped the Israelites overcome the obstacles presented by their enemies as they rebuilt the temple and the walls of Jerusalem and set up the law as the foundation of society. Restoration is the key theme as these books trace the restoration of the temple (Ezra 1–6), the community (Ezra 7–10), Jerusalem (Neh. 1–7), and the covenant (Neh. 8–13).[3] The books show intense interest in the role of the Persian kings. Most often this interest is directed toward demonstrating how God sovereignly worked through the kings to carry forward his plan of restoration.

Esther

The purpose of the book of Esther is to show that God can accomplish his purposes just as easily through "coincidences" as he can through grand miracles of deliverance. Though he works behind the curtain, he is just as much in control. Events that others see as chance or fate can be seen as signs of God's sovereignty to believers. One of the most obvious ways this purpose is accomplished through the book is through the use of irony and reversal. The book thrives on hidden information:

- Haman hides the identity of the people he wishes to destroy when he procures the decree from the king.

- Esther hides her Jewish identity.

- The king hides the identity of the one he wishes to honor.

- Esther hides the reason for the banquets.

- Esther hides the identity of the people for whom she is seeking protection.

- Mordecai hides his relationship to Esther.

Irony and reversal are also seen in numerous details, for example:

- Haman thinks he is being honored by Esther when in reality he is being set up.

- Mordecai refuses to honor Haman; Haman is forced to honor Mordecai.

- Haman is hung on his own gallows constructed for Mordecai.

The significance of the irony is that it demonstrates that there is always more going on than meets the eye and more in the works than any one individual understands or is aware of. God's control cannot be calculated, God's solution cannot be anticipated, and God's plan cannot be thwarted, because no one has all the information. God is still in the business of miracles, but more often than not, they are "miracles of circumstance" occurring behind the scenes in ways that could never be anticipated. Theologians today call this "Providence." Even the absence of the name of God in the text of Esther serves to accentuate the fact that God's work is taking place behind the scenes—it is another piece of hidden information. Just as Esther hid her Jewishness then worked behind the scenes for deliverance, so the book hid God's name, yet he worked behind the scenes for deliverance.

UNDERSTANDING HISTORICAL LITERATURE

History, Objectivity, and Truth

When the Israelite authors wrote this historical literature, what were they doing? What did they seek to accomplish? In the Original Meanings section, we noted that Israel's historiography was focused on how God had acted in history. Events, as the result of divine activity,

> When we affirm that the historical literature is true, we are accepting both the accuracy of the report of events (story line) and the perspective of the author about those events (plotline). The story line might be what is most basically called history, while the plotline could very appropriately be called theology.

served as revelation that the historical literature interpreted. As a result, the truth value in historical literature cannot be assessed simply on the factuality of the events (e.g., the Israelites really did leave Egypt amid a sequence of plagues); it must extend to the author's perspective of the significance of those events (e.g., that God brought them out of Egypt by his mighty power to bring them to the land he had promised them). This is the distinction between the story line and the plotline. When we affirm that the historical literature is true, we are accepting both the accuracy of the report of events (story line) and the perspective of the author about those events (plotline). The authors do not and cannot report everything that happened. They report only as much of the story line as is necessary to convey the plotline. The truth of the plotline is more central to the nature of Scripture than the truth of the story line, though both need to be affirmed. The story line might be what is most basically called history, while the plotline could very appropriately be called theology. Of course, this distinction is artificial, for the two are inseparably entwined. In our culture, we are used to measuring historical accuracy by criteria such as objectivity and comprehensiveness. Whether or not these are appropriate criteria for modern historiography, they cannot be applied to biblical historiography, for neither objectivity nor comprehensiveness was seen as an essential value to the task.

The Power of Story

As discussed in the opening chapter, the Bible presents us with stories about God that help us to know him. How do these stories work?[5] We may believe that God is sovereign—but that does not mean that we have a complete grasp of all of the implications of God's sovereignty. Story has the ability to fill in the spaces. How God's sovereignty is demonstrated will help us understand the nature of his sovereignty. When we see his power over nature, as at the Red Sea, and his control over kings and empires, as in destruction of Sennacherib's army outside of Jerusalem (2 Kings 19:35), we can gain a greater appreciation for the extent of God's sovereignty. But our understanding can become even more sophisticated as we move from those overt acts of power to the more subtle examples. God's sovereignty is shown working behind the scenes in a book like Esther, and it is seen to operate even through the evil choices that people make as in the Joseph story (see Gen. 50:20). Finally, we also increase our understanding of God's sovereignty by observing situations in which

Egyptian Account of the Battle of Qadesh*

My army came to praise me, their faces amazed at seeing what I had done. My officers came to extol my strong arm, and likewise my chariotry, boasting of my name, thus: . . . You are the son of Amun, achieving with his arms, you devastate the land of Hatti by your valiant arm. . . . You are great in victory in front of your army. . . . O Protector of Egypt, who curbs the foreign lands, You have broken the back of Hatti forever.

Hittite Account of the Battle of Qadesh†

At the time that Muwatallis took the field against the king of the land of Egypt and the country of Amurru, and when he then had defeated the king of the land of Egypt and the country of Amurru, he returned to the country Apa.

*COS, 2.5A.
†ANET, 319.

Archaeology and the Bible

Beginning in the mid nineteenth century, the science of archaeology began to develop and produce data and artifacts that contributed to the interpretation of the Bible. The results of archaeology were quickly put to use both by apologists who emphasized anything positive and by skeptics who emphasized anything negative. And so, before long, the discipline of archaeology became integral to the study of the Bible. Still today there are those who claim that archaeology proves the Bible to be true as well as those who claim that archaeology has proven the Bible is flawed.

When weighing the role of archaeology in understanding the Bible, we must keep in mind a number of important perspectives.

Archaeological data need to be interpreted. Determinations about basic data such as the date of layers and artifacts, the occupational history of a site, or even the identification of a site sometimes require the judgment of the archaeologists. Often there may be reasons for disagreement. Caution is therefore advised before any conclusion comes to be considered a fact. Presuppositions about the Bible, about history, and about the role and methods of archaeology (just to name a few of the categories) can have a significant impact on conclusions archaeologists draw.

Archaeology deals in fractions. Only a small percentage of material has survived in the ground, and only a small part of that has been dug up. And at any given location, only a small percentage of the site is excavated. This means that conclusions can be skewed by considering only the narrow slice of the available data.

Absence of evidence is not evidence of absence. Since archaeology deals in fractions, it is risky to extrapolate. The fact that there is not yet any conclusive archaeological evidence of a long Israelite presence in Egypt does not mean that the Israelites were never there. The fact that no contemporary inscriptions name Joseph, Moses, Solomon, or Esther does not mean that they did not exist.

Much depends on how hard one is willing to try to reconcile data with the Bible. Those who do not consider the Bible a reliable source are not concerned when archaeological finds or conclusions appear to contradict the Bible.

Bethshean.

Copyright: ROHR Productions Ltd.

Sanctuary in the southern Israelite town of Arad dating to the ninth century with incense altars and standing stones.

Z. Radovan, Jerusalem

They simply add it to their list of evidence for the Bible's unreliability. In contrast, those who consider the Bible to be reliable will seek out solutions (hopefully plausible ones) for whatever difficulties might arise. When archaeologists claim that there was no walled city at Jericho in the time of Joshua, belief in the Bible's integrity will motivate one to cross-examine the archaeological finds and methods to see how conclusive those claims are. It would also be appropriate to look carefully at the biblical record to make sure it is being interpreted correctly and to reconsider interpretive issues such as the chronological system that suggests the date of the battle. Such measures will be undertaken only by those who attach value to the reliability of the biblical record. In the process of assessing the data that are available to us, we cannot afford to be naïve about the nature of the biblical literature nor about the nature of the ancient literature.

Archaeology can only verify certain kinds of information. Archaeology could theoretically provide all sorts of information about the Israelite sojourn in Egypt, the ten plagues, the exodus from Egypt, and the travels through the wilderness,[4] but even then it could never prove what God's role was. For the Bible, it is not enough to know that certain events took place or that certain people existed. The Bible's principal claims concern what God has done, and that is beyond the reach of archaeology to confirm or deny.

Archaeology is a discipline independent of biblical studies. Though archaeology in the Middle East has often served those in biblical studies, and at times in its history has been motivated and undertaken by those whose interests were in biblical studies, it is not an arm of biblical studies. It is a scientific discipline that is driven by its own ends and means. This is why some today are uncomfortable with the label "biblical archaeology"—archaeology cannot be carried out with integrity if it is just targeting the Bible. As a science, it has a much larger task to fulfill as it focuses on recovering the material culture and successive lifestyles of the peoples of antiquity.

NAME	LANGUAGE	SUBJECT	DATE OF ORIGIN	BIBLICAL SIGNIFICANCE
Laws of Hammurabi	Akkadian (Old Babylonian)	Collection of Babylonian laws	1725	Illustrates ancient Near Eastern law
Merneptah Stele	Hieroglyphic	Military accomplishments of Merneptah	1207	First mention of the name "Israel"
"House of David" Inscription	Aramaic	Syrian conquest of region	9th c.	Earliest mention of David in contemporary records
Black Stele	Akkadian (Neo-Assyrian)	Military accomplishments of Shalmaneser III	840	Pictures Israelites paying tribute
Sennacherib Cylinder	Akkadian (Neo-Assyrian)	Military accomplishments of Sennacherib	686	Describes siege of Jerusalem
Cyrus Cylinder	Akkadian	Decree of Cyrus allowing the rebuilding of temples	535	Illustrates the policy by which Judah also benefited

Copyright: ROHR Productions Ltd.

Megiddo.

he does *not* resolve a crisis. When we note that God's sovereignty did not prevent the godly king Josiah from being killed in battle (2 Kings 23:29) and did not prevent the unjust execution of Naboth by Jezebel (1 Kings 21), it becomes clear that sovereignty may not always be expressed in expected ways. God's sovereignty is not compromised by these incidents, but we learn that we cannot always anticipate how God's sovereignty will be expressed.

PEDESTALS AND ROLE MODELS

God has not given us the Bible with the intention that we put the heroes of the faith up on pedestals of awe and reverence. In contrast, we find that the characters portrayed in the text are shown to share many of the human weaknesses with which all of us struggle.

Editorials, Campaign Speeches, and History

We cannot legitimately speak of "right" perspectives or "wrong" perspectives concerning history. To do so would assume a commonly accepted absolute criterion. Perspectives, perceptions, and feelings exist or do not exist. It is rarely a simple matter to label them right or wrong. In this light *any* historiography should, by rights, be referred to as "perspectives on history." Any historiography must, in some sense, be viewed as an editorial column.

The setting or purpose that motivated the compilation of the record can be an important indicator of how the record is evaluated. As a modern example, a campaign speech is a setting in which the hearer expects to receive more propaganda than reliable information. The high interest in self-promotion, the capability of concealing and misleading, and the total absence of negative information all would confirm a propagandistic intent. An ancient example could be found in commemorative inscriptions honoring kings' successful ventures. Again the three criteria converge to confirm a clearly propagandistic intent. Certain types of records, then, give us cause to anticipate whether or not there is a propagandistic intent.

Even when we are impressed with the faith of Abraham, the humility of Moses, or the courage of Esther, we dare not idolize them. We cannot afford to view them as superhuman—they were people who struggled with uncertainties and made mistakes just as we do. Stories are not in the Bible because the people portrayed were perfect or because they saw everything clearly and responded to God in just the right way every time. Instead, their stories are in the Bible because God worked through them. Indeed, God worked through their successes as well as their failures. Following in the footsteps of Abraham's faith only gets

Michaelangelo's idealized David.

us as far as Abraham. Though we might think that such an aspiration directs our gaze to as high a pinnacle as we dare imagine, the Bible calls us to a different vision. As Hebrews 12:2 encourages us to "fix our eyes on Jesus, the author and perfecter of our faith," so when we study the Old Testament, we should take our marching orders from Deuteronomy 4:32–35, 39:

> Ask now about the former days, long before your time, from the day God created man on the earth; ask from one end of the heavens to the other. Has anything so great as this ever happened, or has anything like it ever been heard of? Has any other people heard the voice of God speaking out of fire, as you have, and lived? Has any god ever tried to take for himself one nation out of another nation, by testings, by miraculous signs and wonders, by war, by a mighty hand and an outstretched arm, or by great and awesome deeds, like all the things the LORD your God did for you in Egypt before your very eyes?
>
> You were shown these things so that you might know that the LORD is God; besides him there is no other. . . . Acknowledge and take to heart this day that the LORD is God in heaven above and on the earth below. There is no other.

In the end, then, we are not seeking simply a deeper knowledge of fellow fallen mortals. Consequently, we would suggest that the stories of the heroes of the Bible are in the Bible not for their own sake, but because they are part of God's story. The historical literature may look like stories about Noah, Ruth, or David, but in the end they are stories about God. People are the bit players; God is the focus. When we apply the Bible to our lives only through the role models provided by its characters, we miss out. The message of Daniel 1 is not that since Daniel ate healthy food, you should eat healthy food too. Such an emphasis is not teaching what the Bible is teaching. When this approach is used, human wisdom is masqueraded as God's authority, and in the process, what the Bible is really teaching can be easily missed. In this Daniel passage, for instance, the point concerns the sovereign protection God extends to Daniel in crisis situations.

We must take care not to attach the authority of the text to things it never intended to teach. For example, it is very possible to learn much about leadership from a study of Nehemiah. In the end, however, there is no indication that the author of Nehemiah was preserving and presenting his material so that readers could be instructed in leadership. That being the case, when leadership is taught from the book and life of Nehemiah, the authority of Scripture is not being tapped. Leadership is an important quality and one that is worth learning about, but one may just as well learn about it from the life of Abraham Lincoln or John Calvin. There is no special merit in learning it from Nehemiah simply because his story is in the Bible while the others are not. The presence of Nehemiah's story in the Bible does not necessarily endorse his style of leadership or approve his leadership decisions. What makes the Bible unique is the things that it teaches with the authority of God. In the case of Nehemiah, the teaching of the book would concern such things as God fulfilling his promises of restoring the city of Jerusalem and his sovereignty in the way his plan was carried out through the yieldedness of Nehemiah. Though many of the principles interpreters derive may be sound, the book of Nehemiah is not God's authoritative guide for leadership.

This is not to say that Scripture's teaching has nothing to do with the human characters. The authors of the Bible take note of Abraham's faith, of Job's righteousness, and of Ruth's faithfulness, and certainly those things are commendable to emulate. But that must not take the focus off God. Each of these narratives seeks to reveal something about God. There is no question that many of us could grow and mature if we accepted the challenge to be like Joseph. There is much to admire about this man. He possesses an integrity to which we can all aspire. Of course, the same could be said of Mother Teresa. As interpreters of the Bible, we cannot stop at the question "Does this person have admirable qualities that I could benefit from emulating?" We must go to the next step of asking, "Is the Bible presenting the character of this person as a model to be emulated?" If it is not, then the admirable qualities that we may observe in a Joseph or a Moses or a David are no different than the admirable qualities of any other individual we would read about in history or literature.

What makes the Bible different from all of these others is its authoritative teaching. As we have mentioned before, though every detail of the text is inspired and has a role to play, incidental details of the text do not carry authoritative teaching on their own. We sometimes look at a passage like Hebrews 11 and take it as a guide to what we are supposed to do with the Old Testament. Hebrews 11, on its authority, presents characters of the Old Testament as role models of faith. It does not thereby suggest that the original contexts presented them as role models. With the inspired text of Hebrews 11 to guide us, we can be confident of the role model value offered there. But Old Testament texts are rarely so clear. Solomon is not offered as a model of setting up an administration (1 Kings 2); Esther is not offered as a model for how to change government policy (Est. 4–7); David is not offered as a model for how to get out of a rough spot (1 Sam. 21:10–15), though each is very successful and receives no condemnation for his or her conduct. We must take our lead carefully from what can be determined to be the agenda of the text.

Were the Judges Godly Leaders?

The judges were raised up by God to bring deliverance to the Israelites in their troubled times. But people who are raised up as

Spirit of the Lord

The spirit of the Lord empowered a number of the judges to do their work (Gideon, Jephthah, Samson). It is also the spirit of the Lord who gave kings their authority (Saul, David). Prophets likewise prophesy under the influence of the spirit of the Lord. Since the Israelites had no revelation concerning the Trinity, they would not have thought of the spirit of the Lord the same way Christians do—as the third person of the Godhead. In Ezekiel the spirit of the Lord is seen to parallel the hand of the Lord (2 Kings 3:15; Ezek. 1:3; 3:14, 22; et al.; cf. 1 Kings 18:46 KJV). In that sense, it is likely that the Israelites considered the spirit of the Lord to be a somewhat less personal "it" rather than a "he." The spirit of the Lord was understood by the Israelites not as a separate entity, but as an extension of God's power manifested through someone that gave them ability or authority that was recognizable as supernatural. The spirit of the Lord in the Old Testament empowers but does not indwell (John 14:17); gives authority but does not regenerate.* It is not unlikely that the Holy Spirit was behind at least some of the activity attributed to the spirit of God in the Old Testament. Peter sees the action of the Holy Spirit at Pentecost as a fulfillment of the prophecy of Joel concerning the spirit of the Lord being poured out (Acts 2:16-17). In the case of Joel 2:28 then, the Holy Spirit was behind the activity attributed to the spirit of the Lord.

*Genesis 15:6 indicates that Abraham was counted righteous before God, but this is not the same mechanism as in the New Testament, nor does it achieve the same final result.

deliverers do not necessarily have to be aware of the role they are playing or of the fact that God is using them (perhaps even despite themselves). A very clear example of this occurs in Isaiah 45:1–4, where God indicates that he will be using Cyrus to bring relief to Israel "though you do not acknowledge me" (v. 4). Understanding that it is well within the range of God's sovereignty to use whomever he chooses, we discover that there is therefore no pressure to consider the judges to be theologically sound or spiritually mature. This makes it much easier to acknowledge some of their dreadful mistakes (Jephthah), syncretistic beliefs (Gideon), and carnal behavior (Samson). We do not learn how to behave from observing the judges—we learn that God in his sovereignty can bring deliverance from even the most unexpected quarters and that he can use us to carry out his plan even though we may not be perfect.

Goliath to Bathsheba: Will the Real David Please Stand Up?

David can also appear to be a bundle of contradictions. He is the author of many psalms in which his hunger for God is evident. He went out against Goliath in faith and was God's chosen king. He was the most prominent forefather of Jesus. We are prone to practically wilt in our admiration: "What a godly man!"

But let's turn over a few pages. He lied to the priest about his situation (1 Sam. 21:2), which led directly to the execution of almost the entire priesthood (1 Sam. 22:22). He worked as a mercenary for the Philistines, wiping out entire villages so that he could preserve the lie he was telling his Philistine master concerning who his military targets were (1 Sam. 27:8–12). He took Bathsheba because he was filled with lust and because he could, and when she got pregnant, he arranged for the death of her husband (2 Sam. 11). We could give numerous other examples of this sort. This is not an attempt to smear David—these are simply part of the Bible's picture of him. We do not handle the Bible well if we elevate the good and ignore the bad, putting a whitewashed David on a high pedestal and making it our personal aspiration to be like him.

So where is the "real David" to be found? Is David the psalmist a hypocritical fraud who is "found out" when we discover his adulterous ways?

Clay figurine of a woman bathing.

The sling was an effective weapon in experienced hands. David used the sling when shepherding to keep wild animals away.

Is his adultery simply a blip on the screen, an isolated error that we must forgive and forget as we consider the godliness that characterized the span of his life? How can the giant-killing psalmist be the same person as the adulterous, deceptive mass murderer?

All of these elements can be merged into a single personality when we understand that David was impulsive. His impulsive tendencies led him to great heights of faith and to deep valleys of sin. We could explore each facet of his life and see this at work, and we could discuss how certain qualities in each of us have the potential for resulting in good as well as evil. But all of this would miss the point. Psychoanalysis is not the path to understanding what the Bible is teaching. We must focus on God and not allow ourselves to become distracted by the circus of curiosities. The Bible wants us to see God working both with "good David" and "bad David." God was building his kingdom and revealing his kingship. David was at times an instrument and at times an obstacle. Our response should not focus on how we should or should not be like David, but how we can be instruments rather than obstacles as God builds his kingdom.

THEOLOGICAL PERSPECTIVES

God Leads the Armies

Like numerous gods in the rest of the ancient Near East, Yahweh was seen as a divine warrior who fought on behalf of his people. Sometimes his weapons are described as lightning bolts or hailstones.

God Leading Armies*

Thutmose III (Egypt): "With joyful heart I turned back in a southerly direction, having celebrated for my lord [Amun-Re] who had ordained the victories and who put the dread of me . . . in my lifetime. Among the foreigners he placed the fear of me so that they might flee far from me."

Murshili II (Hittite): "I, my majesty, went to Arawanna and attacked Arawanna. The Sungoddess of Arinna, my lady, the victorious Stormgod, my lord, Mezzulla and all the gods ran before me and I overcame all of Arawanna."

Sargon II (Assyria): "The inhabitants of Samerina . . . did battle, I fought against them with the power of the great gods, my lords. . . . I caused the awe-inspiring splen-

The central figure is bearing the battle standard of the deity representing the idea that the deity is leading them into battle and will bring victory.

dor of Aššur, my lord, to overwhelm the people of the land of Egypt and the Arabians."

*COS, 2.2B; COS, 2.16; COS, 2.118D.

At other times he triumphs through the person of the king or mighty warriors. In the crossing of the Red Sea, the sea itself becomes a weapon in his hand as he overthrows the Egyptian chariots. Throughout the historical literature, one of the principal titles used for God is "Lord of Hosts" referring to his role as the commanding general of heaven's armies. This role was established from the first pages of the historical literature as God sent one of his heavenly captains to communicate to Joshua the battle plans for Jericho (Josh. 5:13–15).

The theological controversy that surfaced in the events surrounding the establishment of the monarchy had to do with the role of God in military matters. When the leaders of Israel came to Samuel to request a king (1 Sam. 8), they indicated that they needed a king to lead them in fighting their battles. God's reflection on this request was that it represented a rejection of him (1 Sam. 8:7). The opposite inclination can be seen in David's attitude. When he is first seen in action, it is in the battle against Goliath, during which he trusted the Lord to fight the battle and bring victory. Yahweh is portrayed as supreme over other gods and as the only one who is in control in the midst of military conflict.

Kingship and Covenant

One of the most important theological developments in the narrative literature is the formation of the Davidic covenant. In this covenant the main emphasis is on kingship. David had been chosen as king, and the covenant promised a dynastic line for him. He and his descendants would enjoy the favor of God, and they in turn were to reign as his vice-regents, shepherding God's flock. David and his sons were to rule in such a way that God's kingship would be revealed through them. As they exercised wisdom and justice, God would be recognized as the source of those qualities. As they were faithful, God would demonstrate his sovereignty over the nations by establishing Israel's dominion. The covenant stood as an important link between God and the Davidic line as God continued to reveal his nature. This link reached its zenith in Jesus Christ, who, as Messiah, was the Davidic king, and as the Son of God, was the ultimate revelation of God's kingship.

Divine Abandonment

God's special presence in Israel and with Israel was one of the most central elements in its theology. It was expressed most clearly in the theology of the tabernacle/temple as God was understood to have taken

Davidic Covenant

- Dynastic line established under Yahweh's blessing
- Son will succeed David and build temple

up residence in their midst. The temple was seen as securing Israel's possession of the land and guaranteeing God's blessing. Unfortunately, this at times resulted in the superstitious belief that viewed the temple (or the ark of the covenant) as a talisman or good luck charm. In Jeremiah 7 it is clear that the Israelites of Jeremiah's time had concluded that as long as Yahweh's temple was in Jerusalem, the country was safe from the Babylonians. But this mentality had appeared over four hundred years earlier in the time of Samuel. When the Israelites were doing battle with the Philistines, Eli's two sons, the priests Hophni and Phinehas, decided to take the ark into the fray, anticipating that the ark's presence would help bring victory. Instead, the Philistines won, the two priests were killed, and the ark was taken by the enemy.

In the ancient Near East when a city or an army was defeated, the most logical explanation was considered to be that the god of the victor had defeated or in some other way overpowered the god of the vanquished. But as early as 2000 BC an alternate explanation began to be offered—that the deity was not defeated, but had abandoned the city. In literature from Mesopotamia, there is no motivation for the abandonment—it is simply the arbitrary decree of the divine assembly. In contrast, God's revelation of himself had left Israelite theology no room for this view of fickle fate.

As mentioned in the presentation of the plotline above, when the ark was taken by the Philistines, Yahweh had not been overpowered, nor had he simply abandoned Israel's army because it had been decreed. He abandoned them because of their unfaithfulness. This came at the end of the long judges period, during which God had repeatedly refused to go before Israel's armies and had allowed them to be subjugated to various enemies. But now he not only abandoned the army, he abandoned the land, and it was overrun by the Philistines.

> The temple was seen as securing Israel's possession of the land and guaranteeing God's blessing.

You, O LORD, reign forever;
   your throne endures from generation to generation.
Why do you always forget us?
   Why do you forsake us so long?
Restore us to yourself, O LORD, that we may return;
   renew our days as of old
unless you have utterly rejected us
   and are angry with us beyond measure.

Lamentations 5:19–22

Through the monarchy period, there continued to be occasions when Israel (or Judah) suffered defeat at the hands of enemies as God refused to go before their armies, but throughout that time, his presence remained in Jerusalem as the ark stood in its place in Solomon's temple. It was in the prophetic messages of Ezekiel, a contemporary of Jeremiah early in the sixth century BC, that warning came again that God was preparing to abandon the temple and his people (portrayed in Ezekiel 1). Their repeated sins and their constant unfaithfulness to the covenant were about to bring upon them the curses of covenant violation (see Deut. 28:15–68). The book of Lamentations is filled with the sadness that resulted from God's abandonment of the temple and Jerusalem and the resulting destruction by the Babylonians. Yahweh had abandoned their armies, the city, and the temple. As a result, the people lost the land and were taken into exile. Nevertheless, both Ezekiel 48:35 and the postexilic prophets Haggai and Zechariah anticipated the return of God's presence (Hag. 2:6–9; Zech. 1:16).

Lessons from the Exile

The exile serves as a watershed for Israelite theology. Even though the law and the covenant had by now been around for nearly a millennium, many of their main components had not been successfully integrated into Israelite religious thought and practice. As they trailed off into exile, they were struck with the realization that the covenant curses were not just rhetoric. Yahweh took the covenant very seriously. Rather than accepting the conclusion that Yahweh had been overpowered, a faithful remnant recognized that the exile was punishment for their unfaithfulness and determined to return to Yahweh, renew the covenant, trust in his sovereignty and grace, and wait patiently for restoration. When Cyrus decreed that they could return to their land and rebuild the temple, they praised God for a second chance.

Ezra reading the law.

Susanna Vagt and Alva Steffler

In the postexilic period, we find a transformed Israel. It has finally gotten beyond the inclination to worship other gods, and we see the achievement of the monotheistic ideals represented in the law. The Israelites have a clearer view of God's kingdom as they come to realize that the spiritual dimensions of that kingdom are more important than the physical dimension represented by a Davidic king on the throne. They have a firm commitment to the centrality of worship and to maintaining the holiness of the temple—led in both by the Levites. They have come to recognize God's law as the actual foundation of society as it had been intended to be, rather than as some elusive theoretical ideal. In effect, the law became the characterizing feature of their society instead of a countercultural program that sought to transform society.

The exile had confirmed the messages that the preexilic prophets had proclaimed. The doom they had announced had come. The positive aspect of that was that there was therefore hope that the restoration of which the prophets had spoken could also be anticipated. Such thinking was bolstered as they were restored to their land but then seemed to fall short as they continued to be under Persian control. As they progressed further into the postexilic period, they came to realize that the restoration was not going to come all at one time, but was going to stretch over long eras of history (Dan. 9). And so they settled in with a growing hope that focused increasingly on a messianic expectation when the kingdom of God would bring Israel back into a position of political prominence.

Israel's Vision of History as Theology

The books of Chronicles combine the elements of story and sermon to offer a theology of hope for the future through an understanding of the past. The past then becomes a way to understand God, and its study becomes an occasion for worship as the chronicler unfolds his commentary on the faithfulness of God in the past. As a story, Chronicles unfurls the rich fabric of the tapestry of Israel's role as God's covenant people. The book likewise features the hallmarks of a sermon (see "Sermon Characteristics," below) as the author makes repeated references to his authoritative sources, focusing most notably on two words

Sermon Characteristics*

1. Must appeal to recognized source of authority.
2. Proclaims a theological teaching about the nature, character, promises, work, or power of God.
3. Calls for response (e.g., repentance, obedience).
4. Employs rhetorical devices to arouse interest and draw in the audience.

*Adapted from Rex Mason, "Some Echoes of the Preaching in the Second Temple? Tradition Elements in Zechariah 1–8," ZAW 96 (1984): 223–25.

from God (the Davidic covenant in 1 Chron. 17:3–14 and the response to Solomon's dedicatory prayer in 2 Chron. 7:11–22).

The hope that results from the book is founded on the conviction that God is orchestrating history in accordance with his plan. Thus an understanding of history is achieved through an understanding of the nature of God. Chronicles portrays God with the following attributes and roles:

- Sovereign rule as creator (cf. 2 Chron. 20:6)
- Providential intervention as sustainer (2 Chron. 20:12)
- Election of Israel (1 Chron. 16:13, 17)
- Faithfulness to his covenant promises (1 Chron. 17:18–24)
- Responsiveness to prayer (2 Chron. 6:40; 7:12)

Angels and Demons, Cherubs and Seraphs

In the biblical worldview, a wide array of supernatural creatures populates the cosmos. Where the polytheistic religions of the ancient world had their pantheon of deities and divine messengers, Israel had angels, from powerful deliverers to routine deliverymen who served God. Angels are by definition emissaries or messengers and as such constitute only one category of supernatural entity. The only two angelic names given in the text of the Old Testament are Gabriel and Michael.

The only hint of anything close to guardian angels is found in Psalm 91:11–12. In the ancient Near East, it was, of course, deities rather than angels who served as guardians. Mesopotamians believed that personal gods or family gods offered special care and protection that the great cosmic or national deities would not be bothered with. The protection that was expected in the ancient Near East was against demonic powers that were believed to be the cause of illness and trouble. Related to that was the danger of magical spells and hexes that could be pronounced against someone. Infant mortality was attributed to demonic influence, and demons were believed to be prowling about not only in dark or deserted places, but also in alleys and doorways—even by the doorways of temples. There is evidence that Israelites believed in demons, but neither in the Old Testament nor in the ancient world is there any identification of demons with fallen angels.

Other supernatural creatures in the Old Testament are the cherubs and seraphs. Merging biblical descriptions with archaeological discoveries indicates that the cherubs are

Ivory from eighth century Syria of two winged creatures.

composite creatures (having features of a number of different creatures, like the Egyptian sphinx), often with four-legged animal bodies and wings. The cherubs appear in ancient art with some regularity as guardians flanking the thrones of kings and deities. The supernatural creatures known as seraphs occur only in Isaiah 6, but the serpents that plagued the Israelites in the wilderness also go by that designation, and Isaiah twice refers to flying serpents (NIV, "darting" 14:29; 30:6). There is therefore good reason to think of the seraphs in the form of winged serpents. Since the Hebrew root *sarap* is usually associated with "burning," there is also good reason to associate these creatures with fire. Ancient Near Eastern literature offers some support for these portrayals. Fiery serpents are well known in Egyptian art and literature. There the serpent, or uraeus, adorns the crown of pharaoh and sometimes is pictured with wings (usually either two or four). It is not unusual for them to have hands, feet, or faces. Serpents in an upright position with wings also decorate the throne of Tutankhamen. Many seals decorated with winged uraei have been found in excavations in Palestine dating to this period, so we know that the Israelites were familiar with this motif.

- Justice (2 Chron. 19:7)
- Goodness (2 Chron. 30:18–20)
- Mercy (2 Chron. 30:9)

All of this is designed to persuade people that creation and history are in the hand of God and that time and circumstance are his servants. The hope that derives from this conviction is nurtured in renewed worship. The result is this: A sound understanding of history unwraps theology; a sound understanding of theology stimulates worship; a sound understanding of worship nourishes hope; a sound understanding of hope brings renewal.

History

Theology

Worship

Hope

Renewal

REFLECTIONS

1. What are the important theological premises underlying the conquest?

2. Why were the Israelites continually attracted to Canaanite religions?

3. What theological truths are revealed in the judges cycle?

4. What went wrong with Saul's kingship?

5. Was David a good king or a bad king?

6. What is the theological significance of the temple?

7. What is the significance of the fact that the historical literature includes the failures as well as the successes of its main characters?

8. What are the significant differences between the perspectives of Kings and Chronicles?

9. What are the principles for using historical figures legitimately as role models?

10. What is the significance of the exile (both in terms of its causes and its results)?

11. How can the same God who said, "You shall not murder" (Ex. 20:13) also give the command to totally wipe out the Canaanite cities? What are the implications for the idea that the law shows what God is like and that we should seek to be like him?

12. What impact does archaeology have on convictions about the accuracy of the biblical text?

13. Is there such a thing as "holy war" for Christians today?

14. How are the covenant curses of Deuteronomy 28 related to the author's purpose in the historical books?

15. How would the historical books of Samuel and Kings reflect on the paradigm for kingship offered in Deuteronomy 17?

Notes

1. By the end of the period, Samson was more distant from God than the people to whom he was bringing deliverance.
2. This is not dissimilar to the differences between how the different gospels cover the life of Christ.
3. H. G. M. Williamson, *Ezra, Nehemiah* (Dallas: Word, 1985), xlviii-l.
4. We say "could" because archaeology has not yet provided any of that.
5. For a review of the elements of story see Pentateuch, Bridging Contexts, p. 83.

CHAPTER

CONTEMPORARY SIGNIFICANCE

3 HISTORICAL LITERATURE

HISTORY SEEMS BORING AND IRRELEVANT TO ME — HELP!

It is not hard to love the stories of Joshua and Jericho or David and Goliath. Even in longer narratives, such as those of Esther or Ruth, we are captivated by deep characters and intriguing plots. But anyone who has tried to read straight through Kings or Chronicles knows that the narratives mentioned above are the exception not the rule. By the time we finish the litany of nineteen kings of Israel and a similar number from Judah, the names have become a blur and it has become difficult to find anything that looks like plot or character development. To narrative literature that features little plot or character development, some modern readers are quick to attach swift critique: "Boring!"

It gets worse. In our postmodern society, history itself, biblical or otherwise, has lost much of its appeal. The values of postmodernism are much more inclined to be rooted in the present than in an understanding of the past. Even given the cliché that those who don't learn the lessons of history are doomed to repeat the mistakes, the past may seem irrelevant to those who are focused on the present or the future.

Hopefully, information gained in the earlier discussions of historical literature has already begun to remedy these perceived problems. Biblical narrative literature is not simply a record of or discussion of the past. It is God's revelation of himself. Do you want to know God? Listen to his story. How can anything be more relevant to us than stories about the creator of the universe? This is not the study of the past—this is the study of a person.

Consider for a moment a comparison between a history of World War II and a biography of Winston Churchill. There would of necessity be a lot of overlap between them. Both would include reports of events that were significant in the war. From our vantage point in history, both of these books would be talking about the past. But there would be a very real difference between them as well. The goal of the history book would most likely be to offer the reader insight into the events of the war. The goal of the biography would be to gain an appreciation of Winston Churchill, in some measure through the events of the war.

Given this distinction, it might be helpful to think of the historical literature in terms of a biography (autobiography!) of God. Now some people dislike reading biographies as much as they dislike reading history. But here is the difference: Winston Churchill is dead and has no direct impact on my life. In contrast, there is no one more important in our day-to-day lives than God. Nothing is more important than knowing him. Knowledge of God can never be irrelevant.

> **Knowledge of God can never be irrelevant.**

In light of this focus on the historical literature as God's story, when we turn our attention back to issues of plot and character development, again a little reorientation of our expectations is necessary. If, for instance, we are looking for character development and plot in the story of King Shallum (2 Kings 15:13–16), we will be extremely disappointed. If we shift our focus, however, to consider plot and character development in terms of God, we will find different results. The part of the story concerning Shallum blends in with the parts of the story concerning the other kings, and together they show God working with Israel through the ups and downs of the monarchy period. As each king takes his place in the pattern of the monarchy, a pattern of God's interaction and response also develops. We do not need to look at the Shallum story in isolation, but we see it as contributing to the overall picture of God developed in Kings.

If you are one of those people to whom history seems boring and irrelevant, the "historical literature" in the Bible can be salvaged by a shift of focus. Imagine viewing a documentary on the life and career of a great basketball player. The production includes clips of all of his great moves and shots; interviews with coaches, opponents, friends, and teammates; analysis of his greatness and his contributions to the sport. All of it is set to moving music with the intention of motivating the audience to respond with appreciation of the greatness of this athlete. Suppose that as you view this tribute, you can freeze it at a point when the hero has leaped into the air and is poised ready to deliver an impressive slam dunk. With the action paused, you now zoom in on the players on the benches. As you examine each face, you begin to evaluate how those players are responding to what is taking place before their eyes. Then you zoom further and begin to explore the faces in the crowd. You see some excitement, some disappointment, some apathy. Perhaps you begin to identify with some of the faces you see while others earn your disapproval. For the sake of analogy, let us take it to extremes. You begin watching the videotape over and over again. Day by day you zoom through the crowd examining face after face, trying to infer how each person is responding to the athlete and thinking about how you can learn from that response. In this obsession, you might lose sight of a simple fact. When the camera zooms in on the people in the background, the image of the athlete paused in the foreground becomes blurry and unrecognizable. Focus has been lost.

This is the same mistake we often make when reading the historical literature. We spend much of our time and effort looking at the people in the crowd—the Abrahams, Esthers, Sauls, Bathshebas, or even the Shallums. And the image of God becomes simply a blur. We cannot afford to become distracted by the bit players or the fans in the stands. The production that is the Bible is designed to invoke a response from us that will enhance our appreciation of the greatness of our God. As we come to know God better through this literature, we can begin to understand what his relationship is to history and how he acts in it. This in turn will help us to know how to see God in our own historical time and to understand something of his involvement. There is precedent for this approach in the Scriptures when the Psalms continually turn their gaze back into history to look for patterns in what God has done in the past so that they can have hope in the present (see especially Psalms 105 and 106). The chronicler does the same as his recitation of history is intended to bring focus, renewal, and hope to his people.

The Bible says that God is love—but what does that tell me about how he will show his love to me? God is holy and hates sin—what are the implications of that when I sin? What should I expect concerning how God will really act in my life today? It is the Bible's job to give us all an idea of exactly that. Just like we get an idea of what a teacher will ask on an exam and how we will be graded on that exam by looking at what the teacher has done in the past, we get our best glimpse of God by looking at how he has acted in the past. Biblical history matters because it is God's story and as such offers us the way to know him. The following scenario will help us to see a wrong way and a right way to use the historical literature of the Old Testament.

SCENARIO: USING HISTORICAL LITERATURE TODAY

Krystyn practically flew back to her dorm room. She couldn't wait to tell her roommate what had just happened. She burst through the door still breathing hard from her run up three flights of stairs. Kelli, her roommate, grinned at Krystyn's red face and felt her excitement as the words began to tumble out. "I was just walking down the hall after class and ran into Dr. Winston." She was struggling to catch her breath. "He said he had something I might be interested in. Well, you know that last design project I turned in? He said he really liked it and had recommended me for an internship at . . . are you ready for this? Hollis—you know, Hollis and Sons Advertising Associates. Can you believe it? This summer! I have an interview tomorrow. Dr. Winston says I should be a shoo-in. Incredible! It's just what I have been waiting for."

Kelli paused for a moment and smiled with joy at her friend's good fortune. But she also paused so that she could choose her next words carefully. "That's great, Krys," she said with true enthusiasm, "but what does this mean for the missions project that we were planning to do together this summer?" As soon as she said it, she knew that it had been too abrupt, and she saw it also in Krystyn's crestfallen expression.

"Oh no! In my excitement talking to Dr. Winston, I forgot all about that. What am I going to do now? I really felt that God was directing us to go on this missions trip, but isn't it God who has dropped this great internship opportunity in my lap? Now I'm confused. What does God want me to do?"

As Krystyn dropped despondently onto her bed, Kelli lay back on her pillow to think. Then she rolled onto one elbow and faced her friend. "Hey, Krys, doesn't the Bible have a guy who wants to find out what God wants him to do? He lays out this fleece or something and then asks God to give him a sign." Krystyn's face lit up. "Yeah, I remember now. It's in Judges; the guy's name is . . . Gideon! Our pastor just gave a sermon on him last month. Maybe I should do something like that—after all, God answered Gideon. We just have to think of some way to do it. Got any ideas, Kell?"

As the two roommates thought through various options, they finally came up with one they both liked. "Okay," said Kelli, "so you will go to the interview at Hollis tomorrow, and if somewhere in the conversation it turns out Mr. Hollis is a Christian, that can be the sign that God wants you to take the internship."

"And if not," Krystyn added, "then I will turn it down and take it as God's leading that I should go on the trip." They finally settled down and slept contentedly.

Kelli prayed for her roommate often during the next day and expected that by that evening they would have a clear sense of God's leading. When Krystyn returned to the room, however, she was more puzzled than ever. "How'd it go, Krys? Tell me everything."

"Well, Mr. Hollis is real nice," Krystyn began. "They really like my work, and the people that I met were friendly. I could learn a lot from them. Everybody was saying how much they would like me to come and be part of the team. It seemed like a great environment to work and learn in."

"Great! But how about the 'fleece'? Did he indicate he was a Christian?"

"That's the problem," moaned Krystyn as she plopped down on her bed and rested her chin in her hands, "he talked about how important honesty was to their company's dealings with clients, and one time he used the phrase 'God willing'—he even talked about some churches that were their clients. But he didn't exactly say he was a Christian."

As the girls sighed audibly in unison, they wondered what they had done wrong. Did they have to devise another fleece? What was God saying?

RECAPITULATION

By this point in the chapter, at least part of Krystyn and Kelli's problem should be recognizable. We have learned that the characters in the historical literature are not intended to serve as role models instructing us by their conduct how we are to act. The fact that Gideon used a fleece to determine God's will must not be taken as a way of telling us that a fleece (or something serving in place of a fleece) should be used for determining God's will. The fact that it worked for Gideon does not suggest that it will work for anyone else. The fact that God used Gideon's fleece to give him guidance does not suggest that he will again guide in that way,[1] or even that he was pleased with Gideon's approach. To the contrary, it is easy to see that the fleece approach puts people in the position of dictating terms to

God. This is never desirable. So here we have a case where trying to follow in the steps of a role model can lead us into unrealistic expectations and even into manipulative methods.

Can the historical literature offer Krystyn any help? Yes, but not by giving her a direct answer to her specific question. If we think back to some of the things we have learned from the historical literature, we will recall that one of the major themes was the sovereignty of God in every circumstance of life. His sovereignty is such that even people who are doing evil can be used to accomplish God's plan. If sin cannot interfere with God's plan, then an innocent, even if ill-advised choice, cannot do so either. If Krystyn can serve God in either position, then it would be difficult to make a "wrong" choice.

Krystyn's job is to pray that God will help her to set all selfish desires aside, express her desire to go where she can serve God best (or get the best preparation for serving God), and ask that he guide her choice in his will. It is God's job to answer her prayer and lead her to the right decision. She has to trust that he will do that through further discussions with friends and advisers, through further exploration of both opportunities, and through the circumstances that take shape. The historical literature can provide for her an understanding of what God is like and how he works out his purposes in the world and in our lives, sometimes in subtle or complex ways. She should make the

God of Judgment, God of Love

People who are used to reading the New Testament sometimes get to the Old Testament and are puzzled or even troubled by the picture of God they find there. Jesus and the Epistles clearly teach love as a lifestyle. Loving enemies and turning the other cheek are offered as the Christian way. God is love; God is forgiving; God is merciful. These are the hallmarks of the New Testament. But in the Old Testament, we often see God acting in judgment. Harsh retribution (Josh. 7:12, 24–26), dramatic punishment (2 Sam. 6:6–7), and strict adherence to rules (Lev. 10:1–2) characterize him in story after story. This should not be viewed as some sort of inconsistency or transformation. The reader must keep in mind that the New Testament has stories such as Ananias and Sapphira (Acts 5:1–10) and the Old Testament has stories such as Jonah and the deliverance of Nineveh (Jonah 3). God's mercy is manifestly present in the Old Testament from the opening pages, when he chose not to destroy Adam and Eve, and continuing through all of his dealings with Israel, which feature century after century of patience and kindness despite its rebellion. He is explicitly presented as a God of love in the Old Testament not only for Israel (Hos. 11:1–4) but for others as well, in which case his love serves as a model for his people (Deut. 10:18–19). In the same manner, he is no less a God of judgment in the New Testament (Heb. 12:18–29). The major reason for the perceived difference is that there are very few contexts in the New Testament that portray rebellion and sin. In the Old Testament these are most prominent in the narrative and prophetic texts. The New Testament only has one book in each of those genres. The Old Testament and New Testament together comprise an integrated revelation of the nature of God.

choice that she senses will give her the best opportunity to serve God considering both short-term and long-term issues. Having made the best decision she can make, she needs to trust that God has led her to that. But even if she continues to wonder whether that is true, she must trust that God can use her in either place when she commits her life and work to him, and that he can use either type of experience to shape her for his future use. There are no dead ends with God.

God's View of Tolerance and Pluralism

Perhaps the most pointed Old Testament passage for addressing these qualities in our postmodern world is Deuteronomy 13. Here the law indicates that if anyone tries to entice the Israelites to worship another God, whether that person is a highly respected spiritual person or a close relative, he or she should be put to death. It should be noted that this is neither a text that prohibits proselytizing nor one that condemns to death all who practice a different religion. It insists on integrity of the faith within Israel. The Old Testament does not seek to convert and to that extent tolerates the existence of other religions. It does not, however, go so far as to suggest that any given religion or god is as valid as the next. In fact, the Old Testament condemns idol worship as worthless (Isa. 41:24–29; 42:17; 44:9–20; Jer. 10:1–16) and characterizes the gods as no-gods (Deut. 32:17). It portrays Yahweh as the only true God—there is no other (Isa. 43:10–11; 44:6; 45:5, 21; 46:9). The concept of equal standing for every variety of religious practice finds no support in the Bible: "I will not give my glory to another or my praise to idols" (Isa. 42:8).

These *massebot* or standing stones were a part of the Canaanite (and Israelite) cultic assemblage. The Bible condemns these items, especially in the writings of the prophets.

How Can We View History Biblically?

Biblical Affirmations of God's Control of History

- Daniel 2:21
- Daniel 4:35
- Isaiah 14:26–27
- Isaiah 40:15–28
- Genesis 45:7
- Genesis 50:20

Our means, be they good or evil, inevitably produce God's ends. All of our human ends are only means to his ends.

When we speak of viewing history biblically, we are referring to deriving a worldview from the Bible concerning how God is involved in historical events day by day. In the secularism of our culture, even Christians who would affirm God's control of history still tend to isolate him from the cause-and-effect flow of events in our world. In one sense, there is good reason for this—we cannot interpret infallibly exactly what God is doing in history. It is important to note, however, that it is not necessary to understand God's overall plan in order to affirm that he is in control and that nothing happens independently of him. When we read of earthquakes, famines, wars, or terrorist acts, we have no way of identifying what God's purposes are, but we dare not think that these are surprises to God or that they happen outside his jurisdiction.

The perspective offered in the Bible insists that though the fall has created a broken world, God's sovereignty takes every expression of sin and brokenness and molds it to his plan and purpose. The Bible delivers a worldview that conveys that God is not responsible for evil. Yet he has chosen to tolerate its existence as he unfolds his plan of reconciliation. In this way, a biblical view of history can offer no explanations of the genocide of the holocaust, the Oklahoma City bombing, the shootings at Columbine High School, the terrorist attack on New York's twin towers, or of anyone's personal tragedies. Instead, it offers a worldview that insists that God's goodness and power are reflected not by negating all daily sin, oppression, and tragedy, but in moving a fallen world toward reconciliation and the consummation of his plan. His power is seen in the inexorable incorporation of all deeds into the flow of his plan. His goodness is seen in the ultimate shape and intentions of his plan. It is not a case of the ends *justifying* the means; it is rather that our means, be they good or evil, inevitably produce God's ends. All of our human ends are only means to his ends. That does not turn our means into his means; it only indicates that our means and his means combine to produce his ends.

How then do we, as Christians, respond to the horrific events and personal tragedies that happen around us? How do we reflect a biblical worldview of history? First, we should not jump to the conclusion that tragedy is punishment from God. That is only one of several possibilities. Instead, we should be prepared to testify to our confidence in God's ability to weave tragedy into his plan and purpose. Second, in times of tragedy, it is common for people to become introspective, to seek an anchor. In trying circumstances, people are most willing to consider the big issues. We can challenge people to consider the condition of the world and of their own lives and to decide that God deserves more commitment. Third, people always want to know "why." We cannot tell them what God is doing or why the tragedies have occurred. We can tell them who God is and what he is like. That is what our Bible study should prepare us for. We should be a voice of encouragement. Armed with a reasoned faith, we should proclaim hope. Disdaining a rush to judgment, we should call for renewal.

1. Don't jump to conclusions.
2. Encourage introspection and looking at the big picture.
3. Affirm God's love and control.

> The fool says in his heart,
>   "There is no God."
> They are corrupt, their deeds are vile;
>   there is no one who does good.
>
> The LORD looks down from heaven
>   on the sons of men
> to see if there are any who understand,
>   any who seek God.
> All have turned aside,
>   they have together become corrupt;
> there is no one who does good,
>   not even one.   Psalm 14:1–3

How Could the Israelites Have Failed So Often and So Badly?

For the most part, Israel's failures showed an inability to allow the revelation they had from God to transform their worldview. There was a particular role given to God/the gods in the ancient world that served as a cultural default. When we look at the Israelites from the vantage point of outside observers who have not been programmed with the same cultural defaults, it is hard for us to understand how they could be so unsuccessful at transcending those defaults. We can only gain an appreciation for their predicament when we allow ourselves to become aware of the cultural defaults that we are burdened with and how often we fail to transcend them. In fact, like the Israelites, we are usually unaware that we suffer under them, and we are incapable of working past them even when their reality becomes painfully obvious. What are the cultural defaults we have trouble rising above? Secularism, materialism, narcissism, hedonism, rationalism, skepticism, naturalism, practical existentialism, shallow relationships, lack of commitment, the drive to leisure and entertainment, elevation of the individual, obsession with rights—need we go on? There would be much that the Israelites would see in our cultural defaults that often drive us away from God's claims on us. They would be equally perplexed regarding how we could be so blind to them, so incapable of rising above them, and so stubborn in our conformity to these aspects of our culture that we know are counterproductive to faith and godliness. So, if we want to understand Israel's continual failure, the place to start is the mirror.

Before we address today, it might be of interest to assess the "miracle factor" in the Old Testament. There are seven primary categories of what we would be inclined to call miracles, and we will find that each one occurs less frequently than we might think.

1. *God speaking directly to individuals.* The primary examples of this are the prophets, but in many cases the text is unclear about whether God spoke to them directly or through media such as dreams. Aside from the prophets, God conversed with fewer than a dozen individuals: Cain, Noah, Abraham, Jacob, Moses and Aaron, Joshua, Samuel, and Job. God appeared to Solomon in a dream, communicated to David through prophets, and spoke to Gideon (as well as seven others) through the Angel of the Lord. We would also have to count the handwriting on the wall and the lecture given by Balaam's donkey. This is a very elite group, and most of them experienced hearing from God directly on only one occasion.

2. *Acts of deliverance.* The parting of the Red Sea, Daniel in the lions' den, and the story of the fiery furnace are well known, but other examples are difficult to find. We could perhaps include the ravens feeding Elijah during the famine.

3. *Acts of judgment.* The destruction of Sodom and Gomorrah, the plagues on Egypt and on the Philistines when they had the ark, the collapse of Jericho's walls, and the destruction of Sennacherib's army are the most prominent examples. In addition, there are individual cases of punishment (Nadab and Abihu, Korah, Achan, Uzzah, Miriam, Uzziah, and Nebuchadnezzar are the major examples).

4. *Healing.* A few individual cases of healing can be found in the Elijah/Elisha narratives, and Hezekiah was also miraculously healed. In addition, we read of the large-scale situation in the wilderness where people were healed from snakebites by looking at the bronze serpent.

5. *Covenant signs.* The parting of the Jordan (for Joshua, Elijah, and Elisha) is about the only covenant sign other than all of the miracles in the wilderness (manna, quail, water from rock, guiding pillar). Probably also in this group, however, are the cases of babies born to barren women (Sarah, Rebekah, Rachel, Hannah).

6. *Prophetic signs.* A number of isolated miscellaneous signs comprise this group: Moses' rod turning into a snake, the shadow of Ahaz's tower moving backwards, an axhead floating, a hail storm in summer, Jeroboam's hand withering and the altar splitting, Elijah's sacrifice combusting, and the storm starting and stopping on cue in Jonah.

7. *Blessing.* The two examples of individuals being taken by God (Enoch and Elijah) would fit in this category.

Considering the scope of nearly a thousand chapters of text and several millennia passing by, this is not a huge list. In addition, a quick survey reveals that a large proportion of these took place during the lifetimes of Moses and Elijah/Elisha. The point is that miracles are not so frequent in the Old Testament as we might assume. It only seems that they are more common because they are so noticeable and extraordinary and because we focus so much attention on them in our preaching and teaching of the Bible.

Another issue to address is the definition of *miracle*. The Israelite (and we would say biblical) worldview is that God is integrally involved in everything that happens. What we are inclined to call "natural laws" are only a description of God's regular operations. Since God is

> When our fathers were in Egypt,
>   they gave no thought to your miracles;
>   they did not remember your many kindnesses,
>   and they rebelled by the sea.
>
> **Psalm 106:7**

seen as the operating system of the cosmos, it would be inappropriate to speak of him intervening in nature — he cannot intervene in something that is defined by his activity to begin with. As a result, we often end up calling a miracle anything for which we do not have a scientific explanation. In some cases (e.g., some of the plagues), it may be possible that given a modern scientific observer, a scientific explanation would be possible. The fact is that God brought them about and accomplished his purposes through them whether a scientific explanation could be offered or not.

> "A wicked and adulterous generation asks for a miraculous sign!" (Matt. 12:39)

God is just as much involved in the operation of the cosmos today as he ever was. It is possible that our ability to identify scientific processes has reduced the range of phenomena that we would be willing to call miracles. One of the most significant lessons taught in the book of Esther is that God is quite capable of providing deliverance or carrying out any other part of his program without resorting to what we would call miracles. God works in different ways in different periods, and we must be content with God's choices. Only a very few individuals (relatively speaking) got to rub shoulders with Jesus while he lived on earth, and we should not wonder at why we cannot experience that too. Our responsibility is to respond faithfully to the ways God does choose to work in our time, in our world, and in our lives.

> "If they do not listen to Moses and the prophets, they will not be convinced even if someone rises from the dead." (Luke 16:31)

© 1998 PhotoAlto

How Should We View the Bible Historically?

In previous sections, we have identified the events of history as revelation of God (since he is in control of history) and biblical historiography as revelation offering an explanation of what God is doing in history or how God can be seen in the events of history. If these are accurate perceptions, we receive some important guidelines concerning our evaluation of the literature.

In the climate of our postmodern world, there is a heightened skepticism concerning the factuality or reality of some of the people and events that comprise the story line of the Bible. Though doubt concerning whether Adam and Eve really existed has been expressed for centuries, the list has been growing. It is not unusual for scholars today to question whether anyone prior to the division of the kingdom really existed. This would therefore cast doubt about Solomon, David, Samson, Gideon, Joshua, Moses, Joseph, Jacob, Abraham, and Noah. In addition, individuals such as Job, Esther, and Jonah are frequently considered legendary if not entirely fictional.

The first question we must ask is, "Is the theological message of the Bible compromised if it uses legendary or fictional characters?" What if Jacob did not wrestle with an angel? What if Joseph was not sold into slavery in Egypt by his brothers? What if the Red Sea did not really part? What if God did not really speak to Abraham or write the tablets on Mount Sinai? We would contend that it does indeed make a very big difference. If God's revelation of himself is given through the things that he did in the lives of people, the revelation would be negated if the events did not happen or the people did not exist. If God did not speak to Abraham, there is no covenant. If there were no covenant with David, Messiah is a man-made idea or a literary construct. If there were no Esther or no parted Red Sea, God's deliverances did not take place. If these are things that God did not do, then they reveal nothing about God. If the Bible does not reveal God to us, we know nothing about God but what we can infer from the world around us, and the Bible is just an old, though venerated, piece of sectarian literature.

The second important question comes from the opposite direction: "Why would anyone think that the things recorded in the Bible did not happen or that the people did not exist?" Skepticism or incredulity could arise from several directions. Perhaps the most common dismissal arises from a philosophical standpoint. In the culture in which we live, secularism and humanism pervade the cultural

> "Unless I see the nail marks in his hands and put my finger where the nails were, and put my hand into his side, I will not believe it." (John 20:25)

worldview. Consequently, it is easy to be suspicious about the reality of that which is spiritual or supernatural. Rationalism is inclined to smile condescendingly at the naïveté of the people of antiquity and to dismiss their reports as reflections of their superstitions.

From an experiential standpoint, most of us would admit that we have never encountered the sorts of situations the Bible regularly records. It is human nature to be dubious about occurrences that are outside of one's experience. Nevertheless, it betrays a certain arrogance in a person if he or she would even tacitly suggest that there is nothing that could transcend their own world of experience.

From a literary standpoint, our modern world features a wide array of vaguely nuanced literary genres, and the boundaries between them are not always clear. Documentary and historical fiction, for instance, merge together in what has been dubbed *docudrama*. But

Spiritual Warfare

Spiritual warfare is evident on two levels in the Old Testament. In the first level, God's human representative is confronting human representatives of other spiritual powers. The two most familiar examples are the confrontation between Moses and Pharaoh's magicians (who represent the magical powers of the Egyptian gods; Ex. 7), and Elijah's confrontation of the prophets of Baal (1 Kings 18). In the second level, spirit beings are in conflict with one another. The clearest reference to this sort of warfare is in Daniel 10:13, where an angel (presumably Gabriel) was aided by the archangel Michael when he was detained for twenty-one days by the "prince of Persia."

In the Old Testament and the ancient world at large, it was believed that there was a linkage between events taking place on earth and those taking place in heaven. When armies fought, it was accepted that the gods of those armies also fought and the victor among the gods would bring victory to his people as well. In this sense, all warfare was spiritual warfare.

Today we often define spiritual warfare as a combination of these two. We think of Christians as God's human representatives confronting spirit beings: "For our struggle is not against flesh and blood, but against the rulers, against the authorities, against the powers of this dark world and against the spiritual forces of evil in the heavenly realms" (Eph. 6:12). This passage is not suggesting that believers should take on the powers of darkness in single-handed combat. It only indicates that the enemy is neither our own human fallenness nor human opponents. Instead, the battle is still being waged on two levels. There is no such thing as a purely human adversary. Every conflict against evil has a spiritual dimension.

The demon Pazazu. People of the ancient world believed that demons were the cause of many ailments and misfortunes.

Z. Radovan, Jerusalem

Potential Historiographic Subgenres

• journalistic
• epic
• didactic
• propagandistic
• theological

even in the world of the past, we are aware of many instances in which legendary material developed and took hold to the extent that it has become difficult to distinguish legend from history. It is not that literature used to be simple and has become complex—it is just that the complexities of modern literature are different from those of ancient literature, making it easy for the modern reader to be perplexed about the signals and conventions that make up the culturally imbedded rules for reading ancient literature.

The issues ultimately and inevitably come back to presuppositions. If we believe that the Bible is God's revelation of himself and that it has authority, we are committed to its truth and accuracy. At the same time, we must think of its accuracy in terms of the sort of literature it contains and the intentions of the authors. Historical literature is a broad category and may contain a variety of subgenres, each of which has to be read differently (see "Potential Historiographic Subgenres"). It is our responsibility to accept the plain statements of the text without reservation, to accept the supernatural affirmations in the text with the eyes of faith, and to express unreserved confidence in the fidelity of the literature without the skepticism of rationalism. At the same time, we cannot afford to be naïve about the nature of the literature or to impose upon it expectations that would be foreign to its authors.

Our Goal

Faith without guile

Inquiry without naïveté

REFLECTIONS

1. Is historical literature free to use hyperbole if it could be recognized as such by the original audience? How does that affect the authority and reliability of the text?

2. Is the theological message of the Bible compromised if it uses legendary or fictional characters?

3. Should we expect God to do miracles in our lives today?

4. How do God's stories from the past help us to understand God today?

5. How should we proclaim God's sovereignty in history when faced with tragic current events?

Biblical Characters: Ahab and Jezebel, David, Deborah, Eli, Elijah, Elisha, Gideon, Hezekiah, Jehu, Jephthah, Jeroboam, Jeroboam II, Joshua, Josiah, Rehoboam, Samuel, Saul, Solomon, Uzziah

Extrabiblical Characters: Artaxerxes, Belshazzar, Cyrus, Darius, Hazael, Nebuchadnezzar, Sargon II, Sennacherib, Shalmaneser III, Shishak, Tiglath-Pileser III, Xerxes

Peoples: Aramaeans, Assyrians, Babylonians, Hittites, Mitannians, Persians, Philistines, Phoenicians, Sea Peoples

Biblical Places: Babylon, Bethel, Bethlehem, Damascus, Dan, Gibeah, Gibeon, Hazor, Hebron, Jericho, Jerusalem, Mount Tabor, Nineveh, Samaria, Shiloh, Susa, Tyre, Valley of Elah

Extrabiblical Texts: Babylonian Chronicles, Black Stele of Shalmaneser, Cyrus Cylinder, House of David Inscription, Limmu Lists, Merneptah Stele, Mesha Inscription, Sennacherib Prism

Concepts: Davidic covenant, historiography, judges cycle, theocracy

GOING TO THE NEXT LEVEL

Bill Arnold and Bryan Beyer, *Reading from the Ancient Near East* (Baker).

Victor Hamilton, *Handbook on the Historical Books* (Baker).

Alfred Hoerth, *Archaeology and the Old Testament* (Baker).

Alfred Hoerth, Gerald Mattingly, and Edwin Yamauchi, eds., *Peoples of the Old Testament World* (Baker).

David Howard, *Introduction to the Historical Books of the Old Testament* (Moody).

Walter Kaiser, *A History of Israel* (Broadman and Holman).

Kenneth Kitchen, *On the Reliability of the Old Testament* (Eerdmans).

V. Philips Long, *The Art of Biblical History* (Zondervan).

Eugene Merrill, *Kingdom of Priests* (Baker).

Ian Provan, V. Philips Long, and Tremper Longman, *Biblical History of Israel* (Westminster John Knox).

Wolfram von Soden, *The Ancient Orient* (Eerdmans).

Marc van de Mieroop, *A History of the Ancient Near East* (Blackwell).

John H. Walton, Victor Matthews, and Mark Chavalas, *IVP Bible Background Commentary: Old Testament* (InterVarsity Press).

Notes

1. In the same way, we don't try to follow stars even though God led the Magi by that means.

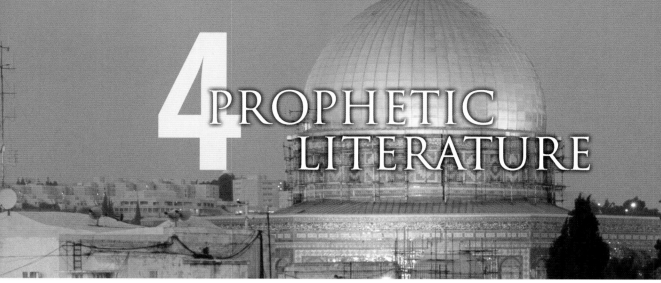

4 PROPHETIC LITERATURE

Dome of the Rock, Jerusalem.

ORIENTATION

- Prophecy should be seen as proclamation of God's plan rather than prediction of the future.
- Message and fulfillment are separate issues.
- Prophets understood and communicated their message.

YAHWEH FOCUS

- God responds to small steps in the right direction.
- God patiently calls his people to return to him.
- Rulers and empires are part of God's choreography of history.
- God responds to trust.
- God requires faithfulness and justice in his people.
- God's plan spans the entire scope of history.

"Prophetic literature is more interested in revealing God than in revealing the future."

KEY VERSES

- Isaiah 55:6–7   Seek the Lord
- Jeremiah 31:31–33   New covenant
- Lamentations 3:22–23   God's faithfulness
- Ezekiel 36:22–23   Holiness of God
- Daniel 4:34–35   Sovereignty of God
- Hosea 10:1–2   Israel's faithlessness
- Joel 2:28–32   Day of the Lord
- Amos 5:14–15   Call to return
- Obadiah 15   God's judgment on nations
- Jonah 3:10   God's mercy
- Micah 3:8–12   Role of the prophet
- Nahum 1:15   Future deliverance
- Habakkuk 3:16–18   Submission to God's plan and timing
- Zephaniah 3:11–13   Restoration of remnant
- Haggai 1:8   Rebuild the temple
- Zechariah 1:14–17   God's continued concern for Jerusalem
- Malachi 3:1–3   Purification to come

KEY PLOTLINE TERMS

- indictment
- judgment
- instruction
- aftermath

- message
- fulfillment
- preclassical prophecy
- classical prophecy

- apocalyptic
- day of the Lord
- messianic prophecy

ORIGINAL MEANING

Story Line of the Prophets in Their Times

Literary Perspective

BRIDGING CONTEXTS

Purpose of Prophetic Books

Prediction, Prophets, and God

Fulfillment and Revelation

Theological Perspectives

CONTEMPORARY SIGNIFICANCE

Scenario: Read Today's Headlines in the Bible

Thinking about Prophecy

Indictment Today

Judgment Today

Instruction Today

Aftermath Today

Recapitulation

PROPHETS		CRISIS PERIOD
PRECLASSICAL PROPHETS Moses, Deborah, Samuel, Elijah, Elisha	800	
Hosea, Amos Jonah Isaiah, Micah	700	ASSYRIAN CRISIS
Nahum, Habakkuk, Zephaniah Jeremiah, Ezekiel, Daniel	600	BABYLONIAN CRISIS
Joel, Obadiah Haggai, Zechariah Malachi	500	PERSIAN CRISIS
	400	

1 ORIGINAL MEANING

Many misconceptions about prophets and prophecy interfere with a proper understanding of these biblical books. People commonly think of prophets as those who utter mysterious predictions about the future. As a result, their books may be treated as encoded or mystical guides to events that will occur centuries later. One of the problems with this view is that it obscures the role of God. Another is that it forces onto prophecy an imbalanced perspective too heavily focused on the future.

In the Old Testament, prophecy is a message from God, more precisely, a proclamation of God's perspective and plan. A prophet is best understood as a spokesperson for deity—a mouthpiece for God, though not a passive one. If we use the analogy of a college course, prophecy is like the course syllabus that provides the professor's perspective on the course and her plan for the course. A student assistant who comes to the class and distributes the syllabus to class members fills the prophetic role. The assistant is not offering his own perspective or ideas about the professor's plan, but is only delivering the final product. The assistant may not fully agree with the plan and may fail to grasp all of the aspects of it, for it is not his plan—it is the professor's.[1] So as we begin the study of the prophets, we should think of the prophets as those who proclaim the divine plan in all of its fullness.

We do not know how prophets generally received their messages. Introductions to prophecies, such as "The word of the LORD came to me," offer very little help, but we know that the prophets were sufficiently confident of the source of their message that they unhesitatingly declared, "Thus says the LORD." Consistently in both the Old and New Testaments, the messages of the prophets are understood to

> **Prophets:**
>
> Those who proclaim the divine plan in all of its fullness.

be mediated by the Spirit of the Lord (for samples see Joel 2:28 and 2 Peter 1:20–21). Their messages were often poignant and poetic, compelling and controversial. Some trained to be prophets while others found their prophetic calling discomfiting.

STORY LINE OF THE PROPHETS IN THEIR TIMES

During the major periods of biblical prophecy, the prophets arose in times of crisis and need. As the times of crisis came more frequently and were more serious, the prophets took on a greater prominence in the biblical record. Beginning in the eighth century BC, prophecies were recorded and preserved, sooner or later to find their way into the biblical canon. The prophets from the eighth through the fifth centuries BC whose oracles are so preserved are called the classical prophets, and they have their own distinctive characteristics. The prophets from before that time are referred to as the "preclassical prophets."

Preclassical Prophets

Though Abraham is once described as a prophet (Gen. 20:7), the first Israelite prophet of stature is Moses. Unless we count Moses' blessings on the twelve tribes recorded in Deuteronomy 33, we have no prophetic oracles from Moses. Nevertheless, he stands as a recognized mouthpiece for God who, by virtue of that role, provided leadership for Israel during the crisis of the exodus from Egypt and the wilderness period. A non-Israelite contemporary prophet, Balaam, provides four oracles (Num. 22–24) that proclaim God's plan in the midst of the crisis that developed between Israel and the Moabites as God's people approached the land.

The only named prophet during the judges period is Deborah (Judg. 4–5), who was an instrument of God during the Canaanite crisis of her day. As the text moves into the historical books dealing with the Israelite monarchy, we find individuals such as Samuel, who presided over the transition to monarchy. He was God's spokesman in the anointing of the first two kings of Israel, Saul and David. Once the monarchy was established, the preclassical prophets' role often focused on advising the king, whether their advice was welcome or not. In this role as the conscience of the monarchy, we see Nathan, who both advised and condemned David (2 Sam. 7, 12), as well as numerous relatively unknown prophets named in passing in the books

Period	Function	Audience	Message	Examples
Pre-monarchy	Mouthpiece-leader	People	National guidance Maintenance of justice Spiritual overseer	Moses Deborah
				Transition: Samuel
Pre-classical	Mouthpiece-adviser	King and court	Military advice Pronouncement of rebuke or blessing	Nathan Elijah Elisha Micaiah
				Transition: North—Jonah South—Isaiah
Classical	Mouthpiece-social/spiritual commentator	People	Rebuke concerning current condition of society; leads to warnings of captivity, destruction, exile, and promise of eventual restoration Call for justice and repentance	Writing prophets Best example: Jeremiah

of Kings and Chronicles. Most prominent of the preclassical prophets of the monarchy period are Elijah and his successor, Elisha (see above). The crisis in Elijah's period centered on the attempt of Ahab and Jezebel to replace Yahweh as the divine king with Baal. During Elisha's time, the political and military threat posed by the Aramaeans was the focus. Elisha died just about one generation prior to the inauguration of the classical period.

Classical Prophets

Classical prophets continued the same function of offering advice and/or proclaiming condemnation of the king, but the main thrust of their oracles expanded well beyond the royal court as they became the social commentators of their day. We find that many of their messages were addressed to the people at large, though they still offered advice and condemnation. As a result, it is in the works of the classical prophets that we begin to hear of the threat that there will be

Artist's reconstruction of Nimrud (Kalah) on the Tigris.

© The British Museum

Artist's reconstruction of the temple complex at Babylon.

Courtesy of the Oriental Institute of the University of Chicago

Artist's reconstruction of the Ishtar Gate of Babylon where the ceremonial procession took place.

Courtesy of the Oriental Institute of the University of Chicago

invasion, destruction of cities and sanctuaries, deportation, and exile. It is therefore also from these that we begin to hear of the eventual return of a remnant, restoration to the land, and the emergence of an ideal king, the Messiah (Anointed One).

The first crisis of the classical period comes as a result of the establishment and expansion of the Assyrian Empire (see also pp. 164–65). The earliest of the "classical prophets," Amos and Hosea, began their ministries in the decades just preceding the Assyrian threat. The people of the northern kingdom, Israel, would not have considered themselves to be in a crisis situation. Amos and Hosea tried to warn them of the rottenness that was pervading their society and of the judgment that loomed on the horizon. The prophet Jonah also belongs to this period and was associated with the northern kingdom.

The Assyrian crisis impacted the northern kingdom first, so that is where we see the earliest prophetic activity. The Israelite kings and people were unresponsive to the word of the Lord, and the crisis overtook them quickly. They were forced to pay tribute as early as 743 BC, were invaded by the Assyrians in 732, and by 722 were gone—cities destroyed, people deported, absorbed by the burgeoning empire. Within a couple of years from when the Assyrian Empire began receiving tribute from Israel, classical prophecy spread to the southern kingdom of Judah. The earliest of the classical prophets of Judah were Isaiah and his contemporary Micah.

Isaiah received his call to office in 739 BC, the year King Uzziah died. He was an adviser to King Ahaz, who chose to ignore him, and to King Hezekiah, who experienced a remarkable deliverance from the Assyrian armies when he followed Isaiah's advice. The Assyrian Empire remained in power well beyond the time period of Isaiah and Micah, but once the wicked King Manasseh (Hezekiah's son) came to the throne of Judah (he ruled for the entire first half of the seventh century), there was no record of a continuing prophetic voice.

By 630 BC the Assyrian Empire was noticeably weakening. Though this would have looked like the end of a crisis, in reality it was only a transition to the next crisis, the Babylonian period. As the Assyrian crisis dissipated, the prophets returned. Habakkuk, Zephaniah, Nahum, and Jeremiah all began their ministries while the Assyrians lingered, and Jeremiah continued into the heart of the Babylonian crisis. These prophets proclaimed the downfall of Assyria and the rising threat of Babylon. The Babylonians extended their control into Judah in a number of stages, with each stage involving deportations at some level. Jeremiah was the most important voice during this time. He was called as a prophet as a teenager at a critical juncture in history. By 630 the Assyrian Empire had lost most of its influence and Ashurbanipal was on the brink of relinquishing control. Consequently, Judah had much more freedom, and in 628 the first phase of King Josiah's reform was initiated. The winds of freedom were also blowing in Babylonia, and in 626 the

Idols

If we take a close look at the indictment oracles of the prophets, one topic that is addressed with some frequency is idols. Idols served a central role in the worship and theology of the ancient Near East. One of the most important reasons why idols were prohibited in Israelite religion was that almost every use of the idols was based on the premise that the gods had needs. The gods' need of clothing was addressed as the idols were dressed in expensive and elaborate garments. The gods' need of housing was met in the luxurious temples that were built to house them. The gods' need of food and drink was supplied through the sacrifices and libations made by king, priests, and people. (This does not suggest that the people believed that the gods were totally incapable of providing for themselves, though in some of the literature, the gods are viewed as highly dependent on human worshipers.) As a result, it was not uncommon for people to believe that by meeting the needs of the gods, they were in some way obliging the gods or that, at the very least, the gods' gratitude would be expressed in bountiful ways. This created an environment ripe with the potential for manipulation or negotiation that derives from mutual dependency. In short, the idols were associated with a religious worldview in which the gods had limitations and could be bought or gently coerced.

In prophetic oracles such as those found in Isaiah 44 and Jeremiah 10, the idols are exposed as powerless and

The god Baal striding forth with lightning and mace; found in his temple at Ugarit.

Gold plated idol of Canaanite god from Ugarit.

Erich Lessing, Courtesy of Art Resources

the process that brought them into being as inherently flawed. Idols were generally carved from wood and then overlaid with gold. Just as Christians believe that the Scriptures were brought into being through a process that interweaved divine and human involvement and resulted in a divine product, so in the ancient world, people believed that though human artisans were involved in the making of idols, in the end, the product was divinely brought into being. In fact, the artisans threw their tools into the river as they declared that they had had no role in manufacturing the image. Technically speaking, an idol was not actually thought to be the god. Rather, people believed that the image became identified with the deity in much the same way as some Christian traditions believe that the bread and wine of the Eucharist become identified with the body and blood of Christ.

Relief of El the head of the Canaanite pantheon.

Erich Lessing, Courtesy of Art Resources

Babylonians declared their independence from Assyria and put their own king, Nabopolassar, on the throne. This was the first step in what would lead to the final downfall of Assyria and the rise of the Neo-Babylonian Empire. In the five years from 630 to 625, the world had turned upside down—mighty Assyria nearly gone, a fledgling empire on the horizon, and the beginning of reform in Judah. Jeremiah's call came in 627.

While Jeremiah continued as the most significant voice proclaiming God's message to those still in Judah in the early part of the sixth century, Ezekiel functioned among the exiles in Babylon. As with the Assyrian crisis, the waning days of the Babylonian Empire witnessed little prophetic activity. Yet throughout the Neo-Babylonian period and into the early days of the Persian period, an important prophetic voice was

Sign-Acts

In modern society, we have been inclined toward what is called "conceptual language" that represents reality in fixed and abstract ways. Postmodern society is leaning more toward "symbolic language" that is more concerned with feelings, imagination, and experience.* This latter approach is also more common in the ancient world. It not only accounts for the communication style of the prophets; it also recognizes the emphasis on stories and rhythms that we have been trying to demonstrate as the way that much of the Old Testament delivers its message to us.

In the Mari texts from over a millennium earlier than Ezekiel, prophets were already using symbolic actions and wordplays as a medium for their prophetic message. In one instance, a prophet devoured a raw lamb to announce an imminent danger that could devour the land.† Among the biblical prophets, Ezekiel used more symbolic actions than any other (more than a dozen instances; see especially chaps. 4, 5, 12, 21, 24). His life and his actions become part of his prophetic message. He not only spoke the word of the Lord, he dramatized the divine plan in creative visual ways. Daniel Block describes sign-acts as "dramatic performances designed to visualize a message and in the process to enhance its persuasive force so that the observers' perceptions of a given situation might be changed and their

beliefs and behavior modified."‡ Some of the symbolic acts were designed to shock the audience with the hope that their callousness could be penetrated as the judgment drew near (Ezek. 4:12–17).

Image and Word:

Examples of the Use of "Multimedia" among the Prophets

Nathan:	parable + declaration, 2 Samuel 12:1–11
Ahijah:	dramatic action + declaration, 1 Kings 11
Elijah:	declaration + miracle, 1 Kings 18:20–46
Elisha:	miracle + declaration, 2 Kings 4:1–7
	declaration + miracle, 2 Kings 5:8–14
Hosea:	living parable (marriage to Gomer, chaps. 1–3) + declaration (chaps. 4–14)
Jeremiah:	living parable + declaration, 13:1–11
	object lesson + declaration, 18:1–10, 19:1–13
Ezekiel:	object lesson + declaration, 4:1–5:17
	allegory + declaration, 15, 17, 24:1–14
	living parable + declaration, 24:15–27
Zechariah:	vision + declaration, 1–6
Malachi:	disputation format (truth claim→audience rebuttal→prophetic declaration)

*Pierre Babin, *The New Era in Religious Communication* (Minneapolis: Fortress, 1991), 149–51.
†J. J. M. Roberts, *The Bible and the Ancient Near East* (Winona Lake, IN: Eisenbrauns, 2002), 228–31.
‡D. Block, *The Book of Ezekiel, Chapters 1–24* (Grand Rapids: Eerdmans, 1997), 166.

sustained by Daniel. Taken to Babylon in 605 BC when Nebuchadnezzar first assumed control of Syro-Palestine, Daniel was to be trained for a role in the Babylonian court. He took a stand from the beginning that established his integrity and commitment to his convictions, and he had repeated opportunities to testify to the power of Yahweh over one of the greatest empires of history, persuading one of the most successful kings the world has known. Daniel interpreted Nebuchadnezzar's dreams and condemned his pride. He announced the fall of the Babylonian Empire to Belshazzar on the eve of its destruction by interpreting the handwriting on the wall. When the Persians took over, he was given high office even though he was then in his eighties, and he refused to change his prayer habits, thus disobeying a decree that had been designed to ensnare and destroy him. His famous survival of a night in the lions' den gave continued testimony to the sovereign power of Yahweh.

When the Babylonian Empire collapsed in 539 BC, the Persians came to power and the dramatic international changes occasioned another series of prophetic messengers. The crisis of the Persian period, however, was quite different from the previous two. Rather than a policy of deportation and exile, the Persians sponsored a program of return and restoration. Though the Israelites continued to chafe under foreign rule, the Persian regime was not repressive, nor did it threaten their land or their worship. The more significant crisis of this period could be called a corporate identity crisis. Are we still God's covenant people? Has God rejected us? When will God's promises come true? What is required of us in this time and in this situation? Will we have a king again? What about the temple? These were some of the questions that perplexed them and that the prophets addressed.

Along with the group that returned from exile to the land were the prophets Zechariah and Haggai. It is likely that the prophets Joel and Obadiah were also from this period, though their books do not offer firm chronological information. These prophets were active in the last decades of the sixth century. This left only Malachi in the fifth century, who brought a conclusion to the era of classical prophecy.

LITERARY PERSPECTIVE

Oracles were often introduced with "Thus says the LORD" or "The word of the LORD came to X saying. . . ." The oracles take several different literary forms, including legal disputation (Hos. 4:1–3; Mic. 6:1–5), parables (Isa. 5:1–7), lament (Jer. 8:18–9:2), and woe (Isa. 28:1–4). Most important, however, is the recognition of the various types of oracles.

760 Amos
760 Jonah
750 Hosea
740–700 Isaiah
730 Micah
650 Nahum
630 Zephaniah
630 Habakkuk
627–575 Jeremiah
593–570 Ezekiel
605–535 Daniel
520 Haggai
520 Zechariah
500 Joel
500 Obadiah
480 Malachi

4 PROPHETIC LITERATURE

Types of Oracles

The messages that the prophets delivered often fell into four general categories. The first category is *indictment*. One of the roles of the prophet was to identify offenses or errors of the king or the people. For a king, this might involve not relying on the Lord or failing to rid the land of false worship. Kings of northern Israel were guilty of sponsoring worship that was contrary to the law. Obviously, indictment focused on the past or the present. The offenses could be religious, political, or personal.

Often coupled with indictment, the second category is *judgment*. These oracles give either general or occasionally specific information about what God is going to do to punish the offenses named in the indictment. Sometimes, especially in postexilic prophecy, the prophets were not announcing future judgment, but were identifying a current

Day of the Lord

The expression "the day of the LORD" was used by the prophets to indicate the time when the current state of affairs would be replaced by the Lord's intended order of things. Most of the oracles in the prophetic literature represent movement toward this ideal condition. What becomes plain as prophecy unfolds is that the new state is to be achieved not through one immense intervention of God (though such an intervention may be involved in the last step), but through a process of dealing with inequities that have become a great threat to the desired end.

The result of this is that there may be numerous "days of the Lord" before *the* day of the Lord that will inaugurate a new order that will never again be at risk or destabilized. In this way, the overthrow of the Assyrian Empire can rightly be considered a day of the Lord; likewise the fall of Babylon. The destruction of Jerusalem and the temple surely qualified as a day of the Lord, as did Josiah's campaign to reform the priesthood.

Some background can be gained by comparing this concept with the annual Mesopotamian enthronement festival known as the *akitu.* During the course of this festival, the deity determined the destiny of his subjects and reestablished order as he had done long ago when he defeated the forces of chaos. In fact, the Babylonian creation account *Enuma Elish,* which recounts Marduk's defeat of Tiamat and his elevation to the head of the pantheon, was read during the course of the festival. Though the texts never refer to the *akitu* festival as the "Day of Marduk," there are some similarities. For example, the Day of

Yahweh may be viewed as the occasion on which Yahweh will ascend to his throne with the purpose of binding chaos and bringing justice to the world order. The destinies of his subjects will be determined as the righteous are rewarded and the wicked suffer the consequences of their rebellion and sin. For Israel there is no firm evidence that this was represented in a regular ritual, but it is rather reflected in a historical expectation.

In the day of the Lord, justice is done. This is a positive time for those who have been victims, but a day of reckoning for those who have been oppressors. It has political, social, spiritual, and cosmic ramifications and can include reversal or restructuring of any number of conditions. For example, overlords will serve those who were formerly their vassals; the poor will be elevated over the rich who had exploited them; people will again call on the name of the Lord, and there will be darkness even at midday. This reversal is a common motif in prophetic literature dealing with the day of the Lord and is called a "world upside down."

The people of Judah and Israel had always anticipated that the day of the Lord would be a time of rejoicing for them. They expected that their enemies would be destroyed and their nation would be exalted to become a chief of the nations, with a Davidic king ruling over a vast empire. Early on, prophets like Amos doused such optimism by insisting that the Israelites would be counted among God's enemies who were ripe for punishment. Thus the day of the Lord became widely proclaimed by the prophets to convey God's approaching judgment on Israel and Judah.

condition as God's judgment (e.g., Hag. 1:7–11). Judgments were most often political but could also be spiritual or economic. These oracles focused mostly on the future but occasionally on the present. The future judgment that was announced was usually considered imminent rather than in the distant future. Nevertheless, it was not usually something that would be expected to happen in the immediate future (i.e., the next week or month). Judgment announced by the prophets could be postponed in some cases. Judgment oracles are more common than any other type of oracle. They were the most unpopular and often put the prophets at odds with the king or people. As the spokesman, the prophet was at times implicated in the messages that he brought such that an oracle of defeat by enemies could lead to a charge of treason.

On much less frequent occasions, the prophets instructed their audience concerning what they needed to do. Often these *instruction* oracles would consist of general advice, such as "Return to the LORD" or "Repent." The postexilic prophets have a higher proportion of instruction oracles and deal with more specific issues (cf. Malachi).

Finally, the fourth category can be called *aftermath* oracles. These address what God's plan includes in the aftermath of the announced (or

CATEGORIES OF PROPHETIC ORACLE

Categories	Description	Oracular Preexilic Emphasis	Postexilic Emphasis
Indictment	Statement of the offense	Focus primarily on idolatry, ritualism, and social justice	Focus on not giving proper honor to the Lord
Judgment	Punishment to be carried out	Primarily political and projected for near future	Interprets recent or current crises as punishment
Instruction	Expected response	Very little offered; generally return to God by ending wicked conduct	Slightly more offered; more specifically addressed to particular situation
Aftermath	Affirmation of future hope or deliverance	Presented and understood as coming after an intervening period of judgment	Presented and understood as spanning a protracted time period Religious: Now Socioeconomic: Potential Political: Eventual

The Western Wall.

Z. Radovan, Jerusalem

experienced) judgment. In most cases, they are messages of deliverance, hope, restoration, and promise. In just a few cases, however, prophets will speak of trying times yet to come in the restoration period (e.g., Ezek. 38–39; Zech. 14). Aftermath oracles, along with judgment oracles, are the ones that look to the future and that are most logically associated with fulfillment. Nevertheless, other categories at times are named as being fulfilled.[2] The aftermath oracles attach more easily to a midrange or distant future.

Once it is understood what a prophet has to say in each of these oracular categories, the message of the prophet can be summarized.

Apocalyptic Literature

Apocalyptic prophecy is a specialized form of prophetic literature that developed as a subcategory of classical prophecy and became

Dreams, Divination, and Prophecy

Dreams, divination, and prophecy are all means by which deities were believed to communicate their instructions or plans to certain humans in the ancient world. Prophecy was common in Israel, dreams were occasional, and divination was prohibited. Divination involved using a mechanism (often the entrails of sacrificed animals) to receive information from deity—usually answers to specific questions. The closest procedure allowed to the Israelites was the use of Urim and Thummim—the oracular stones that the high priest could use when an inquiry needed to be made to Yahweh (Ex. 28:30; Num. 27:21). What are the differences between these various methods?

© The British Museum

Model of a liver used by diviners to read omens from the liver of sacrificed animals.

1. Divination was initiated by human beings seeking information. For both dreams and prophecy, the human recipients could take steps that would prepare them for receiving the communication from the deity, but God would have to initiate.

2. Divination usually dealt with yes or no questions, while the other two procedures could accommodate longer and more specific communications.

3. Dreams and divination both required trained technicians to interpret the resulting message. Prophecies were also subject to interpretation, but despite potentially complex or obscure aspects, the basic message was typically much more transparent.

4. Divination was forbidden because the practitioners of it operated from a worldview contrary to that promoted in the Bible. This worldview assumed that there was a realm of knowledge and power outside of the gods. In this view, the diviners were considered to be powerful in their ability to coerce the gods or work around them. The axis of power was associated with the practitioner. In short, divination was too closely associated with the realms of magic and occult power. Prophecy is not like mantic divination, which required knowledge and training in specialized literature (e.g., spells or omen texts) or the use of magical rituals (spoken words, prescribed actions or gestures), but instead was premised on direct inspiration by the deity. Dreams were often used for outsiders, uninitiated, or those who had no access to prophets.

common toward the end of that period. This subgenre, found primarily in Daniel and Zechariah in the Old Testament and in Revelation in the New Testament,[3] has a number of distinguishing features. Apocalypses often involve visions portraying an angelic interpreter who guides the prophet and converses with him. The angel may show the prophet events in the heavenly realms or in select locations on earth to convey certain realities and activities. He will then offer an

Oracles and Prophecy in the Ancient World

Since Christians believe that there is only one God, and since they understand that prophecy contains messages from that God, they are often inclined to think that prophecy in the Bible was a unique phenomenon. While we may be justified in thinking that any prophecy outside the Bible was fraudulent, the fact remains that biblical prophecy is part of a long tradition of prophecy in the ancient Near East. Even the Bible makes this fact known to us in narratives about Balaam and other narratives about the prophets of Baal sponsored by Ahab and Jezebel.

The most prominent corpus of prophetic messages is found in about fifty letters preserved on tablets found in the royal archives of the town of Mari. These date to early in the second millennium BC (contemporary with the events of Genesis). The letters report to the king prophecies that were brought to the attention of local officials. The prophecies come from various deities and instruct the king in military matters and other issues of government policy. Occasionally they call for certain rituals to be performed.

A second corpus of nearly thirty oracles comes from the Neo-Assyrian period (seventh century, soon after the time of Isaiah). The primary deity is Ishtar of Arbela, and the prophecies typically forecast victory and prosperity for the king in his various undertakings. Some of the oracles are collected on large tablets that served as archive copies, while others are smaller texts concerning single oracles. The oracles are fairly brief, ranging from a sentence to a paragraph or two at the most. The prophetic oracles that are known from the ancient Near East are similar to the prophecies that have been referred to as "preclassical."

Prophets were often identified as madmen—a consequence of the fact that it was not unusual for them to receive their messages while entranced. One of the titles used for prophets in Akkadian literature is *muhhu,* which is usually translated "ecstatic." Nevertheless, prophets were taken very seriously. The very act of speaking their word was considered determinative in bringing their message to reality. This was

© The British Museum

An Assyrian prophecy text.

true regardless of the social standing of the prophet. Some prophets were part of the temple personnel or on the king's council of advisers. But it is not at all unusual for the prophet to be a layperson or a commoner. In Babylon or Assyria, the word of the prophet would be subject to confirmation. This was accomplished by using divination procedures. The question would be posed as to whether or not the message was to be received favorably, and the divination priest would look for the answer to be "written on" the entrails of the sacrificed animal.*

---

*Adapted from J. Walton, V. Matthews, and M. Chavalas, *The IVP Bible Background Commentary: Old Testament* (Downers Grove: InterVarsity Press, 2000), 581–82. For discussion and translation of these ancient Near Eastern prophetic texts see Martti Nissinen, *Prophets and Prophecy in the Ancient Near East* (Altanta: SBL, 2003).

Mari Prophecy

Ahatum, the servant girl of Dagan-Malik, fell into an ecstatic trance, and she spoke as follows, saying, "Zimri-Lim, even though you have neglected me, I will bend over you in love. Your enemies I will deliver into your hand."*

---

*From J. J. M. Roberts, *The Bible and the Ancient Near East* (Winona Lake, IN: Eisenbrauns, 2002), 193.

interpretation of that which the prophet is shown. In the process, he may unveil a future time of trouble and/or deliverance. One of the most noticeable characteristics of this literature is its use of symbols, significant numbers, and mythological images. It draws heavily on both biblical and extrabiblical literature. It tends to schematize periods of history and numbers.

It is important to recognize, however, that each detail in an apocalyptic vision does not necessarily carry symbolic significance. Even the details that do carry symbolic significance may not be transparent to us. A second important principle to remember is that the apocalyptic vision is not the message itself, but rather is the vehicle or occasion for the message. So, for instance, the message of the first vision of Zechariah (1:7–17) is not that there are going to be four horses of different colors in a myrtle grove. The message is laid out very clearly in verses 14 through 17. The apocalyptic vision is simply a medium. The symbols are occasionally part of the revelation (e.g., horns = kingdoms in Dan. 7:24) but more often serve to conceal or obscure certain aspects of the events portrayed in the vision.

An artist's reconstruction of Zechariah's lampstand following R. North.

Susanna Vagt

Postexilic Issues

As groups returned from exile to resettle in the land of Israel, many issues had to be resolved. The first and most important was the issue of monotheism. The law and the prophets had long endorsed monotheism, but prior to the exile, the acceptance of this important tenet was halfhearted in the best of times. The shock of the destruction of Jerusalem and the temple appears to have finally made the necessary impact, as those returning from Babylon seem at last to have grasped the big picture. We see a stronger commitment to monotheism and a realization of the implications for their worship and behavior. With the influence of Ezra, there is a reorientation to the law of Moses as the foundation of their society.

A second issue that the returnees had to cope with was their continuing political status as a province of the Persian Empire. Without a king, their attention shifted to the important leadership roles of the priests and the Levites. Related to this, the temple took on an even greater role than it had had previously. The people of Judah began to realize that the presence of God established a spiritual kingdom that was of higher significance than the physical kingdom. They came to understand the restoration in terms of a theocracy rather than as dependent on a monarchy. Yet at the same time, nationalism surged and they longed for their independence.

Susanna Vagt

The winged figure of Ahuramazda, who was the supreme god of Zoroastrianism, a religion practiced primarily in Persia.

A great concern in this period was assimilation. The Israelites who had remained behind in the land had intermarried with peoples that the Assyrians and Babylonians had resettled in their territories. During the years while one segment of the people was in exile, the others had then become hopelessly assimilated. This group eventually came to be referred to as the Samaritans and were looked on as outcasts. Yet at the same time, those who returned from exile did not always see the importance of remaining ethnically distinct from the other inhabitants of the land. Both Ezra and Nehemiah had to deal with this obstacle to the covenant as the pros and cons of inclusivism were debated and tested.

Finally, the book of Chronicles built the historical pattern of retribution that urged the people to recognize that in the past, obedience and faithfulness brought the favor and blessing of God, while turning away from God and his covenant had brought nothing but pain, death, and destruction.

The postexilic prophets had the task of helping the remnant of Israel understand its identity and priorities in the aftermath of the confusion of the exile. The confusion was represented in three different conclusions about the exile. The first alternative was to conclude that Yahweh their God had forsaken them and wanted nothing to do with them. Those who reached such conclusions would have simply resorted to the local deities with whom they had so long flirted. A second alternative was to conclude that Yahweh had been defeated by the more powerful god(s) of the Babylonians. The natural response to this conclusion would be to acknowledge the superiority of the Babylonian gods and worship them. The third alternative was the one encouraged by the prophets both before and after the destruction of Jerusalem. This view accepted that the destruction was not God's problem, but theirs. Consequently, they needed to recognize that their sin and unfaithfulness to the covenant had brought God's judgment and he wanted them to be repentant and to return to him.

National Lamentation

The book of Lamentations is included among the prophets in the English Bible and has traditionally and popularly been connected with Jeremiah, though no claims of authorship are made. The book is a genre unto itself in the Bible, although there are close parallels in the literature of Mesopotamia. These laments are legitimate literary vehicles for prophecy in that they identify the calamity as the judgment of God, identify the offenses of the people, and express hope for restoration. Though they are not oracles in the sense that they are presented in the context of "Thus says the LORD," the prophets use a wide variety of poetic genres to deliver their messages. As with prophetic messages, these laments arise in the context of crisis and offer insight into God's plan in light of the crisis.

REFLECTIONS

1. Discuss the differences between classical and preclassical prophets.
2. What is the significance of the labels *mouthpiece* and *spokesperson*.
3. What parts of their revelation did the prophets understand? What might they not have understood?
4. How does apocalyptic prophecy relate to classical prophecy?
5. In what ways can the postexilic period be considered a time of crisis?
6. In what ways was Israelite prophecy different from other prophecy in the ancient world?

Notes
1. For fuller development of this analogy, see Bridging Contexts, p. 252.
2. For instance, Hosea 11:1 is in an indictment oracle, yet it is identified as being fulfilled in Matthew 2:15.
3. There are also a number of apocalyptic works from the period between the Old and New Testaments and from the period just after the New Testament.

CHAPTER

BRIDGING CONTEXTS

PURPOSE OF PROPHETIC BOOKS

In the most basic sense, the purpose of the prophetic books was to collect the oracles of those individuals who were considered to be the true prophets of God. Beyond that, however, many of the prophetic books show clear evidence of having been carefully edited so that they are not simply anthologies of oracles, but convey a literary and/or theological purpose. Such purposes are sometimes evident in the themes of the prophet or in the arrangement of the oracles.

Isaiah, Jeremiah, Ezekiel, and sometimes Daniel are traditionally referred to as the "major prophets" because of the length of their books. Hosea through Malachi make up the Book of the Twelve and are traditionally referred to as the "minor prophets."

Isaiah (740–700 BC)

The purpose of the book of Isaiah is to demonstrate the trustworthiness of the Lord. The first king whom Isaiah served, Ahaz, did not trust the Lord. He ignored Isaiah's advice and followed his own schemes. This led to defeat and servitude at the hands of the Assyrians. Ahaz's son, Hezekiah, in contrast, trusted the Lord, and Jerusalem was delivered from Sennacherib and the Assyrians. In the second half of the book, the exiles are also encouraged to trust the Lord to bring deliverance, responding like Hezekiah rather than like Ahaz.

A significant theme is hope in a future ideal Davidic king. From the exaltation of Jerusalem (Isa. 2), to the child who is to reign (Isa. 9), to the peace and stability of the reign of the Davidic heir (Isa. 11), to the role of the Servant (Isa. 42–53), the prophet supplies the template for much of the development of the messianic profile.

Jeremiah (ca. 627–575 BC)

The purpose of the book of Jeremiah is to call the people of Judah back to faithful dependence on the Lord. He warns them of the punishment of exile that is coming quickly upon them at the hands of the "foe from the north," which ends up being the Babylonians.

Jeremiah is commonly known as the weeping prophet as a result of his dismay at the message of judgment he is obligated to bring to his people as they are poised precariously on the brink of destruction. In the context of long-term theology, however, his greatest contribution is found in his proclamation of the new covenant (Jer. 31:31–33). As this unfolds, it becomes the basis of the covenant initiated by Christ with his church.

Lamentations

The book of Lamentations is not connected to a particular prophet, though tradition sees it as composed by Jeremiah. It records a number of poems that express the sadness of the people of Judah over the tragedy of the destruction of Jerusalem in 586 BC. The people weep from the feeling that God has abandoned them. The poems show the people's sense of guilt, confession, and repentance as they realize how deeply they have hurt God by their sin and unfaithfulness.

Ezekiel (ca. 593–570 BC)

The purpose of the book of Ezekiel is to tell the Israelites that destruction of the city of Jerusalem is coming. Ezekiel is already in exile, but he warns the people still in Israel that the Lord's presence is about to depart from the temple leaving the people exposed to Babylonian invasion. Ezekiel prophesies concerning a new covenant just as his contemporary Jeremiah did. But probably one of the most important themes in the book is to be found in the oft-repeated refrain, "Then you will know that I am Yahweh." He constantly anticipates the time when the people will wake up and return to the Lord. He sees a people reborn in the vision of the valley of dry bones (Ezek. 37). Following the fall of Jerusalem and the destruction of the temple, he tells of a future restoration including a vision of a glorious new temple. He sees a time when God's presence will return to the temple (Ezek. 40–48).

Daniel (ca. 605–535 BC)

The purpose of the book of Daniel concerns the sovereignty of God. As Daniel and his friends trust the Lord, he shows himself able to protect and deliver. Daniel's visions proclaim God's sovereignty over kings, nations, and empires. At the same time, his prophecies tell the people of Israel that the kingdom they are waiting for will be longer in coming than expected. In the meantime, they are to live out their faith in the midst of an unbelieving world, trusting in God for deliverance and protection.

MINOR PROPHETS

Prophet	Approx. Date BC	Message or Major Theme
Hosea	750	God's love for Israel
Joel	500	Day of the Lord
Amos	760	Israel's injustice
Obadiah	500	Judgment on Edom
Jonah	760	God's compassion
Micah	730	Judah's injustice
Nahum	650	Judgment on Nineveh
Habakkuk	630	Judgment on the Babylonians
Zephaniah	630	Day of the Lord
Haggai	520	Priorities and the construction of the temple
Zechariah	520	Comfort for Judah and call to repentance
Malachi	480	Israel's relationship with God

Messianic Prophecy

In light of the distinction we have made between message and fulfillment (see "Fulfillment and Revelation," pp. 252–54), we would do well to ask whether messianic prophecy should be defined in terms of one or the other or both. Since there are prophecies that New Testament authors indicate are fulfilled in Christ but show no indication that the original author or audience understood them in messianic terms (e.g., Hos. 11:1), it would seem more appropriate to identify messianic prophecy in terms of fulfillment. In this case, any prophecy fulfilled by Jesus would be labeled messianic. Then we do not have to be concerned with whether the prophet was intentionally speaking of Jesus or not.

The next question to ask is whose identification of fulfillment counts? If we want authoritative and sure identifications, we must find them in inspired literature—that is, the New Testament. Beyond those, we may find other fulfillments that have been accepted as true by consensus throughout church history that we consider to have a high degree of plausibility (e.g., Gen. 3:15) and would therefore label as messianic. Without the support of text or tradition, the identifications become speculations that may rarely warrant our support.

Perhaps it would be valuable then to list messianic prophecies in several distinct categories.

In those cases where we can identify messianic intentions in the message (class I), the information might be quite general in nature. It could be compared to a job description for the pastor of a church—the job description has a particular function in mind rather than a specific individual. But when the individual is found, it will not be a surprise that he looks a lot like the job description.

Finally, what role does messianic prophecy play in apologetics? We would have to admit that the messianic prophecies in classes IV and V would not carry much weight with someone who did not acknowledge the credibility of the New Testament authors or the church. Looking only at those Old Testament passages, they will see little to persuade them that Jesus is the Messiah. When we investigate how Matthew used messianic prophecies, however, we will find a different sort of apologetic than we are accustomed to. We might call it a secondary apologetic. The primary evidence of Jesus' claims is to be found in his life and teachings. Once these provide sufficient data to suggest the plausibility of the hypothesis that Jesus is the Messiah, the secondary evidence is presented to demonstrate that the claim is in accord with Old Testament prophecy, going beyond the well-established expectations even to some fulfillments that no one had ever considered.

Class	When Recognized	Key Elements	Examples
I	Recognized as messianic by the prophet when spoken (in message)	Davidic King Anointed	Isa. 9:6; 11:1–16; Jer. 23:5–6; 30:9; Ezek. 37:21–28; Amos 9:11; Mic. 5:2–5; Zech. 9:9
II	Recognized as messianic by later Old Testament authors (becomes part of expectation)	Quoted in later class I context	Gen. 49:10; 2 Sam. 7:12–16
III	Recognized as messianic during intertestamental period	Found in the literature such as the Apocrypha, Pseudepigrapha, and Dead Sea Scrolls	Num. 24:17–19; Deut. 18:18–19
IV	Recognized as messianic by New Testament authors after the fact (in fulfillment)	If fulfillment had not taken place, Christ's messianic claim would have been suspect	Ps. 22; Isa. 7:14; Hos. 11:1; Zech. 12:10
V	Recognized as messianic by the church after the fact with no support from text	Tradition and consensus important to establish credibility, but lower in level of authority	Gen. 3:15

Book of the Twelve

The Christian tradition has labeled the twelve prophetic books following Daniel in the Protestant canon the "minor prophets." As Augustine noted, the Twelve are not of lesser importance than prophets like Isaiah or Jeremiah, but they are called "minor" because of the brevity of their writings. Prior to New Testament times and continuing today, Jewish tradition has understood this prophetic collection as a literary unity known as the Book of the Twelve. It is counted as a single book in the Hebrew canon and tells the "spiritual history" of the divided kingdoms of Israel and Judah. The story line of the Book of the Twelve begins and ends with the threat of divine judgment in the day of the Lord and a call to repentance in the exhortation to "return" to Yahweh. On a positive note, the Book of the Twelve tracks the story of worship renewal and the return of a remnant of the Hebrew community to covenant relationship with Yahweh. On a negative note, the Book of the Twelve tells the story of covenant violations by the people of God—as both the kingdoms of Israel and Judah are swept into exile. The plotline of the Book of the Twelve is held together by the repeated themes of social justice, worship renewal, God's sovereignty, and the ultimate restoration of a unified Israel under Davidic kingship. Each book has its own contribution to make to this plotline, but we have identified two books, Jonah and Habakkuk, for more extensive comment, particularly since they most clearly differ from the normal pattern of collected oracles.

Jonah

Jonah is quite different from the other prophetic books in that it contains mostly narrative, includes a psalm, and has only one short oracle (3:4). Since it is principally a narrative about a prophet rather than a collection of oracles, it is essential that we consider its purpose in light of the narrative form.

Jonah is a reluctant prophet. He thinks that he can avoid his commission by fleeing in the opposite direction. Despite his one-way ticket to Tarshish, God brings him back by special carrier (a large fish) before he even reaches his destination. There is no one in the book who is less responsive to God's word than Jonah. Both the sailors and the Ninevites acknowledge the power of God with far less information to go on than this Hebrew prophet.

The town of Joppa today.

Jonah offers theological justification for his reluctance in Jonah 4:2: He knew God would be compassionate, and in Jonah's opinion, the Ninevites were not deserving of compassion. The message of the book emerges when God puts Jonah in the position of having received compassion that he did not deserve (the benefit of the plant, 4:6). Since Jonah resented God's undeserved compassion on the Ninevites, God took away the benefit of the plant to see whether Jonah would respond consistently ("Oh well, I didn't do anything to deserve that anyway!"). Instead, Jonah was just as angry about losing his undeserved benefit as he was about the Ninevites getting theirs.

The book of Jonah teaches that compassion and grace are not given by God based on what we deserve, but based on our responsive steps in the right direction. When people respond to God, he responds to them. This is an important message to include among the prophetic books, in which the prophets are continually giving oracles of judgment against Israel and Judah. What does God expect for them? Even small steps in the right direction will bring gracious and compassionate responses.

Habakkuk

A second minor prophet book that easily moves beyond themes to purpose, Habakkuk, has a much higher incidence of oracular material. Of particular interest, however, is the way the book focuses on a central issue—the justice of God's dealings with nations. The book opens with a prayer of lament: Why does God tolerate such injustice in his people? The Lord's answer is an oracle of judgment against Judah at the hands of the Babylonians. This answer perplexes Habakkuk, for he cannot understand how God's justice can be satisfied by using a wicked nation that is even worse than Judah to bring punishment upon them. After God replies that the Babylonians too will be punished in due course for their wickedness, the book closes with a prayer of praise and submission to God's plan.

Watchtower in the Samaritan hills.

PREDICTION, PROPHETS, AND GOD

When many people think of prophecy, they think of prediction—the telling of the future before it happens. Though the prophets of the Old Testament often give information about the future, the word *prediction* is inadequate to describe what their messages are. The prophets are simply messengers; the messages they deliver about the future are not their messages, but God's. Therefore, it would not be technically accurate to speak of the prophets as "predicting"—they are simply delivering a message from God. Would it be more appropriate to say that God is predicting? In general, perhaps we could, but not in the sense that the word is meaningfully used in English. When someone "predicts" something, the usual implication is that the person doing the predicting is not in a position to influence the outcome. The "prediction" would lose its force if the one predicting could make the prediction come true. If we think of the word in these terms, it could truly be said that God does not, indeed cannot, predict—for there is nothing outside of his influence. Alternatively, when someone indicates that certain future events will occur in an area that is under his or her control, instead of a "prediction," we call it a "plan." This is a much more acceptable descriptive term for prophecy—it is the proclamation of God's plan. The plan as it is proclaimed by the prophets is intertwined with Israel's history and founded on the covenant—particularly its blessings and curses (Deut. 27–28).

The term *plan* is also more suitable for two additional reasons. First, it encompasses not only the prophecies concerning the future, but also those that concern the past and present of the prophet and his audience. Second, it helps us to understand what is happening when a prophecy about the future is revoked or changed. For instance, when we understand that Jonah's message to the Ninevites was a proclamation of God's plan rather than a prediction concerning what would happen in forty days, we can see that the response of the Ninevites could have occasioned a change in God's plans.

Prophets and Missionaries

Often the popular misconceptions about prophets lead people to think of them as something like missionaries. So, for instance, if the main objective of the prophets is understood in terms of leading people to repentance and delivering a message of hope, it would be easy to compare them to missionaries who try to do the same as they spread the gospel message. In light of what we have learned about the prophets, however, this equation becomes problematic. The two elements most emphasized by missionaries would fit into the oracular categories of instruction (repentance) and aftermath (hope). These are the two least frequent oracle types among the prophets, who spend twice as much time proclaiming indictment and judgment. Moreover, it was not unusual for the prophets to omit instruction and/or hope altogether—something no missionary would do.

The contrast becomes more striking when we consider specifically the example of Jonah, who, oddly enough, is the one most frequently associated with missionary work. A moment's thought, however, will reveal the differences:

1. Jonah does not want to go, so much so that he flees in the opposite direction.
2. The only message Jonah preaches in the book is coming destruction—no call to repentance, no hope for deliverance, no instruction about God—in fact, God is not even mentioned in Jonah's proclamation.
3. Jonah is disappointed and angry when the people of Nineveh respond favorably.

In short, then, Jonah does not have a missionary attitude, he does not have a missionary message, and he does not have a missionary objective. It is not enough to say that he is delivering a message of God cross-culturally—so was Moses with the plagues. Likewise, it is not enough to base such a conclusion on the result, that is, Nineveh's repentance. That was a panic response to a threat, not an acknowledgment of the claims of God on their lives or an acceptance of his lordship. The only "salvation" they experienced was that the destruction of their city was delayed. There was no blood of Christ to claim, and no indication is given that they intended to become people of the covenant, accept Yahweh as their God, and throw away their idols.

Christians and missionaries who go out to represent Christianity often identify their call as serving as a "light to the nations." The phrase comes from Isaiah, where the Servant of the Lord was called a light to the nations (Isa. 42:6; 49:6; 51:4). Since the phrase is drawn from the prophetic literature, there may be a temptation to use it as a common identifying mandate for both prophets and missionaries. As a description of the Servant of the Lord, the term is appropriately applied to Jesus by Simeon in Luke 2:32. Paul in turn takes it up as his commission in Acts 13:47 as may every Christian (Matt. 5:14). Consequently, it is an appropriate objective for missionaries, but the prophets are never called that. In the end, we do justice neither to prophets nor to missionaries by putting them in the same category.

The analogy of a syllabus in a college course was introduced in the Original Meaning section (see p. 231). The following comparisons develop the analogy further:

1. The syllabus represents the professor's plan, not her predictions of what will occur on each day.

2. The syllabus is meant to be reliable and normative but also is characterized by a certain amount of fluidity or flexibility at the professor's discretion.

3. A student assistant who handed out the syllabus would not be mistaken as the source of the plan, but would be understood as a messenger. The syllabus is not the messenger's opinion of what the professor will be doing in the course.

4. The primary role of the syllabus is to inform students about the nature of the course and, ultimately, about the nature of the professor—the course schedule that indicates certain topics to be addressed on certain dates is only one mechanism for achieving that goal. By publishing her plan for the course, the professor expects that the students will come to know her, her desires for the course, and her expectations of them. It is not unimportant, but is of secondary significance that they come to "know the future."

5. The syllabus is intended to be clear, not cryptic or mystical, as it communicates the plan for the course. The professor knows what she is talking about, and she expects the students to understand. She further expects them to respond by shaping their own plans to coincide with her plans and expectations.

FULFILLMENT AND REVELATION

God generally did not reveal to the prophets details of how their prophecies would be fulfilled. Occasionally a few specifics were given (e.g., the identity of the enemy who would bring destruction), but that is the exception rather than the rule. If prophecy is understood as proclaiming God's plan, fulfillment could be understood as how that plan actually worked out in history. For example, the plan could be that God would punish the Israelites for their covenant violations by bringing an invading army against them to take away their covenant benefits. The fulfillment would be that the Babylonians invaded Israel (on three different occasions) and eventually destroyed Jerusalem and the temple, killed their king, took many into exile, and annexed them into the Babylonian Empire. Or for another example, the plan could be that God would supply a true and just king who would usher in an idyllic age of peace and prominence for Israel. The fulfillment would entail matching up those expectations to particular individuals and particular times in history, including association with the Messiah, Jesus Christ. Both of these examples concern God's plan for the future. But prophecy could also identify God's plan in past or present events. In these cases, however, one would not usually anticipate fulfillment.

In light of these observations, the distinction to be made is that the *revelation* of God through the prophet to his people entailed a plan, not usually the details of the fulfillment of that plan. We could say, then, that the *revealed plan* constituted the *authoritative message* of the prophet. This message was understood by the prophet, was communicated to and understood by the audience, and can be understood by any subsequent interpreter of the biblical text through the common principles of reading and interpretation. This message does not change, and it carries the authority of God's Word throughout time.

When it comes time for later biblical authors (either in the Old Testament or the New Testament) to identify or discuss the fulfillment of the plan, they in effect are providing a new level of authoritative message. Often they are not trying to clarify what the original prophet's message was; they are offering God's revelation of how fulfillment has transpired. Even when the fulfillment takes a very different path from what anyone in the prophet's time could have understood, the fulfillment does not change the original message. In this way, the Old Testament prophet's message must be distinguished from the fulfillment of that message. Since the New Testament authors who identified fulfillment were inspired, we have no cause to doubt their identifications even if we could not have come to them ourselves through the prophet's message.

What is important when we read the Bible is to understand the revelation God is offering through his Word. In the prophetic oracles, that revelation is connected to the message of the prophet, and that is what we ought to focus on. In New Testament texts, the revelation of God sometimes entails identifying fulfillments of those prophecies and, in those texts, that legitimately becomes our focus. The point is that it is a mistake to read prophecy only in light of its fulfillment as if that is the only thing that is important.

If we are careful to maintain the distinction between the prophet's message and the fulfillment of that message, we will be able to preserve the integrity of both the Old Testament in its context and the New Testament as it goes about its business. The Old Testament is the revelation of God by virtue of an authoritative message of the prophet proclaiming the plan of God. The New Testament is the revelation of God by virtue of the authoritative message of the author proclaiming the fulfillment of that divine plan. In the Old Testament, the message does not include fulfillment; in the New Testament, the message often *is* the fulfillment. Neither can be ignored, and neither determines what the other must be.

THEOLOGICAL PERSPECTIVES

Yahweh Delivers

It is fitting that it is in the book of Isaiah, whose name means "Yahweh delivers," that we find the most extensive development of this great theological theme. We have already noted that the prophets were especially active during times of crisis. Particularly at those times it becomes important to believe that the God in whom one trusts is able to bring deliverance from crisis. The watershed event that demonstrated the sovereign power of God to deliver his people from their enemies was the Assyrian siege of Jerusalem in the time of Hezekiah (Isa. 36–37). All aid from possible human sources had been cut off. All hope that the Assyrians might just go home or be stopped before they got to Jerusalem had been dashed. No one entertained any prospect of outnumbered, undersupplied Judah defeating the powerful Assyrian armies of trained and experienced warriors. Yet Yahweh vanquished this proud foe by means of an effortless overnight annihilation.

This act of God stands as a testimony throughout the period of classical prophecy to what Yahweh is able and willing to do. The later generations that faced equally "invincible" armies from Babylon or Persia could theoretically be confident that Yahweh could deliver them in like manner if only they would be faithful to the covenant and rely on him to save them.

This emphasis in the Old Testament is often referred to as redemptive history. As God shows himself able and willing to deliver Israel from slavery, oppression, invasion, and exile, he establishes the redemptive aspect of his character. This aspect emerges in a new light in the New Testament as Jesus comes to provide redemption not just from crisis, but from the universal human plight and destiny, sin and death.

Temple Will Not Shelter

In the time of Jeremiah and Ezekiel, when Judah was falling under the devastating blows of the Babylonians, it was common for the Israelites to believe that the presence of the temple and the ark in Jerusalem would save them. By now the temple of Yahweh built by Solomon had stood for four and a half centuries. The logic was that God would not allow his temple to be humiliated and des-

Artist's reconstruction of the siege of Lachish by Sennacherib from the wall reliefs found in Sennacherib's palace.

ecrated by armies that marched under the banner of powerless gods. Defeat would be a sign of his weakness, destruction an indication of his impotence. This amounted to a belief that God had a reputation to protect and that he was under some sort of binding obligation to protect the temple and Jerusalem.

Jeremiah 7 records the prophet's famous temple sermon. Here, standing at the gate of the great temple in Jerusalem, Jeremiah warns the people that their rituals mean nothing to God if they fail to change their ways. A common belief in the ancient world was that the gods needed the sacrifices that people brought to the temple. The Israelites repeatedly adopted this same mind-set, believing that as long as they performed the rituals that met their God's needs, he would in turn protect them—a mutual dependency. Jeremiah argued forcefully against this misconception: "Will you steal and murder, commit

Jeremiah gave one of his object lessons at the potter's shop (Jer. 18).

adultery and perjury, burn incense to Baal and follow other gods you have not known, and then come and stand before me in this house, which bears my Name, and say, 'We are safe'—safe to do all these detestable things? Has this house, which bears my Name, become a den of robbers to you? But I have been watching!

declares the LORD" (vv. 9–11). The Lord pointed out through Jeremiah that a previous Israelite temple of Yahweh in Shiloh had suffered destruction when the Lord abandoned it because of the wickedness of the people, and Jerusalem should expect no different treatment.

Ezekiel picks up the theme as that book opens with a vision in which the prophet sees the great chariot/throne of Yahweh. The vision resumes in Ezekiel 10 as the glory of the Lord departs from the temple and Jerusalem. In the ancient world, the gods were sometimes seen to abandon their temple as a captain might abandon his sinking ship. Here Yahweh's abandonment is not an act of desperate flight but is disciplinary action against his faithless people. His departure signals that he will no longer fight for or protect his people, thereby leaving them vulnerable to their enemies. More than a century earlier, Isaiah had conveyed this same idea using the imagery of a vineyard that had been tenderly cultivated and diligently protected. But when it failed to yield produce, its hedge was taken down and its wall dismantled so that there would be nothing to prevent its being trampled and ravaged (Isa. 5:1–7).

Ezekiel's Temple Vision

Model of Ezekiel's Temple.

Jablonowski www.pauljab.net/temple

Just as the book of Ezekiel opened by proclaiming the abandonment of the temple and its subsequent destruction, the book ends with a vision of a restored and ideal temple (Ezek. 40–48). The main point of this vision is found in the concluding words: "The name of the city from that time on will be: THE LORD IS THERE." All of the detailed architectural discussion of these chapters becomes in effect a work of concept theory. As an analogy, imagine a seminary student being asked to write a church constitution for a course that would reflect all the important ideals and values of how a church could best serve, honor, and worship God. Since the people of Ezekiel's time had failed to maintain a sanctuary that honored the holiness of Yahweh, Ezekiel laid out this concept design that would capture and reflect God's holiness in all its resplendence. There is no hint in these chapters that this temple would or should be built. It comes in a vision but also offers a vision of an ideal environment for God's presence in the midst of his people that will declare his glory.

> Walk about Zion, go around her,
>   count her towers,
> consider well her ramparts,
>   view her citadels,
>   that you may tell of them to the next generation.
> For this God is our God for ever and ever;
>   he will be our guide even to the end.
>
> *Psalm 48:12–14*

Eschatology

Eschatology refers to the study of the end times, or the last days—the final period of history as we know it. Our Christian eschatology is filled with discussion of topics such as the Rapture, the Great Tribulation, the Antichrist, the millennial kingdom, and the battle of Armageddon. Theologians dispute which of these are going to be literal as opposed to those that are figurative, symbolic, or spiritual. They develop different models for the order of events and discuss what will characterize each of them. These models and conclusions are based on interpretations of prophetic passages from the Old Testament and from the book of Revelation. They require the interpreter to construct a sequence of events, a plot, that will incorporate the anticipated fulfillments of the prophecies.

Few interpreters pause to ask, "What did Israel's eschatology look like? What sort of fulfillment would they have anticipated for the 'last days'?" In this question, several of the components immediately disappear. Few would claim that the Rapture, for example, could be found in the Old Testament. Other topics, such as the Great Tribulation, the Antichrist, and the battle of Armageddon would be seen only by some and only in passing, relatively obtuse passages. In contrast, the center of Israelite eschatology was the land. Their hopes for the future were vested in peaceful and secure existence in a productive land. They looked forward to a kingdom of God on earth that would rule over the world from Jerusalem through an ideal heir to the Davidic throne. All tyranny would be eliminated and oppressors put down. This kingdom would be characterized by harmony and covenant faithfulness.

In the Israelites' view, this is not the end of history but is understood more as the final frontier of history—the fulfillment of history—rather than as a transition to the eternal state. It is not the finale; all else is prelude. They believe that it will last forever, but not in the same sense that we think of eternity. For them it is a continuing status quo with no anticipated ending, better described as perpetual rather than eternal.

It is no surprise, given additional revelation and the events of the New Testament, that our eschatology looks considerably different from that of Israel. This is not a problem. We should exercise caution, however, about commandeering statements from Old Testament prophecy and repackaging them for our own eschatology as if that is what the prophets were speaking about.

	AMOS	ISAIAH	JEREMIAH	EZEKIEL	MISCELLANEOUS
BABYLON		13:1—14:23 Destruction: like Sodom and Gomorrah; no survivors	50—51 Captivity; destruction; humuliation; desolation; ruin		Habakkuk 2:6—17: Destruction; disgrace
PHILISTIA	1:6—8 Remnant will perish; destruction	14:29—32 Helpless famine; defeated from north	47 Conquered from north; destruction; mourning remnant	25:15—17 Destruction; remnant cut off	
MOAB	2:1—3 Fire; death	15—16 Devastation; ruin; mourning; some remnant	48 Desolation; shame; exile; laughingstock; future restoration	25:18—11 Captivity	
DAMASCUS	1:3—5 Cut off; exile	17:1—3 Ruin, but a remnant left	49:23—27 Helpless; destruction		
EGYPT		19 Civil war; economic decline; military defeat; conquered by Assyria	46:1—26 To be conquered by Nebuchadnezzar	29—32 Overcome by Babylon	
EDOM	1:11—12 Fire	21:11—12 Devastation; but possibility of survival	49:7—22 Flight; ruin; object of horror; like Sodom and Gomorrah; desolation	25:12—14 Laid waste	Obadiah: Destruction; no survivors
TYRE	1:9—10 Burning of citadels	23 Destruction; conquest; restoration after 70 years.		26—28 Overthrown; mourning; destruction	
AMMON	1:13—15 Exile	49:1—6 Desolate heap; possessed by Israel; exile; future restoration		25:1—7 Destruction	
NINEVEH					Nahum: Control of Judah ended; besieged, destroyed, plundered

One of the most important themes of the prophets is found in the idea that all of the events of history are in the hands of Yahweh. This includes all of the actions of the nations, from the great empires like Assyria and Babylon, to the major powers like Egypt, and to all of the minor countries that surrounded Israel like Edom and Moab. Many of the prophets specifically targeted the nations surrounding Israel (see "Oracles to the Nations," below). It was important for the Israelites to understand that their God is in control, especially when they were feeling like the helpless and threatened victims of powerful enemies and opportunistic neighbors.

The theology of the prophets is that Yahweh is never overmatched. If enemies succeed, it is because Yahweh is using those enemies to discipline his people. The marauding empires do not reflect a world run amok; they are part of a well-orchestrated plan by the master strategist, who is being faithful to his covenant (blessings *and* curses) and who can be seen in the process as both just and merciful. The theology is expressed most clearly and eloquently by Isaiah:

> Who has measured the waters in the hollow of his hand,
>   or with the breadth of his hand marked off the heavens?

Oracles to the Nations

When Jonah was given a message about Nineveh, he went to Nineveh and delivered that message. Nahum was also given an oracle about Nineveh—but there is no suggestion that he went there to deliver it. Isaiah (chaps. 13–23), Jeremiah (chaps. 46–51), Ezekiel (chaps. 25–32), Amos (chaps. 1–2), and Zephaniah (chap. 2) each have a series of oracles against foreign nations, while Obadiah, Nahum, and Habakkuk each target one specific foreign nation (Edom, Nineveh, and Babylon respectively).

There is no reason to think that these prophets became itinerant preachers traveling around the ancient world delivering their messages of doom to the nations. For example, when Amos offered his series of oracles, he ended with Judah and Israel. One gets the impression that all of these were offered at the same time and that the Israelite audience listened with glee as the prophet pronounced judgment on all of their enemies one by one. But in the end, his attention turned to Israel and he proclaimed its doom as well. These oracles can then be seen as rhetorical devices to attract the audience's attention. In this way of understanding these oracles, the literary and theological intention of them is not to serve notice to the nations, but rather to convey to the Israelites that God is sovereign over the destiny of the nations—that all they do is under his control. As a result, even though the content of these messages is indictment and judgment against the nations, more often than not they offer a message of hope to Israel. Its enemies would be brought to justice. This alternative sees these oracles as functioning for the benefit of Israel. Literarily they would be categorized as judgment oracles; functionally they would be categorized as aftermath oracles.

© edenpics.com

Who has held the dust of the earth in a basket,
    or weighed the mountains on the scales
    and the hills in a balance?
Who has understood the mind of the LORD,
    or instructed him as his counselor?
Whom did the LORD consult to enlighten him,
    and who taught him the right way?
Who was it that taught him knowledge
    or showed him the path of understanding?

Surely the nations are like a drop in a bucket;
    they are regarded as dust on the scales;
    he weighs the islands as though they were fine dust.
Lebanon is not sufficient for altar fires,
    nor its animals enough for burnt offerings.
Before him all the nations are as nothing;
    they are regarded by him as worthless
    and less than nothing.

Isaiah 40:12–17

In this passage, Yahweh's sovereignty over the nations is seen in the same terms as his sovereignty over the cosmos. It is furthermore clear that the exercise of this sovereignty is not a struggle or seen as a difficult task—the nations are nothing but dust. Rather than the usual ancient concept of the nations being represented by various gods who struggle against one another with the stronger gods bringing dominion for their respective countries, all authority is in the hands of Yahweh.

God's Love for His People

The prophets often use the analogy of human relationships to communicate God's love and care for Israel. Ezekiel uses the analogy of an abused and orphaned girl abandoned by the wayside who is taken in and given shelter and provision (Ezek. 16). Hosea adopts the imagery of a faithless wife who is disciplined yet graciously given new opportunities to be faithful (Hos. 1–3). In another analogy, Hosea likens God to a caring father:

"When Israel was a child, I loved him,
    and out of Egypt I called my son.

But the more I called Israel,
    the further they went from me.
They sacrificed to the Baals
    and they burned incense to images.
It was I who taught Ephraim to walk,
    taking them by the arms;
but they did not realize
    it was I who healed them.
I led them with cords of human kindness,
    with ties of love;
I lifted the yoke from their neck
    and bent down to feed them."

Hosea 11:1–4

His love is shown in his faithfulness, but also in his willingness to carry out discipline for their own good. All of these aspects can be seen in Yahweh's impassioned declarations in Isaiah:

"For your Maker is your husband—
    the LORD Almighty is his name—
the Holy One of Israel is your Redeemer;
    he is called the God of all the earth.
The LORD will call you back
    as if you were a wife deserted and distressed in spirit—
a wife who married young,
    only to be rejected," says your God.
"For a brief moment I abandoned you,
    but with deep compassion I will bring you back.
In a surge of anger
    I hid my face from you for a moment,
but with everlasting kindness
    I will have compassion on you,"
    says the LORD your Redeemer. . . .

"Though the mountains be shaken
    and the hills be removed,
yet my unfailing love for you will not be shaken
    nor my covenant of peace be removed,"
    says the LORD, who has compassion on you.

Isaiah 54:5–8, 10

Only too late does Israel recognize both its failures and Yahweh's faithfulness:

> Because of the LORD's great love we are not consumed,
>   for his compassions never fail.
> They are new every morning;
>   great is your faithfulness.

Lamentations 3:22–23

God's enduring love and faithfulness are also demonstrated in the promise of a "new covenant" (Jer. 31:31–34), in which he will forgive the Israelites' sins. In this new relationship, the knowledge of the Lord will be more accessible and more natural because he will "put [the] law in their minds" (literally "entrails") and "write it on their hearts." In the ancient world, the same type of wording is used when the gods communicate their will through divination. The diviner priests ask the deity to write their answer to the inquiries on the entrails of the animal that is being sacrificed. By writing the law (= his revelation) on the hearts of his people, God will be revealing his will and plan to them. As a result, they will know him. God's discipline of his people thus leads to even greater acts of grace.

Social Justice*

A number of the prophets addressed the issue of social justice, and for Amos and Micah, it was their main theme. The prophets called on the Israelites to police their own society and to purge the institutions and the systems of injustices inherent in them. Beyond calling individuals to act justly, the prophets held the leadership and the wealthy classes accountable for preservation of justice for all levels of society. They were responsible for making good laws and enforcing them through an effective court system that was free from corruption.

Righteousness and justice went together in the ancient world and went beyond the functioning of the court system. They were carried out by means of social legislation and social reforms that would proactively care for the weak and protect them. They were characterized by kindness and mercy, and they led to peace, equity, personal freedom, and an end to oppression through exploitation. Doing righteousness and justice therefore involved helping the poor and needy by (1) providing for them, (2) defending them from those who would exploit or oppress them, and (3) delivering them from the power of the oppressor.[1]

A citizen of Lagash living in debt, or who had been condemned to its prison for impost, hunger, robbery or murder—their freedom he established. Uru-inimgina made a compact with the divine Nin-Girsu that the powerful man would not oppress the orphan or widow.*

*COS 2.152.

Justice and the Nations

The Old Testament theology concerning the way God treats the nations can be illustrated if we use the example of an old-fashioned balance scale with trays connected to either end of a rocker beam balanced on its center point. If we envision such a scale for God's handling of sin in the temporal-material frame, we will have a cogent picture of Israel's general theology. One tray represents evil, the other side, good. As a nation did that which was right, weights would be placed on the "good" tray. As a nation did that which was sinful or wrong, weights would be placed on the "evil" tray. One additional feature of this system is that under the evil tray is a button that sounds an alarm. The idea is that when evil sufficiently outweighs good, the alarm sounds and God prepares to carry out judgment. Some important principles go along with this imagery:

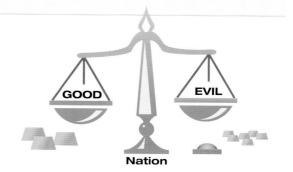

1. If the nation responds by changing its behavior to begin filling the good side, God's hand of judgment can be stayed (as in Jonah).
2. Good weights have more influence than wicked weights (i.e., they weigh more, Deut. 5:9–10).

3. Even though the scale may rock back and forth, the evil tray is not emptied except through judgment. This is true even when God acts graciously to forgo judgment (Ex. 32:34).
4. Finally, from everyone to whom more is given, more is required (Luke 12:48). This means that for Israel it would take less wickedness for the evil side of the scale to trigger the alarm and bring God's judgment—in effect raising the position of the alarm.*

---

*It is important to note that this is not presented as a system that concerns eternity or salvation from sins. It represents only how God responds to sin on earth in human time, and it primarily applies to corporate groups rather than individuals.

REFLECTIONS

1. Discuss the significance of the syllabus analogy. What are the best insights the analogy offers? Identify some places where the analogy breaks down.

2. Discuss the centrality of the temple and its importance in Jeremiah and Ezekiel.

3. Why is God's sovereignty over the nations important to the prophets?

4. How would you define messianic prophecy? Why?

5. How should messianic prophecy be used in apologetics or witnessing?

6. How do Israelite concepts of eschatology differ from ours?

Notes

1. Moshe Weinfeld, *Social Justice in Ancient Israel and in the Ancient Near East* (Minneapolis: Fortress, 1995), 17–44.

CHAPTER

CONTEMPORARY SIGNIFICANCE

SCENARIO: READ TODAY'S HEADLINES IN THE BIBLE

"There are a lot of reasons for my faith," Greg explained to the small group of buddies that had gathered in his dorm room. "One of them is the way the Bible anticipated a lot of the events that are tearing apart the Middle East day after day."

"Come on, Greg," sneered Karl, "you don't really expect us to buy this Nostradamus-type stuff do you?" What is this, 'Isaiah and His Psychic Friends Network'?" Everybody laughed at that.

"No, you've got it all wrong," Greg groaned in exasperation. "For example, God said that the Israelites would return to their land and become a nation again. Who would have thought that could happen in 1200, or in 1500, or even in 1900? In fact, they almost didn't even survive Hitler. But look at what happened in 1948. This is not something to take lightly. There they are!

"Another thing, Jesus said that people all over the world would hear about him—and just look at how the Bible is being translated into language after language. I tell you, it can't just be coincidence. Prophecies are being fulfilled all the time."

"Interesting, Greg," Bruce admitted. "So I am curious—if your Bible is so smart, tell us what it says is going to happen next."

"Well," Greg stalled a bit, trying to remember some of the prophecies they had talked about in his small group, "Daniel talks about a statue with ten toes, and since the legs of the statue represented the fourth kingdom, the Roman Empire, then the toes must represent a reconstituted Roman Empire, a European confederation something like the Common Market. And in the Middle East, one of the next big events is the rebuilding of the temple as predicted in Ezekiel."

Calvin's
Institutes

Without knowledge of God there is no knowledge of self (I.I.2).

God bestows the actual knowledge of himself upon us only in the Scriptures (I.VI.1).

"We'll have to see Gregory, ol' boy, if that black-covered crystal ball of yours is right. But tell us one more thing—how soon do *you* think it will be until this return of Christ that you have talked about?"

Chuck sounded sincere in his question, so Greg thought for a moment. "Well, this is 1972, so I wouldn't be at all surprised if Christ returned before we hit 1980." Then the conversation turned to other things, and the topic never came up among them again. And everyone forgot about it except Greg—and Chuck.

Chuck graduated two years later and went on to get an MBA. He met a girl who had been raised a Baptist but had drifted away in college. They talked about religion every once in a while, even went to church now and then, Christmas and Easter mostly. The year 1980 came and went. "Huh," said Chuck, "I guess Greg was just one of those crazy guys you run into at college," and he went on with his life.

Meanwhile Greg also noticed the passing of years. And he remembered his offhand prediction in his dorm room all those years ago. And as he taught his Sunday school class, he warned them not to get drawn into speaking on the Bible's account so carelessly. As he looked back at that conversation, he realized that it had not given his buddies reason to be drawn to the faith, but reason to confirm their doubt. There must be a better way to proclaim God's plan.

Thinking about Prophecy

Most people who grow up in church think of the prophets from two approaches. The first, *apologetics*, is an approach that has remained prominent throughout the entire history of the church. In this, the fulfillment of prophecy serves as evidence of the divine authority of Scripture and, more specifically, of the deity of Jesus Christ. The second, *eschatology*, is interested in prophecy as a guideline to the end times. It is true that prophetic literature has important contributions to make to both of these areas—and they represent significant issues (see "Messianic Prophecy," p. 247, and "Eschatology," p. 257). But the mistake that is evident here is that as these two approaches have monopolized the use of prophetic literature, other valid and important approaches have been neglected.

These two approaches have something in common—both focus on fulfillment. Indeed, most people raised in the church have come to believe that the relevance and significance of prophetic literature are to be found in fulfillment. As we have explored prophetic literature in the previous sections, we have discovered that in addition to fulfillment, there is the important issue of "message." We have also discovered that only two of the categories of oracles (judgment and aftermath) carry with them any anticipation of fulfillment. Moreover, we have learned that the prophetic literature itself rarely carries any indication within it of what fulfillment will look like. As a result, we concluded that the authoritative word of God in the prophetic books is to be looked for and found in the message rather than in the fulfillment. If all of this is true, then an approach that focuses primarily on fulfillment is consistently going to miss the authoritative word of God represented in the message of the prophetic literature.

Is there relevance and significance in the *message* of the prophets? For instance, what can it mean to us as twenty-first-century Christians that God is going to bring judgment on the Philistines (Amos 1:6–8)? To answer this we have to return to the most basic and fundamental point that we have been making chapter after chapter. If we are to view the Old Testament as God's authoritative word of revelation, then our greatest attention needs to be paid to the revelation of God that it offers. God is capable of revealing himself through an endless variety of media and literary genres. The greatest obligation that we have when we come to the prophetic literature or any biblical literature is to come to know God better. There is nothing more relevant and nothing more significant than the knowledge of God.

Based on what we can learn about God from the Old Testament prophets, what would prophets of today say to us? Before we answer that, we should briefly pause to ask, "Are there still prophets today?" To a large extent, the answer is going to depend on how the word *prophet* is defined. We have been using the definition of a prophet as a "mouthpiece" for God. There is a difference that can be drawn perhaps between the idea of a messenger for God and a mouthpiece for God. A messenger is speaking a word on behalf of God, giving a message that calls people to God and reminds people of who God is and what he expects. Many people today serve as messengers for God in this way, and prophets did these things too. A mouthpiece goes beyond this, however, by speaking the very words of God. Thus the prophets can say, "Thus says the LORD," whereas no one today can say that unless he or she is quoting Scripture.

Certainly God, through his Holy Spirit, gives messages to modern-day preachers who exercise their spiritual gift of prophecy—but there is no movement to add their sermons to the Bible alongside inspired Scripture as the canonical, authoritative Word of God. The prophets as mouthpieces were the instruments for the very word of God, and there is no one today who has that same status and whose words have that same authority. But since the prophets were revealing God through their messages, they can still speak today. Our access to their message for today comes through the four oracle categories. As we examine each of these categories, we should remember that most of the prophetic messages were to a corporate group rather than to individuals, yet each individual shared in being responsible for the group's behavior. This was in addition to each person's responsibility for his or her own behavior. In today's Western societies, individualism is the norm, and we have very little sense of corporate identity or corporate responsibility, but the prophetic messages should not be removed from their corporate focus.

INDICTMENT TODAY

Indictments identify those things that God hates or those attitudes and actions that displease him. God has not changed, and human nature has not changed, so we will find much in the indictments of the prophets that we recognize. We can identify five major categories.

1. Unfaithfulness to God

For the Israelites, unfaithfulness to God could be seen generally in their violations of the covenant, which could be understood as disobedience to the law and particularly as their worship of other gods. We live under the new covenant, so our covenant responsibilities are broader—the law of Christ, which calls on us to be imitators of Christ. When we treat this responsibility lightly or make little attempt to conform our lives to Christ, we fall under the same indictment as the Israelites.

Above all else Christ calls on us to love God, love our neighbors as ourselves, and love one another within the body of Christ. One of the ways that we keep this covenant of love is by being channels of the grace of God to those around us. Philip Yancey's book *What's So Amazing About Grace?* stands as a powerful call for Christians to view themselves not just as beneficiaries of grace, but as agents of grace, dispensers, not collectors.[1] We were not designed to be cisterns, but aqueducts. The grace that God brings into our

The Roman Aquaduct which brought water to Caesarea from the slopes of Mt. Carmel near Tel Mevorah.

Z. Radovan, Jerusalem

lives is a grace that should be evident in us as we live lives of grace. As Yancey points out, this means that we should stand ready to forgive as we have been forgiven; to be charitable in our attitudes toward those with whom we disagree; to exude grace to everyone around us. Unfortunately, most of us would have to agree with him that such grace is often not associated with Christianity.

> Mark Twain used to talk about people who were "good in the worst sense of the word," a phrase that, for many, captures the reputation of Christians today. Recently I have been asking questions of strangers—for example, seatmates on an airplane—when I strike up a conversation. "When I say the words 'evangelical Christian,' what comes to mind?" In reply, mostly I hear political descriptions: of strident prolife activists, or gay-rights opponents, or proposals for censoring the Internet. I hear references to the Moral Majority, an organization disbanded years ago. Not once—*not once*—have I heard a description redolent of grace. Apparently that is not the aroma Christians give off in the world.[2]

It is too easy for us to flow through life with a Great Commission vigor, winning the world to the grace of God but never letting the grace of God show in how we act. As a result, many find the church an uncomfortable place to be, the last place to come for comfort and acceptance. But our God is a God of grace. If we desire to be like him, we need to go beyond being people who are saved by grace to being people who are characterized by grace. Then we will make an impact on our world; and through us, all the nations of the world will be blessed. "The world thirsts for grace. When grace descends, the world falls silent before it."[3] But we consistently fall short, and the indictment of the prophets comes upon us—God is displeased with those who are unfaithful to the calling of the covenant.

2. Oppression of Defenseless

There is much to be proud of in the financial aid that our nation offers to its disadvantaged and outcast through government social programs. It would be easy to cite statistics of the huge sums of money that the United States gives to developing countries to try to relieve poverty and famine. We might stand tall as we recount the commitment to human rights and human dignity that we seek to enforce worldwide. Furthermore, our churches do not stand idle as organizations such as World Relief operate around the globe, and neighborhood food and clothing pantries seek to address the needs in our own cities. Prison ministries reach out in love, and it is not difficult to find those who have given generously and sacrificially to needy causes. Despite successes, oppression of the defenseless remains one of the easiest offenses for us to identify with today.

Widows, Orphans, Aliens, and Slaves

The prophets called on their Israelite audience to provide justice for the underprivileged and vulnerable members of society. Widows and orphans had no one to provide for them. "Aliens" refers to non-Israelites living in the land. These would include refugees, ones who had been prisoners of war, and immigrants. Slaves were usually debt-slaves—Israelite farmers who had fallen on hard times and had to sell themselves or their families into service so they could survive. There is no debt-slavery per se in our culture, and though there are still widows and orphans, they typically do not face the desperate conditions those in the ancient world faced. Society has made better provision for their protection. Perhaps the closest class to those described in the text would be found in illegal immigrants and migrant farmers.

Rather than discuss the similarities and differences of the particulars, it is important for us to explore what we do with the Old Testament when there are significant differences from our own cultural circumstances. We must start where we have begun nearly every discussion—with the understanding that we are reading the text as God's revelation of himself. This takes us back then to the first sentence in this box, which articulates the principle that served as the premise for the divine Word. The text may address social situations of the past, but God's will is never antiquated. God desires that justice be maintained, and that includes prominently the care and protection of the defenseless—those who have little recourse in life and whose desperate plight has come upon them through no fault or choice of their own. God is revealed as one who cares for the marginalized—this is the "good news" of the prophets. Our responsibility then becomes to discern what this knowledge of God demands of us in our own cultural context.

This does not mean that we must immediately become avid proponents of government programs like the welfare system or march for new immigrant naturalization laws— though if injustice were found in these institutions, it would be a biblical response to speak out and act against it. Government solutions do not always bring redemptive results.

Whatever the injustice, we learn that God is not pleased when his people stand idly by and turn the other way when society tramples those who are powerless to do anything about it. Redemptive strategies are going to focus on people above programs. They will focus on caring for people and restoring their dignity and self-worth rather than just throwing money with strings attached their way.

Tithing and Stewardship

Tithing was an obligation in ancient Israel. Similar to taxes today, it was not an option. Many people today wonder whether we are still required to give a tithe to God. What does the Bible teach that is relevant to our contemporary situation?

Giving a tenth of one's produce to deity was commonplace throughout the ancient world. The tithe was a means of revenue collection in both secular (i.e., taxation) and sacred contexts. In the Bible, occasional tithing is practiced before the law by both Abraham (Gen. 14:20) and Jacob (Gen. 28:22). Leviticus 27:30–33, Numbers 18:8–32, and Deuteronomy 14:22–29 contain the most complete descriptions of Israel's tithing laws. The tithe "belongs to the Lord" and is used to support the priests and Levites and to assist the poor. Since the economy of Israel was based on agriculture and herding, the tithes were typically taken from flocks, herds, and crops (including not only grain, but wine and olive oil as well). These were turned over to the temple for use and redistribution. In Malachi 3:8–12 the prophet rebukes the people for withholding the full tithe.

Though our entire religious and social system has changed since Israelite days, some things never change. God is entitled to be acknowledged by our gifts to him, and we are obliged to be conscientious stewards of all that God has given us. In this way, it is seen that tithing is simply a way of talking about our stewardship. The rationale behind stewardship is that God is the creator and giver of life and resources. Our use of these ought to reflect our recognition of his ownership, while our giving from these resources ought to reflect our gratitude to the one who gives freely to us. Our giving to God demonstrates our priorities and serves to honor God. Faithful stewardship is a worldview and serves as a measure of spiritual maturity. Stewardship involves not only how we give of our time and our resources; it also involves how we *use* our time and resources.

In our society, we enjoy a standard of living that is incomprehensible to most of the rest of the world. What are the demands that stewardship imposes on our extraordinary financial and material resources? Our attitude toward financial resources must reflect a balanced worldview. Specifically, our spending must be evaluated to determine whether it reflects God's priorities and whether it honors him. How do we identify God's priorities? Would they include items that provide convenience and comfort? Would they preclude items considered luxuries? The Bible does not offer clear-cut answers to these questions, and different individuals will arrive at different answers.

While the Bible does not demand that everyone live a spartan lifestyle or make a vow of poverty, a biblical worldview prohibits us from succumbing to reckless self-indulgence. We should not buy something "because we can afford it"; nor should our purchases be justified by reference to our station in society. The fact that our friends own certain things or that advertising tells us we need certain things should not dictate what our spending decisions should be. Our standard is not society's values, but God's values. Perhaps we should be more willing to be content with the "functional" rather than the "state-of-the-art" or that which is the current trend. Advertising tries to convince us that prestige is a worthwhile objective and that it can be achieved by inducing envy in others. In contrast the Bible identifies envy with sin, suggesting that we should therefore not attempt to stimulate it in others. Conspicuous consumption or selfish extravagance cannot be reconciled with good stewardship. The entertainment that we enjoy must be God-honoring. Responsible stewardship requires discipline, sensitivity to the needs of others, denial of possessiveness, resistance to the consumerism that pervades our culture, and above all, constant evaluation of our priorities and motivations. Income that is available to us that exceeds our basic needs ought to be the basis for proportionate giving above and beyond the benchmark percentages. Each spending decision should be made by first asking, "Is this a reasonable way to spend the money God has made available to me?" Each acquisition ought to be preceded by asking the question, "What is my motive for owning this?"

The mandate of the Old Testament tithing system indicates that 10 percent is an appropriate level of giving to express gratitude to God for what he has done for us. We show gratitude to God as the source of our goods by dedicating a portion of our goods to him and by becoming a source of goods to others (cf. also Acts 2:44–46; Heb. 13:16). Is the situation any different now that we are not under law? In the New Testament, Paul encourages contributions not as obligatory, but as gifts (2 Cor. 9:5). Tithing can therefore not be considered an obligation of law, but that does not mean that it is not an obligation of stewardship. How are we to show our gratitude to God other than by giving back a portion? If 10 percent was considered an acceptable portion by God as an expression of gratitude then, why should we view it any differently today? We might consider 10 percent as a benchmark just as we consider 15 percent a benchmark for tipping. The extent of the customer's gratitude and appreciation is demonstrated in the size of the tip. It would be considered the ultimate rudeness or the consummate insult to leave no tip at all. So it is to God if we return no portion to him. In addition, there are occasions when the situation calls for a contribution exceeding the benchmark. In these cases, it is appropriate that giving be proportionate, according to the individual's ability (Acts 11:29). Is the faithful steward under obligation to tithe? Not in a legalistic way; but it is the least we can do to show our appreciation to God for what he has given us. Further, we should not be satisfied with the tithe when God begins to prosper us beyond the needs of our normal and necessary expenses. Our stewardship should grow as God continues to provide above and beyond our needs. As mentioned earlier, our determination and success as stewards are measures of our Christian maturity and commitment.

In conclusion, stewardship is a worldview that is not limited to finances, nor to giving. It involves our use and giving with regard to natural resources, time, skills and abilities, and material and financial resources. We must be aware of our stewardship responsibilities in each of these areas. We cannot exercise our stewardship in one area and assume that our obligation taken care of. Giving of our time is not a substitute for giving from our financial resources. Conversely, giving money cannot take the place of giving our skills and abilities. We must be careful to be faithful stewards in all aspects of our lives.

Point

"Jesus sat down opposite the place where the offerings were put and watched the crowd putting their money into the temple treasury. Many rich people threw in large amounts. But a poor widow came and put in two very small copper coins, worth only a fraction of a penny.

Calling his disciples to him, Jesus said, 'I tell you the truth, this poor widow has put more into the treasury than all the others. They all gave out of their wealth; but she, out of her poverty, put in everything—all she had to live on.'" (Mark 12:41–44)

Counterpoint

"Woe to you, teachers of the law and Pharisees, you hypocrites! You give a tenth of your spices—mint, dill and cummin. But you have neglected the more important matters of the law—justice, mercy and faithfulness. You should have practiced the latter, without neglecting the former." (Matt. 23:23)

Amos (2:6–8; 5:10–12; 8:4–6) and Micah (2:1–2; 3:1–3; 6:10–12; 7:2–3) are particularly forthright in their indictments of social injustice. Their indictments did not concern the lack of generosity, nor did they suggest that all should share equally in society. Their concerns focused mainly on how power was wielded in the system. The New Testament picks up the prophetic call first in Jesus' teaching as he informs his disciples that caring for the poor and the outcast is the same as caring for him (Matt. 25:34–46). James follows up in his condemnation of status privileges (James 2:1–13). We continue to live in a system in which the poor are neglected and power is regularly abused by those with the money or status to carry out their agendas. Even apparent acts of generosity can be used as a means of wielding power over nations, classes, and individuals. We have witnessed the destructive power of our political system, of the media, of corporate America, of the judicial system, of the organizations of corruption, of our special interests groups, and yes, even of our churches. Power still is abused; power still corrupts. We continue to stand under the indictment of the prophets.

3. Devaluing, Depreciating, Degrading, Demeaning Deity

The Israelites were guilty of devaluing, depreciating, degrading, and demeaning God through their idolatry, their syncretism, and their refusal to adhere strictly to monotheism. These are not the only ways to demean deity—they were simply the ones most consistently practiced by the Israelites. The prophetic condemnation of these actions reveals to us a God who is outraged when the practices of his people not only fail to honor him, but actually degrade him.

Syncretism involves a mixing of worldviews. Idolatry is premised on the exploitation of a god with needs. The God of the Bible, the triune God, does not have needs, nor does he have patience with those who corrupt their religious beliefs with the godless philosophies and values of their fallen cultures. One has only to look at our own society's values to recognize the problem. Individualism, relativism, naturalism, globalization, hedonism, consumerism, and narcissism all leave their indelible marks on our religious practices and define our resulting lack of commitment. In other words, the extent to which we are influenced or characterized by those is the extent to which our commitment to Christ suffers. If our thoughts are full of ourselves and our plans, the environment of our minds has no room for another to be adored. It is too easy to allow God to drift to the outer edges of our personal world and make something else our center of gravity.

In the church, it is also true that the triune God must be firmly in the center of who we are and what we do. The church is not about tolerance; the church is not about rights; the church is not about racial reconciliation; the church is not about political agendas or social causes; the church is not about food pantry programs, marches, demonstrations, work camps, or potlucks. We cannot allow our picture of God to be trivialized into a "God-of-my-Cause" idea.[4] Many of these may be noble causes, and the church should not just cloister together behind locked doors, sitting in dusty, half-empty pews and singing hymns. But we cannot allow any distraction, as worthy or necessary as it may be, to usurp the central role from Christ.

> Effective fasting is dependent on what you *are* doing while you are not eating.

Fasting

Does God listen better to hungry people? From the way many Christians practice fasting, we might conclude that they think that. What is fasting all about, and how does it work? We get some important clues from the prophets. In Zechariah 7 questions about fasting prompt the prophet to give a lecture about justice. What is the connection? In Isaiah 58:1–12 the same connection is made but with a little more information given. The prophet chides his audience for their inconsistency—while they fast they continue to exploit their workers and quarrel with one another instead of caring for the needs of others. What we discover from these passages is that it is not the skipping of meals that is important—it is what you do instead of eating that makes the difference.

If a loved one were in a serious accident with her life hanging by a thread, it would not matter if it were lunchtime; you still would rush to the hospital. You would probably miss several meals and not even notice because your priorities had been dramatically altered by the circumstances. Fasting works on the same principle. It represents a shift in priorities that overrides the most basic of physical needs in response to the more important spiritual needs required by the circumstances.

In the Old Testament, the religious use of fasting is often in connection with making a request before God. When an employee has to put together a proposal for a client contract, he may work overtime, skip meals, and lose sleep to make sure that everything in the proposal is exactly as it should be. This diligence is part of a conscientious approach to an important meeting. The principle is similar when we talk about fasting in preparation for presenting our petitions before God. The importance of the request causes an individual to be so concerned about his or her spiritual condition that physical necessities fade into the background. In this sense, the act of fasting is designed as a process leading to purification and humbling oneself before God (Pss. 69:10; 102:4). Fasting is not an end in itself; rather, it is disciplined training in preparation for an important event.

Fasting is the discipline that we undertake when we have our mind set clearly on the goal. It focuses on our spiritual condition so that we can go to God in petition well prepared. If the petition is like a recital, fasting is like the practice. If the petition is like a race, fasting is like the conditioning workout. It is a discipline, but not for the sake of practice or conditioning alone—it has the race or the recital in mind.

> "When you fast, do not look somber as the hypocrites do, for they disfigure their faces to show men they are fasting. I tell you the truth, they have received their reward in full. But when you fast, put oil on your head and wash your face, so that it will not be obvious to men that you are fasting, but only to your Father, who is unseen; and your Father, who sees what is done in secret, will reward you." (Matt. 6:16–18)

4. Misplaced Reliance

The Israelites were prone to rely on political alliances and military strength when it came to national policy. When it came to their personal safety and security, they tended to put a lot of stock in ritual performance. Isaiah and Jeremiah had much to say on these issues. God expects to be relied upon, and when we fail to do so, we profess our doubts in him or our elevation of something else above him. In our day, self-reliance is probably more common than any other sort of reliance. It is not only pervasive, it is encouraged and prized. It is something of which people are likely to be proud. On the corporate level, we rely on our military might and on our political system. We rely on our economic strength and stability, on our government, and increasingly, on technology. The constructive question is to what extent we rely on any of these above God. When we succumb to overreliance on any of these, we come under the indictment of the prophets.

5. Confused Priorities

Haggai and Malachi both pointed out that the Israelites were more interested in their own comfort and advancement than in their commitments to God. They withheld what rightfully belonged to the Lord; they gave him damaged or inferior goods as gifts; they neglected the building of his house as they concentrated on improving their own circumstances; and they conveniently ignored God's design for families as they pursued their own desires. Again, as the prophets lead us to understand God's displeasure about these behaviors, we learn of God and we find ourselves challenged as we stand condemned alongside the Israelites.

Do not be deceived: God cannot be mocked. A man reaps what he sows. The one who sows to please his sinful nature, from that nature will reap destruction. (Gal. 6:7–8)

JUDGMENT TODAY

There has been no shortage of those willing to see natural disasters, epidemics, or even terrorist acts as God's punishment on a wayward people. Without an authoritative prophetic voice, however, it has become much more difficult to be certain what events in history should be considered the judgment of God. Despite such limitations, we can be sure that God is still in the business of judging.

In Bridging Contexts (p. 263) we used the illustration of a scale to discuss God's handling of sin in the temporal-material frame. We have no reason to think that God's procedures on this matter have changed since ancient times. It is just that now we have no universally recognized mouthpiece of God to proclaim with Scripture's authority that God's judgment is fast approaching or to identify a present event or circumstance as the judgment of God.

USDA photo

It is not necessary for us to know what God is going to do to be convinced that God will judge wickedness and rebellion. It is not necessary for us to be told that a particular occurrence is the punishment of God for us to find in that occurrence a reason to take sober stock of our behavior and pursue a path of repentance and reform. The Old Testament prophets have given us a glimpse of the types of behaviors that provoke God's judgment and of the kind of judgment that God uses. These are sufficient for us to be warned. Knowing God and seeing him in action in the pages of Scripture, we take his commitment to discipline and justice very seriously.

INSTRUCTION TODAY

Relatively little instruction is found in the pages of the prophets, presumably because the Israelites already knew well what was expected of them. The covenant was their heritage. In most cases when instruction is offered, we will find it as relevant to our situation as it was to theirs. Repenting, returning to the Lord, giving him his due, turning away from empty ritual, purifying ourselves, seeking the Lord, doing justice—these are timeless mandates that God has always laid before his people.

Still, we will often have to make adjustments as we think of how to respond to the instruction of the prophets. For example, when they speak of turning away from empty ritual, they talk about the worthlessness of idols or the mechanical offering of sacrifices. Neither idols nor sacrifices are part of our worship, yet we still have to struggle with being focused and properly motivated in our worship. It is easy to tune out and just let the service roll by us—whether that service is enthusiastic worship choruses or quiet liturgical recitations. The instruction of the prophets for us is to resist the tendency for our worship to degenerate into something that is mechanical or self-serving.

AFTERMATH TODAY

In the aftermath oracles, God gives hope and tells of his plan. It was an encouragement to the people to discover that all of the things that seemed to be going wrong should not be taken as an indication that God had lost control. His plan was going forward and could not be thwarted. This is the *message* of the aftermath oracles, and they offer the same hope and encouragement to us as they did to the Israelites. Herein lies the primary relevance and significance of this element of the prophetic word.

But what about *fulfillment?* Granting that it may not offer the primary relevance of the prophetic literature, it still must have some role to play. After all, Jesus expected the people of his times to have recognized the signs. How then should we think about fulfillment?

The popularity of the Left Behind series at the end of the twentieth and beginning of the twenty-first centuries indicates the strong interest in fulfillment of prophecy. A similar phenomenon occurred a generation earlier in the wide circulation of books by Hal Lindsay, par-

> Therefore, I urge you, brothers, in view of God's mercy, to offer your bodies as living sacrifices, holy and pleasing to God—this is your spiritual act of worship. Do not conform any longer to the pattern of this world, but be transformed by the renewing of your mind. (Rom. 12:1–2)

Image and Word, Sign and Symbol Today

The church must begin to consider alternative forms of communication for our changing world—and the prophets can lead the way. It is important to note that postmodern forms of communication have much in common with premodern communication. Where modern communication has been verbal, cognitive, linear, and idea-based, pre- and postmodern communication is image driven, affective, and experience-based. In this new (and old) environment, signs and symbols can prove to be effective tools for communicating divine truths. A sign, such as baptism, is an action or event that offers a visible representation of a reality or value. A symbol, such as a dove or a lamb, is an object that provides a visual representation of a reality that points beyond itself. Every company that uses a logo understands the power of image. What do signs and symbols accomplish or communicate? Five areas may be mentioned:

1. Affiliation or identification with a group (fish or cross as a mark of Christianity).
2. Documentation of an important event (communion as memorial celebration).
3. Instruction in spiritual truth (syllabus analogy earlier in chapter).
4. Bridge to other dimensions of reality (apple with skin, fruit, and core as analogy of the Trinity).
5. Aesthetic contemplation for enhancing emotion and imagination (ceiling of the Sistine Chapel).

© Philip Coblentz/Brand X Pictures/PictureQuest

ticularly *The Late Great Planet Earth*. How should we respond to books such as these that explore the details and scenarios of fulfillment?

We have recognized that our ability to identify any given contemporary event as fulfillment is limited and flawed. We can try to make connections, but certainty is often difficult. More problematic is the idea of anticipating what fulfillment will look like when it comes. We do a disservice to God's Word if we offer our own speculative interpretations of fulfillment as if they represent the authoritative teaching of the Bible. Perhaps we can make some progress by looking at a few sample passages in relation to fulfillment that can help us to see some nuances.

1. Fulfillment Can Happen When No Fulfillment Is Expected

In John 11:49–52 the high priest Caiaphas says, "It is better for you that one man die for the people than that the whole nation perish" (v. 50). John, the gospel writer, explains that this was an unwitting prophecy that would be fulfilled in Jesus' vicarious sacrifice. Caiaphas was not even a prophet, but even prophets could at times make statements that no one would think required fulfillment but that ended up being fulfilled.

In Hosea 11:1 the prophet is explaining about the history of God's work on behalf of Israel. In that context, he is speaking for God as he says, "When Israel was a child, I loved him, and out of Egypt I called my son." Neither Hosea nor the people of his time, nor the people in the centuries following Hosea would have thought that that statement contained anything that needed to be fulfilled. There would be no anticipation of a future son being called out of Egypt. Yet Matthew identified such a fulfillment when Mary and Joseph brought Jesus back from Egypt (Matt. 2:15). As a result, we must conclude that there may well be some statements in Scripture that we would not think offer any information about the last times yet will be fulfilled in such a way as to play a significant role in the events that transpire.

2. Fulfillment Can Occur in Stages or Stretch Further Than Expected

Years before the fall of Jerusalem and the deportation of the people, Jeremiah had indicated that the exile would last seventy

"Tell us," they said, "when will this happen, and what will be the sign of your coming and of the end of the age?" (Matt. 24:3)

"When you see a cloud rising in the west, immediately you say, 'It's going to rain,' and it does. And when the south wind blows, you say, 'It's going to be hot,' and it is. Hypocrites! You know how to interpret the appearance of the earth and the sky. How is it that you don't know how to interpret this present time?" (Luke 12:54–56)

years (Jer. 25:11; 29:10). In Daniel 9 Daniel is praying about the end of the exile, for he realizes that the seventy years must nearly be completed. The resulting prophecy, however, says that while the return will indeed be very soon, the expected restoration will not come immediately, but will be spread over seventy *weeks* of years. What they would have thought was clear in the prophetic word, ended up being not as clear as they thought. This idea can also be seen in prophecies that are split up. The signs that are listed in Joel 2:28–32 would be read as occurring together in connection with the day of the Lord. At Pentecost Peter quoted the verses indicating that they had that day been fulfilled (Acts 2:16–21). Yet not all of the signs were present, and New Testament authors continued to look forward to the day of the Lord. Therefore we would have to conclude that part of the prophecy was fulfilled but another part remains to be fulfilled. The same could be said of Isaiah 61 when Jesus quoted the first couple of verses as being fulfilled in his ministry (Luke 4:18–21; 7:18–23), while the remainder of the chapter clearly is not. Similarly, Paul and the other apostles expected the soon return of Christ (Rom. 13:11–12; James 5:8–9; 1 Peter 4:7), but their anticipation of how prophecy would be fulfilled turned out to be mistaken. These examples do not suggest deception or unfaithfulness on God's part, only that human beings have at times placed too much confidence in their ability to read the future from the prophecies.

3. Expectations Drawn from Statements Considered Clear in the Text Sometimes Are Not Realized

The problem concerning fulfillment reaches its apex when we have to deal with prophecies that do not seem to have been fulfilled at all, and the opportune moment has come and gone. For example, Zerubbabel and the audience of his day would have considered Haggai 2:21–23 to be perfectly clear:

"Tell Zerubbabel governor of Judah that I will shake the heavens and the earth. I will overturn royal thrones and shatter the power of the foreign kingdoms. I will overthrow chariots and their drivers; horses and their riders will fall, each by the sword of his brother.

"'On that day,' declares the LORD Almighty, 'I will take you, my servant Zerubbabel son of Shealtiel,' declares the LORD, 'and I will make you like my signet ring, for I have chosen you,' declares the LORD Almighty."

Readers would understandably expect the prophecies concerning world dominion (e.g., Isa. 2:1–4) to come true during the reign of King Zerubbabel, the anointed Davidic ruler who had been long anticipated to bring restoration and the fulfillment of all the covenant promises. Within a few years of this prophecy, however, Zerubbabel had disappeared from the scene with no trace of his fate left in the written record. Does this make Haggai a false prophet? No, not at all— it only demonstrates our inability to discern the shape fulfillment must take.[5] A second example can be found in Isaiah 11:15–16:

Signet rings were individually designed for kings and high-ranking officials and served as a symbol of authority when stamped.

Z. Radovan, Jerusalem

> The LORD will dry up
> the gulf of the Egyptian sea;
> with a scorching wind he will sweep his hand
> over the Euphrates River.
> He will break it up into seven streams
> so that men can cross over in sandals.
> There will be a highway for the remnant of his people
> that is left from Assyria,
> as there was for Israel when they came up from Egypt.

A simple reading of this text would easily lead one to the conclusion that the northern kingdom would experience a grand and visible return from their captivity in Assyria. In comparing it to the exodus, one would immediately recall the plagues and the parting of the sea that indicated the powerful acts of God on their behalf. Unfortunately, we search in vain for any recognizable return from Assyria, and there is no more searching for the ten lost tribes with the hopes that they could somehow still return; neither is there any longer an Assyria from which they could return. The point is not to disparage the faithfulness of God or the reliability of his prophets; it is rather to demonstrate that the supposed "clear" readings of prophetic texts that are used to frame the future are not always as clear as we think them to be. This might be a problem if the significance of the prophets were to be found in fulfillment rather than in the message. So, in this passage, the message is that God will restore his people. He will do it in such a way that it will fit with the imagery of the text. We should not think that we have the imagery figured out.

4. Fulfillment Can Be Narrower or More Defined Than Necessary or Anticipated

In this category we will consider three well-known prophetic passages—Isaiah 7:14; Micah 5:2; and Zechariah 9:9. If we investigate the expectations of the Jews of the first century BC concerning the Messiah, what will we find? Will their checklist of qualifications include (1) must be born of a virgin, (2) must be born in Bethlehem, and (3) must ride into Jerusalem on a donkey? In fact, the only hint we see of any of these is when the advisers to Herod responded that the Christ was to be born in Bethlehem (Matt. 2:4–6). Nevertheless, all three of these were fulfilled very specifically by Jesus; and subsequently, we view these as important messianic prophecies. But if Jesus had not ridden into Jerusalem on a donkey, or if he had not been born of a virgin, no one would have thought to use those prophecies as arguments against the claim that he was the Messiah. Alternate, more general explanations could have been offered for each of them. Zechariah 9:9 could easily have been fulfilled by any king coming humbly and peacefully—that is what riding on a donkey indicated. In Micah 5:2 the importance of Bethlehem was that it indicated a new beginning for Davidic kingship. A continuing Davidic dynasty would have found the king born in Jerusalem. The

Aerial view of Bethlehem, the birthplace of Jesus.

idea of being born in Bethlehem was that this was a new start, a new David. A peaceful king would not necessarily have to ride a donkey for the thrust of the prophecy to be fulfilled, nor would a new David necessarily have to be born in Bethlehem—yet Jesus fulfilled both more specifically than necessary.

Finally, Isaiah 7:14 is similar to the above examples in that the language that it uses does not specifically require a miraculous virgin birth in order to be fulfilled in general terms. The context of Isaiah shows this by referring to a contemporary child who fulfilled the prophecy (Isa. 7:16–17) yet was clearly not the result of a miraculous virgin birth. As in the above examples, however, Jesus' fulfillment followed a much narrower reading of the text than would have been required.

Just as there were some prophecies that were not fulfilled in the detail that would have been expected (categories 2 and 3 above), so these last examples show that others were fulfilled in more detail than would have been expected. Both categories show us the hazard of feeling any great confidence in our ability to anticipate the shape of fulfillment.

5. Prophecies Are Not Limited to One Fulfillment

When we look at current events and try to decide what might represent the fulfillment of prophecy, we can be confused by the fact that some prophecies might be fulfilled multiple times. Daniel 9:27, for example, refers to the abominations of one causing desolation. There was and is widespread agreement that this was fulfilled by Antiochus Epiphanes in 167 BC, when an altar to Zeus was placed in the temple. Nevertheless, in Matthew 24:15 Jesus makes it clear that they are still to look for fulfillment.

In a similar way, the prophecies about Israel returning to the land were fulfilled by means of the decree of Cyrus in 538 BC, after which a great number returned and rebuilt cities, walls, and temple. This possession of the land (with all its restrictions) came to an end with the Roman destruction of Jerusalem in AD 70. It was nearly 1900 years later when Jews again

Arch of the Titus, panel from the arch depicting Roman soldiers in triumphant procession carrying the Golden Menorah and other artifacts looted from the Jerusalem Temple before its destruction. Detail showing the Golden Candelbra which stood in the temple.

Z. Radovan, Jerusalem

returned to their ancestral land—a second fulfillment. Yet even now it cannot be said with certainty that the current possession of the land is the final fulfillment of the prophecies. Is it not possible that through some circumstances they could lose the land again and return again?

6. Terminology Can Be Repackaged

In Isaiah 65 the prophet speaks of a new heaven and new earth. Likewise, in John's vision in Revelation 21, he sees a new heaven and new earth. The question is whether they are talking about the same thing or whether Revelation 21 represents a repackaging of some of Isaiah's concepts. Isaiah offers a picture of the messianic kingdom, but it is a kingdom on earth within history. This is clear because death still exists (Isa. 65:20) and children are still being born (v. 23). In contrast the new heaven and new earth in Revelation are connected to the eternal state where there is no death (Rev. 21:4). When such repackaging can take place, it becomes difficult to trace ideas from the Old Testament to the New Testament or from prophecy to fulfillment.

---

1 Maccabees 1:20–21, 24, 29–30, 37, 41–42, 44–50, 54 (NRSV)

Antiochus returned in the one hundred forty-third year. He went up against Israel and came to Jerusalem with a strong force. He arrogantly entered the sanctuary and took the golden altar, the lampstand for the light and all its utensils. . . . Taking them all, he went into his own land. He shed much blood and spoke with great arrogance. . . .

Two years later the king sent to the cities of Judah a chief collector of tribute, and he came to Jerusalem with a large force. Deceitfully he spoke peaceable words to them, and they believed him; but he suddenly fell upon the city, dealt it a severe blow, and destroyed many people of Israel. . . . On every side of the sanctuary they shed innocent blood; they even defiled the sanctuary. . . .

Then the king wrote to his whole kingdom that all should be one people and that all should give up their particular customs. . . . And the king sent letters by messengers to Jerusalem and the towns of Judah; he directed them to follow customs strange to the land, to forbid burnt offerings and sacrifices and drink offerings in the sanctuary, to profane sabbaths and festivals, to defile the sanctuary and the priests, to build altars and sacred precincts and shrines for

Coin bearing the image of Antiochus Epiphanes IV.

©Copyright 1995 – 1999 Phoenix Data Systems, portions copyright 1999 Imspace Systems Corporation

idols, to sacrifice swine and other unclean animals, and to leave their sons uncircumcised. They were to make themselves abominable by everything unclean and profane, so that they would forget the law and change all the ordinances. He added, "And whoever does not obey the command of the king shall die." . . .

Now on the fifteenth day of Chislev, in the one hundred forty-fifth year, they erected a desolating sacrilege on the altar of burnt offering.

These examples are all designed to demonstrate that prophecy is not supposed to provide a sure guide to the shape of fulfillment. Prophecy's purpose is not to reveal the future (though it sometimes does so); it is intended to reveal God and his plan.

What does this understanding of prophecy suggest for our reading of the book of Revelation? In the Original Meaning section we laid out two important principles:

1. The vision is not the message, but the occasion for the message.

2. Symbols are designed to conceal, not reveal, so the revelation is to be found either apart from the symbols or in interpreted or transparent symbols.

This is not the place to enter into a detailed discussion of the book of Revelation, but if the focus should not be on the details of the vision, or on the meanings of the symbols, or on the determination of fulfillment, what is left—what is the message? Can we discern the message of Revelation without reconstructing a plot underlying the vision that offers an interpretation of the symbols and an explanation of fulfillment? We think so. Like the Old Testament aftermath oracles, the book of Revelation offers hope and encouragement in times of crisis. The worthiness and exaltation of Christ pervade the book, and we should find encouragement in knowing that history, even the grand culmination of history, is in his hands. Christ and his saints will prevail; victory will be won. These concepts are much more important than our ability to forecast the shape of the future.

RECAPITULATION

We should return briefly to the scenario concerning Greg and his dorm buddies. What should he have done? First, he probably should have been more guarded in his use of prophecy as he discussed it with his friends. It is true that many prophecies have been fulfilled, but some of those will only be persuasive to the eyes of faith. Overall, it is important not to present biblical prophecy as some sort of crystal ball to tell the future. Even Christ was guarded in his use of it as he directed people's attention to the warnings rather than to predictions.

Second, when challenged to use the Bible to predict the future, he should have turned his friends' attention to prophecy's revelation of God rather than dabbling in prognostication. Specifically, it would have been prudent to discuss God's control of history and the idea that he has a plan that he is working out. Finally, if that stimulated their curiosity, he could invite them to a few study sessions in the prophetic literature—particularly Isaiah 40–49.

1. What role should fulfillment play in our study of Old Testament prophecy today?

2. Is there a distinction between the Old Testament role of prophecy and the New Testament spiritual gift of prophecy? What are the implications of your answer?

3. What are some of the indictments the prophets would have had of our generation and culture?

4. How do we devalue God today?

5. Based on the picture of prophecy given here, what should our eschatology look like?

6. Do we have an obligation to tithe today?

7. Under what circumstances and using what guidelines should we participate in planned fasts?

8. What action do the prophets call us to in relation to the poor in other countries today? What about the poor in the inner-cities?

KEY REVIEW TERMS

Biblical Characters: Amos, Baruch, Daniel, Ezekiel, Hosea, Isaiah, Jeremiah, Jonah, Micah, Zechariah, Zerubbabel

Extrabiblical Characters: Belshazzar, Cyrus, Darius the Mede, Nebuchadnezzar

Peoples: Ammonites, Edomites, Moabites

Extrabiblical Texts: Mari prophecy texts

Concepts: aftermath, apocalyptic, classical prophecy, day of the Lord, fasting, fulfillment, indictment, instruction, judgment, message, messianic prophecy, preclassical prophecy, tithing

GOING TO THE NEXT LEVEL

C. Hassell Bullock, *Introduction to Old Testament Prophetic Literature* (Moody Press).

Robert Chisholm, *Handbook on the Prophets* (Baker).

Joel Green, *How to Read Prophecy* (InterVarsity Press).

Abraham Heschel, *The Prophets* (Jewish Publication Society).

Gordon McConnville, *Exploring the Old Testament: A Guide to the Prophets* (InterVarsity Press).

D. Brent Sandy, *Plowshares and Pruning Hooks: Rethinking the Language of Biblical Prophecy and Apocalyptic* (InterVarsity Press).

Willem Van Gemeren, *Interpreting the Prophetic Word* (Baker).

Notes

1. Philip Yancey, *What's So Amazing About Grace?* (Grand Rapids: Zondervan, 1997).
2. Ibid., 31.
3. Ibid., 282.
4. Donald McCullough, *The Trivialization of God* (Colorado Springs: Navpress, 1995), 27–28.
5. Deuteronomy 18:20–22 concerns primarily the straightforward specific prophecies that the prophets used for signs of their authenticity. Anything long term would not be easily measured by such criteria.

5 WISDOM LITERATURE

Gulf of Aqaba near Eilat.

- Wisdom must be learned from those who are wise.
- Wisdom involves the development of an orderly worldview, and the fear of the Lord is the beginning of wisdom.
- The retribution principle is an inadequate foundation for understanding how the world works.
- Self-fulfillment is unachievable and is not a worthy pursuit.
- "Normal" cannot be defined as when everything is going well.

"Wise words must be wisely used by wise people in order to result in wisdom."

"One of the persistent cultural myths is the myth of fulfillment — the promise that, on this earth, the fullness of all I truly need and all I really desire awaits. And it's not just a Hollywood myth. It's a Christian one, too. Maybe it's especially Christian."*

*Mark Buchanan, "Stuck on the Road to Emmaus: The Secret to Why We Are Not Fulfilled," *Christianity Today,* July 12, 1999, 55–57 (quote from p. 56).

YAHWEH FOCUS

- If we believe that God is wise, there is good reason to believe that he is just.
- God delights in blessing the faithful, and he is committed to punishing the wicked, but this cannot be reduced to a mechanical formula.
- God administers the world in wisdom, and from his sovereign wisdom, justice results.
- Both prosperity and adversity come from the hand of God.

KEY VERSES

- Job 28:20–28   God's wisdom and our wisdom
- Proverbs 3:5–6   The way to wisdom
- Ecclesiastes 7:14   Prosperity and adversity both from God's hand
- Song of Songs 8:6–7   The power of love

OUTLINE

ORIGINAL MEANING

What Is Wisdom?

Retribution Principle

Story Line: Job

Literary Perspective

BRIDGING CONTEXTS

Proverbs and Truth

Purpose Book by Book

Theological Perspectives

CONTEMPORARY SIGNIFICANCE

Scenario: Retribution Principle Today

Recapitulation

When Life Goes Wrong

Seeking Fulfillment in Life

Proverbs and the Family

The Power of Sex

KEY PLOTLINE TERMS

- wisdom
- theodicy
- retribution principle

ORIGINAL MEANING

The wisdom literature of the Old Testament is concentrated in the books of Job, Proverbs, and Ecclesiastes. Several wisdom psalms in the book of Psalms are also included (1, 14, 19, 23, 24, 36, 37, 49, 52, 53, 62, 73, 78, 119), as well as many other psalms that pick up wisdom themes. Finally, the book referred to as the Song of Songs or the Song of Solomon is also counted in this category. The rationale for its inclusion is not obvious, but in the end, not illogical. Wisdom literature can at times be recognized by the form that it uses, such as proverbial sayings. More frequently it is characterized by particular themes associated with what is known as wisdom in the ancient world. Prominent among these themes are questions concerning finding meaning in life, order in the world, and most common of all, human suffering. For example, how does God dole out prosperity or misfortune? How can the world of experience be reconciled with the supposed justice of God? The term used to describe this last question is *theodicy*. In the Old Testament, the issue of theodicy is addressed through what is often called the "retribution principle," which is treated in detail below.

WHAT IS WISDOM?

When we look at the vast number of topics covered under the heading of "wisdom," it is easy to despair of finding common ground, for the heading covers artisan skills, scientific knowledge, etiquette, philosophy, psychology, politics, sociology, and jurisprudence just to name a few. Furthermore, the text insists on more than one occasion that the fear of the Lord is the beginning or foundation of wisdom. Does this suggest that none of those disciplines could be successfully engaged without fear of the Lord?

5 WISDOM LITERATURE

Theodicy: Literature that seeks to reconcile God's justice to the reality of a world where people experience suffering and evil.

Perhaps we can best capture the biblical way of thinking about all of this by thinking in terms of worldview integration. In the ancient world, including Israel, *order* was an important value. Creation brought order to the cosmos; law brought order to society; etiquette brought order to human relationships; politics brought order to governance and authority. Ancient wisdom can then be understood as the pursuit of understanding and preserving order in the world. The people of the day wanted their worldview to fit together like a puzzle—fully integrated with each piece placed in proper relation to the others. In Israel, people saw the fear of the Lord as the keystone to this integration process. Order in the cosmos could only be understood through acknowledgment of the one who brought order. Order could

Authors of the Bible

Do we know who all of the authors of the Bible are? The short answer to that is no. In times past, however, it was considered important to be able to assign authorship to each book. This was because the authority of the book was in part reiterated by associating it with known authoritative voices (e.g., the prophets). Consequently, tradition is filled with associations of books with particular authors. Some of these offer internal rationale (e.g., David with Psalms or Solomon with the Song of Songs) while others offer only the most fragile of circumstantial evidence (e.g., Jeremiah with 1 and 2 Kings).

Pentateuch

The tradition of Moses as the author of the Pentateuch is strong both in the Old Testament and in the New Testament (see "Authors and Books," p. 70). The text offers strong confirmation that Moses should at least be considered the speaker, author, or editor of a large portion of the Pentateuch, although occasional statements appear to require a later hand (e.g., Gen. 12:6; 36:31; Deut. 34).

Historical Books

The historical books offer the least information about their authorship. The traditional authors such as Samuel (for the books of Samuel) or Jeremiah (for the books of Kings) enjoy little ancient or textual support as authors and have generally been so identified by nothing more than the prominence of their roles. All major characters are referred to in the third person. In addition, no later biblical litera-

Z. Radovan, Jerusalem

Bulla with an impression from the seal of "Baruch, son of Neriah, the scribe."

ture offers any suggestion as to authorship. Many today believe that Joshua, Judges, Samuel, and Kings were all edited together during the exile or soon after it. This group is therefore sometimes labeled the "Deuteronomistic History," since it reflects the theological themes of Deuteronomy. As a result, modern writers typically refer to authors such as the deuteronomist (Joshua–Kings) or the chronicler (Chronicles).

Prophets

It is appropriate to assume that the prophets to whom prophetic writings were attached were the ones who delivered those messages. That does not necessarily mean that the prophet was the one who wrote down the message or who compiled the book of those messages. It should be noted that the prophets are at times referred to in the third person. In Jeremiah we are told that a scribe named Baruch served as his secretary (Jer. 36:4). In Isaiah many believe the first five chapters to be a digest of the oracles that stretched throughout his career. If this is true, it would suggest a later editor. Some believe that a few of the prophetic books may have had additional prophecies added on at a

only be preserved in society and in life by understanding God's requirements and expectations. In this way, wisdom can be seen to transcend the basic knowledge or skill related to particular disciplines.

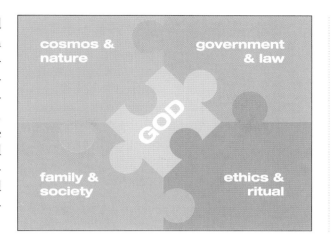

later date, perhaps by generations of followers of the prophet, but criteria have not been clearly established so that such determinations could be made with confidence.

Wisdom

It is no surprise that Solomon is connected to a number of the wisdom books of Israel. Sections of Proverbs are explicitly attributed to Solomon (1:1; 10:1; 25:1). He is mentioned by name in Song of Songs (1:1, 5; 3:7, 9; 8:11–12) possibly as author. In Ecclesiastes the first person pronoun is used for one describing himself as the son of David, king in Jerusalem (1:1, 12), giving the strong impression that Solomon is thus identified, though his name is never used.

Writing a cuneiform tablet by pressing a wooden pointer into wet clay.

Z. Radovan, Jerusalem

Excerpt from Talmud about Authorship (Baba Bathra 14b–15a)

Who wrote the Scriptures? Moses wrote his book and the section of Balaam and Job. Joshua wrote his book and [the last] eight verses of Deuteronomy. Samuel wrote his book, Judges and Ruth. David wrote the Psalms, with the collaboration of ten elders, namely, Adam, Melchizedek, Abraham, Moses, Heman, Jeduthun, Asaph, and the three sons of Korah. Jeremiah wrote his book, Kings, and Lamentations. Hezekiah and his associates wrote Isaiah, Proverbs, Song of Songs and Ecclesiastes. The Men of the Great Assembly wrote Ezekiel, the Twelve, Daniel and Esther. Ezra wrote his book and the genealogies of the Book of Chronicles down to himself and Nehemiah completed it.*

*Quoted from A. Cohen, Everyman's Talmud (New York: Schocken, 1975), 142–43. This represents a very early tradition and many of these conclusions are not considered valid today.

RETRIBUTION PRINCIPLE

The retribution principle is the most prominent theme in the wisdom literature. It is a system developed to try to understand how the world works, or more specifically, how God works in the world. The principle in its most basic form maintains that the righteous will prosper and the wicked will suffer. Derived from this principle is the inference that those who are prospering must be righteous and those who are suffering must be wicked.

By positive treatment, we mean that a person's fortunes show evidence that he or she is receiving favor at the hands of God. By negative treatment, we refer to the appearance that the person is out of favor with God and suffering punishment.

Article 1 of the retribution principle (see "Retribution Principle" chart below) was at the foundation of the covenant blessings and curses pronounced on the people of Israel (Deut. 28). Simply put, obedience brings blessing; disobedience brings curse. It is also reiterated in many different forms throughout the Old Testament (e.g., Ps. 37:9). In contrast, article 2 is never affirmed by the text but was believed by many Israelites. In the book of Job, the friends are explicitly basing their conclusions that Job has acted wickedly on the fact that he is suffering. Logically speaking, article 2 could only be true if article 1 were true all the time. Their experience told them that article 1 was not always true (Ps. 13), yet to abandon article 2 would

RETRIBUTION PRINCIPLE

	OBSERVED	EXPECTED
ARTICLE I	Positive Behavior (e.g., righteousness)	Positive
	Negative	Negative Treatment (e.g., suffering)

	OBSERVED	INFERRED
ARTICLE 2	Positive Treatment (e.g., prosperity)	Positive
	Negative	Negative

throw their worldview, particularly their theology, into chaos. This is because the retribution principle stood as their defense of the justice of God.

The Israelites had no revelation concerning reward or judgment in the afterlife (see pp. 366–70). Consequently, in their understanding, God's justice had to be carried out on this earth (see Ps. 27:13). They knew that neither reward nor judgment was necessarily doled out moment by moment (Ps. 37:25–26), so there could be time lapses. These, of course, applied to article 1—waiting for good or ill to come to those who deserved them.

Judgment scene from the Egyptian Book of the Dead. Each person's heart was weighed against a feather. If the heart was heavier, the person would be fed to the goddess Ammit. If the heart was lighter, the person would move into the afterlife.

© The British Museum

Since the retribution principle was understood as a reflection of God's administration of justice, proportionality was an important factor. It would not represent justice if a serial killer were merely assessed a small fine. In article 1, if someone committed blatant and/or unconscionable offenses, severe repercussions were expected. In article 2, if someone suffered extreme loss or hardship, especially if it came upon them suddenly, it was logical to assume that the judgment of God had fallen. This, of course, was exactly what happened to Job.

STORY LINE: JOB

Most wisdom literature has no story line because wisdom seldom uses the genre of narrative as its medium. Exceptional in this sense is the book of Job. The dialogues and discourses of the book are hung on a frame narrative that offers the setting for the philosophical discussion. This narrative has two locations: one on earth and one in heaven. As viewed from a human perspective, the narrative concerns a prosperous man who is meticulous in his conduct. He is prominent in his world and is widely considered a paragon of righteousness (though not an Israelite). A series of tragic disasters strikes him suddenly and dismantles his world. He loses family and possessions and is afflicted with a painful disease.

The heavenly scene that undergirds this narrative informs the reader that Job's misfortune was engineered by the heavenly accuser who challenged God's policy of prospering righteous people. The accuser insinuated that righteousness was compromised if one could conclude that those who were supposedly practicing it could be considered as being "bought" by God's favors and blessings. Thus the earthly story line is explained in some degree to the reader by means of the heavenly story line (of which the characters in the narrative are never made aware).

As Job ponders his bereavement, he is willing to accept his fate stoically as the hand of God that brings good or ill as he will. His friends and remaining family are not as content with this answer and press him to think through the implications of his current destitution. The first half of the book presents the dialogues between Job and his friends. His friends insist that his suffering is evidence that he has offended God. Since his suffering is great and came on suddenly, it must indicate some great sin. Job, in repeated responses, dismisses his friends as ignorant and pleads with God to meet him in some sort of adjudication of his case. The second half of the book presents discourses from Job, Elihu (apparently an Israelite representative to the

Satan in Job

In ancient belief the world was full of supernatural powers, known and unknown, good and evil, active and passive. Today we live in a modern world that scorns those who believe in the supernatural. Yet Christianity has historically affirmed the existence of demons, angels, and the archenemy, Satan. What did the Israelites know about Satan? To what did they refer when they used the term?

Satan is one of the few words that English has borrowed from Hebrew. In the Old Testament, it finds usage both as a verb and a noun. As a verb, it means "to oppose as an adversary" (Pss. 38:20; 71:13; 109:4, 20, 29; Zech. 3:1). As a noun, it can be applied to a human being, thus designating him or her an adversary (e.g., 1 Sam. 29:4; 1 Kings 11:14, 23, 25). Finally, in the category of most interest here, the noun is applied to supernatural beings (fourteen times in Job 1–2; three times in Zech. 3:1–2; and once each in Num. 22:22, 32 and 1 Chron. 21:1).

Given this range of occurrences, it would be logical to assume that a supernatural being would have been given this designation as a description of his function, that is, as

a heavenly adversary. This finds confirmation in the fact that in most of the cases where the noun is applied to a supernatural being, the definite article is attached to it. In English when we refer to someone by means of a proper name, we do not use a definite article (e.g., Sarah, not "the" Sarah). In this practice Hebrew behaves identically. Therefore we must conclude that the individual in Job should be identified as "the accuser" (description of function) rather than as Satan (proper name).

If we had no name for this individual and had to build his profile from the text of Job, what conclusions could we draw? First, we would observe that the satan comes among the sons of God. It is clear, therefore, that he has access to the heavenly throne and that he is counted among the members of this heavenly council. Second, the satan does not initiate the discussion of Job; he merely offers an alternative explanation of Job's righteous behavior. This represents a more limited view of the satan than we have now, since there is no tempting, corrupting, depraving, or possessing.

discussion judging by the name), and finally, God himself. After drawing the discussion to its resolution, Job's prosperity is restored in greater measure than he originally enjoyed.

LITERARY PERSPECTIVE

The Righteous Sufferer in Ancient Literature

In the ancient world, people were much more convinced that the divine realm actively controlled the fate of humanity. Consequently, everything had a reason (rather than just a cause). The theme of the righteous sufferer was repeatedly taken up in their philosophical quests for understanding. As early as 2000 BC, scenarios were developed in wisdom literature to consider the plight of a man who in his own mind, and in the estimation of all of those around him, was above reproach yet had come to experience a tragic sequence of events. This genre is represented in Mesopotamia in four specific works that span over a millennium from approximately the time of Abraham to roughly the time of David and Solomon:

Man and His God—a Sumerian text of a questioning sufferer.

University of Pennsylvania Museum (neg. #T4-474)

1. Man and His God (Sumerian, 2000).

2. I Will Praise the God of Wisdom (*Ludlul bel Nemeqi*, Akkadian, fourteenth–twelfth centuries BC).

3. Babylonian Theodicy (Akkadian, about 1000 BC).

4. Dialogue of Pessimism (Akkadian, uncertain date, probably late second millennium BC or early first millennium BC).

The importance of these pieces is that they help us to explore how Israel's neighbors thought about these issues and to evaluate how Israel's thinking compared. The resolution offered in the works from Mesopotamia generally takes the form of questioning whether there is any such thing as righteousness and whether the gods think of righteousness in the same terms that people do.

If people were uncertain about what the gods considered righteous behavior, it would be easy for them to have misconceptions about whether they or anyone else were truly righteous. If offenses could be committed without a person's knowledge, it would be easy to fall under condemnation unwittingly. These were options that existed for considering the gods to be *inscrutable*—beyond the ability of human perception and not offering any clear revelation of themselves. Alternatively, the gods could be considered *unscrupulous*—guilty of running an inconsistent system that did not make any claims to justice. The ancients may have felt this at times in their hearts, but they generally believed that the gods were interested in doing justice after their own fashion.

As Israel's wisdom literature considered the question of the righteous sufferer, particularly the book of Job, it could move beyond the typical ancient Near Eastern options because God had revealed himself. There should therefore be no misconceptions about what he considered righteous, and there would be less chance of unwitting sins (though see Ps. 19:12). Moreover, though absolute righteousness may have been considered impossible, the book of Job leaves no possibility for thinking that Job is lacking in righteousness.

Literature of Job

The book of Job is rightly considered a literary masterpiece. It is highly structured and multifaceted, featuring a number of different literary genres. Short narrative sections begin and end the book (Job 1–2; 42:7–17). The midpoint of the book (Job 28) is a hymn to wisdom. The first major segment of the book is introduced by a lament

STRUCTURE OF JOB

Prologue (1–2)

Job's Lament (3)

Three Dialogue Cycles (4–27)

Hymn to Wisdom (28)

Three Discourse Cycles (29–41)

Job's Closing Statements (40:3–5; 42:1–6)

Epilogue (42:7–17)

(Job 3) and filled out by three cycles of dialogue (Job 4–14, 15–21, 22–27). In each cycle as each friend speaks, Job offers a response until the last cycle, where only two friends speak. Thus there are three speeches of Eliphaz (Job 4–5, 15, 22), three speeches of Bildad (Job 8, 18, 25), two speeches of Zophar (Job 11, 20) and eight speeches of Job (Job 6–7, 9–10, 12–14, 16–17, 19, 21, 23–24, 26–27). After the hymnic interlude in Job 28, the genre shifts to discourse. Here there are three speakers (Job, Elihu, and God) each offering a series of discourses. Even within these discourses there is a variety of genres, including Job's extended oath of innocence (Job 31) and God's animal sketches. In all of this diversity, the book evidences a highly structured unity in which each section is literarily and rhetorically integrated into the whole.

Ancient Sumerian Proverb: "To speak, to speak is what humankind has most on heart."

All the Wisdom of the East: Proverbial and Didactic Literature

First Kings 4:29–34 offers a description of Solomon's wisdom and judges it "greater than the wisdom of all the men of the East, and greater than all the wisdom of Egypt" (v. 30). This shows that the biblical author is aware of the great wisdom traditions of the ancient Near East. When the text states that Solomon "spoke three thousand proverbs and his songs numbered a thousand and five" (v. 32), it is not necessarily suggesting that he composed all of those. Alternatively he could be seen as both a composer and a collector. Wisdom is gained by being encountered and absorbed in keeping with the respect of tradition that noted that there is nothing new under the sun.

University of Pennsylvania Museum (neg. B11372)

Proverbs for Sons and/or Daughters?

In the modern West, with our recently developed sensitivities to political correctness and inclusive language, the constant address of the advice to "my son" in Proverbs is deemed antiquated and in need of adjustment by some, while others consider it offensive and nothing short of chauvinistic. Some translations have adapted by adding "daughters" to the admonitions. The law required children to honor both their father and mother (Ex. 20:12). The Egyptian Teachings of Ptah-hotep and the Aramaic Words of Ahiqar also direct the father's advice to his son, showing that to be the norm in the ancient Near East. "Son" may also be understood more broadly as the one who received the saying, thereby not requiring blood relation. The omission of daughters simply reflects the reality that royal sons were generally educated, while royal daughters typically were not. The advice in many cases is just as appropriate to daughters as to sons, but the text reflects the cultural context in which it operated.

When we explore the long-honored traditions of wisdom in the ancient world, we are not surprised then to find many similarities to Israelite wisdom literature. Egyptian literature favors the "Instruction" form in which advice is given from the elder (usually king) to the younger (usually son). Over a dozen pieces are known with the earliest predating Abraham by many centuries and the latest extending beyond the Israelite exile and the last of the prophets. Mesopotamian wisdom literature includes fables (rare in the Bible) but also preserved collections of short proverbs, sometimes referred to as "aphorisms" (Sumerian as well as Babylonian). These memorable digests of wisdom often use simile, metaphor, analogy, contrast, or cause and effect to make their point. The Old Testament uses many of the same forms and occasionally shows striking similarity in content as well.

The Meaning of Life: Philosophical Literature in the Ancient World

The book of Ecclesiastes is sometimes referred to as pessimistic or speculative literature. Literary expressions of despair can be found in the ancient Near East in works such as the Egyptian Harper Songs and in the Mesopotamian Dialogue of Pessimism. But this assessment only picks up one aspect of Ecclesiastes, which, on the whole, is more dialectic. That is, it weighs the pessimistic conclusions about life under the sun against the more hopeful prospects connected with God-centered living. Leland Ryken has identified the book as "quest literature."[1] As such it would have some similarity to the famous Gilgamesh Epic in which Gilgamesh goes on a quest for immortality and in the process explores the meaning of life. Despite this common theme, however, Gilgamesh is a narrative while Ecclesiastes is reflective philosophical discourse.

Love Songs in the Ancient World

Examples of love poetry are known as early as the Sumerian mythological literature (third millennium) concerning the god Dumuzi, but much closer parallels are found in a group of Egyptian love songs from the period of the judges (Egyptian nineteenth and twentieth dynasties, 1300–1150 BC). These love songs were typically performed at festivals and share many of the features found in Song of Songs.

The Literature of Song of Songs

Many interpreters have concluded that the book is a dramatic production that features alternating speakers (individuals or groups). Some translations have gone so far as to identify the supposed speakers in the text (laid out as a play would be), though the Hebrew text does not offer such guides other than in the grammatical forms used for verbs and pronouns (masculine/feminine, singular/plural). Once someone decides to read the book as a drama, further decisions must be reached concerning the character list and the detailed reconstruction of the plot. This poses a number of difficulties in that there is disagreement whether there is one lead male character (king or shepherd) or two (king and shepherd). Even if that matter could be resolved, the details of plot are not easily worked out. It is not even clear whether a linear, sequential plot would be intended or something more circuitous.

Alternatively, the book could be considered a unified anthology in which several originally independent love songs were editorially woven together (note the repeated charge "Do not arouse or awaken love until it so desires," Song 2:7; 3:5; 8:4). In this case, there would be neither a unified plot nor a consistent cast of characters. The love poetry then would have a different purpose than to tell a moralistic story. This will be explored in more detail under Bridging Contexts.

REFLECTIONS

1. If wisdom is connected to bringing order out of chaos, how does wisdom relate to all of the various areas of life?

2. Why is creation such an important theme in the wisdom literature?

3. How important is the authorship of biblical books?

4. Trace the various aspects of the retribution principle through the wisdom literature.

5. Discuss the relationship of the retribution principle to the covenant blessings and curses.

6. Discuss how the ancient Near Eastern perspective on the retribution principle differs from the Israelite perspective.

7. How does the portrait of Satan in Job compare and contrast with the portrait of Satan in the New Testament?

Notes

1. Leland Ryken, *How to Read the Bible as Literature* (Grand Rapids: Zondervan, 1984), 126.

BRIDGING CONTEXTS

To bridge the gap in time and culture between the ancient Israelite wisdom literature and our own day, we need to understand the role of wisdom literature as Scripture. Wisdom literature is not like the commands of the law or the facts of narrative. It is not set forth as "Thus says the LORD" as in the prophets, nor is it even like the exhortations of the New Testament letters. How did the Israelites see this literature as the authoritative teaching or revelation of God?

The answer to such a question must be approached by gaining an understanding of the literature. For example, it would be a mistake to consider the book of Job to be simply a sad story about a good man who had problems. Though there may be reasons to argue in favor of the historicity of Job, we may be sure that the text's driving purpose is not to tell you Job's story. Job's story is a means to an end. Each wisdom book has its own way of communicating, and we cannot get to its truth until we first understand how the literature worked in the culture. It is best to start with Proverbs.

PROVERBS AND TRUTH

The first important point to establish is that a proverb by definition is a generalization. A generalization is considered useful when it is *usually* true. A generalization is not a guarantee or a promise. We know that this is the case with English proverbs. For instance, we consider the proverbial statement "Crime doesn't pay" to be true. Does that mean that there is never an instance in which crime pays? Of course not. The adage is a generalization, and we accept it as that when we recognize it as a proverbial saying.

Biblical proverbs work in much the same way. When Proverbs 22:6 states, "Train a child in the way he should go, and when he is old he will not turn from it," it is not making a promise or offering a guarantee. It is generally true that children will adopt in large measure the values with which they were raised. Are there exceptions? Of course. Does that expose the proverb as false? No—it is a proverb, not a promise. As a proverb, it advises the wise parent to raise a child well, and it offers a sense of confidence that the result will be a responsible adult ready to pass the value system on to the next generation.

Sometimes proverbs seem to present contradictory perspectives. In English consider these pairs:

Birds of a feather flock together.
Opposites attract.

Too many cooks spoil the broth.
Two heads are better than one.

He who hesitates is lost.
Look before you leap.

A bird in the hand is worth two in the bush.
A man's reach should exceed his grasp.

Is only one in each set true? It would be better to recognize that each is true in given situations. In other words, sometimes wisdom would counsel, "Look before you leap," whereas in other situations wisdom would recognize that "He who hesitates is lost." Both are true when wisely applied to the situation at hand.

The Old Testament has a similar example. In Proverbs 26:4–5 the advice is first given to restrain from answering a fool according to his folly lest you become like him. The very next verse turns it around and says that a fool *should* be answered according to his folly so that he not become wise in his own eyes. Again, we would have to conclude that both are true. The wise person would know which advice would be best to follow in any given situation.

These observations imply that proverbs not only teach wisdom, but they require a certain level of wisdom to be used successfully. Wise words must be wisely used by wise people in order to result in wisdom. Proverbs says as much when it observes: "Like a lame man's legs that hang limp is a proverb in the mouth of a fool" (26:7), and "Like a thornbush in a drunkard's hand is a proverb in the mouth of a fool" (26:9).

Wise words must be wisely used by wise people in order to result in wisdom.

How then is one expected to gain wisdom if it takes wisdom to learn wisdom? It must be taught by one who is already wise. In this way, we can understand the setting of proverbs as wisdom that is taught. It is a curriculum that is not meant as a self-study program. In some senses, it could be compared to a catechism in that it provides a framework for introducing and remembering important lessons.

How then are proverbs true, authoritative revelation from God? First, we must ask what would make a proverb false. One way would be if it were to propose its teaching based on a misguided value. Examples of these are found in the ancient Near East: "Do the wish of the one present; slander the one not present" or "The man who does not sacrifice to his god can make the god run after him like a dog."[1] In our modern context, any proverb that promoted multiplying sexual partners or affirmed that the pursuit of money or power should have highest priority would be considered false.

Scribes in training.

Education in Israel

Scribal education presumably taught reading, writing, literature, mathematics, law (for drawing up legal documents) and diplomacy (for royal correspondence). Schools for this sort of training would have been under the sponsorship of the temple or the palace. Besides the disciplines already named, royal sons logically would be taught history, protocol, etiquette, and the skills necessary for ruling wisely. After the invention of the alphabet in the first half of the second millennium, literacy had become more widespread, but there are still differences of opinion as to what proportion of the population was literate. Though schools existed in the ancient world before the time of Abraham, they were often informal and limited to the elite. The evidence for such schools in Israel is sparse, but sufficient to conclude that they existed at least by the eighth century. There was certainly nothing like public education.*

---

*Adapted from James Crenshaw, *Education in Ancient Israel* (New York: Doubleday, 1998); Daniel J. Estes, *Hear My Son* (Grand Rapids: Eerdmans, 1997).

National Geographic

5 WISDOM LITERATURE

A deaf husband and a blind wife are always a happy couple.
Don't offer me advice; give me money.
First secure an independent income, then practice virtue.[2]
Whoever dies with the most toys wins.

These are false because the values they espouse are worldly and flawed. A true proverb, then, is not one that describes something that is always true without exception, but one that will move the student toward the development of godly values.

There remain, however, some proverbs that run counter to our sensibilities or that we would consider unacceptable to our modern way of thinking. A number of proverbs, for instance, make derogatory statements about women (e.g., 11:22; 21:9, 19; 27:15–16; 30:20). Does this give us cause to label the book chauvinistic? Perhaps a few additional observations will be helpful: (1) There are many more derogatory statements made about men than about women (e.g., 10:10; 14:17; 16:28; 18:13; 19:3, 15, 24; 20:6, 19; 21:24–26; 29:22; not to mention that many of the negative characters of the book, such as the fool and the sluggard, are consistently male). (2) We must admit that there are negative characteristics of both women and men that are legitimate targets of proverbial sayings. (3) The book frequently praises wives (e.g., 18:22; 19:14; 31:10–31), compares women favorably in contrast to men (e.g., 11:16), and puts mothers and fathers on an equal plane (e.g., 23:22; 30:17). There is nothing here to compromise the truth of these proverbs.

A second area of controversy has focused on the method of disciplining children by beating them with a rod (13:24; 22:15; 23:13–14; 29:15). It should be noted first of all that the rod was the most extreme form of child discipline and therefore could be used in Proverbs for rhetorical effect. Proverbs at times use hyperbole to make their point. For example, 23:2 tells the glutton to put a knife to his throat when he dines with a ruler. Second, it should be noted that using a stick for discipline was widely accepted in the ancient world as appropriate to some circumstances. The Aramaic Words of Ahiqar from seventh-century Assyria contain a proverb very similar to Proverbs 23:13–14. "Withhold not your son from the rod, else you will not be able to save [him from wickedness]. If I smite you, my son, you will not die, but if I leave you to your own heart [you will not live].[3] Finally, the balance can be seen in Proverbs 19:18–19, where discipline results in hope, not in physical jeopardy, and the man who is acting out of temper must be dealt with severely. Abusing children is never condoned, but effective discipline is consistently called for even to the point of inflicting low threshold physical pain when necessary.

Finally there are the proverbs that might be considered distasteful in their manner of expression (e.g., 26:11; 30:33). Colorful language is one way to make a proverb memorable, which is, after all, the point. The biblical proverbs do not stoop to the profane or obscene modes of expression that are found in other wisdom literature of the ancient world.

In conclusion, we must be careful to interpret proverbs without falling prey to any misconceptions about what they are or about what they seek to accomplish. They promote virtues, expose vices, and advance wisdom as a means of character development that is founded on the fear of the Lord.

PURPOSE BOOK BY BOOK

Proverbs

The book of Proverbs has been discussed at length above. The purpose of the book is to collect the wisdom of ancient Israel and through it to offer insight into and examples of the wisdom that will result

The Ideal Wife?

Proverbs 31:10–31 is an acrostic* poem illustrating wisdom in the woman's world. The woman who is described sounds wonderful. She also sounds impossible! For centuries many women have read this passage and aspired to be that woman. They often have experienced a sense of frustration and failure—even damaged self-esteem—when they felt unable to "rise to the Bible's standard." How could they ever succeed at becoming a "Proverbs 31 woman"? Men have exacerbated this situation by using the passage as the basis for their expectations of their wives (not to mention by delivering guilt trips from the pulpit). Whether men are looking for suitable candidates or making demands of their wives, the ideal always seems far removed from reality. It is a sad state when they finally marry, "resigned to settle for something less."

Is Proverbs 31 giving guidelines for an achievable ideal? Is it a job description? Does it represent what women should aspire to and what men should seek? We would suggest not and propose an alternative suitable to the literature. Consider rather than using the label "ideal," understanding the portrait as "composite." In this view, the chapter contains twenty-two (one for each letter of the alphabet) observations or illustrations about wise or productive women. What are some of the forms wisdom will take in female guise? That is what this chapter explores.

A woman should aspire to be wise. To the extent that she is engaged in activities addressed in this chapter, wisdom will give her an idea of how to conduct herself. Men should find wisdom in a woman attractive. But this is not a checklist; neither does it exhaust all of the forms that wisdom could take. It represents "the ABCs of womanly wisdom."

*In alphabetic acrostics such as this, the first letter of each line represents the successive letters of the alphabet.

from or guide one to the fear of the Lord. It functioned to shape character and promote virtue. Its wisdom is intended to promote a secure and functional family and society in that both are founded on the fear of the Lord. The "fear of the LORD" is the way Israelites expressed what was at the center of their worldview. In the polytheistic setting of the ancient world, it was not unusual for the people to believe in the existence of many gods. Even some Israelites would have believed that other gods existed. So it would not be enough for the Israelites to center their worldview on the belief in Yahweh. Fear of Yahweh meant that they worshiped him and that they embraced the unique nature of Yahweh as it had been revealed to them. That is, the "fear of the LORD" assumed the adoption of the picture of Yahweh as distinct from the ways that their neighbors imagined their gods (for summary of the differences, see "Key Theological Distinctions between Israel and Its Neighbors," p. 106). Consequently, an Israelite saying that he "feared Yahweh" would be making a worldview statement at the same level of someone today identifying herself as a theist, deist, agnostic, or atheist.

Divine inspiration can be credited with guiding the author in selecting already composed proverbs for inclusion. Any that were original compositions devised by the biblical authors would have resulted from inspiration in the traditional ways.

Job

The complexity and the significance of the book of Job require that we spend a little more time on examining its purpose than we have spent on other books. Since the book sometimes uses the language of a courtroom, we will organize our comments using that format.

The Indictment. The first item that needs to be addressed is to determine who is on trial. That question can be answered by identifying what the charges are. Here we have to differentiate between the perspective of the characters and the perspective of the literature. The book begins with a scene in heaven that serves as the basis for the way the argument of the book is designed. But since none of the human characters has any knowledge of the heavenly events, they all play out their parts with a different perspective. In the heavenly scene (Job 1–2), Job is charged with nothing except perhaps questionable motives. His righteousness is stated from the beginning, and neither God nor the accuser suggests that Job's behavior is anything short of righteous. Instead, we find that the charges are being made against God. The accuser suggests that God's policy of blessing righteous people creates a reward system that actually hampers righteousness (1:9–11). His point is that if people are being rewarded for righteousness, it is difficult to discover whether they are truly righteous or whether they are simply conforming their behavior to what is required in order to enjoy blessings. In short, he is charging God with maintaining a flawed system—calling God to account for his policies. The specific policy that is challenged is the one we have called the retribution principle—that the righteous will prosper and the wicked will suffer (see pp. 292–93). God gives the accuser permission to test the policy by taking away Job's blessings to see if he will still act righteously (1:12; 2:6).

When Job begins to suffer, the second charge against God falls into place—and it is the opposite of the first. Based on the thinking that is the foundation of the retribution principle, Job's charge is that it is unjust of God to allow righteous people to suffer (7:11–21). The

The accuser claims that the policy of prospering the upright is counter-productive to true righteousness; Job claims that the policy of allowing the upright to suffer is contrary to justice.

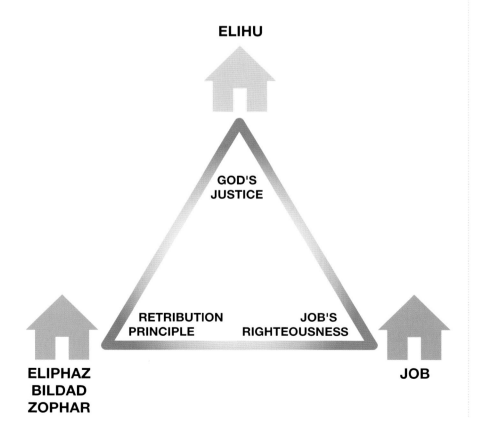

nature of the trial has now come into focus: The accuser claims that the policy of prospering the upright is counterproductive to true righteousness; Job claims that the policy of allowing the upright to suffer is contrary to justice. So we can see that the charges are made against God, and it is his policies that are on trial. It would appear that God loses whichever way he goes. Having said all of this, we must again reiterate that since the human characters know nothing of the scene in heaven, it seems to all of them that Job is on trial—and they play their roles with that frame of mind. The book, however, operates at a different level.

The "Courtroom." The setting is not a physical courtroom but the realm of philosophy. The context of the discussion is the retribution principle. The setting juxtaposes three claims: (1) that God is just; (2) that Job is righteous; and (3) that the retribution principle is true. When the book opens, these three are all givens, accepted by all as true. As the book takes shape, however, it becomes logically impossible to maintain all three claims. If we think of the courtroom as a triangle with one of these claims in each corner, we will see that each of the parties gravitates to a home base that it will defend at all costs, and that one of the other corners will be questioned.[4]

The three friends set up their home base by the retribution principle. They affirm the principle throughout their speeches in many different ways. Since they are not inclined to question the justice of God, they end up proposing that Job's righteousness has been compromised, though they are not aware of any shortcomings. It is the logic of their worldview (the retribution principle) that tells them it must be so.

Job anchors his perspective in his own righteousness—that is at least something of which he can be sure. Since he knows of no alternative to the retribution principle, he affirms its truth and ends up questioning the justice of God (see 40:8).

The fourth friend, Elihu (Job 32–37), positions himself firmly in the corner of God's justice. In doing so, he does not entirely discard either the retribution principle or Job's righteousness. He redefines the parameters first by expanding the retribution principle: In his view, misfortune is not limited to punishment for wrongdoing—it can also be preventative as it detects a deviation from the right path and preempts the grave error. Using this expanded definition, he is able to affirm Job's past righteousness but press the claim that Job's self-righteous response to his misfortune indicates a flaw in his character that the misfortune is drawing to the surface. He therefore avoids

Appeasement Theology

- Assume deity is angry.
- Assume offense cannot be confidently identified.
- Confess to anything and everything.
- Offer gifts to soothe anger.
- Anticipate returning to favor and receiving blessing.

discarding one of the corners by reshaping two of them. All three human parties, then (initial friends, Job, and Elihu), can be seen to be operating in the context of this triangular setting. In addition, it is this setting that has framed the indictment, since the charges against God made by both the accuser and Job assume that God's policy is accurately represented by the retribution principle.

The Trial. What would have to happen for God to lose the case? First, the quickest route would have been if Job had succumbed to his wife's advice: "Curse God and die!" (2:9). This would have demonstrated that the benefits and rewards were central in Job's thinking. The second way God could have lost the case would have occurred if Job had followed the advice of his friends and adopted the strategy of appeasement. The rationale of this strategy was that since deity was inscrutable and had not offered any guidance as to what pleased or displeased, people could not really discern what offense they might have committed. Consequently, when circumstances made it evident that deity was angry, the only thing one could do was seek to appease that anger. If one could readily embrace the idea that he or she had offended deity and somehow make amends, then the blessing train could start rolling again. If Job followed this advice, it would confirm what the accuser had claimed—that Job was not really concerned with true righteousness; he was only interested in doing whatever it would take to gain God's favor and blessings. If Job could be shown to think in that way, it would prove the accuser's charge that God's policy was flawed. Job, in contrast, maintains his integrity precisely by withstanding this path of least resistance (27:1–6). Either of these results would have proved the accuser's point, allowing him to emerge the victor.

What would have to happen for God to lose against Job's charges? Job would be victorious if the retribution principle were allowed to stand unaltered or unnuanced. This course of nuancing was the one that Elihu began to follow. Since Job thinks that he is on trial, he is striving for his own victory. He thought that he could win by brute force: First, by trying to cajole or coax God into appearing in court, and second, to use God's silence to his own advantage by pronouncing his oath (Job 31). In this negative oath, Job made detailed claims of his innocence with regard to numerous possible offenses, tacitly calling down God's punishment if any of his statements were false. This was the opposite of what his friends had advised (blanket confession). If God remained silent after Job's oath, his silence would stand as an affirmation of Job's innocence and, logically, as an admission that the misfortune of Job was undeserved.

> **Two Ways God Could Lose Based on Job's Choices**
>
> 1. Curse God (wife's advice).
> 2. Appease God (friends' advice).

The only way Job can win the case that he thinks he is involved in (concerning his own righteousness) is if God admits, on the basis of the retribution principle system, that he had acted unjustly. In this way, if Job wins (the retribution principle stands and Job's righteousness is affirmed), God loses.

The Parties and Case for the Prosecution. Job's charges are pressed in his frustration that God refuses to answer the subpoena. How can the charges be answered if God will not come to court? As with many of the readers of the book, Job thinks that he is on trial, and certainly in his friends' eyes, he is. The friends think that Job is on trial, so they press their charges of wickedness against him. In fact, however, in the perspective of the literature, they are unwittingly representing the accuser's charge against God. They do this through the advice they offer Job to simply admit to wrongdoing so that he can be restored to favor. With this advice they become champions of the conventional wisdom of the ancient Near East, which placed a high value on appeasement, as discussed above. So here we find the two parties of the prosecution: Job is pressing his own case against God, while the friends are pressing the accuser's case against God by advising a course of action for Job that will demonstrate the accuser's point to be true.

The Parties and Case for the Defense. As in many trials, the case can rest on the strength of one witness. Even though Job is one of God's prosecutors, he is also, unknown to him, the star witness for God's defense. What he does or does not do is going to make or break the case against God. The other party for the defense is the fourth friend. Like the other friends and Job himself, Elihu is under the impression that Job is on trial, and he mounts an impressive and irrefutable accusation against Job. Elihu's position serves as an introduction to God's ultimate defense because it begins to loose God from the restrictions inherent in the retribution principle. He proposes that the conventional formulation of the retribution principle is too simplistic. Elihu does not buy into the strategy of appeasement and so differs from the other friends. His is the only name that is Hebrew, so it is possible that he serves in the book as a representation of the best that Israelite thinking had to offer—more sophisticated than the ancient Near East at large represented by the other friends but still tied too closely to the retribution principle.

The case for the defense actually begins, however, in Job 28, the Hymn to Wisdom. Literarily this stands as an interlude between the dialogues and the discourses. The speeches of the friends represented the cutting edge of wisdom in the ancient world. The implication of the Hymn to Wisdom is that although the friends have exhausted their case, the voice of wisdom has not yet been heard. The hymn indicates how difficult true wisdom is to find and how profound God's wisdom is. The discourses of Job (Job 29–31) and Elihu (Job 32–37) each set up the final defense in their own way as indicated in previous paragraphs. Job's oath stakes a final claim to the retribution principle system and shows that he has not been able to think outside that box (with the exception of the slight progress made in Job 24), while Elihu's begins the qualification of the system. In God's self-defense (Job 38–41), the retribution principle system is shown to be simplistic and is dismantled. If we go back to the triangle as representing the courtroom, we could say that God insists on a change of venue—a new setting in which the trial will be conducted. He discards the triangle.

> If we believe that God is wise, there is good reason to believe that he is just.

The justice of God's policies is what is under investigation. God does not try to defend his justice in his discourses because, as becomes clear, no one is in a position to assess his justice. To assess God's justice in running the world, someone would have to have all the information about how the world was run. God's speeches make

Leviathan

The book of Job deals with several fantastic creatures, but perhaps the most intriguing, and the one treated in most detail, is the leviathan. Some have considered the leviathan of Job 41 as an actual beast, others as a mythical creature, still others as actual beasts being used metaphorically to represent cosmic forces. Those who see it as an actual beast tend to favor either crocodile or dinosaur. Those who see the leviathan as a mythical creature look to the creatures featured in ancient Near Eastern literature, such as the seven-headed dragon pictured on seals. In Isaiah 27:1 the leviathan is counted among mythical beasts that are used by the prophet to represent national foes. The close correspondence between Isaiah 27:1 and a Ugaritic mythological text strengthens the idea that it has seven heads. The Ugaritic text reads, "When you smote Lotan the fleeing serpent, you made an end of the twisting serpent, the mighty one of the seven heads."* Psalms also indicates that the leviathan has more than one head (Ps. 74:13–14), making the identification with an actual beast extremely difficult (though it should be noticed that in Job words like *tongue*, *jaw*, and *neck* are used in the singular [Job 41:1, 2, 22]). Additionally, Job 41:21 suggests that the leviathan breathes fire.

Given the data, there would be cause to identify the leviathan as a cosmic beast. Like the phoenix in Greek mythology, this would be a creature who represents something, specifically the cosmic evil associated with the primeval sea. But in addition, it could be considered a spiritual reality. Like the cherubim, who are considered by people who take the Bible seriously as "real" creatures, you would not expect to encounter it or find it in a zoo. It is mythical in design (griffin-like characteristics), functions in the divine sphere, and inhabits the supernatural realm. Yet it is portrayed in sculpture and relief throughout the ancient world. Leviathan would be similarly understood in Israel. Whether cosmic creature or supernatural beast (or both), the contention in Job 41 that God can tame the fearsome leviathan is evidence of his establishment of justice in the cosmic or supernatural realm.

---

*COS, 1.86:265.

it plain that no one possesses such information (40:8–14; 41:11). The conclusion of the matter and the point the book intends to make is that the world is too complex for us to be able to have all the information that we would need to affirm that God is just. We do have enough, however, to affirm that he is wise. If we believe that God is wise, there is good reason to believe that he is just.

The Verdict. Job demonstrated that his righteousness was not simply a pursuit of blessing and prosperity. Consequently, the accuser's charge against God's policy of blessing righteous people was shown to be false. God demonstrated that his wisdom surpassed the simple equations of the retribution principle and that the operation of the cosmos was based on wisdom rather than on the premise of the retribution principle. Consequently, Job's charge of injustice premised on the retribution principle was also shown to be false. God's policies were thus vindicated, and he showed his renewed commitment to them by again heaping blessing on Job.

But how is this not a reiteration of the retribution principle? The difference is that in this new view, the retribution principle is not of a system that is the foundation of the world. It does not represent a guarantee or a mechanical cause-and-effect process. It is God's delight to prosper those who are faithful to him, and it is God's commitment to punish wickedness. That is the nature of God. But this cannot be reduced to a formula. God has created the natural world and maintains it day by day. But that does not mean that the natural world is endowed with the attributes of God. Rain can be used by God to enforce justice, but the rain is not just (38:25–27). He administers the world in wisdom, and from his sovereign wisdom, justice results.

Ecclesiastes

This book, also known as Qoheleth, is one of the most difficult books in the Bible to read and to understand. Its interest is in no less significant a subject than the meaning of life. The quest it investigates concerns whether there is meaning to be found in life "under the sun," or as we would say, "in this life." The answer is that each pursuit investigated (wisdom, wealth, pleasure, power, legacy) has several potential drawbacks: (1) it proves an unworthy pursuit; (2) it is unachievable (i.e., no matter how much of it you get, there is always more to get); or (3) in the end you die anyway, so what is the point? The author therefore adopts the radical conclusion that there is no sense of self-fulfillment that can bring meaning to life, so the best choice is to stop pursuing self-fulfillment. The alternative he offers is the pursuit of a God-centered life. Even though pursuits under the sun may not be capable of providing self-fulfillment or give meaning to life, there is much in life that can be enjoyed as the gift of God.

The book also recognizes that there are many things in life that cannot be enjoyed and would not be called gifts. Ecclesiastes 3:1–8 lays out some of these as contrasts in our experiences. Whether our frustrations in life are great or small, the book establishes that we dare not entertain the idea that life without frustrations is possible. Both prosperity and adversity come from the hand of God (7:14). This discussion concerns a person's expectations of life. No one's life is problem-free, so the book teaches that, without being fatalistic, we ought to adjust our thinking to absorb or even embrace the difficult lessons that life brings our way.

Ecclesiastes' perspective on religion and government is that we should not expect either to solve all of our problems. Regarding the retribution principle, the author observes that it cannot offer any guarantees but that it is prudent to live as though it were absolutely true (7:15–18; 8:10–14). If we approach religion as a means to a smooth, trouble-free life, we will be disappointed. In this way, he discusses only what religion should not be expected to do rather than outlining the positive aspects of religion. In the same line of thought, if we expect the government to provide justice and resolve our insecurities, we will be equally disappointed. The author advises his readers to live under authority but not to expect too much from it (8:1–9).

To summarize the message of Ecclesiastes: Find enjoyment in the gifts of God. It will not suffice to think that "normal" is when everything is going well in life. Both prosperity and adversity are normal

Qoheleth

The Hebrew word translated "Teacher" in Ecclesiastes 1:1, 12 is *Qoheleth*. It occurs only in this context, and its meaning is uncertain. Greek translators of the Bible understood it as relating to a Hebrew verb that means to gather or collect and therefore used an appropriate Greek term that meant something similar; and it is from that word that we get the English title Ecclesiastes. Some have seen Qoheleth as gathering people together for instruction, others as gathering words together as one would gather wise sayings (perhaps like an English anthology). Another possibility is that the book *convenes* a discussion group. This could be represented by several people actually gathering for discussion or by representing several viewpoints (as some modern publishers do in books entitled *Four Views of. . .*). Finally, it is possible that the book gathers various personae or perspectives to discuss the issues at hand. What would be the experience of a king? What would be the experience of a slave? In this way, the book's issues could be turned around and examined from numerous vantage points. Of course, it is possible that the title is not related to the verb at all—language does not always work that way. After all, we do not think of a professor as "someone who professes."

and come from God's hand; both can shape us in important ways. It is normal that we have times of difficulty, because it is a broken world and death is really all that it has to offer. Life is not under our control. Lower expectations, increase contentment. In many ways the philosophy of Ecclesiastes is preparatory for the gospel, though the author had no knowledge of the eventual option that Christ made available as he defeated sin and death.

Song of Songs

Under Original Meaning we discussed the difficulties of reconstructing an underlying narrative to this book and raised the possibility that the teaching of the book is not conveyed through a moralistic story (see p. 299). The power of a country-and-western love song is that anyone can play that ballad with his or her own story in the background. Such songs are not trying to offer biography or autobiography—they are singing about love. Song of Songs does the same. What is the message it wants to convey to the reader about love? There are many potential themes. Love can be described as faithful or as fickle; love can be submissive or controlling; love can be pure or corrupt; love can be likened to hunger or to fever; love can be mutual or unrequited. A given song could focus on any one or any combination of these qualities. Our expectation of the Bible is that it will offer valid thinking and insight about love.

Song of Songs as Allegory?

The most common interpretation of Song of Songs in both Jewish and Christian circles has been an allegorical one. In this approach, the Song is *really* about God's love for his people Israel (Jewish interpretation) or Christ's love for the church (Christian interpretation). One of the early church fathers, Origen (third century), wrote a ten-volume commentary on the book offering verse-by-verse explanation of the allegorical correlations. So, for example, Song of Songs 1:13, "My lover is to me a sachet of myrrh resting between my breasts," is interpreted by the Jewish allegorists as the presence of Yahweh between the two cherubim and by Christian allegorists as Christ between the Old and New Testaments. Origen, along with the Christian allegorists that came after him, believed that the literal level of meaning, or the "plain" meaning, was profane and carnal.

The obvious difficulty to this approach is the subjectivity of the conclusions. In the example above, the only guiding concept is that the male (always representing God) is portrayed between paired objects. Only imagination can provide the details. It is impossible to maintain the concept of an authoritative message in the text if the message is entirely devised by means of the imaginative speculations of the interpreter. This results in shifting inspiration from the text to the interpreter. How are we to choose between one interpreter and another? Which one is inspired? Consequently, even if we were to accept the possibility of an allegorical level of meaning, we would have no biblical guidance as to what that meaning was. The idea of the text is to *reveal*. In allegory, by definition, the meaning is *concealed* with no sure means of getting to that which is *revealed*.

When Song of Songs talks about love, it emphasizes the necessity that love be kept under control despite the passion, the longing, and the anticipation. These characteristics must be controlled because they give love power over a person and that power can work in positive ways to overcome the obstacles of circumstance or work in negative ways as it breaks through barriers of propriety. Love has this power whether applied to young unmarried sweethearts, those who are betrothed, newlyweds, or those married for decades. Its power is not only evident when the flames are burning, but when the flames are dying. This power is addressed directly in Song of Songs 8:6–7: "Love is as strong as death, its jealousy unyielding as the grave. It burns like blazing fire, like a mighty flame. Many waters cannot quench love; rivers cannot wash it away. If one were to give all the wealth of his house for love, it would be utterly scorned."

The love songs preserved in this book illustrate many of the faces of love's power. A wise person must be aware of that power and recognize its faces and its dangers. So in that sense, this is a wisdom book. Love and sex wield incredible power, and the wise person will understand that and learn to harness and discipline that area of his or her life.

Purpose of the Wisdom Literature as a Whole

The diagram below shows how the various pieces of wisdom literature interlock to cover the entire field of wisdom. As discussed in unit 6, the wisdom aspect of Psalms, summarized well in Psalm 1, offers perspective concerning relating with God through the difficulties and uncertainties of life. The psalmist is often confused about the circumstances of his life and seeks God for help, encouragement, deliverance, and vindication—his hope is in God. A wise person will praise God when life is going well and God's hand is evident and will trust God when life is falling apart and God seems distant. Job gives an understanding of the moral structure of the cosmos and proposes that it is based on God's wisdom pervading his creation rather than justice as defined by the retribution principle. Ecclesiastes offers perspective on what our expectation of life should be. Song of Songs focuses on the power of love and sex in our lives. Proverbs helps us to see how to live wisely in society and community.

The diagram also indicates that the overall thrust of the wisdom literature is to help us develop a unified worldview with God at the center. This brings us back to the literature's own claim that the fear of the Lord is the beginning of wisdom. In the New Testament, we find the same concern as Paul exhorts us to "take captive every thought to make it obedient to Christ" (2 Cor. 10:5). We bring order to the chaos of our lives and our world by having this sort of integrated worldview. In Christian education, the importance of this is recognized as we seek to integrate faith and learning, which reflects a commitment to showing how any disciplinary field of study should be informed by our faith and related to our faith. God needs to be the center of gravity in our worldview. Most other biblical literature builds the view of God that needs to be a part of our worldview. Wisdom literature builds the worldview that should result from a proper understanding of God.

THEOLOGICAL PERSPECTIVES

© edenpics.com

Theology of Retribution Principle

As we discussed under Original Meaning (see pp. 292–93), the retribution principle begins with the premise that God is just. If God is just, then righteousness should be rewarded and wickedness should be punished. In our modern theology, we believe that some righteousness and wickedness is judged in this world but that the larger and final expression of God's justice will take place at the final judgment as each person's eternal destiny is ordained. Israel did not yet have very much revelation about this final judgment and alternatives for eternal destiny, so all of their attention focused on this world (Prov. 11:31; see further discussion on pp. 366–70).

When we combine Israel's conviction that God's justice would be reflected in the world and in each person's life with the belief that God is the cause behind all that happens, we can understand the logic that would lead the Israelites to assume that just causes behind prosperity or adversity should be identifiable. Where does this logic break down? Both premises—God as just, and God as ultimate cause—can be accepted unequivocally. The breakdown occurs in the complexity of each. Both are so far beyond our ability to fully comprehend that few situations can be considered transparent.

A biblical perspective can be gained by observing how Jesus reflected on the retribution principle. In Luke 13:1–5 Jesus was informed of a massacre of some Galileans bringing sacrifices to the temple. Alluding additionally to people who had been killed when a tower collapsed, he responded by raising the question as to whether the disasters that befell these people were brought on by some guilt on their part. His conclusion denies the cause-and-effect connection yet affirms that sinners should live in fear of the judgment of God. In this way, God's commitment to maintaining justice is declared, but events are not thereby considered transparent.

In a second important New Testament passage, John 9:1–5, the disciples raise the retribution principle question concerning a man who was born blind. This would be an obvious difficulty because, on the one hand, it would appear that the man's own sin could not have caused his condition, but on the other, it would not seem just for his condition to have been caused by some offense committed by his parents.

Here, rather than use this as an occasion to affirm God's interest in justice as he did in Luke, Jesus uses the question to offer a different approach. His answer to their question is: "Neither this man nor his parents sinned, . . . but this happened so that the work of God might be displayed in his life" (John 9:3). This reply indicates that even when cause cannot be identified and guilt cannot be assigned, attention can be directed toward purpose. Rather than focus on the past, look to the future. Theologically this suggests that God's justice may at times be discerned through an understanding of purpose rather than through an understanding of cause. Some might conclude that this results in a situation where the ends justify the means, but it is more like "We know that in all things God works for the good of those who love him" (Rom. 8:28). This is the difference between just cause and providence. The book of Job had indicated that the cosmos did not operate with every cause and effect based on justice. Job himself never learned the "cause" of his tragedy. But God's providence is

> Not all circumstances are just, but God can bring justice out of circumstances.

demonstrated in his ability to turn any occurrence that is brought on in the context of a broken world and sinful people and to bring his good purposes from it (Gen. 50:20).

Imagine a car that has somehow careened from the smooth highway and has now become an off-road vehicle encountering rough terrain and obstacles of every kind. If the cosmos (the car) and its history (the terrain) are viewed in that way, we will observe that God is still at the wheel and still has his foot on the accelerator. No matter how rough the terrain or how imposing the obstacles, he is firmly in control of the car and is guiding it back to the smooth highway. We are blindfolded passengers and cannot say why this bump or that underbrush is encountered—they are simply part of this difficult terrain. We can only trust that the car is still under the control of the driver. At times, hitting a bush may be preferable in order to avoid a rock or a chasm. Perhaps going up a mountain may be the best way to get to the plain. We place ourselves in the care of the navigator. The conclusion to be drawn from this is that the Bible indicates that we are incapable of discerning cause. Not all circumstances are just, but God can bring justice out of circumstances.

What then of the retribution principle? Is it true? Article 2 could only be true if article 1 were true in every case with no exceptions (see p. 292). Is article 1 true? Yes, but in the same way a proverb is true. When God or the Old Testament authors affirm the principle, they do so as an expression of the nature of God—he is committed to justice. In the proverbial sense by which it operates, the retribution principle should be understood as a statement that explains the nature of God rather than as a statement that explains the nature of the world. As such, the truth of article 1 is not of the sort that would offer guarantees, and therefore article 2 is not true.

Order Out of Chaos: Creation and Wisdom

Even a casual reader would observe that creation is a common theme of wisdom literature. Scholars have often drawn attention to how wisdom literature almost neglects covenant and law in favor of creation. A logical explanation of this emphasis is found in the understanding that wisdom represents orderliness in all matters. Creation is the initial establishment of that order. In the ancient world, order was maintained by the decrees of the gods. One set of decrees in Sumerian thinking included institutions of civilization such as kingship and priesthood, activities such as kissing and traveling, abstractions such as knowledge and fear, behaviors such as deliberation and decision making, technical skills of scribe and carpenter, negative qualities such as deceit and slander—ninety-four in all.[5] Creation involved establishing order at every level and maintaining that order moment by moment. Wisdom involved perception and understanding of that created order. In ancient ways of thinking, creation was not a one-time act that brought some bit of matter into existence in space and time. Creation was the establishment of a functioning cosmos, civilization, and society, and wisdom was the foundation of it. Consider Proverbs 8:22–31:

© edenpics.com

> The LORD brought me forth as the first of his works,
>   before his deeds of old;
> I was appointed from eternity,
>   from the beginning, before the world began.
> When there were no oceans, I was given birth,
>   when there were no springs abounding with water;
> before the mountains were settled in place,
>   before the hills, I was given birth,
> before he made the earth or its fields
>   or any of the dust of the world.
> I was there when he set the heavens in place,
>   when he marked out the horizon on the face of the deep,
> when he established the clouds above
>   and fixed securely the fountains of the deep,
> when he gave the sea its boundary
>   so the waters would not overstep his command,
> and when he marked out the foundations of the earth.
>   Then I was the craftsman at his side.
> I was filled with delight day after day,
>   rejoicing always in his presence,
> rejoicing in his whole world
>   and delighting in mankind.

This section of Proverbs identifies Lady Wisdom as preceding creation and facilitating it. This does not suggest the existence of some goddess consort, but indicates the integral relationship between wisdom and creation with the preeminence belonging to the former. In conclusion, the association of wisdom and creation in the wisdom literature helps us to understand both wisdom and creation more accurately.

REFLECTIONS

1. In what ways are proverbs true? How do we penetrate the truth of a proverb?

2. What are the implications of considering God to be the one on trial in the book of Job rather than Job?

3. Compare and contrast the perspective of Elihu against those of the other three friends in Job.

4. How does the role of Satan compare to the role of the friends in the book of Job?

5. What is the significance of God's blessing Job with doubled prosperity at the end?

6. Does the author of Ecclesiastes believe that one can find fulfillment in a relationship with God? Why or why not?

7. Are the lovers in Song of Songs married? Do they get married? Does the book's message depend upon their marriage?

8. Discuss the idea that the purpose of the wisdom literature is to help us develop a unified and coherent worldview with God at the center. How does it do that?

9. Is the retribution principle true? What are the Bible's claims about the truth of the retribution principle?

10. What are the pros and cons of reading the Song of Songs as an allegory?

Notes

1. Both drawn from Benjamin Foster, *From Distant Days* (Bethesda, MD: CDL, 1995), 371, 387.
2. The first three here were taken from a website by Stephen L. Spanoudis ©1994 on 5/30/02. See www.geocities.com/~spanoudi/quote–05a.html.
3. *ANET* 427–30. Egyptian literature also has a saying, "A son does not die from being punished by his father" (in the tenth instruction of Papyrus Insinger, *AEL* III: 192; 9.9).
4. The triangle idea is developed in M. Tsevat, "The Meaning of the Book of Job," *HUCA* 37 (1966): 73–106.
5. "Inanna and Enki," in COS, 1.161, p. 523.

CONTEMPORARY SIGNIFICANCE

SCENARIO: RETRIBUTION PRINCIPLE TODAY

Barry loved basketball. He had begun playing as soon as he could hold a ball. He spent countless hours out on the driveway practicing shots and moves using the hoop attached to the garage. A pro career was certainly not in the cards, but he had been one of the regular performers on his high school team. Now he was finally here at college. Despite the small size of Barry's high school, the coach had recruited him to come and play at this midsized university. Other schools had seemed interesting to him, but this was the only one that had offered him the chance at some scholarship money. Of course, though, he had to make the team first.

As tryouts approached, Barry became more and more nervous. There was only one spot available on the varsity squad. He was confident that he was better than most of the new recruits, but then there was Jeff. Jeff was already establishing a reputation as "big man on campus." He was clearly popular with both the other guys and the girls, but he gained that popularity in all the wrong ways. He was a bully in the dorm and outside was impressive only because of his reckless and irresponsible lifestyle.

Barry wasn't perfect by any means, but he always tried to do the right thing and was conscientious in his commitment to Christ. As he shared his concerns about the tryouts with his small group at church, they offered to pray for him. Together they looked through the Bible and found verses, especially in Proverbs, that gave him assurances that God blesses the righteous with success while he brings well-deserved disaster to the wicked. Barry felt confident that he could claim the promises of God in these verses and that the result could only be a spot on the varsity team and the finalization of his scholarship. His friends confirmed his thinking and continued in prayer. That big shot Jeff was toast.

The big day came, and Barry's performance was flawless. His shooting percentage was higher than usual; he played aggressively in the two-on-two drill; and in one of the one-on-one contests, he was matched against Jeff, whom he beat by one point with a sweet inside move that he had been practicing. He left in high spirits, but they lasted only a day. The next morning the names of the varsity squad were posted, and there was Jeff's name where he thought his ought to be. God had let him down. God had failed to keep his promise. Maybe God was overrated—why bother? Somehow he couldn't face the option of playing intramural ball—he had lost his heart for the game. Besides that, he had to take a job on the side to make up the money that the scholarship was supposed to cover. It was hard to keep up with his job and with school work, and the latter began to suffer. He certainly didn't have time for church—a lot of good God had done him.

RECAPITULATION

Barry's basketball tryout may have been flawless, but his Bible/theology tryout left much to be desired. He was treating wisdom literature as if it offered promises—guarantees for success for the righteous. As a result, he was viewing the outcome of the basketball tryout as an indication of God's favor and as governed by God's justice. This was never how the wisdom literature was meant to be used, and his misunderstanding had led to the dismantling of his faith. God hadn't failed Barry; rather, Barry's expectations had been misguided. If we are going to avoid the pit that Barry fell into, we need to explore how we should understand those passages in the Bible that present the basics of the retribution principle.

WHEN LIFE GOES WRONG

Some days nothing goes right. But most of us can handle a bad day now and then. Life is much more of a challenge when it is full of days in which nothing goes right. It is even worse when there seems to be no way out. Many people feel trapped by life's circumstances—a family situation that seems irreconcilable and unsalvageable; an illness that is chronic and incurable; or a loss or offense that is irreversible with staggering consequences. When life seems unfair, it is normal for us to look for someone to blame—and eventually the blame works its way back to God. When life goes wrong, it is easy for doubts to arise about whether God really is in control. And if he is, how can he be good, wise, or just? How can we be people of faith when we live broken lives in a broken world?

The wisdom literature intends to help us with these questions, but it chooses a very unusual approach to them in the book of Job. Though we sympathize with Job's plight, it is easier to care about ourselves than it is to care about Job. That is why it was important to demonstrate earlier that God is the one on trial in the book—because when life goes wrong, we feel like standing right there next to Job hurling our accusations at the Almighty. There is a great empty loneliness when we banish God from our world. When the heavens are brass, the silence in which our screams echo is oppressive and deafening. And so we listen carefully when God speaks from the whirlwind. We want to believe that he is good, wise, and just. We cling to such comfort in our misery. We whisper under our breath, "Give us hope; give us a reason to believe."

Broken World

The first step is to acknowledge that we live in a broken world. In the Pulitzer prize–winning play about Job, *J. B.*, Archibald MacLeish's characters powerfully express this brokenness as they consider the Jobs of history:

> There must be
> Thousands! What's that got to do with it?
> Thousands—not with camels either:
> Millions and millions of mankind
> Burned, crushed, broken, mutilated,
> Slaughtered, and for what? For thinking!
> For walking round the world in the wrong
> Skin, the wrong-shaped noses, eyelids:
> Sleeping the wrong night wrong city—
> London, Dresden, Hiroshima.
> There never could have been so many
> Suffered more for less.[1]

© edenpics.com

Why does God allow it? This is a question that has kept many from belief in a good and powerful God. MacLeish again captures the question eloquently.

> I heard upon his dry dung heap
> That man cry out who cannot sleep:
> "If God is God He is not good,
> If God is good He is not God;
> Take the even, take the odd,
> I would not sleep here if I could
> Except for the little green leaves in the wood
> And the wind on the water.[2]

It is a question that has plagued many millions who lived their lives in the shadow of tyranny or suffering and too often died at its hands. Accepting a God who would allow millions of innocent people to be tortured and killed is considered by some worse than worshiping a God who was powerless to stop it. But when we accept the fact of a broken world, we must consider that while God has clearly not resolved the brokenness, neither is he the one who broke it.

Purpose Not Cause

The next step is to take seriously the reorientation to suffering offered by Jesus in John 9:3 (see Bridging Contexts, p. 317). Unless there is some immediately obvious or identifiable cause (e.g., unfaithfulness leading to divorce, drunken driving leading to one's own disability), we should turn our attention away from the past (cause) and look to the future (purpose). Accept the current circumstances however difficult they may be and consider what God can do in you and through you in those circumstances. The question should not be "Why me?" but "How can I serve God from here?" Avoid "Why?" Cling to "What for?"

The example of Joseph in Genesis 37 through 50 is a helpful one. Sold into slavery by his brothers, imprisoned through false accusations, and forgotten by those who had promised to help him—life kept hitting the bottom, and the bottom kept dropping out. Undoubtedly Joseph was often tempted to wallow in self-pity as he looked at the misfortunes that had plagued him and wondered what he had done to deserve this. Where was the God of the covenant? Eventually he discovered God's purpose, but only after fifteen years of hardship and suspense. Finally, as he rose to high position in Egypt and brought

> In times of suffering and trials, we need to turn our attention away from cause and focus on purpose.

deliverance from the famine to his family and to thousands of other families, God's purposes were realized in his life.

Good Out of Evil

The next step is to embrace the hope that God works to bring good out of evil (Gen. 50:20; Rom. 8:28). Can anyone make the claim that he or she is in a situation in which it is impossible to serve God? If we can serve him, good can result. With God there are no dead ends, no forgotten corners, no total disqualifications.

© edenpics.com

Joel Sonnenberg is a modern-day illustration of one who certainly had cause to question God's sovereignty and love. He was not yet two years old when a tragic chain-reaction car accident changed his life forever. When a truck crashed into the back of a line of vehicles stopped at a toll plaza, the car Joel was riding in was engulfed in flames. Agonizing minutes went by before he could be rescued. Though he survived, he was faced with excruciating pain, and even after more than fifty surgeries, he is still severely disfigured. Bitterness would have been easy. But instead of rejecting God as powerless or cruel, Joel has allowed God's love to fill him and has had opportunity to testify to what God can do in someone's life. He has been featured in national news programs such as *48 Hours* and *Public Eye* with Bryant Gumbel.[3] Special reports by Chicago anchor Carol Marin have also followed Joel's story over the years. He graduated from Taylor University in the spring of 2000. The university's website listed some of Joel's achievements and honors: Eagle Scout, Discover Tribute award winner, Western North Carolina Citizen of the Year, and high school student body president, to name just a few.[4]

Like the biblical Joseph, Joel could not have known what God eventually would accomplish through the crises and tragedies of his life. We are not in a position to argue with God about why he sovereignly allows the difficult things that come into our lives.

> "Woe to him who quarrels with his Maker,
>   To him who is but a potsherd among the potsherds
> on the ground.
> Does the clay say to the potter,
>   'What are you making?'

© edenpics.com

Does your work say,
  'He has no hands'?
Woe to him who says to his father,
  'What have you begotten?'
or to his mother,
  'What have you brought to birth?'"

Isaiah 45:9–10

The fact is, however, that whatever people intend for evil or consider evil, God can use to bring about good. God does not promise to shield us from all evil. But we can believe that whatever evil may come, God is able to accomplish good through it. This sentiment may be good in theory and even represent sound theology, but it is easy to doubt that God can bring anything positive out of our circumstances. This is where God's wisdom comes into the picture.

God's Wisdom: Is God Fair?

Parents often tell their children that "life is not fair." If life is not fair, how can God be fair? In God's wisdom, he has allowed a sinful, fallen world to continue to exist. This is reflected in the philosophy of Ecclesiastes: The world is crooked and broken. But God has determined to engage in a salvage operation rather than simply to destroy. Our very existence then already exceeds the limits of fairness. To say it another way, we live only because of God's grace.

We have warped views of fairness. Imagine this scene: A child comes home from school and asks, "What's for dinner tonight?" Mom replies, "Roast beef," at which the child makes a face and whines, "That's not *fair*—we just had roast beef two nights ago!" A dozen retorts come to mind: Is it *fair* that you get your dinner cooked for you every night and never lift a finger to help? Is it *fair* that you get meat for dinner nearly every night? Is it *fair* that many children in the world don't see a dinner like this in a lifetime? Is it *fair* that children starve to death every day while you complain about the frequency with which you get roast beef? The litany could go on and on. We can see that "fairness" can be a relative assessment.

But there is more. Since the world is fallen, by definition it cannot always be fair. The fact that this fallen world is not fair cannot be held against God or be thought to compromise his fairness. Again we must return to the fact of God's wisdom. He does not stop every devious plan of wicked people, but he can always accomplish his purposes despite them. He does not prevent all natural disasters, nor does he always protect his people from their effects—but he can accomplish much in the shadow of tragedy and adversity.

Finally, the New Testament teaches that we endure hardship as those who participate in the suffering of Christ (1 Peter 4:12–13) and anticipate future glory (1 Peter 1:3–7). In conclusion then, we should not expect or ask that God protect us from all misfortune and suffering. When suffering comes, our biblical response includes:

1. Looking for God's purpose through it rather than laboring over its cause.

2. Seeking ways to serve God and grow through the suffering.

3. Expecting God to bring good out of misfortune and hardship.

4. Putting our circumstances in a grace perspective, appreciating the grace God has given.

5. Meditating on the sufferings of Christ for us.

6. Weighing our hardships against the misery of others and against the span of eternity.

7. Trusting God's wisdom.

SEEKING FULFILLMENT IN LIFE

A beautiful, expensive luxury car rolls slowly down the street of an exclusive neighborhood as all the neighbors turn and gawk in admiration. The driver's self-satisfied smirk exudes contentment. The commercial makes its point clearly: You will be the envy of all when you own this car. This is how you say, "I have arrived. I am successful." The implication is that you will finally be able to catch hold of that elusive sense of complete fulfillment by purchasing (or leasing) this impressive vehicle. Or maybe it's the clothes, or the pool, or the house. Lose weight, get rid of wrinkles, build up those abs, get that dream job—the prospect of self-fulfillment is dangled before our eyes

> That is why, for Christ's sake, I delight in weaknesses, in insults, in hardships, in persecutions, in difficulties. For when I am weak, then I am strong. (2 Cor. 12:10)

in increasingly attractive ways day by day as we are bombarded with the enticements and the promise that we can achieve that moment when we sigh, "It doesn't get any better than this."

If Qoheleth lived in the neighborhood through which the luxury car was cruising, he might want to sneak over in the night and slap a bumper sticker on the back of the car: "Eat well, stay fit, die anyway," or "Whoever dies with the most toys ~~wins~~ is dead," or "Hearses pull no trailers."

The advertising in our culture has persuaded us that self-fulfillment can be found, so it goes without saying that self-fulfillment should be pursued. In the rampant unbridled consumerism that we have embraced, we have believed it. We have moralized it (a right not just to the pursuit of happiness, but to happiness itself), we have Americanized it (patriotism through consumerism to strengthen the economy and the country), and we have Christianized it (God wants you to prosper or to enlarge your borders).

We have restructured society in this pursuit. This is evident in our attitudes toward both our work and our leisure. The original premise of work was survival. Occupations such as farming and herding were not pursued to achieve a sense of fulfillment in life—one had to live.

Is It Unbiblical to Be Rich and/or Happy?

The wisdom literature has told us that we cannot expect life to go smoothly, since God has offered no such guarantees. Furthermore, we have learned that adversity and even suffering is to be expected in life. The New Testament goes yet further in suggesting that suffering is a good thing as it helps us to identify with the sufferings of Christ. It also exhorts Christians to give to the poor. As a result of all of this, Christians who have not suffered sometimes are made to feel like they are missing out. Christians who have prospered and are wealthy are made to shoulder the guilt for world hunger. Jesus himself points out how difficult it is for the rich man to enter the kingdom of heaven, and he advises the wealthy young man who inquired about what he needed to do to sell all that he had and give it to the poor.

If we search out the biblical view of wealth and possessions, the wisdom literature adds some important balance to our understanding. Consider the following verses from Proverbs:

The wealth of the wise is their crown. (14:24)

The house of the righteous contains great treasure, but the income of the wicked brings them trouble. (15:6)

Humility and the fear of the LORD bring wealth and honor and life. (22:4)

Do not wear yourself out to get rich; have the wisdom to show restraint. (23:4)

Paul suggests a similar restraint in his advice to Timothy as he disdains those who think of godliness as "a means to financial gain" (1 Tim. 6:5) and observes that "people who want to get rich fall into temptation and a trap and into many foolish and harmful desires that plunge men into ruin and destruction" (1 Tim. 6:9). And so he concludes with his well-known but often misquoted statement, "The *love* of money is a root of all kinds of evil" (1 Tim. 6:10, emphasis added).

What is clear in all of this is that wealth itself should not bring guilt. What the Bible warns about is the pursuit of it and the inappropriate use of it. Wisdom shows restraint, generosity, detachment from one's wealth, and concern for the plight of the poor.

But society has become increasingly complex over the millennia as service, merchant, and professional classes have developed and as technology and industrialization have had their impact. The so-called "Protestant work ethic" was built on the concept of doing one's work in such a way as to feel a sense of accomplishment in working hard and doing a job well. This easily led to the related idea that it would be too mundane to think of work simply as something one had to do to survive—an employee or laborer ought to derive a feeling of fulfillment from achieving that sense of accomplishment.

By the middle of the twentieth century, some women began to wonder why it was that men got the opportunity to find this self-fulfillment in the workplace and they didn't. The workplace held out the hope of power, wealth, and a sense of accomplishment that the home did not provide. It is not a surprise that when the workplace was construed in those terms, it would be viewed as an attractive place to be. So men and women both have taken their quest for fulfillment into the workplace.

At the same time, Americans have more leisure time than any culture in the history of the world, and advertisements tell us that we can achieve a sense of self-fulfillment through the activities, distractions, entertainment, or travel with which we fill that time. Parties are portrayed as happy communities of well-adjusted people relating to each other in healthy and fun ways, rather than the too frequent reality of quarrelsome semiconsciousness or drunken orgies. The weather is always perfect in travel brochures, and there are no transportation delays or cranky children.

So life is portrayed as caring people in challenging jobs that gain them prestige and wealth yet allow them time to play on the weekends and get away to exotic resorts where they and their families of talented, intelligent, and well-adjusted children spend happy hours in quality family entertainment and relaxation. The good life is just around the corner.

All of this flies directly in the face of the teaching of Ecclesiastes, where Qoheleth contends that self-fulfillment cannot be found and should not be sought. From a Christian perspective, we might agree in theory that possessions, fame, or other accomplishments of this world cannot bring fulfillment, even when we cannot resist the subtle (or not so subtle) lure of them and pursue the pleasures of sin for a season. But we may have less certainty when we consider Christian permutations of the quest. Should we expect to find fulfillment in our relationship with God? In Christian service? In self-sacrifice? In family?

When the church began to respond to the migration of women into the workplace, it was interesting to see the tack that was taken. Books and sermons began to contend that women did not need to go to the workplace to find fulfillment when they could find a greater fulfillment in the rearing of children. In other words, rather than denying the validity or exposing the futility of the pursuit of fulfillment, they simply redirected the pursuit. Consequently, we agree that the *fulfillment myth* pervades our society at every level.

Pastor Mark Buchanan writes, "One of the persistent cultural myths is the myth of fulfillment—the promise that, on this earth, the fullness of all I truly need and all I really desire awaits. And it's not just a Hollywood myth. It's a Christian one, too. Maybe it's especially Christian."[5] We are often led to endorse this myth in its spiritualized form, but Buchanan exposes the mirage.

© edenpics.com

Where is this huge, exultant freedom for which Christ set us free? Why do I still fret over downturns in the Asian markets, get irked by reckless or doddering drivers, harbor grudges over petty slights, care more about my rhododendron bush than about the soul of the boy who broke its branches playing street hockey?

As a pastor, I hear and see all the time those who want to have a deeper, richer experience with Christ, but they find themselves instead whiling away their days. Their days pass in a blurring swiftness and yet drag on in a dreary sameness—in jobs they dislike, in relationships that baffle and hurt them, with financial worries and health problems.

They don't feel fulfilled. And they carry a secret dread: Is there more, and I'm the only one missing it? Or worse: Is this it, and everyone's pretending it's enough?[6]

The problem is in our expectations. It begins in our evangelism pitch. Marketing strategies dictate that you have to sell the benefits of your product. So we sell Christianity, no longer as giving up everything to follow Christ (Luke 14:33), but finding a wonderful, marvelous, happy new life in Christ that is characterized by blessing (= health, prosperity, and success), fellowship (= acceptance and fruitful relationships), peace (= no troubles)—the very things the world promises in advertisements. Consequently, people come to Christ feeling that they are buying in to certain guarantees. Yet when Christ speaks of peace, he makes the point clearly: "My peace I give you. *I do not give to you as the world gives* " (John 14:27, emphasis added). In that passage, the gift he is speaking of is the Holy Spirit, who is the Comforter. That was Christ's gift to his disciples as he spoke of his imminent departure; he was not talking about fulfillment.

The fulfillment hype shows up in many different guises, from the obvious excess of the health and wealth gospel to many subtle forms. It is always recognizable as it promotes an expectation of success, whether of a material sort or in spiritual undertakings. Christians disappointed by the lackluster returns on their conversion at times abandon the church and their faith or alternatively wonder what they are doing wrong—where the formula for success broke down. Many blame God for failing to deliver on his promises (though they have forgotten that the promises were made by Christians, not by Christ).

This leads us to what might appear to be a shocking conclusion: We should not expect to find self-fulfillment in our relationship with God. In this conclusion, Ecclesiastes is supported by the teaching of the New Testament. Christians there are plagued by all sorts of difficulties and seem to accept that as their plight. Christ suggests no less as he details the hate and rejection that will be directed toward his followers and the sacrifices they will have to make in the process of being disciples. He never implies that this will give them an inner sense of well-being. Buchanan therefore observes, "The portrait of the faithful is not a portrait of the fulfilled. What defines them . . . is hope."[7]

Does all of this mean that no one finds fulfillment in life or that there is no such thing as fulfillment? No. It is just a question of guaranteed paths and the worthiness of the pursuit. There is no sure path to self-fulfillment, and when experienced at all it is typically fleeting. It cannot be pursued, and it should not be pursued. The fear of the Lord is the beginning of wisdom, and both sides of that axiom are worthy of pursuit. Self-fulfillment is not part of the equation. "Fulfillment is heaven's business."[8]

PROVERBS AND THE FAMILY

Proverbs speaks often of family: raising children, relationships and responsibilities between family members, and enticements that jeopardize the family. It contains observations both about functional and dysfunctional families and what makes them so. It therefore speaks to many issues of today.

Disciplined Sexuality

We live in a culture that prides itself on sexual freedom and offers little censure for fornication or adultery. Movies and TV idealize sex,

> We should not expect to find self-fulfillment in our relationship with God.

and libertarians fight for its free expression. Proverbs, by the nature of its literature, is not inclined to issue dictates. The wisdom it offers comes more often through elaborating the consequences of actions. So rather than lay down the law of what is right and wrong, it portrays the reality of how things work in real-life experiences. Whether the consequences are social, psychological, relational, or physical, the point is made that the price is high when one exercises undisciplined sexual expression.

Disciplined Relationships

In our day, the weakening of the institution of marriage is a by-product of the more insidious reluctance to commit to a relationship. For an increasing number, marriage is simply a convenient temporary living arrangement as relationships become revolving doors. Wisdom seeks order; order in marriage derives from security; security is a consequence of faithful commitment. Marriage cannot simply be viewed as a cultural invention that we can freely shape in whatever way we choose. Proverbs does not argue for marriage over singleness, though in the ancient world, very few would have opted for the latter. It plots the path of wisdom in marriage by noting the obstacles such as laziness, quarrelsomeness, and the lure of the adulteress. Wisdom calls us to overcome the obstacles, resist natural inclinations, and aspire to be extraordinary: "Many a man claims to have unfailing love, but a faithful man who can find?" (Prov. 20:6). This offers the generalization that an individual with the requisite values and virtues is rare indeed. If we look to proverbial literature to give us God's take on values and virtues, then our obligatory response is to adopt those values and practice those virtues.

Proverbs and Sexuality

For the lips of an adulteress drip honey,
    and her speech is smoother than oil;
but in the end she is bitter as gall,
    sharp as a double-edged sword.
Her feet go down to death;
    her steps lead straight to the grave.
She gives no thought to the way of life;
    her paths are crooked, but she knows it not.

Now then, my sons, listen to me;
    do not turn aside from what I say.
Keep to a path far from her,
    do not go near the door of her house."*

Proverbs 5:3–8

---

*See also Proverbs 2:16–19; 5:15–17; 6:23–29, 32; 7:6–27.

Disciplined Children

When pediatrician Benjamin Spock published his book on child rearing in the middle of the twentieth century, it was controversial in its outspoken opposition to physical forms of punishment. Debate subsided over the years as more and more families adopted his strategies. With growing numbers of reported child abuse, it became more and more difficult to identify where the line was between legitimate physical punishment and abuse. Consequently, a society has taken shape in which children can sue their parents and state child protection agencies can remove children from a home when they conclude that physical abuse has taken place. This sounds like a good idea until a basic spanking is defined as physical abuse.

Accompanying this development is the idea that children will grow up just fine if parents will just stay out of their way. Indulgence has thus become the modern parenting strategy of choice. At the same time, pushy, domineering, demanding parents who are living out their unfulfilled hopes for their own lives crush their children's spirits, overburden their children with expectations, and force them to be something they are not. As accurate as that picture may be, the solution is not to be found in a pendulum swing to the other extreme.

Proverbs argues against this strategy as a couple of examples clearly show:

In the biblical author's view, the refusal to discipline children is tantamount to passing a death sentence on them (19:18). He sees the parents' role as active and constructive (22:6) and a necessary ingredient to instruction in wisdom. He favors neither abuse nor permissiveness. Without the potter's hands, the lump of clay remains a lump of clay or falls off the wheel altogether. But a potter who applies too much force will have a misshapen vessel.

These same principles are pertinent to spiritual discipline. Whether spiritual discipline is part of the family structure as envisioned in Proverbs or takes place in a mentoring relationship, we must recognize that there is no room for indulging our natural tendencies. Our spiritual discipline cannot afford to be permissive, but likewise we must avoid the opposite strategy of abuse. Spirituality is not gained by self-flagellation or legalistic prohibitions.

> Folly is bound up in the heart of a child, but the rod of discipline will drive it far from him. (22:15)
>
> The rod of correction imparts wisdom, but a child left to himself disgraces his mother. (29:15)

© Jess Alford/Getty Images

Disciplined Communication

Brothers and sisters mocking one another; children talking back to their parents; men lashing out at wives and children in anger; women gossiping with one another or nagging their husbands; these are the negative stereotypes that all-too-often run true to form in modern families. These undisciplined abuses of words destroy our families and often boil beneath the surface, painful secrets hidden from outside observers. The public face of a family may give the appearance of being well adjusted and on Sundays at church may radiate spiritual health. But "word abuse" may be destroying the infrastructure, resulting in broken victims.

Proverbs has more to say about the wise use of words than almost any other topic. Even though the book does not often comment on the use of words specifically in a family context, its observations can easily be applied to our family situations. Words should not be rash (13:3), contentious (15:1; 21:19), disrespectful (13:1; 20:20), or abusive (9:7–12). Instead, words should build up (15:23). Words have power. Words also betray a person's weaknesses. Nagging may be a sign of discontent or anxiety. Gossip, like slander, seeks to tear down others and thereby indirectly put oneself in a better light. This can easily be seen as a result of vanity, self-righteousness, or low self-esteem. Anger expressed by one who is hot-tempered reveals impatience (14:29). The approach of wisdom will seek to eliminate these character flaws through discipline of one's tongue.

In conclusion, order (wisdom) is to be achieved through disciplined living. A dysfunctional family has had a discipline breakdown at one or many levels. Some final words of Proverbs about discipline in general can stand without comment:

James 3:5–10

The tongue is a small part of the body, but it makes great boasts. Consider what a great forest is set on fire by a small spark. The tongue also is a fire, a world of evil among the parts of the body. It corrupts the whole person, sets the whole course of his life on fire, and is itself set on fire by hell.

All kinds of animals, birds, reptiles and creatures of the sea are being tamed and have been tamed by man, but no man can tame the tongue. It is a restless evil, full of deadly poison.

With the tongue we praise our Lord and Father, and with it we curse men, who have been made in God's likeness. Out of the same mouth come praise and cursing. My brothers, this should not be.

The corrections of discipline are the way to life. (6:23)

Like a city whose walls are broken down is a man who lacks self-control. (25:28)

At the end of your life you will groan,
  when your flesh and body are spent.
You will say, "How I hated discipline!
  How my heart spurned correction! . . .
I have come to the brink of utter ruin."

5:11–12, 14

Copyright © 2001 by Todd Bolen. www.bibleplaces.com

THE POWER OF SEX

The Song of Songs intends to make us aware of the power of sex. This is a relevant topic since our society has stripped off the supposed shackles of sexual inhibition. Sexuality is insistently portrayed in media of every kind, shamelessly exploited in advertising, and brazenly celebrated in the clothes people wear—even in preteen fashions. Sexual choices and sexual orientations are defended as legal rights. The Internet puts pornography at anyone's fingertips, and unless filtered, explicit sexuality is emailed randomly into our homes daily.

The slogan advertisers use is "Sex sells." In our culture, power is expressed clearly in the ability to produce revenue. If sex did not have power, it would not have such a prevalent role in movies and advertising. To economic power we could add interpersonal power. Revealing fashions use sexuality to exert power over others in that they have the ability to stimulate lust. Lust, in turn, is a vice, which weakens the

---

Proverbs Concerning Family Communication

Put away perversity from your mouth;
  keep corrupt talk far from your lips.

Proverbs 4:24

The tongue that brings healing is a tree of life,
  but a deceitful tongue crushes the spirit.

Proverbs 15:4

A hot-tempered man stirs up dissension,
  but a patient man calms a quarrel.

Proverbs 15:18

Better a dry crust with peace and quiet
  than a house full of feasting, with strife.

Proverbs 17:1

A foolish son is his father's ruin,
  and a quarrelsome wife is like a constant dripping.

Proverbs 19:13

one captured by it. Many would object that what they wear is only a reflection of their personal choices about what looks fashionably attractive or feels comfortable. Women who profess to be unaware of how revealing clothing affects men are naïve. Men who claim to be ignorant of how their clothing draws attention to their bodies are deluding themselves. Sexual power is wielded both subtly and explicitly in every segment of our society.

Yet even as we celebrate the ability to incite lust in others, we decry its inevitable outcomes. We are staggered by the burgeoning crimes in which sexual predators use the Internet to seek out those whom they can victimize or exploit in their lust. We express horror at the eruption of the scandal of priests sexually abusing minors. We are well aware of the abuses of sexual power. The question is, where is the line at which wielding sexual power becomes abusive or unacceptable? We condemn the sexual harassment that continues to plague the workplace by jeopardizing the safety of the work environment. Yet if sexual harassment includes using sexuality to exert power over another, we find that the laws provide inconsistent coverage. The unwanted stimulation of someone constantly touching a fellow employee (stroking the arm, massaging the shoulders) is labeled sexual harassment. Yet there is no such label attached to the unwanted stimulation caused by the revealing clothes a fellow employee wears.

Our society has decided that it wants to play with fire but doesn't like getting burned. It wants the freedom and self-indulgence but not the particular uses of sexual power that it is content to label crime or abuse or that lead to disease or unwanted pregnancy. Lust is not considered a problem by our society as long as it does not progress to action beyond certain limits. If lust is not considered a problem, then the stimulation of lust is not considered a problem. In fact, it would appear that our society believes that one's ability to stimulate lust is just as laudable as the ability to stimulate sales. It helps us feel good about ourselves if we are desired (read "lusted after") by someone else.

Unfortunately, the Christian subculture is not succeeding in shielding itself from the problem or withstanding the onslaught from society. A glimpse at the clothing worn by the young people in our youth groups and Christian schools (when there are not regulating dress codes) or a survey of the movies and TV shows regularly viewed by Christians would reveal little distinction between Christians and non-Christians. If we still believe that lust is sin, we should guard against indulging in it or causing it in others. The former should make us careful about what we read or watch. The latter should make us sensitive about what we wear. In all of this, we see the power sex can have over us. Like the Internet filters we spoke of earlier, the wisdom literature should help us set up a filter against destructive influences.

So far this discussion has been about the power of sex in our society. Song of Songs is more focused on the power of love and sex in personal relationships—the power to affect personal choices and impact the course of a person's life. Few cases would illustrate this as persuasively as that of King Edward VIII, who in 1936 gave up the throne of England to marry an American divorcée, Wallis Simpson. This romantic example, however, would have to be weighed against the tragic ones that unfortunately are far more common.

In the Bible, Samson and Solomon are two well-known examples of those who fell prey to the power of love and sex. History is littered with those who gave up families, jobs, faith, and social status as well as forfeiting promises, self-respect, and honor for the love of a man or woman. In today's world, dating relationships are plagued by sexual confusion and expectations, parents are devastated by teen pregnancies, minds are corrupted and perspectives distorted by pornography, children are torn through the departure of an unfaithful parent who has decided the grass is greener in another pasture, and churches are traumatized by staff or prominent members who cannot control their passions. The power has not diminished.

As we become aware of the power of sex and sexuality, and of the inability of lust to constrain itself, we must seek out strategies to avoid its dangers. Such is the path of wisdom. Some schools have rules about clothing or movies, and there may be good reason to follow that route, but we cannot mislead ourselves into thinking that rules alone result in wisdom. Behavior can be legislated and regulated, but wisdom is not gained through such methods. It must be taught.

Sexual Purity

Flee from sexual immorality. All other sins a man commits are outside his body, but he who sins sexually sins against his own body.
(1 Cor. 6:18)

Having lost all sensitivity, they have given themselves over to sensuality so as to indulge in every kind of impurity, with a continual lust for more. You, however, did not come to know Christ that way.
(Eph. 4:19–20)

Marriage should be honored by all, and the marriage bed kept pure, for God will judge the adulterer and all the sexually immoral.
(Heb. 13:4)

1. What is the impact of focusing on purpose instead of cause in times of trial?

2. How should we assess the question of whether God is fair?

3. What is the "fulfillment myth," and how does it affect you?

4. What are some of the ways our lives would change if we were not pursuing fulfillment?

5. Is it permissible to spank children? Is it advisable? Is it mandatory?

6. What are some of the forms that the "house of the adulteress" takes in our society?

7. What are some of the ways the power of sex impacts people today?

8. Are rich people called upon to sell all they have and follow Christ?

9. What are some of the ways in which the teaching of Jesus fits the pattern of wisdom teacher?

KEY REVIEW TERMS

Biblical Characters: Elihu, Job, Qoheleth

Extrabiblical Texts: Babylonian Theodicy, Dialogue of Pessimism, Instruction of Amenemope, *Ludlul bel Nemeqi,* Man and His God

Concepts: retribution principle, theodicy

GOING TO THE NEXT LEVEL

C. Hassell Bullock, *An Introduction to Old Testament Poetic Books* (Moody Press).

James Crenshaw, *Old Testament Wisdom* (Westminster John Knox).

Derek Kidner, *The Wisdom of Proverbs, Job and Ecclesiastes* (InterVarsity Press).

Ernest Lucas, *Exploring the Old Testament: A Guide to Psalms and Wisdom* (InterVarsity Press).

Roy Zuck, *Learning from the Sages* (Baker).

Roy Zuck, *Reflecting with Solomon* (Baker).

Roy Zuck, *Sitting with Job* (Baker).

Notes

1. Archibald MacLeish, *J. B.* (Boston: Houghton-Mifflin, 1958), 12.
2. Ibid., 11.
3. *48 Hours*, a CBS program hosted by Dan Rather aired on September 2, 1999. The CBS program *Public Eye*, with Bryant Gumbel was broadcast in July of 1998.
4. See www.tayloru.edu/upland/campus/news/1999/joel.html from posting on 5/30/00.
5. Mark Buchanan, "Stuck on the Road to Emmaus: The Secret to Why We Are Not Fulfilled," *Christianity Today* (July 12, 1999), 55–57 (quote from p. 56).
6. Ibid., 55.
7. Ibid., 56.
8. Ibid., 57.

6 PSALMS

The plain by Jebel Musa.

ORIENTATION

- The book of Psalms offers poetic reflections on the kingship of God.
- Psalms 1 and 2 introduce the themes of the book carried forward by seam psalms.
- Praise is an expression of joy; lament is a search for peace.
- Trust does not need to understand or approve every action.

KEY VERSE

- Psalm 145:8–20   God's kingship

Our prayers are often dominated by requests seeking benefits. More important would be prayers that focus on building our relationship with God. As we acknowledge who he is and seek his help regarding what kind of people we need to be, we will grow closer to him and be more effective instruments for his kingdom.

YAHWEH FOCUS

- It is important to trust God even when he doesn't seem to hear our prayers—he hears and cares.
- God does not need our praise, but it is right for us to praise him, and he is worthy.
- God is not obligated to us as a result of our worship of him.
- We are in God's image not just intellectually, but emotionally as well.
- God, not the benefits he offers, ought to be the focus of our faith and hope.

KEY PLOTLINE TERMS

- praise psalms
- lament psalms
- wisdom psalms
- covenant kingship

OUTLINE

ORIGINAL MEANING
Summary of Content

Literary Perspective

BRIDGING CONTEXTS
Purpose: Kingship in Psalms

Psalms as Revelation

Theological Perspectives

CONTEMPORARY SIGNIFICANCE
Contemporary Worship and the Psalms

What Do We Expect from God and What Does He Expect from Us?

Scenario: Trusting God When He Doesn't Seem to Hear

Recapitulation

Devotional Use of Psalms

TIMELINE

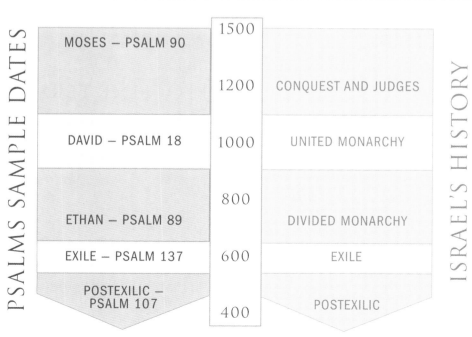

PSALMS SAMPLE DATES		ISRAEL'S HISTORY
MOSES — PSALM 90	1500	
	1200	CONQUEST AND JUDGES
DAVID — PSALM 18	1000	UNITED MONARCHY
	800	
ETHAN — PSALM 89		DIVIDED MONARCHY
EXILE — PSALM 137	600	EXILE
POSTEXILIC — PSALM 107	400	POSTEXILIC

CHAPTER

ORIGINAL MEANING

SUMMARY OF CONTENT

The 150 psalms are arranged in five "books" that are marked in most English translations (1–41, 42–72, 73–89, 90–106, 107–150), each ending with a benediction. In addition, it is likely that the first two psalms serve as an introduction to the collection and the last five serve as the worship climax. The Psalms were written over a one-thousand-year period across the whole range of Old Testament history. They are the backbone of the Old Testament and represent the legacy of Israelite worship and liturgy. In this book, we will find prayers to God by individuals as well as prayers designed for corporate use. Some arise out of historical or personal circumstances, while others address particular liturgical contexts.

In these five books are found some of the most cherished verses of Christendom throughout the centuries. Millions of Bible readers in every walk of life, in countries from around the globe, perhaps suffering circumstances of unimaginable horror have opened these pages and found hope and comfort. Several of the names for God that give us comfort represent metaphors that have been popularized by the Psalms. Shepherd (23:1), rock (19:14), shield (28:7), and fortress (18:2, which lists a number of the titles) come to

Waterfall at En Gedi where David hid from Saul (1 Sam. 24:1).

6 PSALMS

The Pool of Gibeon.

mind most readily. Our hymnals, prayer books, and sacramental ceremonies have drawn so repeatedly from this book that many of the lines have become culturally entrenched.

The Psalms were also deeply entrenched in the Israelite culture and are interconnected with the rest of the biblical text. In the diagram on the next page, we can see how the four other main divisions in this textbook each find a reflection of sorts in the book of Psalms through shared themes. The Law (Torah) that is found in the Pentateuch is pondered and praised in a number of Psalms, with 1, 19, and 119 being the most familiar. Other themes of the Pentateuch include creation and covenant, which are the subjects of Psalms 104 and 89 respectively. The narrative literature that offers perspectives of Israel's history can be beneficially paired with the theological retrospection and introspection of Israel's past found in Psalms such

25 of the Most Familiar Psalm Lines

1. O LORD, our Lord, how majestic is your name in all the earth! (8:1)
2. The fool says in his heart, "There is no God." (14:1)
3. The heavens declare the glory of God. (19:1)
4. My God, my God, why have you forsaken me? (22:1)
5. The LORD is my shepherd, I shall not be in want. (23:1)
6. The LORD is my light and my salvation—whom shall I fear? (27:1)
7. Delight yourself in the LORD and he will give you the desires of your heart. (37:4)
8. As the deer pants for streams of water, so my soul pants for you, O God. (42:1)
9. God is our refuge and strength, an ever-present help in trouble. (46:1)
10. Be still, and know that I am God. (46:10)
11. Great is the LORD, and most worthy of praise. (48:1)
12. Create in me a pure heart, O God. (51:10)
13. May God be gracious to us and bless us and make his face shine upon us. (67:1)
14. How lovely is your dwelling place, O LORD Almighty! (84:1)
15. Sing to the LORD a new song, for he has done marvelous things. (98:1)
16. Shout for joy to the LORD, all the earth. (100:1)
17. For the LORD is good and his love endures forever; his faithfulness continues through all generations. (100:5)
18. As far as the east is from the west, so far has he removed our transgressions from us. (103:12)
19. Give thanks to the LORD, for he is good; his love endures forever. (107:1)
20. Your word is a lamp to my feet and a light for my path. (119:105)
21. I lift up my eyes to the hills—where does my help come from? (121:1)
22. Unless the LORD builds the house, its builders labor in vain. (127:1)
23. How good and pleasant it is when brothers live together in unity! (133:1)
24. I praise you because I am fearfully and wonderfully made. (139:14)
25. Search me, O God, and know my heart. (139:23)

as 105 and 106. The wilderness period and the time of David's reign are among the more frequent topics in this category. Examples of wisdom themes are illustrated in Psalms 37, 49, and 73. Finally, though the Old Testament does not classify Psalms as prophetic, the earliest interpretations of the Old Testament found in the intertestamental literature and the Dead Sea Scrolls both understood certain psalms as prophetic, particularly with regard to the Messiah and his kingdom. This understanding continued in the New Testament and into early rabbinic literature. Given this linkage, it is easy to see how Psalms can serve as a literary microcosm of the Old Testament.

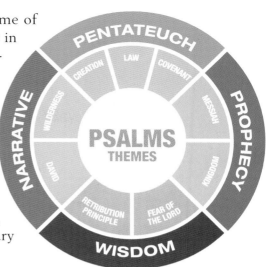

Hebrew Poetry

The Psalms are written in poetic form. If poetry is to be understood and appreciated, the reader must have some knowledge of how the poetry works. It would be a mistake to think that one culture's poetry uses the same conventions found in another culture, so it is necessary for us to consider the mechanics of Hebrew poetry.

The two most prominent conventions of English poetry are meter and rhyme. In contrast, these are much less observable in Hebrew poetry. Scholars have concluded that there are most likely some conventions of meter, but meter is not as central to Hebrew poetry as it is to English. Likewise, Hebrew occasionally uses sound repetition within a line, but repeating the same sound at the end of lines was not considered artistic in Hebrew.

Hebrew poetry places a higher value on the structuring of the piece as a whole. Consequently, conventions such as inclusio, chiasm (or palistrophe), and acrostic are common. *Inclusio* begins and ends a section with the same clause or verse (Pss. 8, 106). *Chiasm* arranges words so that a second line of poetry inverts the order of the first line: "But his delight is in the law of the LORD, and on his law he meditates day and night" (Ps. 1:2). Chiasm is often used to describe the use of this same kind of inversion on the extended level of the paragraph, though technically this is called *palistrophe*. We could think of palistrophe as extending and combining the ideas of inclusio and chiasm. Unlike inclusio, it involves not just repetition of the first and last line, but correlates the second and

second to last, third, and third to last, all the way through the section. It is like chiasm in using inversion so that the order of topics in a series of lines is inverted in the second half (see box). Often there will be a line in the center without a match. This becomes the center of the palistrophe and is usually the most important statement.

In an acrostic, the psalm is structured with one line being composed for each letter of the Hebrew alphabet (Pss. 9, 10, 25, 34, 37, 111, 112, 119, 145). Looking at the first letter of each line would then spell out the alphabet. Psalm 119 is a complex acrostic in which eight lines rather than just one are composed for each letter.

As in English, poetry at times has its own special words, grammar, and rhetorical devices. In the category of rhetorical devices, poetry makes frequent use of imagery, such as personification, simile, and metaphor.

Having made all of these observations, it must be noted that all of the conventions discussed so far should be considered only the supporting cast or occasional features of Hebrew poetry. By far the most prominent feature is *parallelism*. Parallelism is defined as the correspondence between phrases of a poetic line when the second phrase carries forward the thought of the first, but together they form a single statement.

Chiasm

a
  b
    c
      d
      d'
    c'
  b'
a'

LITERARY PERSPECTIVE

Types of Psalms

Psalms can be divided into three major literary categories (genres) with several subcategories as well as several minor categories. The major categories are *praise, lament,* and *wisdom.* An example of a subcategory would be the penitential psalms (e.g., Ps. 51), which are a specialized form of lament psalms. Significant minor categories would include royal psalms (e.g., Ps. 72), Zion psalms (e.g., Ps. 48), pilgrimage psalms (e.g., Ps. 128), and Torah (Law) psalms (e.g., Ps. 119).

Praise psalms occur either as individual expressions of praise, sometimes called Thanksgiving psalms, or as songs for use in corporate settings, sometimes referred to as hymns. Some of the distinc-

Parallelism

Semantic Parallelism (based in word usage)

Using synonyms (2:3; 7:16; 17:1; 24:2)

  24:2   for he founded it upon the seas
        and established it upon the waters.

Using similar terms (1:5; 2:8; 6:1, 2; 7:13; 17:8)

  1:5   Therefore the wicked will not stand in the judgment,
        nor sinners in the assembly of the righteous.

Using matched pairs (2:1; 9:8; 15:1)

  9:8   He will judge the world in righteousness;
        He will govern the peoples with justice.

Using opposites (1:6; 15:4; 37:9, 16)

  37:16 Better the little that the righteous have
        than the wealth of the many wicked.

Progressive Parallelism (based on logical sequence)

Using cause and effect (1:3; 6:7; 7:14; 16:1; 18:36; 37:4, 27)

  37:4   Delight yourself in the LORD
        and he will give you the desires of your heart.

Using sequence (1:1; 3:4, 5; 6:10; 37:29)

  37:29 the righteous will inherit the land
        and dwell in it forever.

Using deduction (4:3; 13:6; 16:8)

  16:8   I have set the LORD always before me.
        Because he is at my right hand, I will not be shaken.

Using metaphors (4:7; 18:31)

  18:31 For who is God besides the LORD?
        And who is the Rock except our God?

Using explanation (5:10, 11)

  5:10b Banish them for their many sins,
        For they have rebelled against you.

Grammatical Parallelism (based on choice of grammatical forms)

Using parallel parts of speech (18:4, 5, 25, 26; 19:7-8)

  19:7-8 The law of the LORD is perfect, reviving the soul.
        The statutes of the LORD are trustworthy, making
          the wise the simple.
        The precepts of the LORD are right, giving joy to the
          heart.
        The commands of the LORD are radiant, giving light
          to the eyes.

Using word order (reverse: 1:2; 2:5; 18:4-5)

  1:2   But his delight is in the law of the LORD,
        and on his law he meditates day and night.

Using ellipses (16:11; 18:41)

  18:41 They cried for help, but there was no one to save them—
        to the LORD, but he did not answer.

tive features of each are summarized in the chart below. The corporate praise psalms typically praise God for who he is or for what he has done for the group (Israel, the faithful, or even all people). This sort of praise is called *descriptive* praise. Individual praise psalms more commonly praise God for what he has done for the psalmist in a particular crisis situation. This type of praise is labeled *declarative* praise.

Lament psalms are characterized by complaint, questions, petitions, and sometimes even imprecations (curses) on the enemy. In lament psalms, the psalmist (or the group he represents) has a problem, and he has come to God seeking help. In many of these psalms, the psalmist wants to know why God has not already come to his aid. He considers himself the "good guy" in contrast to his enemies who are oppressing him. The psalmist does not believe that he has done anything to deserve the troubles he is having, so he is seeking vindication. The element necessary for understanding the psalmist's thinking here is the retribution principle introduced in unit 5 (see pp. 292–93). If the wicked suffer, and the psalmist is suffering at the hands of his adversary, then most observers would assume that he has done wrong and is experiencing the punishment of God. The psalmist's logic now becomes clear—when his enemy is defeated, his own escape or victory will be evidence that he is not being punished by God. That will be his vindication. Lament

Psalm Types Statistics

Some statistics will help us see the distribution of the psalm types in terms of initial indicators:

- 29 corporate praise psalms (hymns) feature an imperative in the first line: Psalms 29, 33, 47, 66–68, 81, 95, 96, 98, 100, 103–7, 111–13, 117, 118, 134–36, 146–50

- 16 individual praise psalms (thanksgiving psalms) feature a proclamation in the first line: Psalms 9, 11, 18, 30, 34, 40, 75, 89, 91, 92, 101, 108, 116, 121, 138, 145

- 55 lament psalms (both corporate and individual) feature a vocative in the first line: Psalms 3–8, 10, 12, 13, 15–17, 21, 22, 25, 26, 28, 31, 35, 38, 42–44, 51, 54–61, 63, 64, 69–71, 74, 79, 80, 83, 86, 88, 90, 94, 102, 109, 120, 130–32, 139–41, 143

- These add up to 100 of the 150 psalms that contain an initial indicator.

- Of the remaining 50 psalms, 14 are wisdom psalms (1, 14, 19, 23, 24, 36, 37, 49, 52, 53, 62, 73, 78, 119), 5 are royal psalms (2, 20, 45, 72, 110), and 9 are pilgrimage psalms (122–29, 133).

- That leaves 22 "exceptions" (smaller subcategories or minor categories or simply one of the major categories without the initial indicator): Psalms 27, 32, 39, 41, 46, 48, 50, 65, 76, 77, 82, 84, 85, 87, 93, 97, 99, 114, 115, 137, 142, 144.

- Of these 22, 8 praise psalms and 6 laments do not feature the initial indicators. There are 2 in the remaining 8 that are good examples of the uncommon mixture of categories (Pss. 27, 144; both begin with praise and then move to lament).

psalms typically conclude with an expression of confidence that God will hear and deliver. From the complaint, the psalmist is able to arrive at a point of praise. The "Psalm Types" chart on the facing page compares the typical characteristics of lament psalms to those of the praise psalms.

Psalm 139: Praise or Lament?

Does it matter whether we identify a psalm as praise or lament? Isn't it self-evident without spending time and energy looking for literary indicators? Yes, in most cases it is self-evident, but there are exceptions, and that is why we cannot afford to neglect these important observations. It matters because we will read the psalm differently depending on whether it is considered a praise or lament psalm. Psalm 139 provides the best example.

Traditionally Psalm 139 has been viewed as a praise psalm. It expresses wonder concerning various important attributes of God in verses 1 through 12. It uses the language of praise in verses 14 and 17. It appears overall to give a very positive picture of God.

Nevertheless, when we use the indicators for identifying psalm types, we find that the psalm begins with a vocative ("O LORD"), it ends with petition (vv. 23–24) and, most importantly, it includes an imprecation against enemies (vv. 19–22). None of these are typical of praise psalms, and it is hard to even imagine what possible role an imprecation could play in a praise psalm. These indicators suggest very strongly that the author intended a lament.

How would the praise elements be justified if this were a lament psalm? On the attributes of God, one only has to read a section like Job 7:17–21 to see that as praiseworthy as these attributes are, they certainly have a "down side" for fallen mortals. If we thought of Psalm 139:1–12 coming from someone who was suffering as Job was, these verses would be read with a different tone of voice.

Once we consider the possibility of reading it as a lament psalm, other supporting observations could be made. For instance, the "hemming in" of Psalm 139:5 is used in other passages as oppressive rather than protective (it is used for laying siege).* The second line of the verse uses language of capture (cf. Job 41:8; Ps. 32:4).† The verb in verse 10 can be positive ("guide") but can also be negative ("lead away captive"). Last, the verb in verse 14

("praise") can also mean "thank." If the psalm is a lament, this verse should be taken like the first twelve. The psalmist does not resent God's attributes and deeds, but he finds them a basis for complaint. He is pointing out that as the perfect judge, God knows all and sees all. Nothing can be done in secret places, and God, as creator, knows all of the psalmist's thoughts and motives. When he exclaims, "How precious to me are your thoughts" (v. 17), the idea is that God's thoughts are inaccessible—not easily gained, thus the psalmist is confused: "What could you be thinking?"

We can see that the way the translator renders the passage can be influenced by how he or she interprets the psalm. The final example of the significance of identifying the psalm type is found in the last two verses of the psalm. If it is a praise psalm, these verses are read as a sinner's plea: "Help me to discover the wrongs that I find it difficult to recognize in myself." If it is a lament psalm, the verses are read as a righteous sufferer's claim of innocence: "Probe as deeply as you want—you will not find offenses that justify my harsh treatment." This latter sentiment occurs occasionally in other psalms (see Pss. 17:3; 26:1–2, both using the same verb for "test").

Whether a person agrees that Psalm 139 is a lament psalm or prefers to retain the traditional reading as a praise psalm, it undeniably serves as an illustration of how differently two people could read the same psalm depending on which category they put it in. The tone and sentiment of the psalm, and especially the final petition, would take on a whole new sense if the lament indicators prevail.

---

*Job refers to this same idea but uses a variety of verbs (Job 3:23; 7:12).

†Again, both use slightly different language.

Wisdom psalms do not have any standard opening lines, though instruction-style introductions such as "O my people, hear my teaching" (Ps. 78:1) or "Hear this, all you peoples" (Ps. 49:1) would be a clear indicator. Wisdom psalms might open with declarations ("The earth is the LORD's and everything in it," Ps. 24:1), observations ("The fool says in his heart, 'There is no God,'" Ps. 14:1), or instructions ("Do not fret because of evil men," Ps. 37:1). Besides the common themes that identify wisdom psalms, an important feature is that they are typically addressed to people rather than to God. In other words, these are not prayers, but teachings.

Hymnic Literature of the Ancient World

All of the peoples in the ancient world prayed to their gods. Like the Israelites, their prayers included lifting praise and voicing complaints. They ascribed similar attributes to their gods that were praiseworthy, and their complaints reflected that they suffered along with Israelites in the common plight of humanity—disease, crop failures, war, injustice, and interpersonal problems all providing occasions for petition to those who were believed to be capable of providing relief. Many such hymns and prayers have

Z. Radovan, Jerusalem

PSALM TYPES*

	CORPORATE PRAISE	INDIVIDUAL PRAISE	CORPORATE LAMENT	INDIVIDUAL LAMENT
INITIAL INDICATOR	Imperative Call to Praise (e.g., "Sing to the Lord a new song")	Proclamation of Intent to Praise (e.g., "I will extol the Lord")	Vocative Opening with Petition (e.g., "Rescue us, O Lord")	Vocative Opening with Petition (e.g., "Vindicate me O Lord")
CORE SECTION	Reason for Praise: 1. Who God is 2. General Acts of God	Narration of Specific Intervention: 1. Describe Crisis 2. Recount Prayer 3. Report Deliverance	Lament Proper: National Crisis	Lament Proper: 1. Enemy 2. Psalmist 3. God
RESPONSE	Instruction	Acknowledge Role of God; Instruction	Petition; Confession of Trust	Petition; Optional: 1. Confession of Sin 2. Imprecation 3. Vow of Praise 4. Expression of Confidence

been recovered through archaeological excavations in Mesopotamia and Egypt. Similarities can be observed in the subject matter and some of the phrasing and ideas, but a number of differences must also be recognized. These are important because they provide insight into the theology of the Psalms.

Praise. One of the elements of Israel's praise literature is not found in the other literatures, the element that we have called declarative praise. This type of praise was an expression of thanks that God had come to the aid of the psalmist in a particular crisis. Israel believed in a God who could and would act in an individual's life, not just by showing favor by bringing blessing (all nations believed that), but by bringing relief from enemies, illness, or troublesome circumstances. It is possible, and even likely, that the Babylonians would believe that their gods could do the same, but so far hymns expressing thanks for such things have not been found.

A second area of comparison in the praise category concerns the nature of descriptive praise. In Mesopotamia the descriptive praise of the deity often enumerated attributes in what was little more than a list:

> O Ishtar, queen of all peoples, who guides mankind aright,
> O Irnini, ever exalted, greatest of the Igigi,
> O most mighty of princesses, exalted is thy name.
> Thou indeed art the light of heaven and earth, O valiant
>   daughter of Sin.
> O supporter of arms, who determines battle,
> O possessor of all divine power, who wears the crown of
>   dominion,
> O Lady, glorious is thy greatness; over all the gods it is
>   exalted.[1]

In Egypt, although enumeration of attributes is not absent, depicting praise in action is a common characteristic of descriptive praise. This is illustrated in the "Great Hymn to Osiris" (see "Selections from Ancient Near Eastern Hymns").

The biblical psalms contain examples of both of these approaches to descriptive praise, but the outstanding feature of the Israelite literature is the imperative call to worship that begins so many of the descriptive praise psalms.

Lament. The differences in the lament genre go beyond the issues of form. The major difference can be found in beliefs about how deity could be offended. In Israel Yahweh was offended by violation of the

- Israelite laments seek vindication; Mesopotamian laments seek appeasement.
- Laments in Mesopotamia are most often connected to incantations.
- Israelites typically claim innocence while Mesopotamians acknowledge guilt.
- Mesopotamians think in terms of ritual offense while Israelites think in terms of ethical offense.
- Israelites remind God of ways in which he has obligated himself while Babylonians seek to bring deity under obligation by ritual.

law and the covenant. Because of the law, Israel knew what God expected, so offenses could usually be identified. In Mesopotamia there was no divinely established law or covenant to define expectations. Babylonians or Assyrians were much less confident that they could figure out what would offend the gods.

In laments the Israelites would generally be insistent that they were innocent and therefore would seek vindication. The Mesopotamians might claim ignorance of having committed any offense but recognized that there were all sorts of possibilities for offense of which they could not begin to be aware. Consequently, they would simply assume that the deity was angry over some unknown or unknowable offense and had therefore aflicted them in some way. Their preferred course of action was to simply confess to anything and everything and in so doing hope to appease the wrath of the angry deity. The laments were often associated with ritual actions or spoken incantations that were expected to exert

Descriptive Praise:

enumeration in Mesopotamia

depiction in Egypt

imperative in Israel

Declarative Praise:

unique to Israel

Selections from Ancient Near Eastern Hymns

Great Hymn to Osiris (Egypt)*
Hail to you, Osiris,
Lord of eternity, king of the gods . . .
Sky makes wind before his nose,
That his heart be satisfied.
Plants sprout by his wish,
Earth grows its food for him,
Sky and its stars obey him . . .
Everyone exults,
All extol his goodness:
How pleasant is his love for us,
His kindness overwhelms the hearts,
Love of him is great in all.

Great Hymn to the Aton (Egypt)†
Thou living Aton, the beginning of life!
When thou art risen on the eastern horizon,
Thou hast filled every land with thy beauty,
Thou art gracious, great, glistening, and high over every land;
Thy rays encompass the lands, . . .
Thy rays are in the midst of the great green sea.
Creator of seed in women,
Thou who makest fluid into man;
Who maintainest the son in the womb of his mother,
Who soothest him with that which stills his weeping.
How manifold it is, what thou hast made!
They are hidden from the face of man.

O sole god, like whom there is no other!
Thou didst create the world according to thy desire,
Whilst thou wert alone:
All men, cattle and wild beasts,
Whatever is on earth, going upon its feet,
And what is on high, flying with its wings.
The countries of Syria and Nubia, the land of Egypt,
Thou settest every man in his place,
Thou suppliest their necessities.

Prayer to Marduk (Babylon)‡
O great lord Marduk, merciful lord!
Men, by whatever name,
What can they understand by their own efforts?
Who has not been negligent, which one has committed no sin?
Who can understand a god's behavior? . . .
Forget what I did in my youth, whatever it was,
Let not your heart well up against me!
Absolve my guilt, remit my punishment. . . .
Let me stand before you always in prayer, supplication and entreaty . . .
Let your heart be reconciled to me
O warrior Marduk, let me sound your praises!

---

*From Miriam Lichtheim, *Ancient Egyptian Literature*, vol. 2 (Berkeley: University of California Press, 1976), 81–86.
†*ANET*, 370.
‡*COS*, 1.114

power over the deity. The laments are also generally introduced by sections of praise. This has led some interpreters to conclude that the Mesopotamian worshipers thought it necessary to flatter the gods before laying out their complaint or petition. Israelite psalms do not usually mix genres in a single psalm, but there are a few exceptions to that rule (e.g., Pss. 22, 27, 144).

When attempts are made to identify offenses, the Mesopotamians were aware that their gods expected them to maintain justice, but they usually assumed that their offense had been in the realm of ritual. Some gods could be offended by eating certain foods. Others had sacred space that had not been recognized but could be trespassed. The possibilities were endless. In this way, the laments clarify the religious and spiritual perceptions and concerns in the ancient world.

The Cantata of Psalms

The biblical book of Psalms is not just a collection, it is a *book*. The evidence suggests that the psalms have been carefully arranged. The arrangement is not by musical style, literary genre, or author, though some groupings can be found for any of these. Neither is it topical or chronological. When researchers looked at the connections between individual psalms, they found that within each of the five books there was always continuity at some level (author, musical style, shared vocabulary, catch-words, etc.). So there was always some similarity between each psalm and its neighbor on either side. But there was no continuity in the transitions from one book to the next. This suggested that there were "seams" between the books. Consequently, the last psalm in each book has been labeled the "seam Psalm" (41, 72, 89, 106, and 145 [since 146–150 serve as the conclusion to the book]). It has therefore been concluded that the books represent stages of composition—perhaps books 1 and 2 at first standing alone with 3, 4, and 5 added one at a time in different periods.

The seam psalms have been interpreted as together containing a somewhat cohesive commentary offering a theological perspective on the history of the Davidic covenant and the kingship of God. In this view, the theme of the book is introduced in Psalms 1 and 2, carried forward step by step in seam psalms 41, 72, 89, 106, and 145 and then climaxed with a praise conclusion in 146 through 150. This message is traced in some detail under Bridging Contexts (see pp. 356–60). What is still controversial is whether each psalm had a role in carrying the larger message forward or if that role was left to the seam psalms. If each psalm had a role, it must be determined how that role is to be identified. If only the seam psalms carry the message, other explanations need to be offered as to why any given psalm was in one book rather than another and whether the ordering of the psalms has any logic behind it.

Z. Radovan, Jerusalem

Titles and Authorship

Many of the psalms are introduced in the Bible by what is referred to as a title. These are not the headings provided by the translation, but are words that are actually in the Hebrew text. Sometimes the title mentions a person's name (cf. Solomon, Ps. 72), sometimes musical direction (for the choir director to the tune of "Lilies," Ps. 69), sometimes a musical genre (maskil, Ps. 89), and sometimes a historical setting (Ps. 18). Some titles include all of the above (cf. Pss. 59 and 60). Literarily, these titles are not poetic and are not part of the composition itself. Most interpreters agree that the titles were not put in by the author but most likely by later compilers or editors, though no information exists to suggest who did so or when it was done. They obviously have a long tradition, since the earliest Hebrew manuscripts (second century BC) already include them.

> **Named Authors of Psalms**
>
> David, Solomon, Moses, Asaph, Heman, Ethan, Sons of Korah

The most controversial aspect of these titles concerns what they communicate about the authorship of the psalms. In some cases the person named in the title is explicitly set forward as the composer (e.g., Psalm 18). But most cases are not that clear. Of the seventy-three titles that refer to David, nine of them contain only David's name prefaced by a rather ambiguous preposition.* An additional eighteen add only a designation of the musical genre.† In the English translations of these titles, the preposition is usually rendered either "of" or "by" but is probably best represented by "belonging to."‡ These psalms could "belong to" David as the composer of them, but that is not the only option. Not all Gregorian chants were written by Pope Gregory. Likewise, it is possible that not all "Davidic" psalms were written by David. On the other side of the equation, however, it would not be logical to designate chants "Gregorian" if he were not connected in some way, and the same is true of Davidic psalms. It is not that important whether David is considered the author, the editor, or the popularizer of the literary or liturgical prototype. Certainly some Gregorian chants were written by Gregory. Likewise, though the phrasing of the title falls short of clearly attributing authorship to him in all but a few cases, there is every good reason to see David as the composer of some, or even many, of the psalms that have his name attached. He is certainly the driving force behind the biblical psalmic tradition, his greatest legacy.

> **All these men were under the supervision of their fathers for the music of the temple of the LORD, with cymbals, lyres and harps, for the ministry at the house of God. Asaph, Jeduthun and Heman were under the supervision of the king. (1 Chron. 25:6)**

---

*Pss. 25, 26, 27, 28, 35, 37, 103, 138, 144.
†Pss. 15, 16, 17, 23, 24, 29, 32, 38, 101, 108, 110, 122, 124, 131, 133, 141, 143, 145.
‡That is how it functions on seals where it precedes a name—it indicates that the seal and the accompanying authorization belong to the named individual.

© The British Museum

The term that we have chosen to describe this concept of an intentionally arranged book of Psalms is "Cantata." A cantata, similar to an oratorio, uses various sorts of musical pieces, some sung as solos and others by a chorus, to treat a particular theme. It presents a connected story by means of the music rather than through the use of scenery or acting. In the books of Chronicles, the author/editor has used various sources to piece together a continuous narrative with particular themes in mind. By using the term *cantata*, we are suggesting that the editor(s) of Psalms have done the same sort of thing using the hymns of Israel rather than narratives. In our modern setting, we are aware that the same story can be told through narrative or through song (e.g., *Les Misérables* or *Phantom of the Opera*). Likewise, the story of the communist revolution could be told through historical narrative, through philosophical treatise, through compiled stories of those who lived through it, or through a musical setting such as the one that focused on the Jewish plight in *Fiddler on the Roof*. There are many ways to tell a story.

REFLECTIONS

1. What is the importance of the five-book structure?

2. Discuss the importance of identifying the authors of individual psalms.

3. Discuss the importance of identifying the historical or ritual setting in which each psalm was composed.

4. Would you consider Psalm 139 a praise psalm or a lament psalm? Defend your choice.

5. In what ways could the Psalms be considered the hub of the Old Testament?

6. What is the importance of identifying psalm types (genres)?

7. What are the differences and similarities between Israelite and ancient Near Eastern psalms?

Notes

1. From "Prayer of Lamentation to Ishtar," *ANET*, 384, lines 2–8.

BRIDGING CONTEXTS

To understand what we are to do with the book of Psalms, we have to have some acquaintance with the theology and worship practices of Israel, as well as a conception of the function of the Psalms in the canon of Scripture.

PURPOSE: KINGSHIP IN PSALMS

Before we discuss what the purpose of the book of Psalms is, it will be helpful to consider some common ideas. The purpose of the composers was often prayer, but that does not mean that we should think of the book of Psalms being compiled as a hymnbook or a Book of Common Prayer. There is no hint or suggestion in the book itself, in the rest of the Old Testament, or even in the New Testament that it is being provided as an authoritative "how-to" guide. First, as noted in Original Meaning, not all of the psalms are prayers (see pp. 341–343). Wisdom psalms are addressed to people, not to God. Second, not all of the psalms that are prayers are ones that we can comfortably or appropriately pray (cf. Pss. 59:10–11; 109:6–15; 137:8–9). Third, when Jesus offered his model prayer, he did not offer a psalm or point to the Psalms. Fourth, it would be difficult to explain the psalms that were repeated if imitation were the idea (see, e.g., Pss. 14 and 53). Finally, the idea that these are presented as model prayers offers no explanation for the careful editing that is evident in the book. In conclusion, though many of the psalms *can* be beneficially used as model prayers either in private devotion or corporate worship, we would be mistaken to think that that is why they are in the Bible. They illustrate what Israelites prayed, but there is no biblical mandate for us to go and do likewise.

What alternatives are there? If they are not given for us to imitate, what are they given for? We have to move beyond the reasons that motivated the composers to those that motivated the compilers, those who took 150 individual compositions and made them into a book that then became a book of the Bible. To understand this, we return to the cantata concept introduced under Original Meaning (see pp. 352–54), where it was suggested that the book of Psalms was compiled to offer a theological perspective on the history of the Davidic covenant and the kingship of God.

Psalms 1 and 2

These two psalms are different genres (1 is a wisdom psalm, 2 is a royal psalm), but they are brought together to serve as an introduction to the book. They may even have been written for that purpose. Despite their genre differences, continuity is evident between them in the inclusio that draws them together ("Blessed . . . ," first line of 1, last line of 2), in shared vocabulary (e.g., "meditates" in 1:2 and "plot" in 2:1 are the same Hebrew word), and in the contrast of "two ways" that they hold in common—(1) the righteous and the wicked; (2) the nations and the Lord's anointed.

A CANTATA ABOUT THE DAVIDIC COVENANT

Introduction Psalms 1–2		
Ps. 1. Ultimate vindication of the righteous		
Ps. 2. God's choice and defense of Israelite king		
BOOK	**SEAM**	**CONTENT**
Book 1	41	Many individual laments; most psalms mention enemies
Book 2	72	Key psalms: 45, 48, 51, 54–64; mostly laments and "enemy psalms"
Book 3	89	Asaph and Sons of Korah collections; key psalm: 78
Book 4	106	Praise collections: 95–100; key psalms: 90, 103–5
Book 5	145	Halleluyah collection: 111–17; Songs of Ascent: 120–34; Davidic reprise: 138–45; key psalms: 107, 110, 119
Conclusion 146–150		
Climactic praise to God		

These two psalms set the stage by laying out the theological grid through which the book is to be read. The horizontal lines of the grid are represented in Psalm 1 in what we have called the retribution principle. The way of the righteous flourishes, while the way of the wicked leads to destruction. This is offered as a given though it will be questioned in many contexts throughout the book. The vertical lines of the grid are represented in Psalm 2, seen in God's support of his anointed against the opposition of the nations, though the book will question this again and again. Through these two psalms, God's justice and sovereignty are established as offering the grid through which the prayers and wisdom psalms of the book need to be viewed. They also together bridge the gap between individual and nation.

Seam Psalms

The seam psalms (41, 72, 89, 106, 145) carry the major responsibility for advancing these themes through the book. Psalm 41 corresponds best with the theme of Psalm 1 and could be seen as the application of Psalm 1 to a life situation, particularly that of David's conflict with Saul. As a result, instead of the peaceful clarity of Psalm 1, Psalm 41 captures the psalmist's faith in the midst of confusion and the unresolved nature of his circumstances.

Psalm 72 is a blessing on the king, apparently Solomon, wishing for him the very assurances that Psalm 2 offered. It could easily be viewed as an enthronement hymn. Of interest is the editorial comment in the last verse of the psalm that this ends the prayers of David.

2 Samuel 7:8–16

"Now then, tell my servant David, 'This is what the LORD Almighty says: I took you from the pasture and from following the flock to be ruler over my people Israel. I have been with you wherever you have gone, and I have cut off all your enemies from before you. Now I will make your name great, like the names of the greatest men of the earth. And I will provide a place for my people Israel and will plant them so that they can have a home of their own and no longer be disturbed. Wicked people will not oppress them anymore, as they did at the beginning and have done ever since the time I appointed leaders over my people Israel. I will also give you rest from all your enemies.

"'The LORD declares to you that the LORD himself will establish a house for you: When your days are over and you rest with your fathers, I will raise up your offspring to succeed you, who will come from your own body, and I will establish his kingdom. He is the one who will build a house for my Name, and I will establish the throne of his kingdom forever. I will be his father, and he will be my son. When he does wrong, I will punish him with the rod of men, with floggings inflicted by men. But my love will never be taken away from him, as I took it away from Saul, whom I removed from before you. Your house and your kingdom will endure forever before me; your throne will be established forever.'"

This is particularly intriguing since there are many psalms still to come that name David in the title.

Looking briefly at these first two books, a case could be made that the books relate to the two stages of David's life (thus the editorial comment in 72:20 would refer to the end of the Psalms editorially arranged as reflections on David's period of history). In this view, book 1 would relate to David's life in exile as the enemy of Saul. Book 2 would reflect on David's reign on the throne of Israel.

Ivory dagger portraying Syrian king seated on throne flanked by Cherubim.

Z. Radovan, Jerusalem

Psalm 89 concerns the Davidic covenant of kingship. As it recounts the specifications of the covenant, it also indicates that there was a covenant crisis. In sequence from the first two books, this third book would reflect a period of jeopardy to the covenant and to the monarchy, whether a specific crisis (e.g., division of the kingdom, threat of the Assyrians) or destruction by the Babylonians.

Psalm 106 is a retrospective look at Israel's history focusing on the failures of the nation and the continued graciousness of God. It ends with a petition for regathering from the nations and therefore could be understood as offering thoughts from the perspective of exile.

Psalm 145 is a psalm praising the kingship of God. It captures both the individual and corporate themes introduced in Psalms 1 and 2 and elevates the kingship of God as a higher priority than the kingship of the Davidic dynasty. It could easily apply to the postexilic period when there is no Davidic king on the throne and the kingship of God has become the preeminent focus.

This sequence of the seam psalms could then be seen as tracing through Israel's history with special attention to Davidic kingship as an instrument of God's kingship. The next question concerns whether or not the themes of the seam psalms are picked up in any way in the interior psalms in each book.

Interior Psalms, Book 1 (3–40)

If it is true that book 1 reflects on the period of David's flight from Saul, how would the individual psalms relate to the theme?[1] A careful reading of the first book will show a significant emphasis on the theme of trouble at the hands of one's enemies. Occasionally interspersed are a couple of psalms of deliverance (18, 30). This book is full of cries for protection and guidance and affirmations of God's strength and ability to deliver. These themes make it very appropriate to the period of David's struggles and follow the theme of Psalm 1 more than that of Psalm 2. They pick up David's despair and confusion but also reflect those occasions when he experienced deliverance in astonishing ways.

Interior Psalms, Book 2 (42–71)

Book 2 has a remarkable number of psalms that can be applied directly to events of David's reign. David came to the throne with the kingdom in utter chaos, having been recently overrun by the Philistines. It is not surprising, therefore, to have a national lament like Psalm 44 near the front of this collection. In contrast, Psalm 45 indicates a secure throne with the expectation of princes and endurance. Psalms 46 and 47 can be seen as hymns commemorating victories such as those experienced by David (see 2 Sam. 8). Psalm 48 specifically turns its attention to Jerusalem, which David conquered and made his capital (2 Sam. 5). Psalm 51 is well known as a penitential reflection of David's sin with Bathsheba. Psalm 53 repeats Psalm 14 and suggests a return to the "enemies" motif. As Saul had forced David into exile earlier in his career, in the latter days of his kingship, he was forced into temporary exile by his son Absalom. In this section of book 2 there are then a whole series of psalms of lament seeking protection and deliverance from enemies. In this way,

Messianic Psalms or Royal Psalms?

A number of psalms focus their attention on the king. They identify him as a specially chosen ally and instrument of God and portray him in idealized terms. In several of these psalms, he is called the "anointed one," which in Hebrew is *mašiaḥ* (*messiah,* cf. Ps. 2:2). Some of these find their way into the New Testament listed as fulfilled by Jesus the Christ (which is the Greek term for messiah; see Acts 4:25–26; 13:33; Heb. 1:5; 5:5–6). Furthermore, in Luke 24:27, 44, it is clear that Jesus saw himself in relation to the Psalms.

Should we say that these psalms are prophesying about Jesus? Or are they simply talking about an ideal king, a position that was later associated with Jesus? To some extent, these questions can be addressed through an understanding of fulfillment. This has already been discussed in the chapters on prophetic literature. Given the view of fulfillment that we presented there, these psalms could be considered as royal psalms in their original context (on the "message" level). Since the Israelite audience thought of the Messiah as a future, ideal, Davidic king, it would be easy to contend that though they read these as royal psalms, they would expect them to be most true of the Messiah. In that sense, it might be helpful to consider these psalms as operating on a level similar to a job description in which the role is described in detail without having a particular individual in mind. Yet when an individual surfaces to fill that job description, there will be an uncanny correlation to the person described in the document.

book 2 can offer reflection of the period of David's kingship in a way that is closely correlated with the narratives of 2 Samuel. The seam psalm passes the kingdom to Solomon and thus ends the psalms pertaining to David's life (72:20).

Interior Psalms, Book 3 (73–88)

Book 3 takes a distinctly corporate turn as it reflects the national struggles of Israel and God's preeminence over the nations. Sin, rejection, and defeat are common themes. Psalm 79 speaks of invasion and defilement of the temple. Psalm 80 seeks restoration, and Psalm 84 finds security and comfort in the temple. These themes are all appropriate to the struggles of the divided monarchy period and the threats that came from the major international powers.

Interior Psalms, Book 4 (90–105)

If the seam psalm at the end of book 4 indeed suggests associating this book with the exile, it is fitting to start with a word from Moses in Psalm 90 reminding the people that the truest dwelling place of Israel is God himself rather than the land that he has given them. It notes God's anger and calls on him to relent. The emerging theme in the psalms of this book is the kingship of God as he reigns over Israel. The Israelites look to God to bring vengeance and forgiveness.

Interior Psalms, Book 5 (107–144)

Finally, the last book begins with praise that God has regathered the Israelites from the nations (107:1–3), suggesting reflection of the postexilic period. Psalm 110 looks for the return of an ideal Davidic king, and Psalm 119 addresses a commitment to the law. Psalms 120 through 134 were written as pilgrimage songs for when the people journeyed to Jerusalem for the great festivals. In book 5 they would have increased poignancy in the context of the great pilgrimage back to Jerusalem out of exile.

These are just a few examples of how the interior psalms may offer additional reflections on the themes carried by the framework of the seam psalms. There is, however, still much work to be done at this level, and no consensus about the role of the interior psalms has developed.

Message of Psalms

We are now ready to draw conclusions about the message of the book of Psalms. Regardless of how the interior psalms are viewed, the introduction, seam psalms, and finale of the book are sufficient to point us in the right direction. Simply put, the message is "God reigns." The reign of God is evidenced throughout Israel's history as he delivers David from Saul, brings him to the throne, and sets up a kingship covenant with him. God's kingship is supreme among the nations but also just in the requirements made of Israel. God's judgment as well as his faithfulness is attested as Israel's destiny unfolds. God's faithfulness to righteous individuals and to his people in their national crises is evidenced in the defeat of enemies, whoever they may be. God is worthy of praise, and he is receptive to the petitions and laments of the righteous. The wise will trust in him. This is how God is revealed in the book of Psalms. The reason why the psalms are Scripture is that they portray God accurately. The reason why so many of them are repeatable is that they affirm this picture of God.

> The reason why the psalms are Scripture is that they portray God accurately. The reason why so many of them are repeatable is that they affirm this picture of God.

Psalms as Revelation

When we read the New Testament Gospels, we are aware that each gospel represents a unique version of Jesus' actions and words edited by the apostle under the direction of inspiration. No one would deny that Jesus' own words would carry the authority associated with inspiration, but the inspiration of the book operates at a second level and lends authority to the editorial message of the apostle as he organizes Jesus' words to his particular purposes. Inspiration is therefore operating at two levels: first to the original words and second to the editorial presentation of those words.

This same phenomenon can be suggested for the Psalms. The psalmists' words expressed in the composition of the individual psalm would be considered the first level of inspiration, lending authority to the contents of the psalm. But a second level of inspiration would be seen in the work of the editors as they arranged the psalms so as to offer a message that transcends the individual compositions. In this way, the Psalms, as in all other books of the Bible, have an authoritative message tied to their canonical form. Such an understanding helps us to handle the book of Psalms as we do all of the other biblical books—by recognizing and taking account of the importance of context.

THEOLOGICAL PERSPECTIVES

Worship in Israel

We often fail to grasp how significantly different the worship practices of Israel were from our own. There is nothing in the Old Testament that functions the way churches do today (see "Temple and Church," p. 123). There was no weekly congregating of believers at a central place of worship in the town. It is probable that there were

Jerusalem and its Temple were the central focus of worship in Israel.

Sabbath observances at the temple, but few people lived close enough to the temple to participate. Even those who came to the temple on such occasions would have been largely spectators to the performance of rituals or liturgies. There is no indication that they thought in terms of gathering together once a week for worship. Liturgies were probably recited in the temple daily in connection with morning and evening sacrifices. Those who came to the temple to sacrifice and pray would have participated, at least as spectators, in those liturgies. But for most of the people, these would be rare privileges. In the common person's experience, psalms were not for periodic worship services; they were for life.

Worship in the Old Testament

Two of the major words for worship in the Old Testament refer (1) to the performance of service and (2) to assuming a position of prostration. Other verbs refer to actions of praise, such as "thank," "shout," "sing," and "proclaim." The worship that consisted of service was performed by the temple personnel. This included everything from officiating at sacrifices to cleaning up the mess that resulted from the sacrifices. Worship activities included performing rituals, reciting liturgies, making pilgrimage, celebrating festivals, and simply coming to the temple to bow before God. All of these activities focus their attention on the temple. The temple represented God's presence in the midst of his people and was viewed as the center from which God ruled the earth. It therefore represented the ongoing enterprises of covenant and creation. These issues were at the center of Israel's worship.

We find our spiritual communities in our churches. There we experience the accountability, support, instruction, and encouragement that enhance our spiritual lives in a unique way. In Israel, each family, neighborhood, and town was to provide such a community twenty-four hours a day, seven days a week. They were God's covenant people living together under God's law and being instructed by God's representatives, the priests and Levites. They did not need a separate community apart from the world as our churches provide for us—Israel as a whole was apart from the world.

One of the ways we think about our religious practice is in terms of what we call spiritual disciplines—prayer, Bible reading, and so on. In fact, the book of Psalms holds a prominent place in those disciplines as it serves as a basis for our prayers and the frequent source for our devotional readings. Whether or not common Israelites could read (a matter of some controversy), they certainly would not have had access to personal copies of their Scriptures. It is even difficult to determine whether Old Testament Israelites had anything they would have thought of the way we think of the Bible. They considered some works to be "sacred writings" (such as the law of Moses), but they would have had little if any access to them. So there could have been nothing like devotional reading of God's Word. Whatever access they had to God's words, they would have had through oral

Worship and Baseball?

If we compare going to the temple to one of our largest traditional public spectacles, major league baseball games, we may find a good analogy. Just as sacrifices were made daily, baseball games occur often and with regularity. A small percentage of fortunate individuals have season tickets, just as some who lived in or near Jerusalem could come to the temple regularly if they had the leisure and inclination to do so. But for many who attend a ball game, they might plan for months, make a long journey, and view the evening as an exciting special event in their lives. Others who live in the general area might make it a family outing just once or twice a season. Still others might get to attend only once or twice in a lifetime. Those in the stands are enthusiastic participants, but only as spectators. They sing the national anthem; they cheer and boo; and they might sing "Take Me Out to the Ball Game" at the seventh-inning stretch. Sometimes rituals take place, like fireworks displays or kids running the bases after the game.

We would have to shift the analogy to other sports to pick up a comparison of priests leading liturgies to cheerleaders leading cheers. Attending a baseball game is also a major investment, just as offering a sacrifice was, and there is often a ritual meal (hot dogs and peanuts). We could extend the analogy even further if we considered the concept of sacred space. The field itself is restricted to the participants, the players. Someone who goes out onto the field without approval will be arrested and ejected from the ballpark. Similarly, there were areas in the temple that were only for the priests. Anyone else who trespassed on that area was ejected. Perhaps this analogy gives us just a small glimpse at the sort of occasion that going to the temple was.

Courtesy of the Museum of Anatolian Civilizations

communication and those parts that they committed to memory, which could have been numerous (cf. Deut. 6:6–9). What about daily prayers? We know that they prayed, but we don't know how often they prayed. Psalm 5 speaks of prayer morning by morning (v. 3) directed toward the temple (v. 7). Daniel practiced praying three times a day, again directed toward the temple (Dan. 6:10). The psalmist also refers to prayers three times a day, at least in times of trouble, though maybe with regularity (Ps. 55:17).

Another important aspect of worship was sacrifice—how often did the common Israelite make sacrifices? Males were expected to make the journey to Jerusalem for three pilgrimage festivals each year. These would be logical times for other sacrifices to be brought as well (e.g., purification offerings or thank offerings). But we have little information about how regularly the Israelites participated in these pilgrimage festivals. It has been pointed out that practical issues such as leaving livestock unattended for a week or two or leaving a settlement with no males to defend it might have precluded consistent participation.

From the standpoint of the temple, many sacrifices would have been made each day: those provided by the king, those made from the temple flocks and herds for corporate purposes, and those brought by whatever private persons may have come to the temple that day. From the standpoint of any given individual, journeys to the temple (sometimes taking many days just in travel) with sacrifices may have been relatively rare occasions.

Vindication vs. Appeasement

As we have already mentioned in Original Meaning, the Israelite psalmists differed from their ancient Near Eastern counterparts by focusing on vindication rather than appeasement. They were not content to think that God was angry at some unknown offense that they had unwittingly committed. Instead, they wanted to be declared innocent of any wrongdoing that might be suggested by their misfortune. This is an important theological distinction that demands our attention. A psalmist asking for vindi-cation must be either incredibly presumptuous in his self-righteousness or well informed about God, the latter being the logical choice. This points out a key difference between the Israelites and, say, the Babylonians, who had such limited revelation and so little confidence about the nature of their gods. Babylonian literature contains prayers directed at any god and asking forgiveness for any of a number of general offenses (e.g., "If I have eaten that which was forbidden by any god, or if I have unwittingly trespassed on ground that was holy to any god, please overlook my sin"; see "Prayer to Every God," p. 104). It also warns us against relapsing into a primitive, misinformed state in which we think of God as irrationally angry, leaving us no recourse but blind appeasement of his wrath. It is true that God is angered by our sin but that anger is different when we have been made aware of what it is

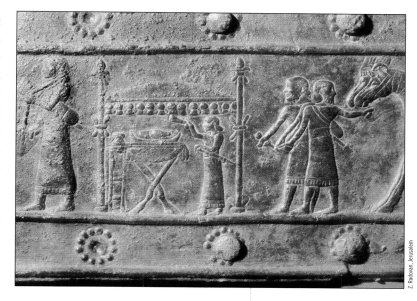

Sacrificial scene on the Assyrian Balawat gates.

that makes him angry. What a mistake it would be to think that God simply wanted to be bought off or that he had no interest in communicating to us what displeased him. The psalmists expected God to act justly, and they called for his justice to be enacted swiftly. They were concerned for God's reputation. Request for vindication assumed God's justice; attempts at appeasement implied that justice was not the issue.

Ritual and Psalms

Did the psalms originate as spontaneous outpourings of the soul, or were they carefully composed? Were the psalms formal liturgy accompanied by ritual, or were they used as stand-alone expressions of piety? There is still much disagreement between scholars on these questions. Certainly some of the psalms were carefully composed—one does not spontaneously utter acrostics. Yet other psalms could easily have been spontaneous. The text of Scripture is suggestive in some contexts that psalms were spoken spontaneously (1 Sam. 2, Jonah 2, Luke 1, 2), though some of these could be recitation of appropriate psalms that had been committed to memory.

On the second issue, it is possible that some of the psalms were used in conjunction with rituals, but there is little cause offered in the text to think that the primary use of the psalms was to accompany rituals. There is even less reason to think

Relief of Tiglath-Pileser III worshiping carved images to procure the support of the gods before a military campaign.

that many of them had been composed with ritual occasions in mind. The Old Testament offers numerous instances in which the Israelites show great interest in commemorating historical events by setting up memorials (Josh. 4, 22; 1 Sam. 7), celebrating festivals (Ex. 12), or composing literary works (Ex. 15; Lamentations). Such evidence gives us reason to believe that historical events, rather than ritual needs, motivated at least some of the compositions of psalms (cf. David's eulogy for Saul and Jonathan, 2 Sam. 1:19–27). The titles of some psalms suggest this very idea (see especially many of the psalms between 51 and 60).

Afterlife Belief in the Old Testament

While we enjoy an assurance of heaven as a place of reward for those who have received God's salvation, we cannot assume that the Israelites shared that confidence. We must rather explore the Old Testament text to discover what concepts they had of the afterlife. Did they believe that there would be reward and judgment in the afterlife? What possibilities existed after death in their understanding? Did they look forward to an eternity with God? What revelation had they received on the topic?

Sheol is the Hebrew term used to designate the place where the dead go. As can be seen in the sidebar "Sheol," the information that can be gleaned about Sheol suggests very little overlap with our current ideas about afterlife.

Another approach to the question concerns what requests the Israelites made of God and how they expressed their hopes, fears, and confidence. There are three phrases that occur in the Old Testament

---

Sheol

1. Those in Sheol are viewed as separated from God (Pss. 6:5; 88:3, 10-12; Isa. 38:18) though God has access to Sheol.
2. Sheol is never referred to as the abode of the wicked alone.
3. Sheol is never identified as the place where all go, but no alternatives are discussed.
4. It is not just a place of human imagination, for God speaks of it as well (Deut. 32:22).
5. Sheol is viewed in negative terms: no possessions, memory, knowledge, or joy.
6. It is not viewed as a place where judgment or punishment takes place, so it is not "hell." The only sense in which it represents judgment is when someone is sent there rather than remaining alive.
7. There is no reference that suggests different compartments in Sheol for the righteous and the wicked.
8. Logically one would not expect a distinction between a place of reward and a place of punishment at this juncture since the ultimate criterion for the distinction as we understand it, the work of Christ, was not yet available.

texts that are often interpreted as indicating an Israelite belief that when they died they would be with God.

1. The reassurance that they would "see his face."

2. Various ways of expressing that the righteous person would not be "abandoned to Sheol," or would be "redeemed from Sheol."

3. The confidence that God will "receive" the psalmist.

Seeing God's Face. Some psalms speak in terms of awakening and seeing God's face (Pss. 11:7; 17:15). In Psalms, however, the motif of going to sleep besieged by enemies and awaking expecting to experience God's deliverance is firmly attested (e.g., Pss. 3:5–6; 63:6; 139:18). In the context, this is not an anticipation of heaven, but of an experience in the temple as Pss. 27:4 and 63:2 make clear. The psalmist expects his deliverance to come when he awakes in the morning (Ps. 139:18).

Redeemed from Sheol. The phrase "abandon me to the grave" (= Sheol, Ps. 16:10) does not refer to the individual being abandoned *in* Sheol, but to him not being consigned *to* Sheol.[2] Consequently, the psalm can be seen to express the psalmist's confidence that rather than reject the psalmist, consigning him to death and the netherworld, God will protect his life by bringing his presence into the psalmist's life and providing perpetual deliverance from his enemies by the power of his right hand.

That having one's life be redeemed from Sheol (Ps. 49:15) means having his life spared is seen clearly in Psalm 30:2–3: "O LORD my God, I called to you for help and you healed me. O LORD, you brought me up from the grave [= Sheol]; you spared me from going down into the pit."

God "Receiving" an Individual. In Psalm 49:15 the psalmist expresses his confidence that God "will surely take me to himself."

If There Were No Heaven

No hope of heaven—imagine that for a moment! Would we give God a chance if there were nothing in it for us? Would we give God our lives if he gave nothing back but himself? Would our lives have a place for God if we were living for today as the psalmists were? It should be our aspiration to respond to those questions with a resounding "yes!"

God asks no less of us than to be our all in all—here and now, day by day. Job was called upon to demonstrate that there is such a thing as disinterested faith—trusting only in God when there are no personal benefits to gain. When all is stripped away and no hope remains; in the dark, in the loneliness, in the emptiness, there is God. That is when faith stands up and is counted.

The verb "take" is the same one that is used of Enoch. It also occurs in Psalm 73:24: "You guide me with your counsel, and afterward you will *take* me into glory" (emphasis added).

Initially, a few comments on the translation of these verses are necessary. In 49:15 the phrase reads simply, "he will take me." "To himself" has been added by the NIV translators. In 73:24 the translation could lead us to the conclusion that *glory* is a synonym for *heaven*, since that connotation is known in English usage. It must be pointed out, however, that Hebrew never uses the word translated "glory" as a synonym for heaven. A more accurate translation would be along the line of the NRSV, "And afterward you will receive me with honor," or, to avoid the need of a preposition all together, "honorably." It should be clear then that there is nothing in either of these passages to suggest that the individual is being taken *somewhere* (i.e., to God or to Glory). But what else can the verb suggest? The answer is to be found in Psalm 18:16–19, where the first line contains the exact same verbal form as that found in Psalm 49:15 (Ps. 73:24 is also the same except for the change from third person to second person). Yet Psalm 18 makes it clear that the phrase means to deliver someone from his or her trouble. So in Psalm 49:15 the psalmist is praying that God would deliver him from his life-threatening situation, and in Psalm 73:24 he prays that he might be delivered honorably—very much like requests for vindication that are found in other psalms.

In all three of the phrases that have been used to support an Israelite alternative to Sheol, we have found that not only is there ambiguity, but that usage in Psalms (where they are primarily found) suggests that the only alternative to Sheol is continued life on this earth. To substantiate the belief in an alternative to Sheol, we would need a clear, unambiguous passage. None of these offer that. But is there anything that would demonstrate that Sheol indeed was the only possibility the Israelites recognized?

Throughout the book, the psalmists consistently expect vindication in terms of deliverance from their enemies. They expect the enemy to be destroyed while they themselves enjoy a long and happy life. There is no indication that they look for deliverance or vindication in terms of being removed to the presence of God. For them, death offers no possibility of vindication. The psalmist considered the suffering of the righteous and the prosperity of the wicked to be a matter of some urgency, as attested by the frequency with which it is discussed. If the psalmists were aware of the existence of reward and punishment in the afterlife, it would be logical to expect that they would relieve the theological tension by alluding to that as a means of sustaining a belief in God's justice (in the long run) despite what was happening in life. The fact that they restrict their attempts at resolution to the temporal sphere stands as strong evidence that that is all they knew. Otherwise, they would be overlooking a fairly simple solution: that everyone would get their just deserts in the afterlife.

Israelites believed that all persons would continue to exist after death in a place they called Sheol. It was not a place where reward or punishment took place. It was not a pleasant place, but there was no torment. God had access to Sheol, but those in Sheol had no access to God. While they had evidences that there may be alternatives to Sheol, they did not profess to know anything about those alternatives, so they could only hope to be spared from Sheol for as long as possible. Thus they saw God's blessing and reward in a long life. Unknown were: (1) the concept of spending eternity in heaven or with God; (2) judgment by God in the afterlife to reward faithfulness and punish wickedness; and (3) punishment of the wicked in hell.

Israel's Hope. What then was Israel's hope? Israelites were aware of individuals such as Enoch and Elijah who "were taken"—presumably to a better place, though the texts do not say. Did faithful Israelites harbor any hope of ending up in a place better than Sheol? Hebrews 11:16 says that Abraham and others of faith "were longing for a better country—a heavenly one." The designation "heavenly" however, refers not specifically to heaven, but to those things that emanate out of heaven—things that are immaterial in nature and possess a spiritual quality. Abraham wasn't just interested in real estate—to him the land was a spiritual inheritance.

It is also important to note that God was gradually offering increased revelation. By the end of the Old Testament period, Daniel was able to tell his audience that "Multitudes who sleep in the dust of the earth will awake: some to everlasting life, others to shame and everlasting contempt. Those who are wise will shine like the brightness of the heavens, and those who lead many to righteousness, like the stars for ever and ever" (Dan. 12:2–3). This served as a bridge to the full development of a theology of resurrection and afterlife that we see in the New Testament.

Few Israelites would have thought that they had any chance of joining the ranks of Enoch or Elijah—so what was their hope for the future? It was in their children, the next covenant generation. Rather than placing their hope in an individual's continuing existence in heaven, they placed their hope in their nation's and family's continuing existence on earth. So, for instance, the Hebrew word that is often translated "eternal" is found parallel to "from generation to generation." It refers to things that are ongoing or perpetual.

The Israelites' faith was not that God had saved them from their sins so that they could go to heaven. Their faith was that God had provided a mechanism by which he could have relationship with them (the covenant, the temple, and the sacrifices). In that way, their faith focused on the end result of a relationship with God rather than on the reward of heaven (see epilogue for more discussion). Likewise, our faith is in the mechanism provided by God (Jesus' death) so that we can have a relationship with him. Relationship is primary; the reward of heaven is simply a by-product of that relationship. The book of Psalms can lead us through this kind of transformation in our thinking.

REFLECTIONS

1. What are some guidelines for using psalms appropriately as model prayers?

2. Discuss the relative importance of the composers' intention and the compilers' intention.

3. What are the strengths and weaknesses of the cantata model?

4. How did worship at the temple differ from worship in our churches?

5. How were the motivations of appeasement and vindication different from one another?

6. How does the absence of revelation about the afterlife impact our understanding of Israelite faith?

7. Is Sheol real?

8. When an Israelite spoke of being redeemed, what did he mean?

9. What hope did the individual Israelite have?

Notes

1. Note carefully that this approach does not suggest that the psalms in book 1 were all *written* to reflect on this theme.
2. This combination of verb and preposition (abandon to) is used elsewhere in Leviticus 19:10; Job 39:14; Psalm 49:14; and Malachi 4:1 and in each case means "consign to."

CHAPTER

CONTEMPORARY SIGNIFICANCE

CONTEMPORARY WORSHIP AND THE PSALMS

Should our worship services be traditional or contemporary? Should we use choruses, worship songs, hymns, or chants? Is it appropriate to use drums and electric guitars, or should the organ be preferred? Is it pleasing to God to use a prayer book or to pray in tongues? Is it biblical to clap when we sing? To kneel when we pray? These are the questions that not only perplex us, but also often divide us. Does the book of Psalms offer us a "biblical" resolution?

Psalms does not tell us *how* to worship, but *whom* to worship. The book does not tell us what worship is, but who God is. Israelite worship is occasionally described, including percussion (Psalm 150), clapping (47), shouting (100), dancing (149), and raised hands (134). But we need to remind ourselves that what is described in Psalms is not always recommended for imitation (e.g., the cursing psalms). Furthermore, the imperatives in Psalms are imperatives to praise, not to praise in certain ways. "Clap your hands" (imperative, 47:1) does not mean that true worshipers must clap their hands. The imperative compels us to engage in worship. The specific action simply reflects how Israel did that. In that sense, this imperative is taken in the same way as those in the next psalm, "Walk about Zion, go around her, count her towers" (48:12).

The book of Psalms will not solve our worship controversies and dilemmas, which typically focus on taste and traditions rather than on biblical or theological propriety. *Is* there a biblical way to worship? Yes—with a "pure heart" (24:4). "Pure heart" refers to the integrity of our motivations and the clarity of our commitment to live holy lives. That is the worship that is pleasing to God. It is

> Psalms does not tell us *how* to worship, but *whom* to worship.

6 PSALMS

important for us to remember that the effectiveness of our worship is not measured by how we feel when we are done. It is too easy to walk out of church asking ourselves what we got out of it. We should be wondering what God got out of it. Our question should be, "How did I do?"

In addition, there are precedents for worship that we can glean from the Psalms. For instance, despite the presence of exuberant worship in Psalms, we cannot afford to ignore the inclusion of the other two psalm categories—lament and wisdom. Lament suggests the appropriateness of coming before God with problems, questions, petitions, humility, and repentance—not just in personal prayer, but in corporate contexts as well. Wisdom psalms indicate the appropriateness of instruction and exhortation in the context of worship. These should not be considered requirements, but ideas offered concerning the range of possibilities that should be considered for well-rounded worship.

What Do We Expect from God and What Does He Expect from Us?

We believe that God answers prayer. We believe that God judges the wicked. We believe that God is pleased by righteousness and grants grace and blessing to those who are faithful to him. But worship is not part of a deal. God does not need our service, and he does not need our worship or praise. We fill no physical, social, or psychological need in God. We are the ones in need. Our needs compel us to seek him. His love motivates him to seek us.

We expect that God hears and cares. We expect that he is just and that he is able to overcome any obstacle. We do not expect that his purposes will always be discernible or that he will always respond the way we want him to. Even some of the psalmist's expectations were misguided. But we should never feel let down or disappointed by God. Our expectations are that God will carry out his plan and fulfill his purposes. He is good, and he is worthy of our praise and worship—that reason, and that reason alone is why we offer it. We expect nothing in return and can harbor no sense that God is somehow obligated to us.

What does God expect from us? Wholehearted commitment, trust, faith, purity, holiness, and obedience, just to name a few—in short, he expects no less an act of worship than the giving of our lives (Rom. 12:1–2). Our words of praise should only serve as tokens of the larger gift, and if they do not, they are empty words. God expects us to renounce our self-centeredness and to recognize his centrality in our lives, in the world, and in history. This is what we were made for, and he expects us to find joy and peace in that recognition. Praise is an expression of the joy; lament is a search for the peace.

> God expects us to renounce our self-centeredness and to recognize his centrality in our lives, in the world, and in history. This is what we were made for.

SCENARIO: TRUSTING GOD WHEN HE DOESN'T SEEM TO HEAR

Carolyn had been ill for as long as she could remember. Her asthma had kept her from many activities growing up. As a little girl, she could only watch as her friends jumped rope. In high school, trying out for the cheerleading squad was out of the question. She had always hoped secretly that she would somehow grow out of it, but it seemed to be getting worse now in college. Some days she couldn't even go outside without having an attack. She couldn't help feeling depressed about it all. One good thing though was how supportive the girls in the dorm Bible study had been. They were really sensitive to her condition and her feelings, and they prayed for her often. They

Should I Curse My Enemies?

The sections or psalms in which the psalmist calls down curses on his enemies are labeled imprecatory. Given the command of Jesus to love our enemies, Christians often find these psalms perplexing. We can solve the dilemma by recalling that in the lament psalms (where imprecations occur) the psalmist is pleading God to bring justice. God's reputation as a just God is at stake. Justice is only accomplished if the punishment is proportional to the offense. How wicked are the psalmist's enemies? Would a badly scraped shin or a painful hangnail be sufficient punishment? What about a broken leg or a serious illness? When the psalmist names particular consequences and calls them down on his adversaries, he is communicating to God examples of some of the forms justice would have to take to measure up to the magnitude of the crimes. In that way, the psalmist could be compared to an attorney in a liability suit suggesting to the judge and jury that his client ought to be awarded so many millions of dollars as a result of the wanton negligence of the company being sued. The attorney would claim that the court must make an example out of the company so that everyone knows that the justice system is not going to tolerate such negligence. The dollar amount is relative to other liability awards and proportional to the seriousness of the offense.

> Our response should not be to pray as the psalmists pray, but to be as concerned for God's reputation of justice as they were.

were studying some of the psalms together, and Carolyn often felt comforted when she read about the struggles the psalmist had and how he depended on God. Only last week, however, they had encountered a psalm that really challenged them. Carolyn had had a particularly difficult day, and in Bible study they found themselves in Psalm 30. Erika read aloud verse 2: "O LORD my God, I called to you for help and you healed me." The room became suddenly quiet as all eyes turned expectantly to Carolyn.

"What do you think, Carolyn?" Erika asked. "We all believe God answers prayer. Maybe if you pray and trust him like the psalmist did, he will heal you of your asthma."

Carolyn didn't feel very sure at all. Was it really that easy? What was the catch? When Erika brought up these questions, Andrea reminded them of the verse they had talked about a few weeks earlier, Psalm 37:4, "Delight yourself in the LORD and he will give you the desires of your heart." For the rest of the Bible study, the girls encouraged Carolyn to trust the Lord and to pray for healing. She appreciated her friends' concern and encouragement, but she left that night still undecided about what to do.

Now a week had gone by, and Carolyn was feeling not only undecided, but also totally confused. Was her reluctance a sign that she lacked faith? If she prayed the psalmist's prayers and shared the psalmist's faith, why shouldn't she experience the psalmist's healing? But something just did not feel right about it all. What was she missing? Bible study was tonight—what was she going to tell her friends? What did God really want her to do?

RECAPITULATION

Carolyn's confusion came in part from an uncertainty about how to use the Psalms. It is easy to see that she and her friends were looking to Psalms as model prayers and to the psalmist as a role model of faith. In this way of thinking, the psalms can become formulas and the psalmists' experiences can be turned into promises. On the one hand, it is important for us to acknowledge that God can indeed heal and that he does answer prayer. But the "desires of your heart" mentioned in Psalm 37:4 do not refer to whatever desires anyone reading the psalm happens to have. The psalm is talking about a very specific desire, and that is identified just two verses later: "He will make your righteousness shine like the dawn, the justice of your cause like the noonday sun." God wants us to trust his wisdom rather than to trust that he will yield to our wisdom. There is nothing too hard for God, but we cannot dictate which hard thing he should do. For Carolyn, the hard thing God might decide to do is help her learn to cope with her condition and use it in her life to strengthen her spiritually and work in the lives of others.

Psalms is full of pleas that appear to be falling on deaf ears:

> O LORD, how many are my foes! . . . Arise, O LORD! Deliver me, O my God! (3:1, 7)

> Give me relief from my distress. (4:1)

> O LORD, heal me, for my bones are in agony. (6:2)

> Why, O LORD, do you stand far off? Why do you hide yourself in times of trouble? (10:1)

> How long, O LORD? Will you forget me forever? (13:1)

> My God, my God, why have you forsaken me? (22:1)

> Let me not be put to shame, O LORD. (31:17)

> Come quickly to help me, O Lord my Savior. (38:22)

> Why must I go about mourning, oppressed by the enemy? (42:9)

> Deliver me from evildoers and save me from bloodthirsty men. (59:2)

© edenpics.com

Yet the psalmist trusted God to respond and to intervene for the good. Numerous psalms testify to the fact that God did exactly that. One of the purposes of Psalms is to provide the basis for just that kind of trust.

Trust is a tricky thing. Think about the trust that children have that their parents will take care of them. Consider the trust that a patient has in a doctor. Trust does not imply an understanding of all of the actions that are being taken. Trust does not expect to receive enough information to give approval of every step. For example, young patients have trouble understanding the concept behind stitches being used to close wounds. The needle seems to inflict more pain—over and over again—and right at the spot that really hurts. The eyes of trust accept that this course of action is necessary to bring healing. The child might feel that the doctor is not listening to his screams. Indeed, the doctor pays no attention to the child's cries with each pass of the suturing needle, but that is not because she doesn't hear—it is because she knows what she is doing.

Even more seriously, consider the patient who is told that the only way infection can be stopped is for a limb to be amputated. The patient must not only trust the doctor's surgical skills, but he must

Spiritual Formation in the Church: Psalmist as Mentor

What used to be called "discipleship" is termed "spiritual formation" these days, which is probably a little more easily understood. A process of spiritual formation will put us on the path to spiritual maturity. The curriculum for this process includes the practice of spiritual disciplines (e.g., prayer and Bible reading) and being mentored or instructed by someone further along. Important elements are accountability and service, and an important result is character development. In what ways can the psalmist serve as a mentor in our spiritual formation?

To the extent that a mentor needs to respond to questions and hold people accountable, the psalmist would have a very limited role. On the other hand, when we think of a mentor as offering an example or guidelines to follow, the psalmist may contribute. We have contended that the Psalms are not in the Bible to tell us what to pray. Nevertheless, the psalmists can alert us to important aspects about prayer.

1. Think about prayer as a community activity—it will keep you aware that you are not alone but are part of the people of God across space and time.
2. Think about praying without concealing frustration and questions—it will keep you humbly aware that you are a work in process.
3. Think about praying concerning what you can do to uphold the reputation of God—it will keep you focused on him rather than on yourself.
4. Think about prayer as a hunger flowing out of a recognition of your need and God's worthiness—it will help to reinforce the fear of the Lord as the beginning of wisdom.
5. Think about prayer as an act of submission—it will keep you mindful of your need to be accountable.
6. Think about prayer as entering God's presence—it will motivate you to holiness.
7. Think about prayer as a quest—it will keep you on the track of seeking God.

trust her judgment as well. He must believe that such a drastic course of action is really the best solution.

Cries of pain and requests for relief are not antithetical to trust, nor do they communicate a lack of trust. Like the psalmist, at times we are led by our circumstances to cry out in distress. Like the psalmists, in our circumstances we must express the deepest outpourings of our trust that God will hear and act, rather than resort to into accusations. The most important focus of Psalms is not to show us a psalmist who trusts, but a God who is worthy of that trust.

DEVOTIONAL USE OF PSALMS

The book of Psalms uses the praise, complaint, and exhortation of God's people to reveal God's character. As readers to whom the authority of God's Word is important, we have the task of submitting to the God who is revealed. Praise psalms extol the attributes and actions of God and compel us to kneel before him. Wisdom psalms explore theological axioms for means to comprehend God's ways. Lament psalms help us to see God through the emotional struggles of a believer in crisis who is thrown to dependence on him.

> **Affirmation of God's attributes is the goal of our devotional reading.**

The historical books help us learn more about God by telling us his stories. In contrast, the Psalms give us a different perspective by helping us come into contact with God through our daily experiences

---

The Use of Psalms in Worship

In the synagogue tradition
- as hymnbook
- as liturgical readings
- as responses to readings of Torah and the Prophets
- as responses to prayers
- as a source for liturgical prayers

In the New Testament tradition
- singing in public worship (1 Cor. 14:26; Eph. 5:19; Col. 3:16)
- private worship (Matt. 26:30; Mark 14:26; James 5:13)

In church history
- singing whole psalms
- as a basis for new hymnody

- as a response to the reading of the Old Testament lesson
- as antiphonal or responsive readings, often in connection to introit, offering, or communion
- in the daily prayer cycle
- in connection with specific festivals or holy days
- in special services such as baptism, marriage, or funeral

All of these are legitimate and profitable uses of psalms that can be adapted to today's practice no matter what the liturgical traditions of any given church might be. We should feel free to use the Psalms creatively to enhance worship in whatever ways we can.*

*Adapted from A. Hill, *Enter His Courts with Praise* (Grand Rapids: Baker, 1997), 205–10.

and the questions that arise from them. When journalists want to find out about a person, they don't just read biographies, they also interview the people who know him or her best. When someone applies for a job, the employer doesn't stop with reading the applicant's resume, but also checks his or her references. These analogies show the difference in how the historical literature and the psalms reveal God to us. Unquestionably, the interviews or references are more likely to be subjective than a biography or resume. But the subjective aspect can be just as important a guide to knowing the individual. The revelation of God through Psalms is a more experiential approach to revelation—that is, God is revealing himself through the way the psalmist experienced him.

We encounter the hard questions in our experiences as we relate to God day by day. We often grapple with affirming God's attributes, not because we have philosophical reservations, but because our experience leads us to question his attributes—his goodness, his justice, or his love. The true affirmation of his attributes comes through acknowledging them even when our life experiences do not seem to support them. That is the long-term effect that Psalms should have on us, and it is why we read the Psalms. This process prepares us for or sustains us through trials and loss. It likewise keeps God in focus and everything in perspective when life goes smoothly.

Furthermore, the Psalms help us to submit in trust to the authority of God by using emotional mechanisms to lift us. Appeal to emotion may not be successful in bringing about long-term commitment,

Prayers of Becoming

While many of the psalms are suitable for use in our own prayers, others are not. As a book that focuses on the issues of prayer, the Psalms can be used to lead us to consider the content of our own prayers. Many of our prayers focus on health needs of loved ones, success in our plans, and benefits that will enrich our lives and bring us success. We must avoid an approach to prayer that focuses too narrowly on what we want to receive from the hands of God rather than what we want to become by the hand of God. The psalmists at times focus on prayers of becoming (e.g., Ps. 51:10-12). Consider adding prayers for the following to your list:

- personal purity in thoughts, motives, and actions
- personal integrity in relationships, responsibilities, and character
- balance in priorities, passions, and worldview
- desire to be an imitator of God, reflecting his attributes
- desire to be representative of godliness, showing his love and fruit of the Spirit
- willingness to testify to God's grace and to be a channel of his grace to others
- wisdom in making decisions and discerning God's will
- submission to one another, God's will, and God's Word
- openness to being changed, shaped, and guided by God
- ability to value other people above yourself and God's glory above your own
- self-discipline (studies, relationships, reactions, words)
- commitment to and effectiveness in service

but it does bring flashes of adoration and appreciation that can never be achieved through rational approaches. Theological lectures rarely move us to tears; but the same concepts put to powerful music can evoke a very emotional response. Our rational side is enriched by expositions of God's justice as illustrated by historical recitation, prophetic announcement, or theological analysis. Our emotional side, however, is often in control when the crises of life come along. That side of us, also created by God and reflecting his image, processes crises by the pouring out of the heart and the experiencing of the depths of pain, yet affirming God's attributes through it all.

We can be encouraged in our own struggles by the psalmist's struggles. By witnessing his distress or euphoria, we receive affirmation of our own emotional responses and encouragement to remain strong through the emotional time of stress. We can be led to be as concerned (or even more concerned) for the preservation of the integrity of the attributes of God than we are for our own well-being.

The Psalms are properly part of God's inspired Word in that they call us to humbly and submissively trust in the person and attributes of God whom they reveal. Submission does not always come through creedal assertion. More frequently it comes through trial, loss, and eventual acceptance. The Psalms lead us in that process. That does not mean that we are only to read them when life is going wrong. We need to read them when all is well so that we will be prepared for when life goes wrong. In doing so, we develop the mental and spiritual habit of trust.

When we sing worship songs together, we remind one another and ourselves of God's attributes. When we report to a person or group something that God has done in our lives, we are bearing witness to one another of God's attributes. In such situations, we do not respond with "I already knew that." We recognize the reminders as playing an important role. The Psalms fill that same role: We remind one another of God's attributes and bear witness to the role of those attributes in our lives. As we do so, we are encouraged to trust him more.

1. What guidelines for worship does the book of Psalms offer us?

2. To what end should we use the book of Psalms in our devotional reading of the Bible?

3. Does the book of Psalms encourage us to curse our enemies?

4. Does the book of Psalms offer any guidance on what we should pray?

5. Why is it that the Psalms give us such comfort?

6. What profile of the Messiah emerges from the Psalms?

7. Discuss the variety of ways in which Jesus can be seen as fulfilling the Psalms.

KEY REVIEW TERMS

- appeasement
- cantata
- declarative praise
- descriptive praise
- five-book structure
- imprecatory psalms
- parallelism
- pilgrimage psalms
- Psalm titles
- seam psalms
- Sheol
- vindication

GOING TO THE NEXT LEVEL

Robert Alter, *The Art of Biblical Poetry* (Basic).

Bernhard Anderson, *Out of the Depths* (Westminster John Knox).

C. Hassell Bullock, *Psalms* (Baker).

Andrew Hill, *Enter His Courts with Praise* (Baker).

C. S. Lewis, *Reflections on the Psalms* (Harcourt Brace).

Tremper Longman III, *How to Read the Psalms* (InterVarsity Press).

Patrick D. Miller, *They Cried to the Lord* (Fortress).

7 EPILOGUE

We have spent a lot of time and energy in the pages of this book trying to understand the Old Testament. We have discovered that this corpus of literature is important in its own right, as it represents a major portion of what we have come to believe is the Word of God that offers his revelation of himself to us. That notwithstanding, we must also recognize that the Old Testament is only the first part of the story—in a sense, the prelude to God's grand climax found in the pages of the New Testament.

PLOTLINE OF THE OLD TESTAMENT CONTINUED TO THE NEW TESTAMENT

The Old Testament ends with Israel caught in an uncertain middle ground. The Israelites had officially returned from exile in Babylon (though many did not return), yet the promised restoration seemed a distant dream. They had no king and no kingdom. They were part of a larger empire with no changes in sight. They had rebuilt the temple and refocused on the

law, but the spiritual platform of the prophets had not been realized. The future was fuzzy and full of question marks. The Persian Empire finally fell in the fourth century BC, but the Greeks simply took over where the Persians had left off. There was a time in the second century BC when Israel briefly regained independence and messianic hopes ran high, but the Hasmonean Dynasty soon deteriorated under political power struggles, and the previous Greek overlords were replaced by Roman ones. Four hundred years went by between the end of the Old Testament and the birth of Jesus.

In the meantime, a number of developments took place. Whether due to Persian or Greek influence, or for other reasons altogether, the concept of reward and punishment in the afterlife took firm hold in Judaism, though it remained controversial. Literature of this period also indicates the expansion of speculation regarding the angelic realm, and we find more discussion of Satan as well. Some of these theological developments received affirmation in the New Testament, so they have become part of the doctrinal profile of Christianity. The concept of the synagogue took shape as a place for teaching and preserving tradition. Significant Greek influence was observable in the Jewish worldview, especially in the diaspora (the Jewish community still spread around the classical world), but there was also a continuing commitment among the Jews to retain their distinctiveness in various ways. The law was at the center of this commitment, and various schools of interpretation of the law arose that came to be associated with sectarian groups such as the Pharisees and the Sadducees, which are familiar to readers of the New Testament. Judaism in this period took shape around three "pillars"—prayer, fasting, and almsgiving—that grew to be considered the most basic responsibilities of the observing Jew.

In all of this, the scene was gradually taking shape that would represent the "fullness of time" (see Gal. 4:4), at which the boldest step in God's plan would be revealed through the wondrous birth of a son to a simple peasant girl. In the birth, life, death, and resurrection of Jesus, the dislocation that came about as a result of the Eden Problem found its resolution, for we can find "relocation" by being "in Christ" (Eph. 2).

HOW DO THE OLD AND NEW TESTAMENTS RELATE?

To answer properly the question of how the Old and New Testaments relate, we must address issues of continuity and discontinuity.

Continuity

Jesus as Fulfillment

In the category of continuity, we recognize that both testaments deal with the same God carrying out his comprehensive plan. Jesus proclaimed the God of Abraham, Isaac, and Jacob and saw himself in the line of Moses, David, and the prophets. He did not offer a revised view of the Israelite God or forge his own path to God. Jesus' teaching was steeped in the tradition of the Old Testament law and covenant. Jesus declared that he did not come to abolish the law and the prophets but to fulfill them (Matt. 5:17). Jesus fulfilled the law and the prophets in a number of different ways. The most familiar way is that many prophecies found their fulfillment in him as he began to assume his earthly role as the Messiah—the anointed ideal Davidic king. A more comprehensive view of his fulfillment is related to the whole concept of the covenant as introduced in the Bridging Contexts section of unit 2 on the Pentateuch (see pp. 90-93). There we suggested that the covenant represented God's program of revelation. In such a view, we can see Christ as the climax of this revelatory program. If the Old Testament (= Old Covenant) is the story of the covenant and is God's revelation of himself, then the New Testament (= New Covenant) can be seen as God's ultimate revelation of himself through his Son (Heb. 1:1–2). Jesus thus fulfills the revelatory plan of God that was introduced by the law and the prophets. As God's ultimate revelation of himself, Jesus, we could say, represents where the law and the prophets were going all along.

View of God

Just as God's revelatory program is stretched across the testaments, so God's consistent, unchanging character is stretched across the testaments. We can give no credence to the popular perception that the God of the Old Testament was a God of vengeance and wrath while the God of the New Testament was a God of grace and love. God's grace and love are readily found throughout the pages of the Old Testament (Deut. 4:32–40; Hos. 11), and God's wrath and judgment play a prominent role in the New Testament (Luke 21; Acts 5:1–11; Heb. 10:26–31; Revelation). It is likewise unacceptable to think that there is a dichotomy in the two testaments represented by "law" in the Old Testament and "grace" in the New Testament. If we agree that the law was part of God's program of revealing himself, it is easy to see that the giving of the law was an act of grace. On the other hand, if we understand Christ as indwelling us as the seal of the new covenant, we accept that he represents the law in our hearts (Jer. 31:33), and his grace is the law that governs our behavior.

Law of Love

Two great commandments were central to Jesus' teaching: "Love the Lord your God with all your heart and with all your soul and with all your mind" and "Love your neighbor as yourself" (Matt. 22:37–39). Not surprisingly, these are also central to the Old Testament (Deut. 6:5; Lev. 19:18). This must then be viewed as establishing a solid line of continuity between the expectations God has of his people across the ages.

Social Justice/Ethics

One of the most common themes of the Bible from the law to the prophets and from the Gospels to the Epistles is the mandate to uphold justice. This is the obligation of God's people in both the Old and New Testaments. Since God is revealed throughout as a God who has compassion on the needy and cares for the widow and orphan, we are called upon to act on his behalf showing mercy in his name (Matt. 25:34–46).

Discontinuity

Despite these major points of continuity, we must also recognize some discontinuity, perhaps better understood as new initiatives that are introduced in the New Testament. Paul talks about several of these in Ephesians and calls them "mysteries" (Eph. 1:9; 3:3–9; 5:32; Col. 1:26–27; 2:2–3). Among the most significant of these initiatives are the work of Christ, the nature of Christ, the coming of the Holy Spirit, and the character of the church. We will discuss each one briefly.

The Work of Christ

As we have discussed in several places throughout this book, the Israelites had no revelation that offered individuals a hope of heaven. They were aware of sin but did not know they could be "saved" from it. The sacrificial system gave them a mechanism to address the sin problem, but they did not see that as offering hope for eternity, only for maintaining relationship with God day by day. There was little if any hint in the Old Testament that God had in mind a greater provision that would settle the matter of sin for eternity. With the eyes of hindsight, we might look back on passages such as the promise of the new covenant in Jeremiah 31:30–33 and make the connection, but the Israelites would not have been able to do so. When we look at a passage like Isaiah 53, we easily see the death of Christ that took the punishment for the sins of all. The Israelites could well have seen the suffering of Messiah because of their sins in that passage, but that is still a long way from the concept that they could be saved from the penalty of eternal condemnation and instead enjoy the presence of God forever. Isaiah 53 gives no hint of a perfect sacrifice that would solve the Eden Problem once and for all.

The Nature of Christ

The Israelites had little to suggest to them that their Messiah would be divine. We look at a passage such as Isaiah 9:6 and conclude that the messianic figure there is called by divine names ("Mighty

God"), but the Israelites would not have read the passage in that way at all. Names in the Old Testament often were statements about God. The name Isaiah means "Yahweh saves"—God's name is in Isaiah's name, but it does not therefore identify him as God. Likewise, the name[1] given in Isaiah 9:6 could easily be read as a statement about God (e.g., "the Mighty God is a wonderful counselor"). The Jews of Jesus' time were expecting a messiah, so it was no shock that he would be called that by his followers. What really upset the Jewish authorities was that he claimed to be one with God. This was not what they expected of the Messiah. It should be noticed that Jesus was not executed because he claimed to be Messiah, but because he claimed to be God (Matt. 26:62–66).

© Glen Allison/Getty Images

The Coming of the Holy Spirit

In John 14:15–27 and John 16:7–15, Jesus promises that the Holy Spirit will come as a counselor after he himself has left. Though the Holy Spirit exists eternally as the third person of the Trinity, in the New Testament, he takes on some new roles that are not found in the Old Testament. In the Old Testament, since the work of Christ had not yet been accomplished, there was no indwelling of the Spirit, nor was the Spirit regenerating those who had been cleansed by the death of Christ. In fact, the understanding of the spirit in the Old Testament was in itself more limited. The spirit of the Lord was understood by the Israelites not as a separate entity, but as an extension of Yahweh's power and authority. In this sense, it was understood as something like the "hand of the LORD" (2 Kings 3:15; Ezek. 1:3; 3:14, 22; et al.; cf. 1 Kings 18:46 KJV) that came upon individuals in special circumstances. In summary, the spirit of the Lord in the Old Testament empowers, but does not indwell; gives authority, but does not regenerate.[2] It is not unlikely that the Holy Spirit was behind at least some of the activity attributed to the spirit of God in the Old Testament, but the Israelites were not aware of any plurality within the Godhead. These initiatives come in the New Testament.

The Character of the Church

Paul gives most attention to the mystery of the Gentiles being included among the people of God. In the Old Testament there were certainly examples of God showing grace to Gentiles by bringing them in as part of his covenant people (Rahab, Ruth). Examples likewise occur in the prophetic literature where future inclusion is anticipated (Isa. 19:18–25). Nevertheless, the nature of the covenant in the Old Testament was by definition exclusive. By the covenant, Israel was elected from among the nations and distinguished from the nations. By contrast, and only through a difficult process, early Christians came to understand the work of Christ as opening the door to invite the Gentiles in on the same basis as the Jews (Acts 10; 11:1–18; 15:1–30; Eph. 2:11–22). The people of God are thereafter connected to a covenant that brings salvation rather than a covenant that has promoted God's revelation of himself through an ethnic group.

© edenpics.com

WERE ISRAELITES "SAVED"?

We have already indicated that Israelites did not think in terms of being saved from their sins or of going to heaven. But did people like Abraham, Moses, and David in fact go to heaven? How did it all work for them if Christ had not yet died, given John 14:6, "No one comes to the Father except through me"?

The concepts associated with salvation are represented in the Old Testament ritual system (see "Salvation Concepts,"), but no permanent, effective mechanism was provided, so Paul could appropriately weave together the concepts of law, sin, and death (Rom. 5:20–21). The law was not intended to be a means of salvation, but a means of revelation. By teaching what God is like, it also teaches the meaning of sin (Rom. 7:7–13). But if the law could not save, how could people in the Old Testament be saved?

The Bible does not take on the task of answering all of our questions about salvation—who was saved and on what basis; its intention is to reveal God. Nevertheless, if we think through the issues carefully, we can arrive at some sound conclusions. Let's begin by a more careful look at the nature of our faith, then we can use that as a basis to understand Israel.

We have a distorted view of our faith if we think of it primarily as a mechanism for a benefit, that is, if we think about having faith

Salvation Concepts

Propitiation: soothing aroma

Atonement: scapegoat

Justification: purging sanctuary

Reconciliation: forgiveness

Regeneration: internalization of the law

Sanctification: "Be holy, for I the LORD your God am holy."

in Christ to save us from sin, death, and hell and to bring us eternal life in heaven. The benefit should be viewed as a fringe benefit and is just a small part of the larger issue of who God is and who he has revealed himself to be. God, in Christ, has provided a mechanism for relationship with him, and we have faith that the mechanism will be sufficient. Our faith is reflected in our life response that seeks out all of the depth of that relationship. Our understanding of salvation cannot be limited to faith in a mechanism for our benefit isolated from faith in God. The mechanism must be understood as providing for relationship, not just benefit. Relationship is primary; salvation is secondary.

With this premise, we can now turn to the consideration of the Israelites' faith. As in our situation, most important was that their faith was in God and his revelation of himself. This faith was demonstrated by their obedience—benefits known or unknown, potential or realized, are secondary. Their faith, then, like ours, was reflected in a life response—they acted on their faith.[3] In the sacrificial system, God had revealed to them a mechanism for continuing relationship to be maintained. Even though their revelation included much less information about mechanisms for relationship, they were asked to have faith in God that the revelation they received was sufficient to provide for the desired relationship. Their mechanisms for relationship were temporary rather than permanent (law, sacrificial system) and were therefore incapable of achieving heaven—Christ is the only way. But if they responded in faith to the mechanisms that God provided for relationship, it is easy to assume that they would have met the criteria for the final and permanent mechanism, Christ's blood, to be applied to them when it became available.

Criterion: Faith in God and the mechanisms of relationship he provides.

INTERPRETING THE OLD TESTAMENT IN LIGHT OF THE NEW AND THE NEW IN LIGHT OF THE OLD

Old Testament in Light of the New Testament

There can be no question that the unfolding of God's plan in the New Testament shed a clarifying light on the Old Testament. But we must be careful to draw a distinction between understanding God's plan and understanding God. The Old Testament is insufficient to provide a comprehensive understanding of God's plan, for Jesus is at the center of that plan. If we are going to the Old Testament to understand its role and contribution to the plan of God, we must be careful to link it to the New Testament development of themes and investigate the fruition of the Old Testament initiatives in the New Testament.

Having said that, we must not conclude that the Old Testament is deficient in the revelation of God that it offers. Christians often make the mistake of discarding the Old Testament simply because the New Testament provides the exciting conclusion. Since we believe that the Old Testament is, in and of itself, God's authoritative revelation of himself, it cannot become obsolete. We cannot afford to ignore or neglect what the Old Testament teaches us about God. As interpreters we then have an obligation to preserve the authority of the Old Testament text. It offered an authoritative revelation of God to Israel without the New Testament, and it continues to offer the same to us today. It would therefore be a mistake to evaluate each Old Testament passage only in light of Jesus. A proper understanding of the text requires us to understand the text as the Israelites would have understood it—in terms of their language, worldview, and theology. That will result in an understanding of God's communication about himself through the Israelite author. Then, as we proceed to understand the contribution of any given passage to our current theology and to the unfolding of God's plan, we can track it into the New Testament and seek the larger perspective that is necessary.

New Testament in Light of the Old Testament

The New Testament writers preach from the Old Testament, quote the Old Testament, allude to the Old Testament, and explain the Old Testament. About one-third of the New Testament is composed of quotations from or allusions to the Old Testament.[4] The themes of the Old Testament serve as a backdrop as well as a foundation to the teaching of Jesus and the apostles. Consequently, we cannot expect to understand the New Testament without some understanding of the Old Testament. A few examples should suffice.

1. Jesus' parable of the Good Samaritan requires the reader to have some understanding of the Old Testament ritual system of purity in which one becomes unclean when coming into contact with a corpse. It also depends on knowledge of where the priest and Levite were going and how that affected their actions. Finally, it

is based on the expectation that the reader will understand the status of Samaritans in the Jewish culture of the day. The history of this extends back to the exile and the postexilic period.

2. Peter's vision in Acts 10 expects that the reader understands the laws about eating certain foods in the Old Testament.

3. The concerns and decisions of the Jerusalem Council in Acts 15 are founded on the Old Testament law and on what is important about it.

4. The book of Hebrews addresses a Jewish audience and assumes that the audience is steeped in the traditions of the Old Testament, such as the exodus, the tabernacle, and the sacrifices.

5. The imagery of Revelation draws widely on prophetic books such as Daniel (e.g., son of man, Dan. 7:13; Rev. 1:13), Ezekiel (e.g., living creatures, Ezek. 1:10–11; Rev. 4:6–8), and Zechariah (e.g., four horses, Zech. 6:1–6; Rev. 6:2–8). Many of the images find their significance in the context of the Old Testament world.

These examples give only a brief glimpse of the degree to which the New Testament is dependent on the Old Testament but are sufficient for the point that we must interpret the New Testament in the light of its Old Testament background.

Interpretation

Interpretation is accomplished by filling gaps. It has been said that "a text is a web of holes joined together by snippets of writing."[5] The question then concerns how we will seek to fill the gaps. Some interpreters believe that the reader cannot help but fill the gaps from his or her own imagination, worldview, culture, and needs. Others believe that they need to look to the text to fill those gaps. In Old Testament interpretation, some would define the "text" as the book being studied; others as the entire Old Testament; and others as the entire Bible. This is where the decision about the relationship between the Old Testament and the New Testament becomes most vital. A third approach seeks the key to filling the gaps in an understanding of the author. Such interpreters seek to understand his mind-set, intentions, or worldview. Though he cannot be cross-examined or psychoanalyzed, it is plausible that he has communicated effectively enough that his words and meaning can be understood.

> **Three approaches to filling the gaps**
>
> - from the reader
> - from the text
> - from the author

7 EPILOGUE

We believe that all three must be blended and must regulate one another. We would suggest that the author has first priority, the text second, and the reader third. So we should not rush to fill in gaps with theology when the author's words are premised on a cultural understanding. Likewise, we should not be too quick to consider "what it means to me" without considering what it meant to the author and what it was understood to mean throughout the history of interpretation. Interpretation should not be privatized or individualized. The text is the tool of the author as he is guided by inspiration, and we must adopt a submissive attitude toward it rather than an exploitative or imperialistic one.

WHAT HAVE WE LEARNED?

In this book we have attempted to approach the Old Testament at four different levels (see diagram below).

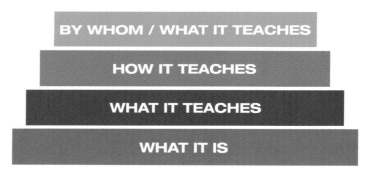

What the Old Testament Is

At the foundational level, we have tried to proceed on an understanding of the nature of the text. We have considered it as inspired by God and therefore as authoritative for our lives. Most of all, it offers the authoritative revelation of God. When someone today publishes a biography of an important person, the book is usually presented as either an authorized or unauthorized biography. The difference is whether or not the subject of the biography was consulted and cooperated with and whether he or she approved of the book's representation of him or her. The Old Testament is not only the authorized biography of God (so to speak); it has the status of an autobiography, though we might say using ghost writers. So autobiographies today might indicate that they were written in collaboration with another author. Everything else we have discussed is based on this idea of what the Old Testament is.

What the Old Testament Teaches

Once we identified the nature of the text, we proceeded to seek an understanding of the focus of the text. We have attempted to identify that which the text primarily wanted to teach. Understanding the Old Testament as God's revelation of himself, it was not difficult to conclude that the primary focus of the text was to teach us about the nature of God. In addition, we have found the text to explore the implications of the nature of God for us and for our world. This involves information concerning creation and the fall, sin and God's attempts to restore relationship. Finally, we have found that the text provides for an understanding of the results of the nature of God—primarily concerning how his nature is reflected in the unfolding of his plan for his creation.

How the Old Testament Teaches

Third, we have tried to introduce students to the methods of the text. With an understanding of the ways in which the Old Testament teaches, we can be equipped with important guides as to how we should study it. We should also be able to adjust our expectations of the text and therefore spare ourselves from unfruitful study. We have learned that the text will pursue its own purposes and that it cannot be expected to answer all of our questions. We have learned that we cannot conscript the text to our own purposes nor commandeer it for lateral service as, for instance, a science text.

By Whom/What the Old Testament Teaches

Last, and least, we have introduced students to some of the details of the text (names, places, dates, etc.). It is regrettable that so many introductions to the Old Testament and so many courses on the Old Testament focus on this level with the result that students easily become overwhelmed. It is true that we need to gain familiarity with the story line of the Old Testament, but the story line is only a means to an end. To go back to an analogy that we used early in the book, the details are but the threads to the grand tapestry of God's self-revelation. Hopefully we can grow more and more familiar with the story line as we study the Bible, but we should never make the mistake of thinking that knowing the trivia is the same as mastery of the text.

OVERALL THEME

If we had to identify the most pervasive theme in the Old Testament, it would probably be "The Presence of God." The Garden of Eden was defined by God's presence. When sin brought expulsion from the garden, the greatest loss was the loss of the privilege of being in God's presence. God's presence was again made possible through the covenant and realized in the tabernacle and temple. Through God's abiding presence, the Israelites experienced God, related to him, and learned of his nature and attributes. The program of revelation was intended to make him known and thereby make a relationship possible. This was done by Christ, who, as Immanuel ("God with Us"), represented God's presence in our midst, and who has also made it possible for us to enter into God's presence once and for all. Those cast into outer darkness will lose the great privilege of experiencing God's presence. In the meantime, we experience the presence of God through the indwelling Christ and through the Comforter, the Holy Spirit. The Old Testament and New Testament offer the revelation of God so that we can be in relationship with God and enjoy his presence forever.

WHAT TO DO WITH IT

If we truly believe that this is what the Old Testament (the Bible for that matter) is all about, we cannot afford to respond to it casually. If we recognize the authority of the text, we must respond to it by submitting to its authority. Submitting to the authority of the Bible means embracing the picture of God that the Bible offers and building our lives around it. How do we do that? Three things should define our life response as we accept the lordship of the God of the Bible. We must live in obedience, live as channels of grace, and live as people of faith, hope, and love.

Live in Obedience

If we were to try to make a list of all the rules in the Bible that should be obeyed, it would be a daunting and intimidating list. Yet even as we looked at it, we would realize that there were responsibilities that we have as Christians that were not reflected on the list. From the very start we have recognized that the Bible is not a book of rules. We must conclude then that obedience to the Bible consists of more than following rules that we might find therein. Principles must also be obeyed. We are to love God (Deut. 6:5) and our neighbor (Lev. 19:18)—whatever it takes. We are to be holy as God is holy (Lev. 19:2)— that is pretty open-ended. We are also encouraged to pursue wisdom (Prov. 23:19; James 1:5). Paul observes that wisdom goes beyond obedience: "Everyone has heard about your obedience, so I am full of joy over you; but I want you to be wise about what is good, and innocent about what is evil" (Rom. 16:19). God has created us in his image, the Bible has revealed God to us, and obedience calls for us to be imitators of God.

Live as Channels of Grace

The call to be agents of grace was discussed in some length in unit 4, Prophetic Literature (see "Indictment Today," pp. 267–68). Why do Christians find it so difficult to be gracious people? For some people, obedience comes much easier than grace. Our desire for justice can easily develop into a judgmental attitude. In the Beatitudes after Jesus urges his followers to "hunger and thirst after righteousness/justice," his next statements offer ideals to make sure that hunger is balanced: As we hunger after justice, we are to be merciful, pure in heart, and peacemakers (see Matt. 5:1–12). All of this is to ensure that even as we seek justice and pursue righteousness for ourselves and our world, we not lose sight of grace.

How do we arrive at that hungering and thirsting after righteousness/justice? The first three beatitudes lead us to the path. Being poor in spirit is a reflection of our regrets for the world's situation. Consequently, we mourn over it, but we also, in meekness, recognize that we cannot fix it by our own power. As a result, we must resist partaking in the world's corruption, and must not pursue power as the means to finding a solution. It is only when we abandon corruption and power that we are in a position to long for justice. The Beatitudes then guide us in how to be people of grace as we hunger for righteousness/justice, and the result is that we will be salt and light to the world around us (Matt. 5:13–16).

Live as People of Faith, Hope, and Love

Faith, hope, and love are the three great qualities that Paul sets before us in 1 Corinthians 13:13. But these simply offer a summary of Old Testament exhortation. The narratives and many of the prophetic oracles call the Israelites to respond to God in faith. This call often finds its foundation in the covenant, and so we are not surprised to find Abraham commended for his faith at the inauguration of the covenant (Gen. 15:6). Hope flows out of the prophetic literature and itself is founded in faith and the covenant. That is, the hope offered to the Israelites is the hope that as they respond in faith, the covenant promises will find their fulfillment. Love is linked to the law. It explores how one loves God and one's neighbor. This aspect is therefore also linked to the covenant, since the law is at the core of the covenant. As a result, we would conclude that in the Old Testament, being people of faith, hope, and love meant being people of the covenant.

The new covenant is likewise the basis for our New Testament faith, hope, and love. Christ is the foundation of the new covenant, and our faith is in him, our hope is through him, and his love is to shine through us. In the covenant, God has revealed himself to us. In the new covenant, he has revealed himself to us through Christ. The expected response of God's covenant people has always been the same: Faith in the God of the covenant, hope in the promises of the covenant, love as the God of the covenant loved us. What we truly believe about God cannot help but change our lives. If we do not want to change, we do not truly believe.

YOU WILL KNOW THAT I AM YAHWEH

In the Pentateuch unit we suggested that the purpose of Scripture was not the revelation of what society's laws should be, but a revelation of what God's holiness looks like. In the historical literature unit, we suggested that the narratives were not primarily intended to be a revelation of historical events, but a revelation of the God who

> "This is what the Sovereign LORD says: Once again I will yield to the plea of the house of Israel and do this for them: I will make their people as numerous as sheep, as numerous as the flocks for offerings at Jerusalem during her appointed feasts. So will the ruined cities be filled with flocks of people. Then they will know that I am the LORD." (Ezek. 36:37–38)

directs history. In the prophetic literature unit, we suggested that the primary intention of the literature was to reveal God, not to reveal the future. In the Psalms unit, we tried to demonstrate that the literature did not intend to reveal model prayers, but to reveal God. The biblical authors do not intend to reveal the details of science or the mysteries of Messiah—they intend to reveal God. Though the Bible contains rules, promises, rituals, and stories, it is important that we see these as means rather than ends. We hope that the point is coming through loud and clear. The result of coming to the Bible should be to leave with knowledge of God and a transformed life and worldview that such knowledge makes possible. Consequently, we will be holy people who live in obedience, who serve as channels of grace, who display an attitude of faith, who hunger and thirst after righteousness and justice, who worship God wholeheartedly, and above all, who love God, one another, and our neighbors as ourselves.

USDA photo

GOING TO THE NEXT LEVEL

David L. Baker, *Two Testaments, One Bible* (InterVarsity Press).

David Dockery, Kenneth Mathews, and Robert Sloan, eds., *Foundations in Biblical Interpretation* (Broadman and Holman).

William Dumbrell, *The Faith of Israel* (Baker).

William Dyrness, *Themes in Old Testament Theology* (InterVarsity Press).

Paul House, *Old Testament Theology* (InterVarsity Press).

Tremper Longman III, *Making Sense of the Old Testament* (Baker).

Brent Sandy and Ronald Giese, *Cracking Old Testament Codes* (Broadman and Holman).

Paul Wegner, *Journey from Texts to Translations* (Baker).

Notes

1. Notice that it is called a name (singular), not names (plural).
2. See discussion in the sidebar "Spirit of the Lord" on p. 203.
3. This is the faith discussed in Hebrews 11, where faith is not presented as leading to salvation, but is seen as faith that results in action or life response.
4. For details see Andrew Hill, *Baker's Handbook of Bible Lists* (Grand Rapids: Baker, 1981), 102–4.
5. John Barton, *Reading the Old Testament* (Louisville: Westminster John Knox, 1996), 218.

APPENDIX

READING THROUGH
THE OLD TESTAMENT

150 OF THE MOST SIGNIFICANT CHAPTERS

Genesis 1–3

Genesis 6–9

Genesis 11

Genesis 12

Genesis 15

Genesis 22

Genesis 27–28

Genesis 32

Genesis 37

Genesis 45

Exodus 1–3

Exodus 7

Exodus 14

Exodus 19–20

Exodus 32

Exodus 40

Leviticus 16

Leviticus 19

Numbers 13–14

Deuteronomy 2–4

Deuteronomy 6

Deuteronomy 10–13

Joshua 1

Joshua 6

Joshua 10

Joshua 23–24

Judges 2

Judges 4

Ruth 1–4

1 Samuel 1

1 Samuel 4–6

1 Samuel 8

1 Samuel 15–17

1 Samuel 24

2 Samuel 5–7

2 Samuel 12

1 Kings 2–3

1 Kings 11

1 Kings 18

2 Kings 6–7

2 Kings 10

2 Kings 17

2 Kings 25

1 Chronicles 28

2 Chronicles 6–7

2 Chronicles 26

2 Chronicles 29–30

2 Chronicles 32–35

Ezra 6

Nehemiah 6

Nehemiah 8–9

Esther 4

Esther 8
Job 1–2
Job 27
Job 28
Job 42
Psalm 1
Psalm 2
Psalm 51
Psalm 89
Psalm 90
Psalm 103
Psalm 106
Psalm 145
Proverbs 1
Proverbs 3
Proverbs 8
Proverbs 15
Ecclesiastes 1–3
Isaiah 1
Isaiah 6
Isaiah 7
Isaiah 9
Isaiah 11
Isaiah 40
Isaiah 42
Isaiah 53
Isaiah 55

Isaiah 58
Isaiah 61
Isaiah 65
Jeremiah 1
Jeremiah 7
Jeremiah 23
Jeremiah 31
Lamentations 3
Ezekiel 1
Ezekiel 8
Ezekiel 18
Ezekiel 36
Daniel 2
Daniel 3
Daniel 6
Hosea 1–3
Hosea 10
Joel 2
Amos 5
Jonah 1–4
Micah 4–5
Habakkuk 1–3
Zephaniah 3
Haggai 1
Zechariah 8
Zechariah 14
Malachi 3

GLOSSARY

Acrostic. A literary feature of poetic compositions in which sets of sequential letters (e.g., initial or final letters of the lines) form a word or phrase or an alphabet.

Anthropomorphism. Describing a deity by terms and concepts that relate to human beings.

Anthology. A collection of selected writings based on keywords or themes.

Apocrypha. A collection of intertestmental Jewish literature, recognized as part of the canon in some Christian traditions (e.g., Catholic).

Apostasy. The renunciation or abandonment of religious belief, whether personal or corporate.

Atonement. To "pay" for sin by means of sacrifice and offering, as a symbol of repentance and confession before God.

Canon. As applied to the Bible, a collection of religious books measured against the standard of divine inspiration.

Chiasm(us). A literary device in which words or phrases parallel one another in reverse order (e.g., a-b-c-c-b-a).

Cosmology. A story about the origin of the world.

Covenant. A contract or treaty that establishes a relationship between two parties.

Cuneiform. A wedge-shaped writing system that developed in the Sumerian culture of Mesopotamia early in the third millennium BC.

Deuteronomistic school. (Hypothetical) Hebrew scribal guild of the seventh century BC responsible for shaping the historical literature of the Old Testament from Deuteronomy to Kings.

Eschatology. The branch of theology concerned with end-time events (i.e., the doctrine of the last things).

Exegesis. The careful and methodical study of a text undertaken in order to understand its meaning.

Exile. The forced removal of Israelites from their land, which resulted from the Babylonian deportations of 597, 587 BC and later. In 538 BC Babylonian Jews were allowed to return home.

Genre. The classification of literature based upon the style or type of writing (e.g., law, poetry, history, prophecy).

Genealogy. The record or account of the ancestry and descent of a person, family, or group.

Ban (Heb. *herem*). A divine law prohibiting Israel from taking plunder from conquered cities.

Hermeneutics. The application of rules and procedures for determining the meaning of written texts, broadly defined as the "art of interpretation."

Historiography. The writing of history or the product of historical writing; a collection of historical literature.

Holiness. The separation from the "mundane" and ordinary for service or worship to God, who himself is wholly separate from his creation.

Inclusio. A special form of the repetition common to Hebrew poetry sometimes called an envelope figure, since by repeating key words and phrases the poet returns to the point from which he began.

Messiah (Heb. "anointed one"). Generally one set apart for a divinely appointed office such as a priest or a king. Specifically, the title identifies a figure prominent in Old Testament prophetic writings who serves as Israel's deliverer-king (realized in Jesus of Nazareth according to the New Testament writers).

Monotheism. The belief in the existence of one God.

Mythology. Stories that explain how the world came into being and how it works.

Omens. Signs that are used to determine what the gods are doing, or what pleases or displeases them, based on a conventional understanding of a linkage between the gods and various phenomena.

Ordeal. A procedure or ritual appealing to the knowledge of God (or the gods) employed to determine the guilt or innocence of a party for a crime committed in secret or a legal case lacking sufficient evidence.

Pantheon. A divine assembly of gods and goddesses formally recognized by a society as participants in the experiences of community life.

Pentateuch. A Greek word meaning "five scrolls, applied to the first five books of the Bible.

Plotline. Identifies and traces the theological message of the Old Testament.

Polytheism. The belief in multiple gods who work together and share jurisdiction in the cosmos.

Retribution principle. A basic theological teaching of the Old Testament that states rewards and punishments are dispensed in accordance with one's obedience or disobedience to God's laws (i.e., "you reap what you sow" principle).

Sacred space. An area made sacred by the special presence of a deity. Generally, it is treated as holy and, therefore, access to it is denied or limited, and it needs to be safeguarded both to retain its holiness and to protect people from harm.

Sheol. The abode of the dead in the Old Testament, either as the grave or some realm in the depths of the earth containing the spirits of the dead.

Story line. A factual summary of the content of the Old Testament informing the reader of what happened.

Suzerain. A superior feudal ruler; an overlord (in a covenant).

Synchronism. A method of establishing a chronology for a person or an event by comparison to other known persons or events where fixed dates have already been determined.

Syncretism. The combining of different forms of religious belief or practice.

Theocracy. A state or a nation ruled directly by God.

Theodicy. The philosophical and/or theological defense of God's goodness and omnipotence in view of the existence of evil.

Theophany. An audible or visible manifestation of god.

Torah. The revelation of God as contained in the first five books of the Bible. The basic idea of the Torah is "instruction in holiness" after the pattern of God's holiness.

Vassal. A subordinate nation or group (usually as a result of a treaty following conquest).

Ziggurat. An architectural representation of the stairway between heaven and earth for the gods.

INDEX

Aaron, 39, 80–81, 222
abortion, 118–21
Abraham, 3–4, 29, 31, 45, 67–68, 71, 92–95, 115–16, 201, 203, 222, 232, 291, 369, 396; and the stars, 90; covenant of, 90–93; in real life, 31
Abram. *See* Abraham
Adam, 3, 28, 71, 218, 404
adoption, 48, 306
afterlife, 293, 366–69
aftermath, 239–240, 251, 266, 276, 283
Ahab, 145–46, 162–63, 187, 233
Ahaz, 149–50, 164, 234, 244
Ahmose, 51
Ahuramazda, 242
Ai, 137
Akhenaten, 46, 49, 156, 157
Akkadian, 11, 19, 160, 295
Alexander the Great, 5, 172
aliens, 269
Amarna, 46, 48, 49, 155, 156; period, 159
Amenemhet I, 50
Amorites, 45, 26, 136
Amos, 147, 230, 234, 237, 238, 246, 258, 259, 262, 272
ANE stories, 84
angels, 15, 210
Antiochus Epiphanes, 281, 282
apocalyptic, 240, 242
Apocrypha, 247
appeasement theology, 308, 309–10, 364–65

Aramaeans, 135, 144, 145, 162, 163, 233
archaeology, 198
archives, 48, 64, 155, 160, 241
ark, Noah's, 28, 67, 74
ark of the covenant, 75, 99, 127, 183, 184, 207–8, 255
Artaxerxes, 47, 172
armies led by God, 205
Ashurbanipal, 47, 49, 64, 150, 166, 167, 174, 235
Ashurnasirpal, 162
Assyria, 5, 47, 150, 151–52, 159, 162–68, 169, 188, 230, 234–36, 238, 254
Assyrian: Balawat Gates, 365; inscription, 168; deportation, 188; prophecy text, 241; treaty text, 150
Athaliah, 145, 146, 149
Atrahasis, 59
authority, 8, 118, 202–3, 226, 253, 275, 361, 377–78, 390, 394
authors, 70; of the Bible, 290
authorship, 62, 70, 197, 243, 253, 290, 291
Azariah (Uzziah), 149, 164

Baal, 33, 145–46, 160, 182, 187, 225, 235
Baal Cycle, 49, 160
Babel, 3, 29, 71, 72; problem, 3, 71, 91–92
Babylon, 5, 45–47, 135, 152, 153, 165–66, 167, 165–69, 170, 188,

235–37, 250, 252–55; fall of, 163, 172, 238

Babylonian: captivity, 5, 153–54, 188, 208, 235; Chronicles, 170; Counsels of Wisdom, 105; creation epic, 49; Dialogue of Pessimism, 104; flood story (*see* Atrahasis); map of the world, 15; siege 5, 153, 245; temple complex, 232; theodicy, 295

Baruch, 290; seal impression, 290

bathing, 204

battle of: Carchemish, 5, 47, 168, 169; Qarqar, 46, 162, 163

Belshazzar, 169, 237, 169

Ben-Hadad III. *See* Hadadezer

Beni Hassan, 31

Bethel, 137, 144

Bethlehem, 92, 280

Bible, 198

biblical: affirmations, 220; law, 120; quotes, 164; theology, 98

blessing, 28–29, 57, 64, 65, 67, 71, 72, 78, 90–93, 95, 182, 185, 195, 207, 222, 242, 251, 292, 372

Book of the Dead (Egyptian), 293

Book of the Twelve, 244, 248. *See also* minor prophets

brick makers, 38

burning bush, 7, 73

calf figurine, 74, 144

campaign tablet (Babylonian), 153

Canaan, 4, 31, 37, 44, 45, 47, 68, 139, 157–60

Canaanite religion, 74, 181, 182, 190, 235

Canaanites, 49, 136, 156, 180

cantata, 352–56

Carchemish. *See* battle of Carchemish

Chaldeans, 45, 166

chaos, 28, 55–56, 67, 72, 80, 86, 102, 182, 238, 316, 318–20

chariot, 52

cherubim (cherubs), 99, 184, 210, 311, 358

chronicles, 174

chronological: reckoning, 163; systems, 147

City of David, 192

classical prophecy, 232, 234, 237, 240

clean, 78, 125

confession, 310

conquest, 4, 132, 136–41, 181–82

cosmology, 57

cosmos, 28, 54, 55, 56–57, 61, 67, 74, 80, 86–87, 90, 102–3, 122, 123, 182, 186, 223, 290, 291, 312, 319; as temple, 86, 87, 90, 102, 186; three-tiered, 56, 86

covenant, 4, 67–68, 71–72, 80–81, 90–97, 106, 117–18, 138, 152, 175, 181, 185, 186, 188–190, 206, 208, 224, 242, 243, 245, 248, 251, 257, 262, 267, 279, 292, 344, 352, 384–88, 394, 396; benefits, 92; kingship, 194, 206, 361; renewal, 5, 48, 54, 64, 81, 152, 185, 190, 195

covenant/revelation blessing, 92

covenant-treaty format, 64

Creation, 4, 28, 55, 57–59, 67, 72, 74, 86, 123, 211, 290, 315–16, 318–20, 344, 362, 393; stories. *See* Enuma Elish and Atrahasis

creationism, 108

Creator, 55, 57, 73, 86, 270

curse, 373

Cyaxares the Mede, 167

Cyrus, 5, 47, 154, 169–71, 172, 204, 208, 281; Cylinder, 154, 170, 199; tomb of, 171

dagger, 358

Daniel, 5, 154, 202, 225, 230, 237, 241, 244, 246, 264, 278, 281, 369

Darius the Mede, 47, 171–72

David, 4–5, 11, 21, 86, 140–42, 160–61, 185, 186, 189, 191–93, 203, 204–6, 244, 279, 353

David (by Michelangelo), 201

Davidic: covenant, 186, 191, 206, 224, 352, 356, 358–60, 384; king, 5, 189, 206, 209, 238, 244–45, 248, 280, 358, 359, 360, 384

Day of Atonement, 76, 79, 101. *See also* Yom Kippur

day of the Lord, 238, 246, 248, 278

Dead Sea Scrolls, 22, 245
demon, 63, 201, 210, 225, 294
destruction, 180
Deuteronomy, 24, 40, 54, 64, 70, 81–82, 121, 132, 219, 290
devotions, 31, 126
discipline, 259, 261, 262, 275, 304, 333
divided kingdom/monarchy, 4, 248, 342, 360
divination, 63, 240, 241, 262
divine figure, 29
dreams, 240

Early Dynastic Period, 41, 50
Ebla, 48
Ecclesiastes, 289, 298, 312–14. *See also* Qoheleth
Eden, 3, 394; problem, 3, 28, 29, 71, 88, 91–92, 97, 98, 123–24, 186, 384, 386
editing, 22, 51, 54, 244, 290, 299, 353, 354–55, 361
editorials, 200
Egypt, 4, 5, 19, 24, 27, 35–38, 47, 50–51, 68, 73, 144, 152, 155–57, 159, 167–68, 169, 197, 258, 277, 350
Egyptian: confession, 310; cosmos, 55; sun god, 55; Tale of Sinuhe, 50
El, 235
Elamites, 45, 48, 166
Elihu, 294, 307–10
Elijah, 145, 187, 188, 230, 233, 255, 369
Elisha, 145, 187, 188, 194, 230, 233
Emar, 48
En Gedi waterfall, 343
Enlightenment, 56, 89, 174–76
Enuma Elish, 55, 238
Esarhaddon, 47, 64, 150, 166
Esau, 31, 34
eschatology, 72, 257, 265
Esther, 132, 195–96, 197, 203, 223
Euphrates, 42, 141, 147, 161
Eve, 3, 71, 89, 218
evolution, 108–13, 108, 113
exegesis, 17–19

exile, 4, 5, 132, 135, 153, 154, 168, 184, 189, 194, 208–10, 234, 237, 242, 243, 244–45, 248, 254, 277, 342, 382
exodus, 4, 24, 52, 73–74, 232; date of, 52
Ezekiel, 5, 154, 208, 230, 236, 237, 244, 245–46, 256; temple, 256–57, 258
Ezra, 5, 132, 155, 195, 208, 242

face value, 13–16, 24, 89
fall, 80, 88–90, 114, 220, 393; of Babylon, 47, 169, 172, 238; of Jerusalem 47, 151–53, 189, 246
families in the ancient world, 32
famine, 35, 72, 220, 325
fasting, 273
First Intermediate Period, 27, 50
fleece, 216–17
flood, 3, 4, 59, 67, 71, 89
fulfillment, 8, 203s, 240, 247, 252–54, 257, 265–66, 276–83, 284–85, 359

Garden of Eden, 29
genealogies, 14, 28, 57–59, 71, 81, 195
Genesis, 24, 28–29, 41, 54, 55, 57, 58, 60, 67, 71–72, 108s; and history, 89; and mythology, 58; and science, 108
genre, 3, 7, 13, 14–15, 83, 89, 225, 226, 243, 266, 293, 295, 296, 297, 346, 350, 352, 353
Gezer calendar, 79
Gibeon, 137–38, 344
Gilgamesh, 49, 58, 59, 60, 298
gods, household, 91
government, 117, 268–69, 291, 313
guides, 83, 85

Habakkuk, 230, 235, 237, 246,
Hadadezer (Ben-Hadad II), 162
Haggai, 154, 208, 230, 237, 246, 250, 259, 274, 279
Haman, 195–96
Hammurabi, 46, 48, 60, 61, 62, 199; prologue, 62
happy, 328

Haran, 42, 45, 168, 169
harp, bull-headed, 45, 354
Hasmonean Dynasty, 383
Hattushili III, 159
Hazael, 46, 162
Hazor, 47, 138, 161
healing, 222, 374–76
heaven, 282, 366–70, 367, 386, 388–89
hermeneutics, 13, 17, 19
Hezekiah, 149, 151–52, 165–66, 168, 188, 234, 244
hieroglyphic, 19, 22
High Place at Dan, 145
historiography, 173–76, 178–79, 186, 196, 200, 224, 226
history, 3, 11–14, 72, 89, 175, 177, 194, 196–97, 200, 209–11, 213–15, 220, 224–26, 259; God's control over, 220; ideas about, 175. *See also* historiography
Hittite: god, 180; instructions, 63, 65; treaties, 65
Hittites, 48, 135, 158–59, 197
holiness, 54, 62, 69, 75, 88, 97, 102, 123–24, 125, 209, 257, 396
Holy Spirit, 98, 123, 203, 266, 330, 386, 387, 394
Horeb, 33
Hosea, 147, 230, 234, 237, 246, 260, 277
Hoshea, 148, 150, 165
house, 32
Hurrians, 159
Hyksos, 27, 51
hymns, 351

Ibbi-Sin, 45
idols, 122, 191, 235, 275
image, 276
imagery, 123, 256, 260, 263, 279, 345, 391
indictment, 235, 238, 239, 251, 267–74, 395
inscriptions: and prophecies, 170; royal, 174
inspiration, 240, 306, 314, 361, 392
instruction, 251, 275–76, 298, 349, 363
intelligent design, 112

Iron Age I, 157, 159–60
Isaac, 31
Isaiah, 151, 164, 186, 188, 230, 233, 234, 237, 244–45, 254, 258, 274
Ishtar Gate in Babylon, 234
Israel (Northern Kingdom), 142–47, 148, 150, 162–65, 188, 234, 238, 248
Israel, 4, 29, 33, 36, 73, 75, 91, 93, 95, 141, 171, 180–81, 185, 189, 195, 206, 209, 245, 254, 259, 260, 344, 360–61, 369, 382; education in Israel, 303; and failure, 221; and kings, 185

Jacob, 29, 31–34, 36, 72
Jehoram, 145–46, 149, 186
Jehoshaphat, 144–45, 149, 186
Jehu, 144–46, 147, 162, 163, 168, 186
Jeremiah, 5, 208, 230, 235–36, 237, 243–45, 255–56, 274, 277
Jericho, 137, 138, 199, 206
Jeroboam, 4, 142, 144, 148, 162, 186
Jeroboam II, 146–47, 148, 149, 164, 186
Jerusalem, 4–5, 47, 137, 138, 141, 144, 149, 150, 151, 153–55, 160, 165, 169, 172, 186, 188, 192, 195, 202, 208, 245–46, 254, 255–56, 282, 362, 364
Jezebel, 145–46, 187, 200, 233; seal of, 146
Jezreel, 42, 152
Job, 18, 116, 289, 292–97, 301, 306–12, 317, 323, 367
Joel, 203, 230, 237, 246
Jonah, 186, 230, 234, 237, 246, 248–49, 251
Jonathan, 141, 193
Joppa, 249
Joseph, 34–36, 51, 86, 324
Joshua, 4, 81, 132, 136, 137–38, 189–90, 206
Joshua the high priest, 154
Josiah, 149, 152, 167–68, 186, 188, 200, 235
Judah (Southern Kingdom), 4–5, 142, 144–46, 149–52, 161,

163–68, 188, 194, 208, 234–36, 245, 248–50, 255, 259
Judean Wilderness, 142
judges, 4, 132, 135, 139–40, 158, 160, 183, 186, 190–91, 194, 203–4, 207; cycle of the, 191; functions of the, 139; results of the, 183
judgment, 181–82, 190, 194, 218, 222, 234, 238–39, 243, 248–50, 259, 263, 274–75, 293, 316, 361, 366, 385; oracle, 238–39, 250, 274–75; scene, 293
justice, 18, 61–62, 70, 105, 121, 139, 182, 191, 206, 211, 239, 248, 250, 262, 263, 269, 273, 274, 289, 293, 296, 308, 311, 313, 316–18, 352, 365, 369, 373, 385–86, 395–97; and the nations, 263

Kadesh-Barnea, 24, 39, 40
Keret, 49
king, presentation of, 144
kingship: in ANE, 44, 318; and covenant, 206; in Israel, 139–40, 185–88, 191, 194, 205, 206, 248, 280, 352, 355, 358, 360
kosher, 78

Laban, 32–34
Lachish, 151, 153, 255
lament oracles, 237, 243
lament psalms, 346–47, 348, 349, 350–52, 372–74, 377
Lamentations, 208, 237, 243, 245
Lampstand of Zechariah, 242
Land, 4, 24, 29, 31–32, 34, 38–40, 43, 51, 68, 71, 80–82, 101, 132, 136–40, 171, 180–83, 188, 189–90, 193, 207, 234, 238, 257, 281, 360, 369
Late Bronze Age, 46, 157–59
law: in ANE, 41, 45, 46, 60–63, 65, 103–6; comparison of, 61; reading the, 126, 208; in Israel, 4, 8, 39, 63, 69–70, 81, 92, 96–97, 103–6, 117–21, 124, 126, 155, 181, 186, 189, 195, 208–9, 238, 262, 267, 270, 290, 318, 344,

351, 363, 383–84, 388; living the, 97
Leviathan, 311
Leviticus, 24, 39, 63, 74–79, 124, 126
Lipi-Ishtar law collection, 61
liturgical year, 127
liver omen, 177, 240
love: songs, 298–99, 315; God of, 218

MacLeish, A. C., 114, 323
major archives, 48s
major prophets, 244
Malachi, 244, 246, 274
Malataya, 103
man and his God, 295
Manasseh, 5, 149, 152, 166, 188, 234
map of the world (Old Babylonian), 15
Marduk, 62, 172, 238, 351
Mari, 45–47, 48, 238; prophecy, 241
Medes, 5, 152, 167–68, 169, 170
Medo-Persian Empire, 170–72
Megiddo, 143, 159, 161, 190, 200
Merneptah, 52, 53, 199
Merodach-baladan, 47, 165–66
Mesopotamia, 29, 41–46
Mesopotamian Land Grant, 95
message, 11, 136, 224, 231–32, 238, 247, 252–54
Messiah, 5, 206, 234, 247, 253, 280, 345, 359, 384, 386–87, 397
messianic: prophecy, 247, 359; psalms, 359
Micah, 230, 234, 237, 246, 262, 272
Middle Bronze Age, 47
Middle Kingdom, 27, 50
minor prophets, 244, 246, 248. *See also* Book of the Twelve
miracles, 195–96, 222
Mitanni, 46, 156–59
Moab, 144, 160, 232, 258, 257
Mordecai, 196
Moses, 4, 7, 19, 24, 36–40, 60, 62, 69, 70, 74, 230, 232, 290; in real life, 37
Mount Carmel, 187

Mount Ebal, 181
Mount Gerizim, 181
Mount Nebo, 40, 70
mythology, 58

Nabonidus, 47, 170–71, 172
Nabopolassar, 47, 167–68, 236
Nahum, 230, 235, 237, 246, 259
names of God, 73
Naram-Sim, 44
Narmer Palette, 48
Nebuchadnezzar, 168–169, 237
Nehemiah, 5, 132, 155, 172, 195, 202
Neo-Assyrian Empire, 162, 164–66
Neo-Babylonian Empire, 167–69, 170
new covenant, 117–18, 245–46, 262, 267, 385–86, 396
Nile, 36
Nimrud, 234
Noah, 3, 28–29
Northern Kingdom. See Israel
Numbers, 24, 39, 80–81
Nuzi, 48; tablets, 48, 49

Obadiah, 239, 237, 246, 259
offering, 75, 76, 91, 95, 101, 275, 282
Old Babylonian period, 45–46
Old Kingdom, 27, 50–51
omen, 177, 178, 240
Omri, 144–45, 148
oracles, 239, 248, 250, 241, 244, 249, 253, 259, 266, 276, 396. See also lament oracles
order, 29, 55–56, 61, 67, 72, 78, 80, 86, 102, 112, 123, 186, 290, 316, 318–20, 332–34
orphans, 269

parallelism, 346
patriarchs, 4, 27, 29, 45, 50, 137
Pekah, 148, 164
Pentateuch, 24, 28, 54, 60, 62, 65, 69, 70, 83, 117, 180, 290, 344
pharaoh, 52
Philistines, 140–41, 183, 204, 207, 359
pilgrimage psalms, 346
plagues, 38, 73, 279

plan, 67, 80, 93, 175, 176, 185, 191, 195–96, 202, 210, 218, 220, 231, 232, 239, 243, 250–54, 276, 372, 384, 389
plotline, 3, 11, 197, 382
pluralism, God's view of, 219
poetry, Hebrew, 345
polytheism, 102, 106
Pool of Gibeon, 344
postexilic, 5, 135, 154–55, 208–9, 238, 239, 242, 243, 358
postexilic issues, 242
praise psalms, 346–47, 347, 348, 350, 377; declarative, 347; descriptive, 347, 350
prayer, 6, 80, 218, 250, 340, 343, 349, 355, 357, 364, 374, 376, 378, 397; of becoming, 378; to every God, 104; to Inanna, 103
preclassical prophets, 230, 232–33
preexilic, 209, 239
priest, 39, 63, 74–76, 86, 88, 95, 97, 100–101, 123, 125–30, 144, 149, 195, 242, 363; in Israel, 77
prophecy, 8, 231–32, 240, 241, 243, 247, 250, 252–54, 265–67, 281, 283. See also classical prophecy and inscriptions and prophecies
prophecy fulfillment. See fulfillment
prophets, 3, 93, 187, 188, 194, 203, 209, 222, 230–32, 231, 244, 250–52, 259, 260, 266, 272, 290, 383–85; and missionaries, 251. See also major prophets, minor prophets, and preclassical prophets
Proverbs, 289, 291, 297–98, 301–3, 305–6, 316, 331, 332, 334, 335; concerning family communication, 335; and sexuality, 332; for sons and/or daughters, 297
psalms, 8, 96, 204, 215, 289, 315, 343–44, 346, 353, 355, 359, 361, 363, 376, 377–79, 397; ancient near eastern, 349–52, 351; lines, 344; types of, 347; in worship, 377. See also lament psalms, praise psalms, seam psalms, and wisdom psalms
Psammetichus, 166
pyramids, 36

Qarqar, 46, 162, 163
Qoheleth, 312, 313, 328–29. *See also* Ecclesiastes
Qumran, 2, 22

Rameses II (the Great), 46, 52, 157, 159
Rebekah, 31
Rehoboam, 4, 142, 149, 161
remnant, 189, 195, 208, 234, 243, 248
Retribution Principle, 289, 292–93, 307–13, 316–17, 321, 347, 357
revelation, 3, 6–7, 13, 15–19, 54–57, 67, 72, 89, 90, 92, 93–97, 117–18, 120, 121, 176, 178, 182, 186, 197, 207, 213, 224, 252–54, 266, 283, 296, 361, 369, 378, 382, 392–95
rich, 328
Rim-Sin, 46
role model, 200–204, 217–18, 374
royal psalms, 346, 347, 359
Ruth, 132, 191, 388

Sabbath and Sunday, 129
sacred: compass, 75, 76–77, 79, 100; space, 74, 76–78, 86, 87–88, 100–102, 121–30, 193, 352; time, 128, 129
sacrifices, 60, 63, 75, 78, 97, 98, 101–2, 126, 130, 235, 255, 364; function of, 102
salvation, 91–95, 118, 266, 388–89, 388; concepts, 388
Samaria, 146
Samaritans, 242, 391
Samuel, 140, 185, 192, 206, 230, 233, 290
sanctuary, 39, 75, 81, 97–100, 121, 124, 144, 282, 388
Sarah, 31
Sargon I, 44, 84
Sargon II, 46, 151, 165, 205
Satan in Job, 294
Saul, 4, 86, 140–41, 185, 192–93, 357
science, 3, 58, 108, 110–13, 198, 393, 397
scribes, 303
scripts, 19, 19

scroll, 6, 21
Sea Peoples, 46, 140, 157, 159, 160, 162
seam psalms, 357–58
second temple, 155
Sennacherib, 46, 151, 165, 166, 168, 172, 188, 197, 199, 222, 244; prism, 166; siege, 151, 164, 165, 166, 168, 173, 188, 255
seraphs, 210
sermon characteristics, 209
Sesostris III, 51
Shalmaneser I, 159
Shalmaneser III, 46, 146, 147, 162, 163, 199
Shalmaneser V, 46, 151, 165
Shamshi-Adad I, 46
Shechem, 34
Sheol, 366, 366–69, 402
ship, 143
Shishak, 144, 161, 184
Shulgi, 45
Shuppiluliuma, 46, 65, 159
sign, 276; acts, 236
signet rings, 278, 279
Siloam: inscription, 152; tunnel, 152
Sinai, 4, 7, 38, 39, 53; map, 60, 74
Sinuhe, 47, 50
slaves, 269
sling, 204
social: issues, 120; justice, 248, 262, 385
Solomon, 4, 21, 141–42, 143, 160–61, 203, 291, 297, 337; cities of, 143; fortifications of, 143; temple of, 192–93
Song of Songs, 298, 299, 314–16, 335–37
Southern Kingdom, 4, 142, 144, 149, 234
sovereignty, 106, 125, 195, 197, 200, 204, 206, 218, 220, 246, 259–60
speeches, campaign, 200
Spirit of the Lord, 203, 387
Spiritual: formation, 376; warfare, 225
standard, 184, 205; of Ur, 45
standing stone, 94, 138, 198, 219
stewardship, 270
story, 6–7, 197; ingredients, 83

subgenres, 226
Sumerian king list, 15
Sumerians, 19, 41
sun god, 55, 58
suzerain-vassal treaty, 65, 402
symbol, 276
syncretism, 188, 272, 402

tabernacle, 39, 69, 74, 81, 97, 98, 99, 100, 186, 206
Tale of Aqhat, The, 49, 160
Tale of Keret (Kirta), The, 49, 160
Talmud, 291
Tel-Dan Inscription, 161
temple, 29, 31, 56, 72, 77, 87, 88, 90, 97, 98, 102, 104, 121, 123, 153, 154, 155, 186, 189, 192–93, 192–93, 207, 208, 209, 237, 245, 255, 256, 281, 363, 364, 394; and church, 123
ten plagues, 38
theocracy, 242, 403
theodicy, 289, 295, 295, 403
theophanies, 7, 115
Thutmose III, 46, 52, 190, 205
Tiglath-Pileser III, 46, 150, 164, 165, 168, 174, 365
Tigris, 43
tithing, 270
tolerance, 18, 219, 273
tomb: of Cyrus, 171; painting, 38
Torah, 24, 344, 403; psalms, 344, 346
Tower of Babel, 72. *See also* Babel
tragedy, 90, 220–21, 317, 327
treaty, 64–65, 82, 150
tribute bearers (Syrian), 51
twelve tribes, 29

Ugarit, 43, 46, 47, 48–49, 95, 157, 158, 159, 160, 235
Ugaritic, 11, 12, 160, 311
united monarchy, 140, 141
Ur, 34, 41, 44, 45, 156
Ur III Period, 27, 44, 45, 46
Ur-Nammu, 44–45
Uzziah. *See* Azariah

Valley of Elah, 183
Valley of Jezreel, 42, 152
vindication, 315, 347, 350, 351, 364, 368
virgin birth, 280–81
votive offering, 41

warrior, 182, 205
watchtower (Samaritan Hills), 250
waterfall (En Gedi), 343
widows, 269
wife, ideal, 305
wilderness of Sinai, 38–40
wisdom, 286, 289; literature, 315; psalms, 289, 347, 349, 355, 357, 373, 377
word, 276; for "king," 19
world, ancient, 42
worldview, 102
worship, 362, 363, 371
woman bathing, 204
writing, 19, 20, 21, 22, 291, 303

Xerxes, 47, 172

Yahdun-Lim, 46
Yahweh, 33, 37, 62, 73, 74, 93–95, 103–6, 122, 139, 145, 152, 175, 177, 178, 182, 185–88, 205–8, 219, 237, 238, 246, 254, 259, 306, 396; the God of Israel, 33; supremacy of, 133
Yom Kippur. *See* Day of Atonement

Zechariah, 154, 208, 236, 241, 242, 246, 273, 280, 391
Zephaniah, 235, 237, 246, 259
Zerubbabel, 154, 278, 279
Ziggurat, 29, 72, 403
Zimri-Lim, 46
Zion psalms, 346
Zoroastrianism, 242